POSUKA DEMIZU

A very fortunate thing happened—lots of Little Bunny merchandise came out, and I have a lot of Bunny samples in my room.

So...I decided to put different earrings on them so that I can differentiate between them.

To put it mildly, it's awesome.

Not only can I tell them apart, their individuality is coming out.

As soon as there are more Emma items, I'm going to line them up nicely. New merchandise is always something to look forward to!

Please look forward to volume 16!

KAIU SHIRAI

Writer Shirai's personal highlights for *The Promised Neverland* fanatics, part 11!

1. Don-doko!! (the original joke came from *The Promised Neverland* anime episode 9—it was an ad-lib by Mr. Ueki, the actor who plays Don)

2. The stuffed animal that laughed along (clue: HA)

3. The eel streamer returns! And Bunny furiously hangs on!

4. The owl that nods knowingly at the boss's words (or maybe it's just eating and not nodding)

Those who found #2 and #4 are hard-core!

Please enjoy this volume!

Posuka Demizu debuted as a manga artist with the 2013 *CoroCoro* series *Oreca Monster Bouken Retsuden*. A collection of illustrations, *The Art of Posuka Demizu,* was released in 2016 by PIE International.

Kaiu Shirai debuted in 2015 with *Ashley Gate no Yukue* on the *Shonen Jump+* website. Shirai first worked with Posuka Demizu on the two-shot *Poppy no Negai,* which was released in February 2016.

THE PROMISED NEVERLAND

VOLUME 15
SHONEN JUMP Manga Edition

STORY BY KAIU SHIRAI
ART BY POSUKA DEMIZU

Translation/Satsuki Yamashita
Touch-Up Art & Lettering/Mark McMurray
Design/Julian [JR] Robinson
Editor/Alexis Kirsch

YAKUSOKU NO NEVERLAND © 2016 by Kaiu Shirai, Posuka Demizu
All rights reserved.
First published in Japan in 2016 by SHUEISHA Inc., Tokyo.
English translation rights arranged by SHUEISHA Inc.

The stories, characters and incidents mentioned in this publication are
entirely fictional.

Printed in Italy

Published by VIZ Media, LLC
P.O. Box 77010
San Francisco, CA 94107

10 9 8 7 6 5 4 3 2
First printing, June 2020
Second printing, April 2021

viz.com

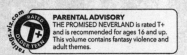
PARENTAL ADVISORY
THE PROMISED NEVERLAND is rated T+
and is recommended for ages 16 and up.
This volume contains fantasy violence and
adult themes.

THE PROMISED NEVERLAND

15

Welcome to the Entrance

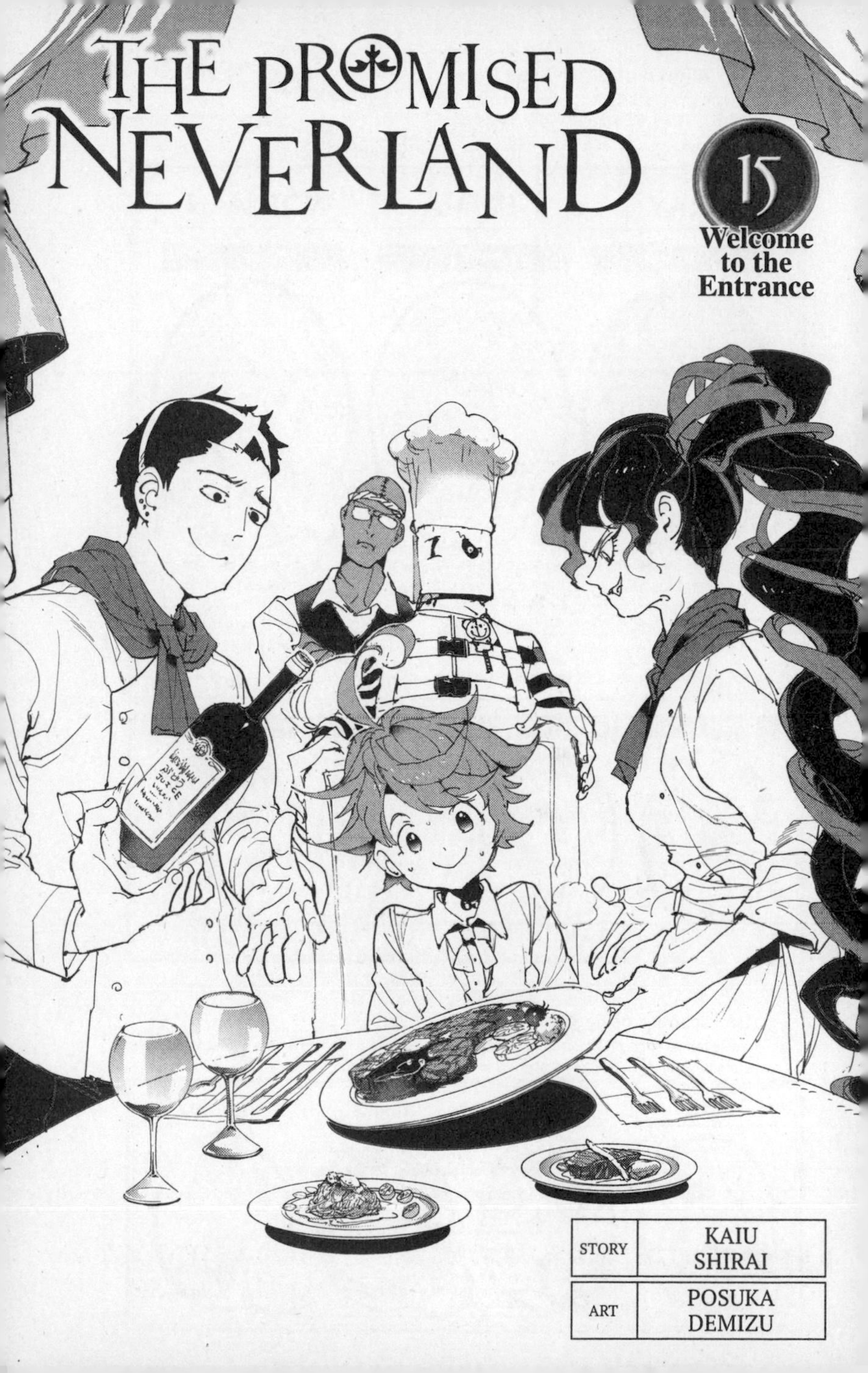

STORY	KAIU SHIRAI
ART	POSUKA DEMIZU

CHARACTERS

The Children of Grace Field House

They aim to free all of the children who are trapped in Grace Field House within the next two months.

RAY

On the Run

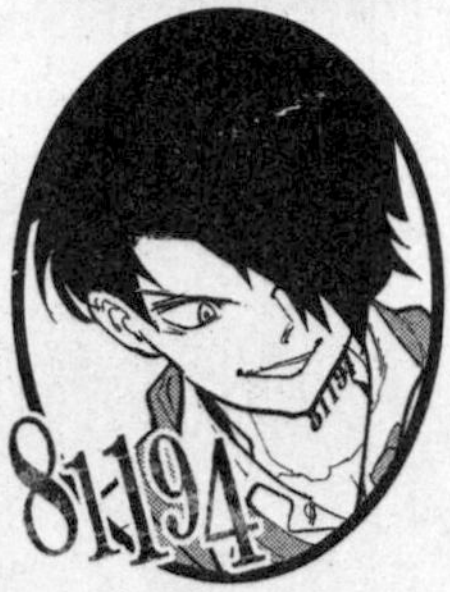
81194

The only one among the Grace Field House children who can match wits with Norman.

EMMA

On the Run

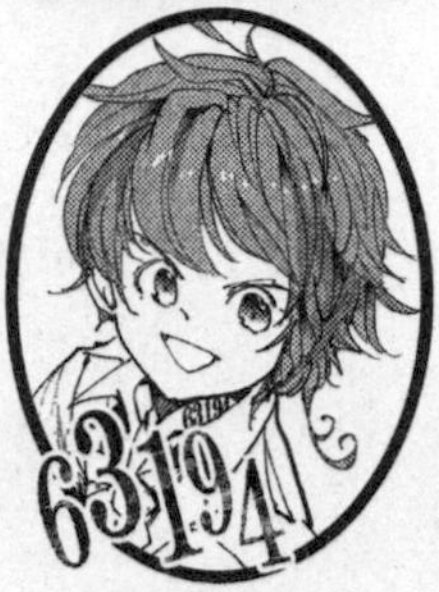
63194

An enthusiastic and optimistic girl with superb athletic and learning abilities.

NORMAN

On the Run

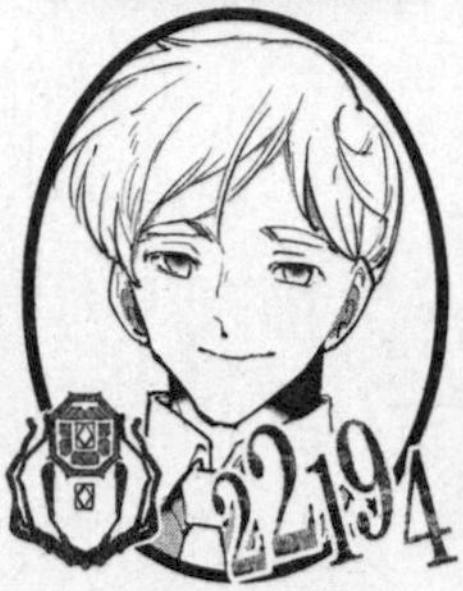
22194

A boy with excellent analytical and decision-making capabilities. He is the smartest of the children from Grace Field House.

CAROL

In Grace Field House

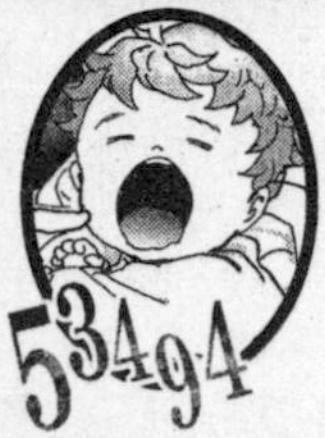
53494

PHIL

In Grace Field House

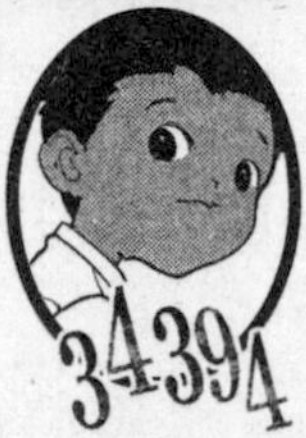
34394

GILDA

On the Run

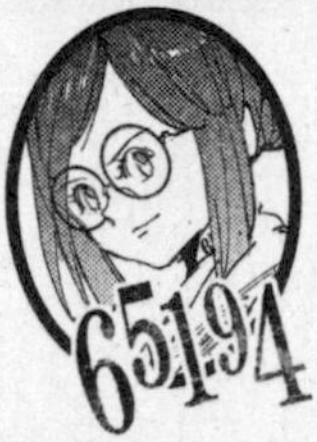
65194

DON

On the Run

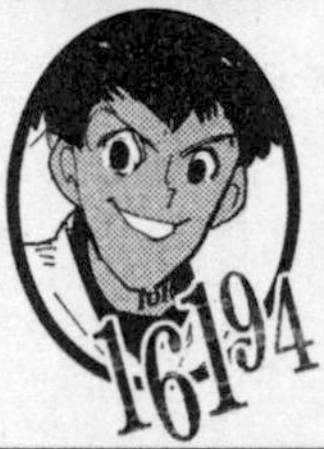
16194

The Escapees of Lambda 7214

They obtained superpowers from being repeatedly experimented on by the demons. They are devoted to Norman and have destroyed many farms with him.

ZAZIE

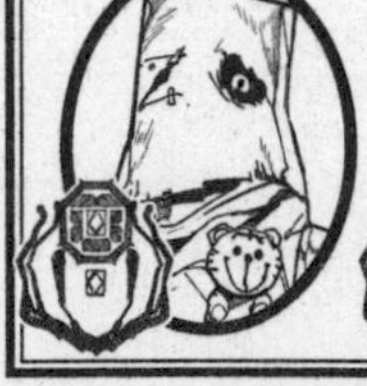

BARBARA

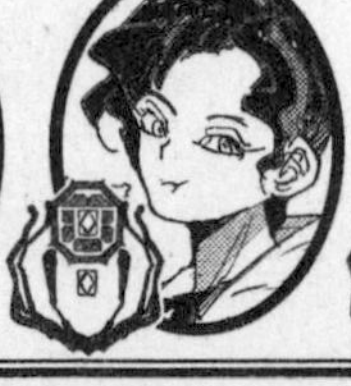

CISLO

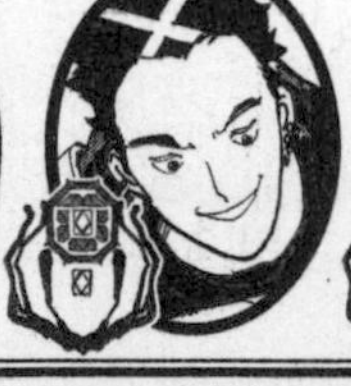

VINCENT

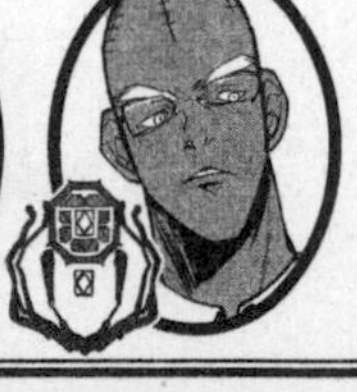

The Ratri Clan
They seek to kill the children who escaped the farms and Goldy Pond as well as the supporters who help them.

PETER RATRI

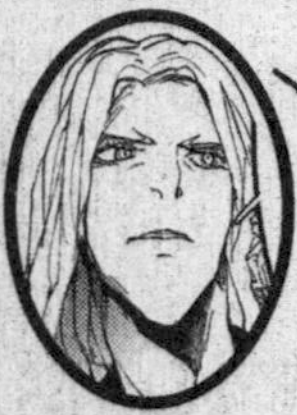

ANDREW

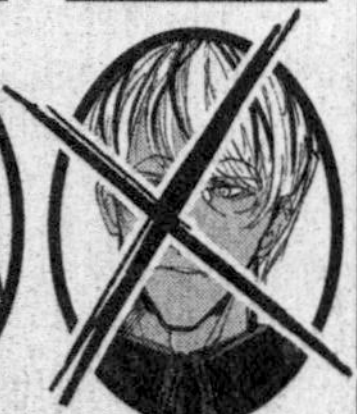

The Escapees of a New Mass Production Farm
They set out on a journey to protect Emma's group but were saved by them instead when they were attacked by a wild demon.

HAYATO

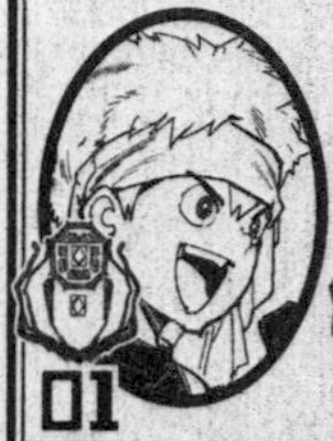
01

JIN

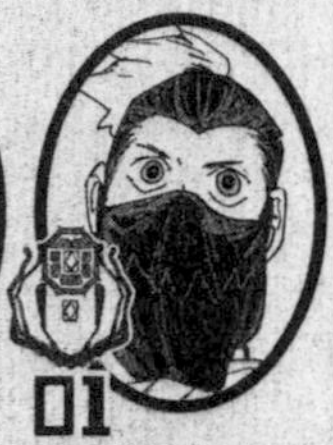
01

???
Said to be located in a mysterious space with a dragon.

???

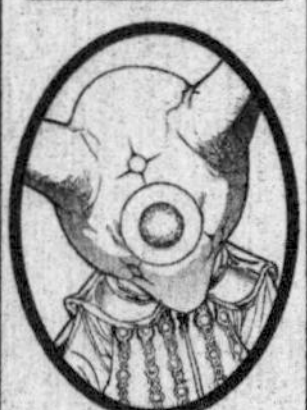

???
Nomadic demons. They are forbidden by their religion to eat humans raised in farms.

MUJIKA

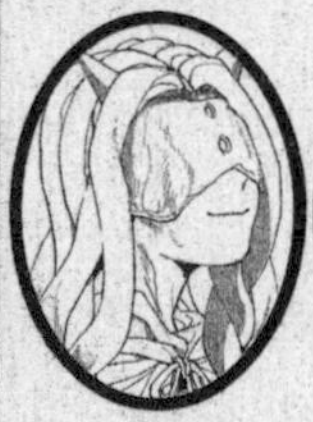

SONJU

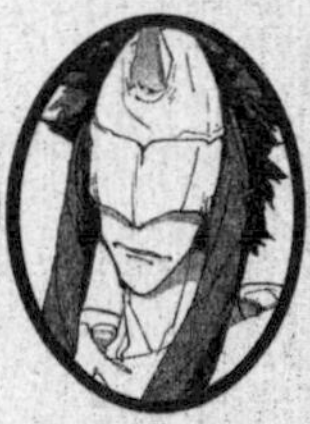

Supporters
They support children who escape by providing tools and facilities.

WILLIAM MINERVA (JAMES RATRI)

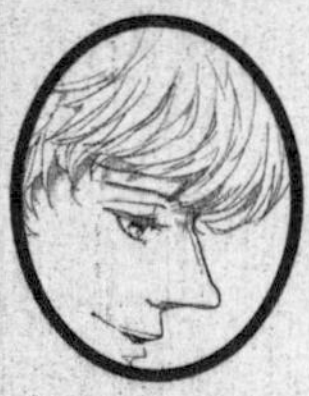

The Story So Far

Emma is living happily at Grace Field House with her foster siblings. One day, she realizes that they are being bred as food for demons and escapes with a group of other children. After meeting new friends and gaining further information, she decides to free all of the children raised in the farms. Her group takes action to achieve this goal and obtains a clue to overwrite the current promise that is the cause of the children being eaten. But just then, they are attacked by the Ratri clan and lose both their allies and their base. With no time to mourn, the group heads to a new location where they are reunited with Norman, who is alive. They find out how he's been using Minerva's name to annihilate the demons.

THE PROMISED NEVERLAND

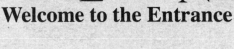

15

Welcome to the Entrance

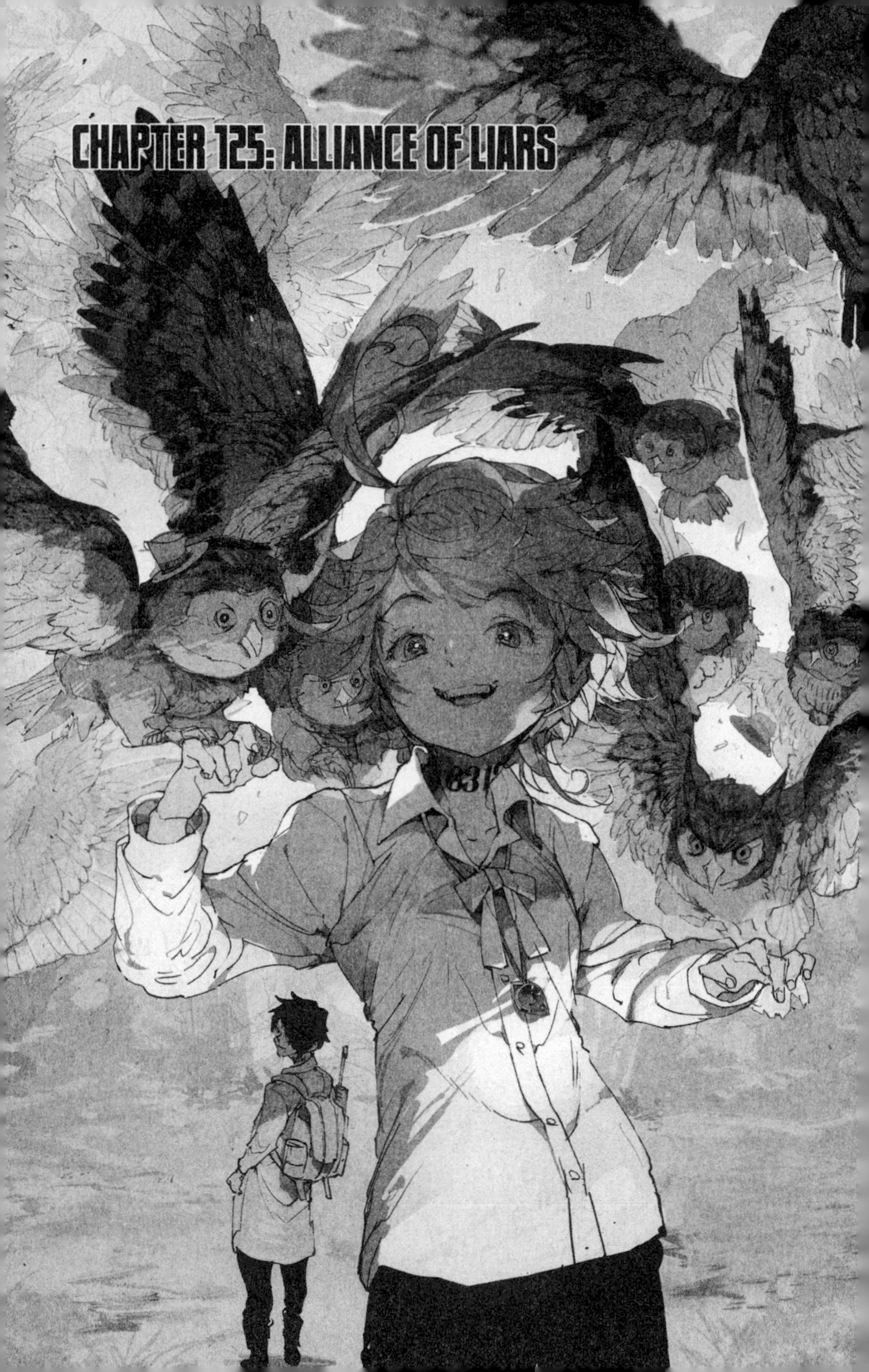
CHAPTER 125: ALLIANCE OF LIARS

STUDY TIME

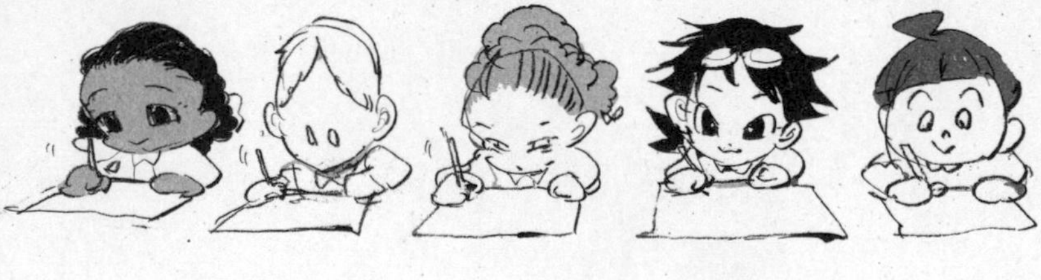

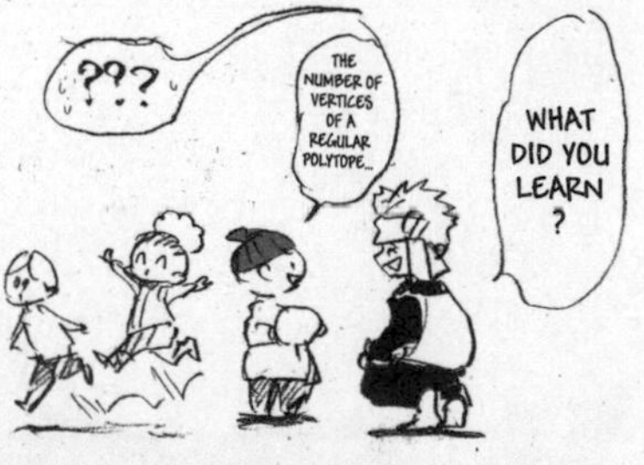
WHAT DID YOU LEARN ?
THE NUMBER OF VERTICES OF A REGULAR POLYTOPE...
???

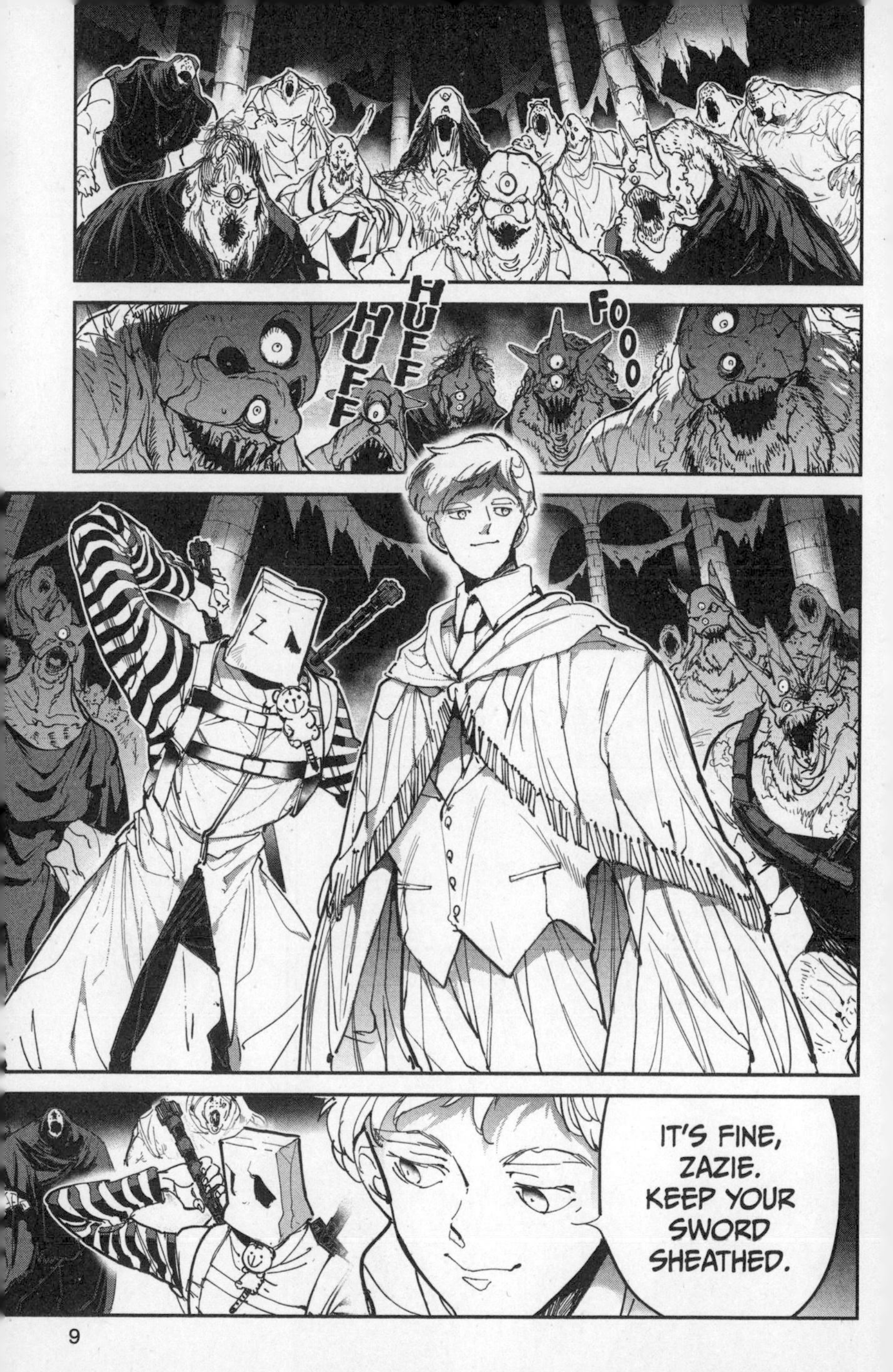
FOOO
HUFF HUFF
HUFF
IT'S FINE, ZAZIE. KEEP YOUR SWORD SHEATHED.

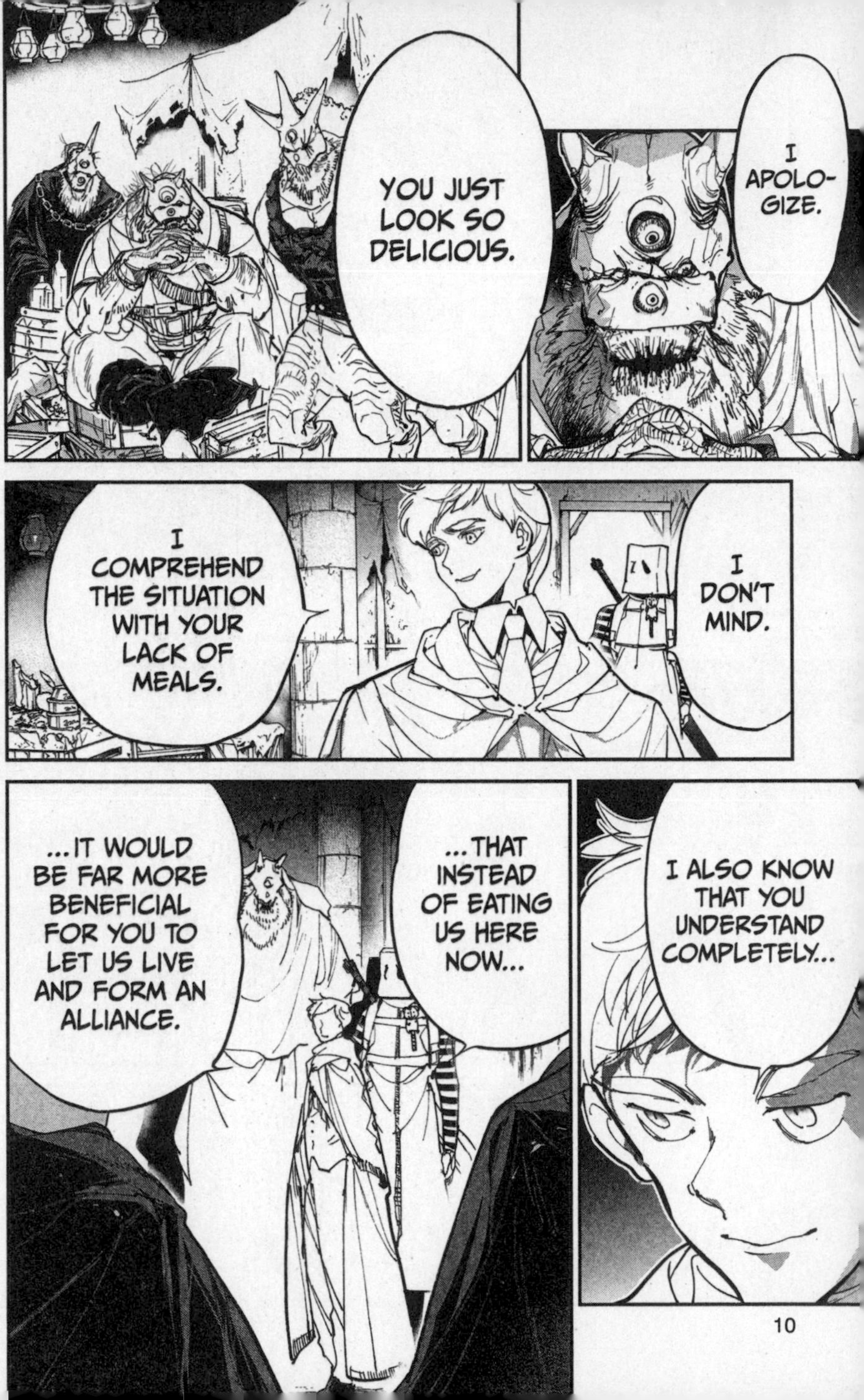
I APOLO-GIZE.
YOU JUST LOOK SO DELICIOUS.
I DON'T MIND.
I COMPREHEND THE SITUATION WITH YOUR LACK OF MEALS.
I ALSO KNOW THAT YOU UNDERSTAND COMPLETELY...
...THAT INSTEAD OF EATING US HERE NOW...
...IT WOULD BE FAR MORE BENEFICIAL FOR YOU TO LET US LIVE AND FORM AN ALLIANCE.

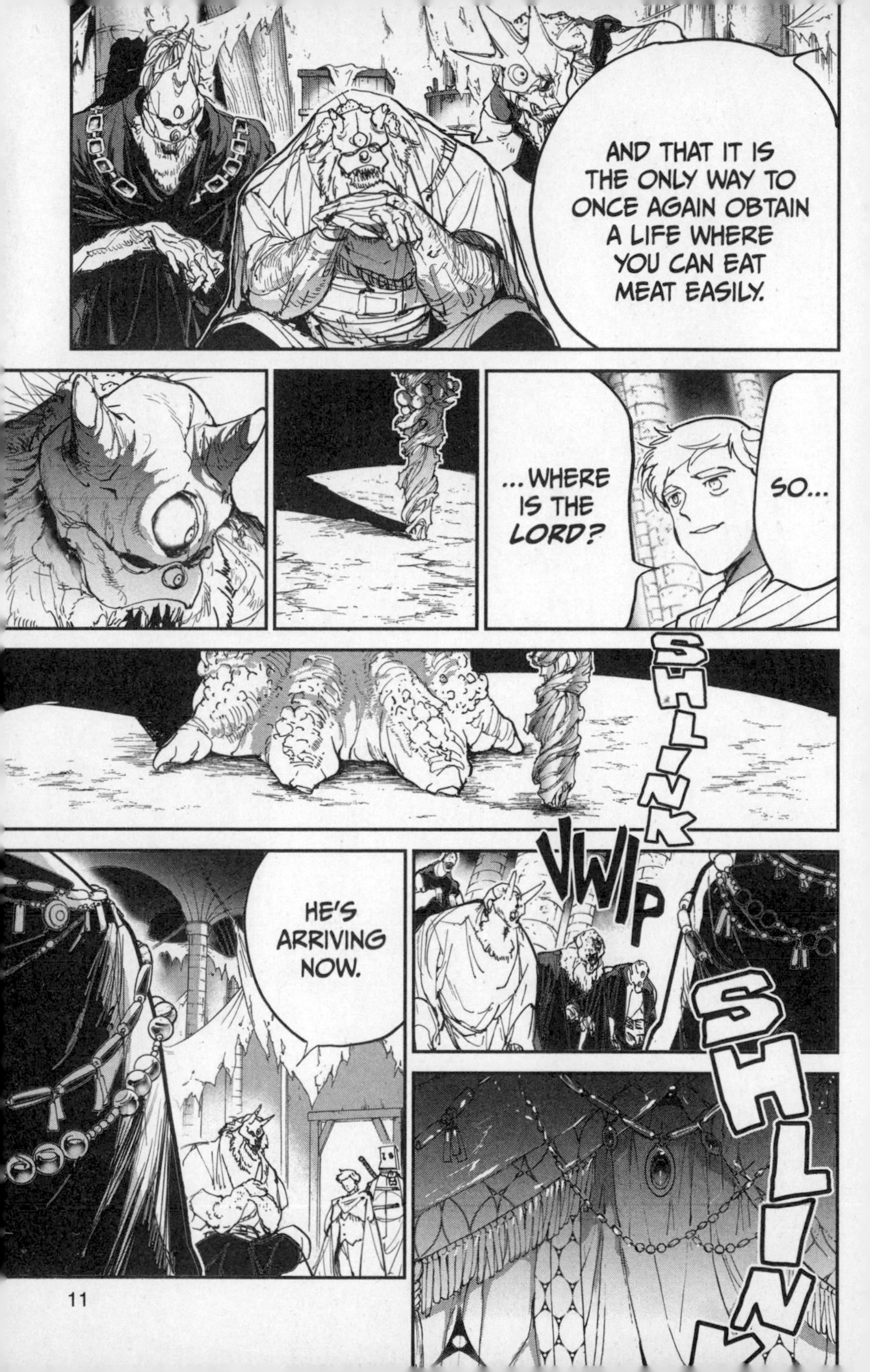
AND THAT IT IS THE ONLY WAY TO ONCE AGAIN OBTAIN A LIFE WHERE YOU CAN EAT MEAT EASILY.
SO...
...WHERE IS THE LORD?
SHLINK
VWIP
SHLIN
HE'S ARRIVING NOW.

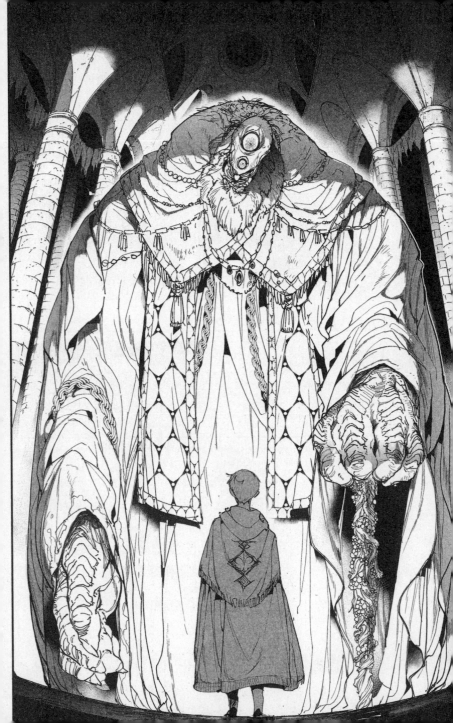

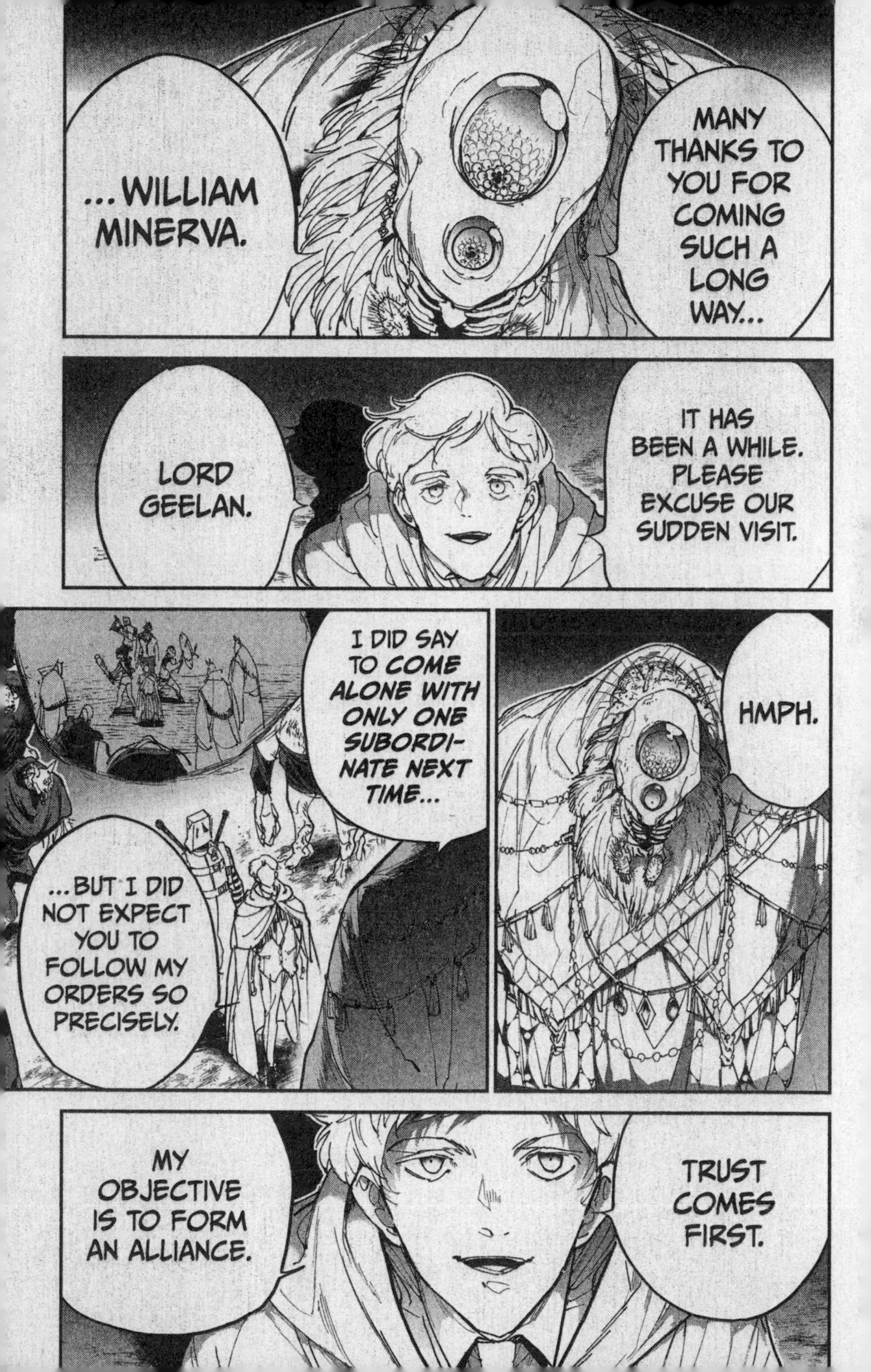
MANY THANKS TO YOU FOR COMING SUCH A LONG WAY...
...WILLIAM MINERVA.
IT HAS BEEN A WHILE. PLEASE EXCUSE OUR SUDDEN VISIT.
LORD GEELAN.
HMPH.
I DID SAY TO *COME ALONE WITH ONLY ONE SUBORDINATE NEXT TIME...*
...BUT I DID NOT EXPECT YOU TO FOLLOW MY ORDERS SO PRECISELY.
TRUST COMES FIRST.
MY OBJECTIVE IS TO FORM AN ALLIANCE.

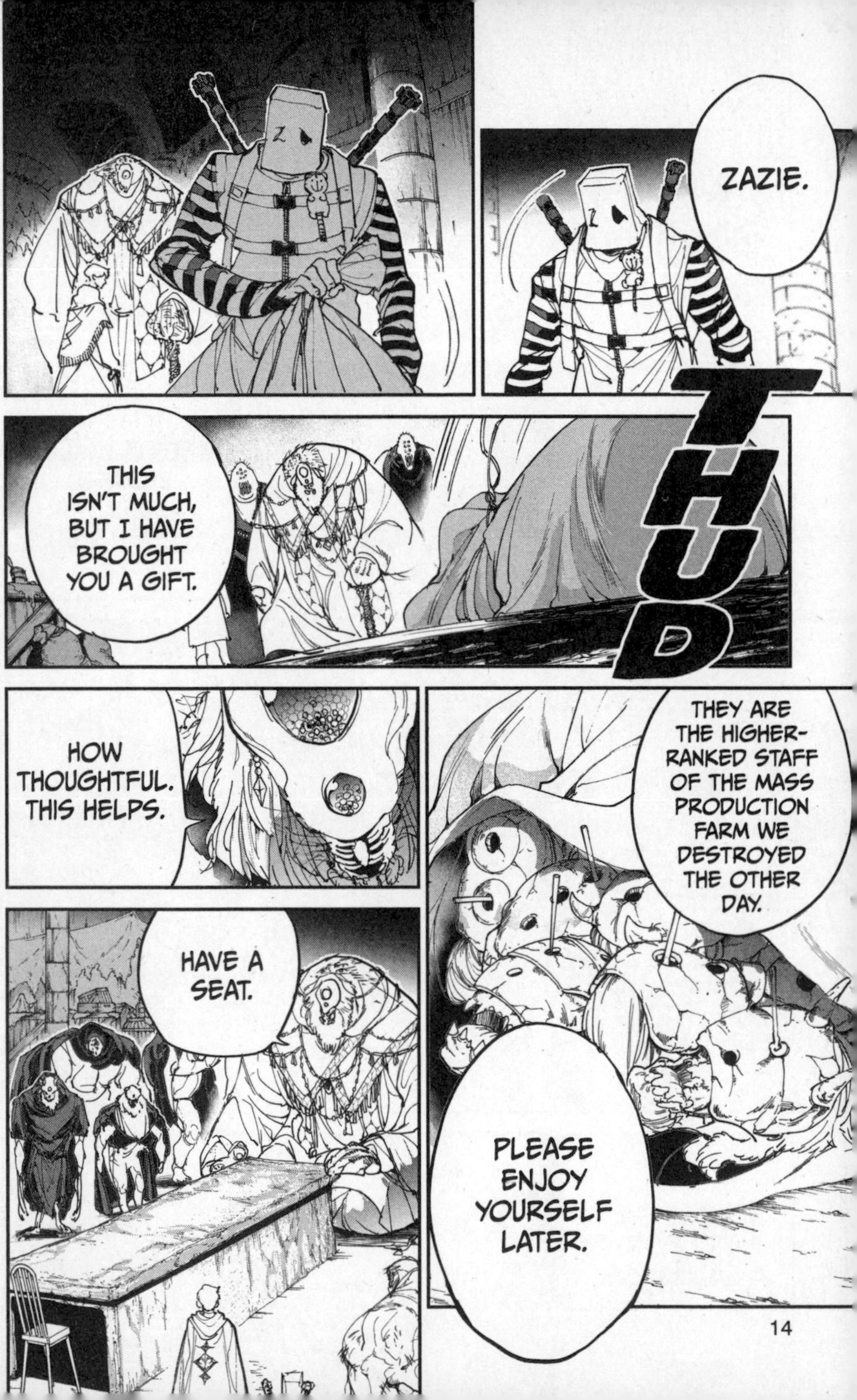
ZAZIE.
THUD
THIS ISN'T MUCH, BUT I HAVE BROUGHT YOU A GIFT.
THEY ARE THE HIGHER-RANKED STAFF OF THE MASS PRODUCTION FARM WE DESTROYED THE OTHER DAY.
PLEASE ENJOY YOURSELF LATER.
HOW THOUGHTFUL. THIS HELPS.
HAVE A SEAT.

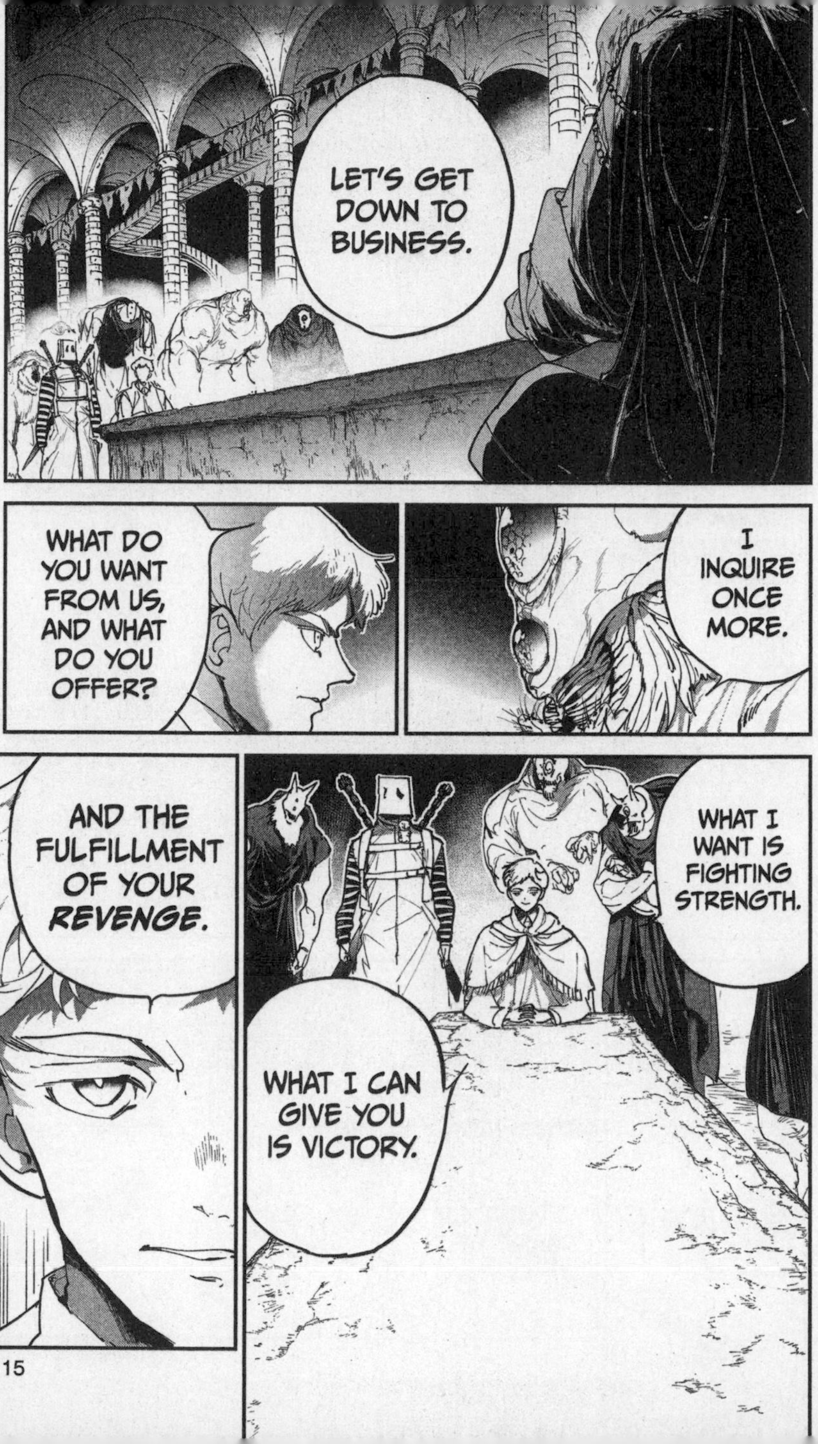
LET'S GET DOWN TO BUSINESS.
I INQUIRE ONCE MORE.
WHAT DO YOU WANT FROM US, AND WHAT DO YOU OFFER?
WHAT I WANT IS FIGHTING STRENGTH.
WHAT I CAN GIVE YOU IS VICTORY.
AND THE FULFILLMENT OF YOUR *REVENGE*.

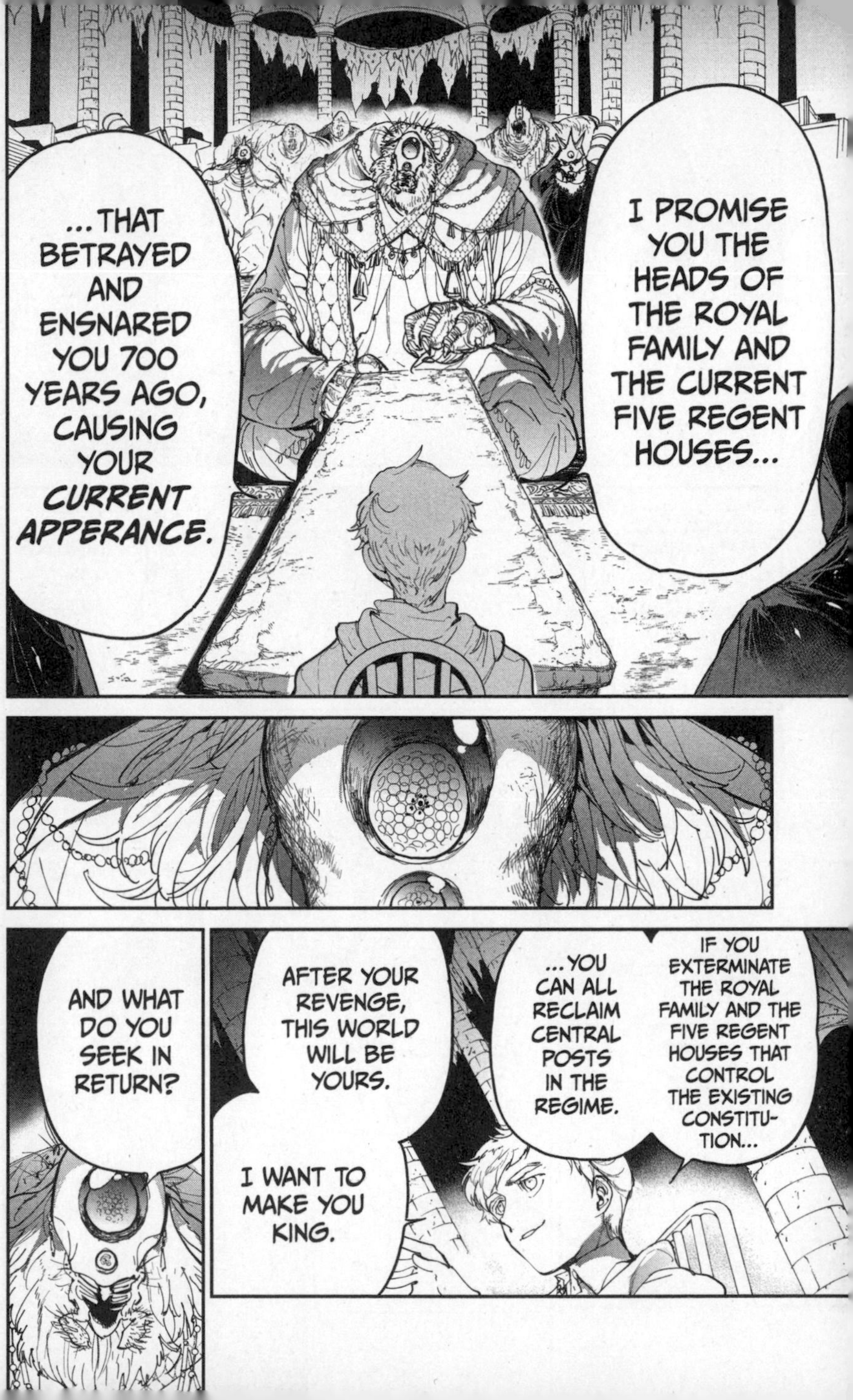
I PROMISE YOU THE HEADS OF THE ROYAL FAMILY AND THE CURRENT FIVE REGENT HOUSES...
...THAT BETRAYED AND ENSNARED YOU 700 YEARS AGO, CAUSING YOUR *CURRENT* APPERANCE.
IF YOU EXTERMINATE THE ROYAL FAMILY AND THE FIVE REGENT HOUSES THAT CONTROL THE EXISTING CONSTITU-TION...
...YOU CAN ALL RECLAIM CENTRAL POSTS IN THE REGIME.
AFTER YOUR REVENGE, THIS WORLD WILL BE YOURS.
I WANT TO MAKE YOU KING.
AND WHAT DO YOU SEEK IN RETURN?

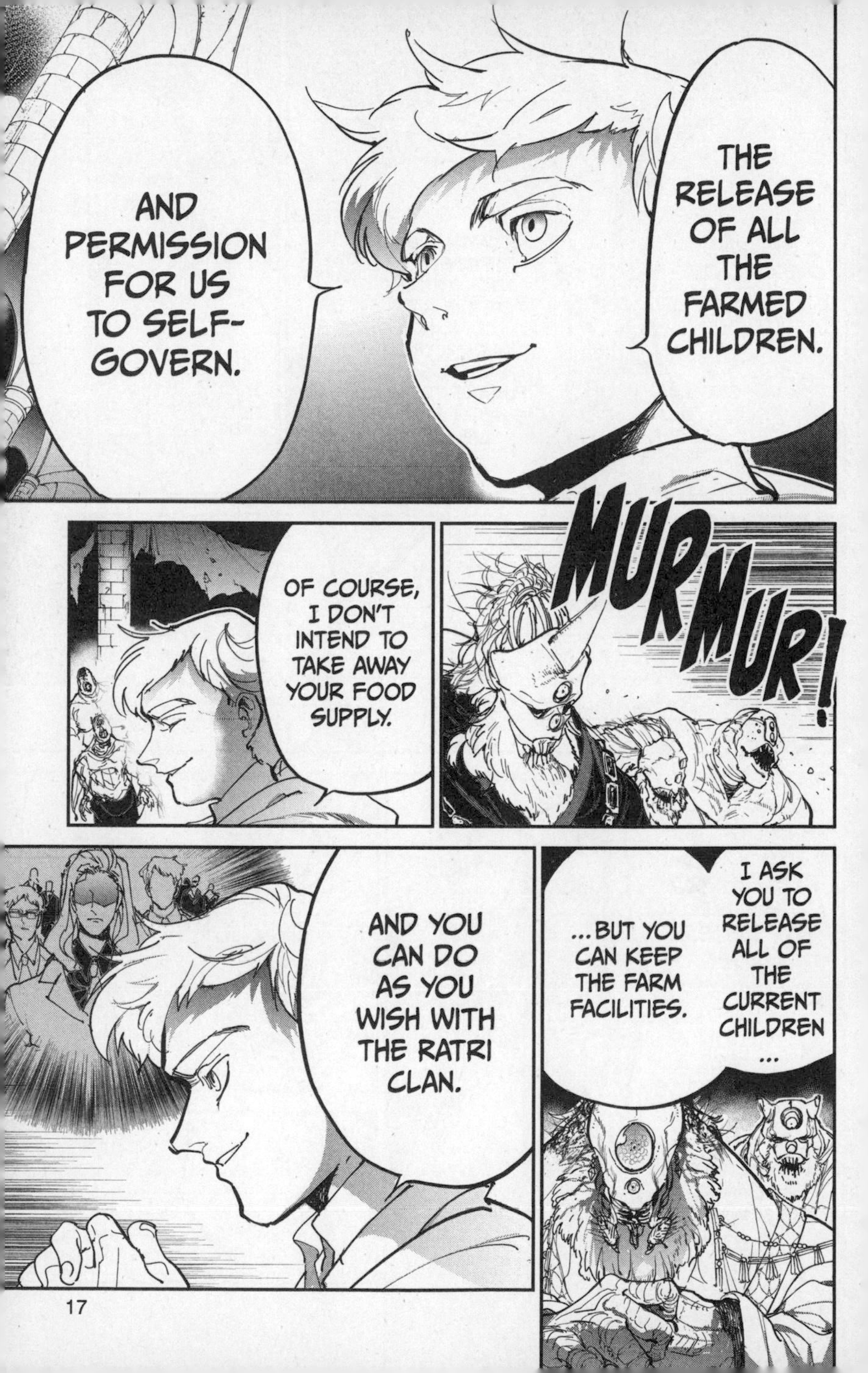
THE RELEASE OF ALL THE FARMED CHILDREN.
AND PERMISSION FOR US TO SELF-GOVERN.
MURMUR!
OF COURSE, I DON'T INTEND TO TAKE AWAY YOUR FOOD SUPPLY.
I ASK YOU TO RELEASE ALL OF THE CURRENT CHILDREN ...
...BUT YOU CAN KEEP THE FARM FACILITIES.
AND YOU CAN DO AS YOU WISH WITH THE RATRI CLAN.

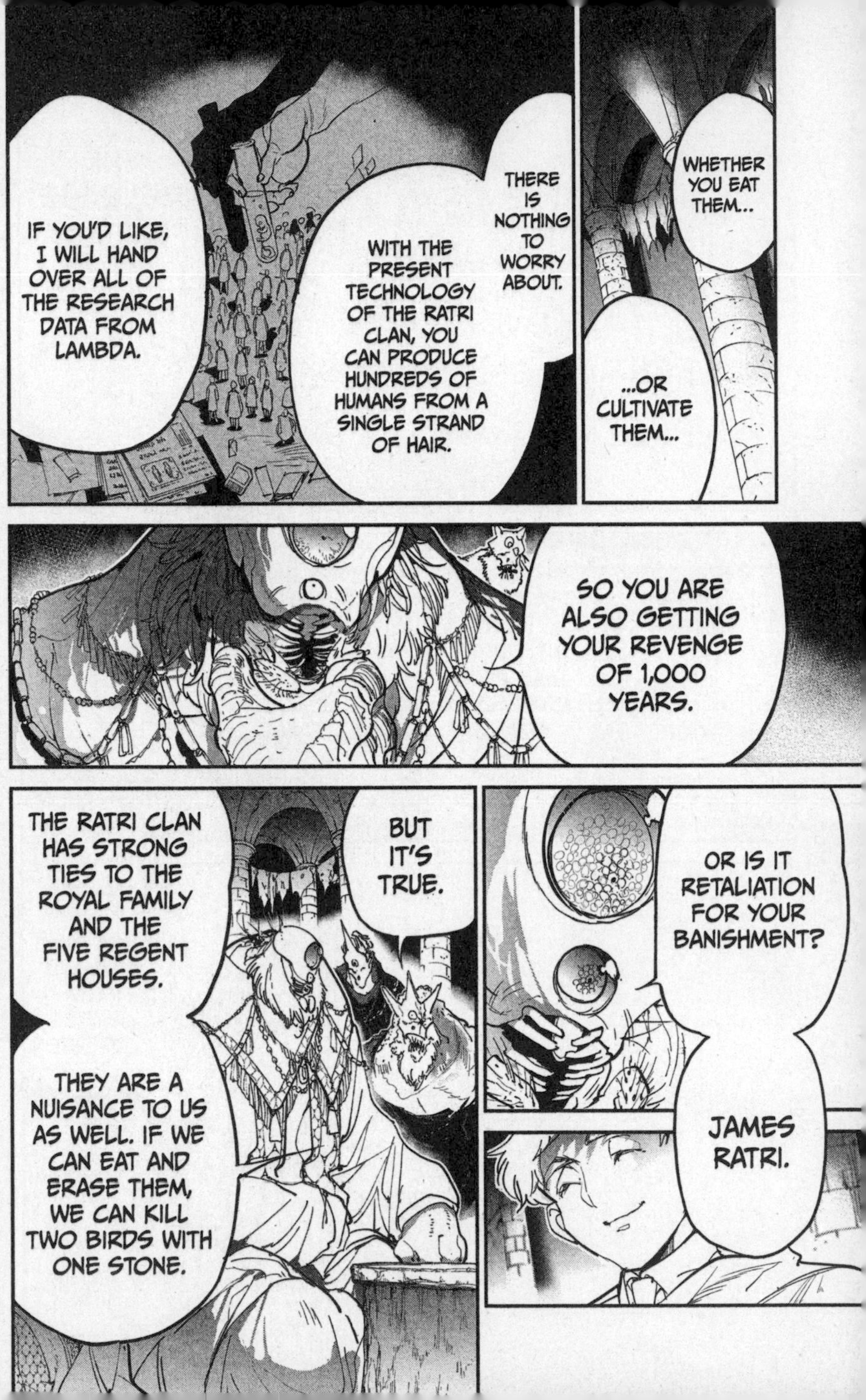
WHETHER YOU EAT THEM...
...OR CULTIVATE THEM...
THERE IS NOTHING TO WORRY ABOUT.
WITH THE PRESENT TECHNOLOGY OF THE RATRI CLAN, YOU CAN PRODUCE HUNDREDS OF HUMANS FROM A SINGLE STRAND OF HAIR.
IF YOU'D LIKE, I WILL HAND OVER ALL OF THE RESEARCH DATA FROM LAMBDA.
SO YOU ARE ALSO GETTING YOUR REVENGE OF 1,000 YEARS.
OR IS IT RETALIATION FOR YOUR BANISHMENT?
JAMES RATRI.
BUT IT'S TRUE.
THE RATRI CLAN HAS STRONG TIES TO THE ROYAL FAMILY AND THE FIVE REGENT HOUSES.
THEY ARE A NUISANCE TO US AS WELL. IF WE CAN EAT AND ERASE THEM, WE CAN KILL TWO BIRDS WITH ONE STONE.

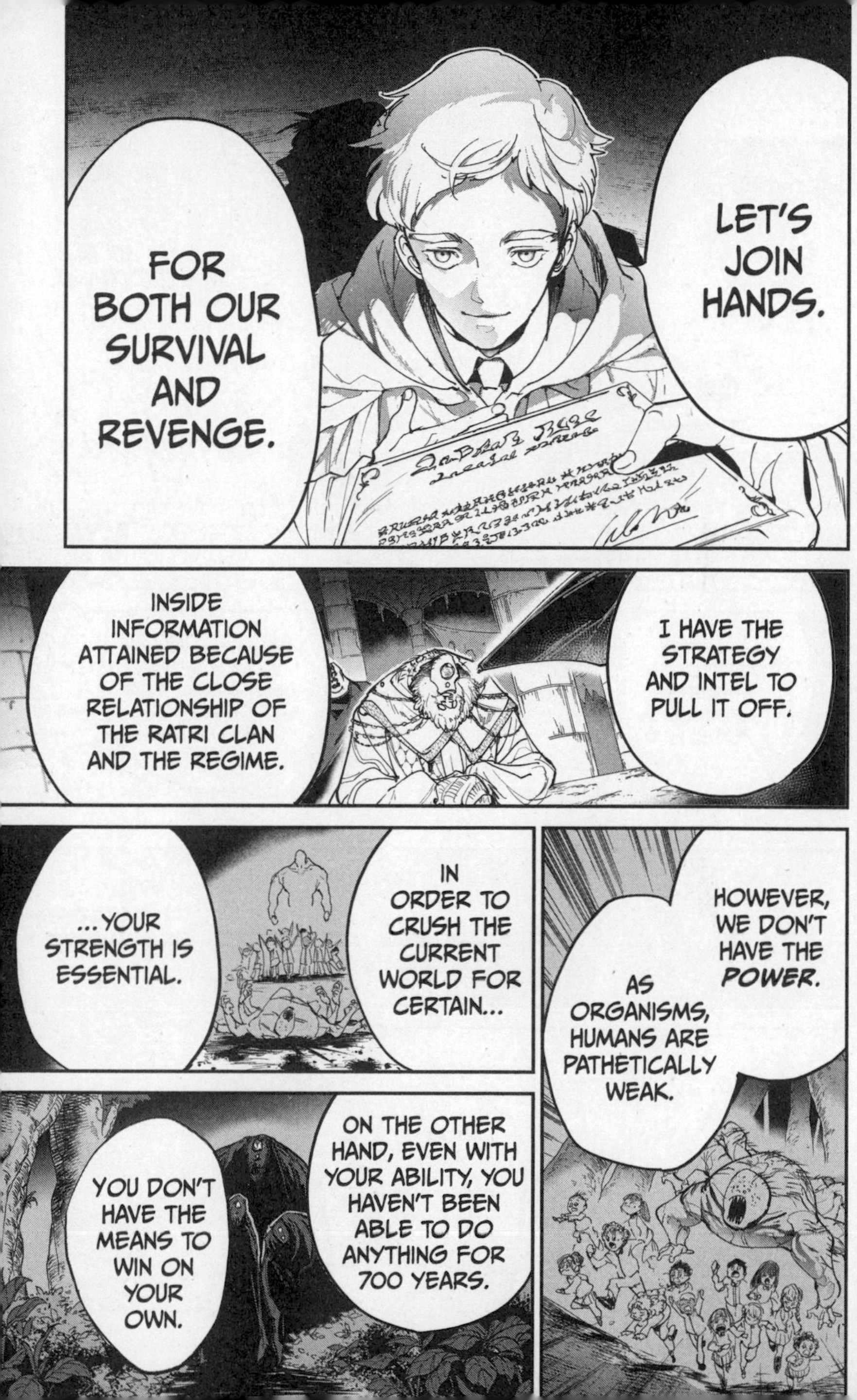
LET'S JOIN HANDS.
FOR BOTH OUR SURVIVAL AND REVENGE.
I HAVE THE STRATEGY AND INTEL TO PULL IT OFF.
INSIDE INFORMATION ATTAINED BECAUSE OF THE CLOSE RELATIONSHIP OF THE RATRI CLAN AND THE REGIME.
HOWEVER, WE DON'T HAVE THE *POWER*.
AS ORGANISMS, HUMANS ARE PATHETICALLY WEAK.
IN ORDER TO CRUSH THE CURRENT WORLD FOR CERTAIN...
...YOUR STRENGTH IS ESSENTIAL.
ON THE OTHER HAND, EVEN WITH YOUR ABILITY, YOU HAVEN'T BEEN ABLE TO DO ANYTHING FOR 700 YEARS.
YOU DON'T HAVE THE MEANS TO WIN ON YOUR OWN.

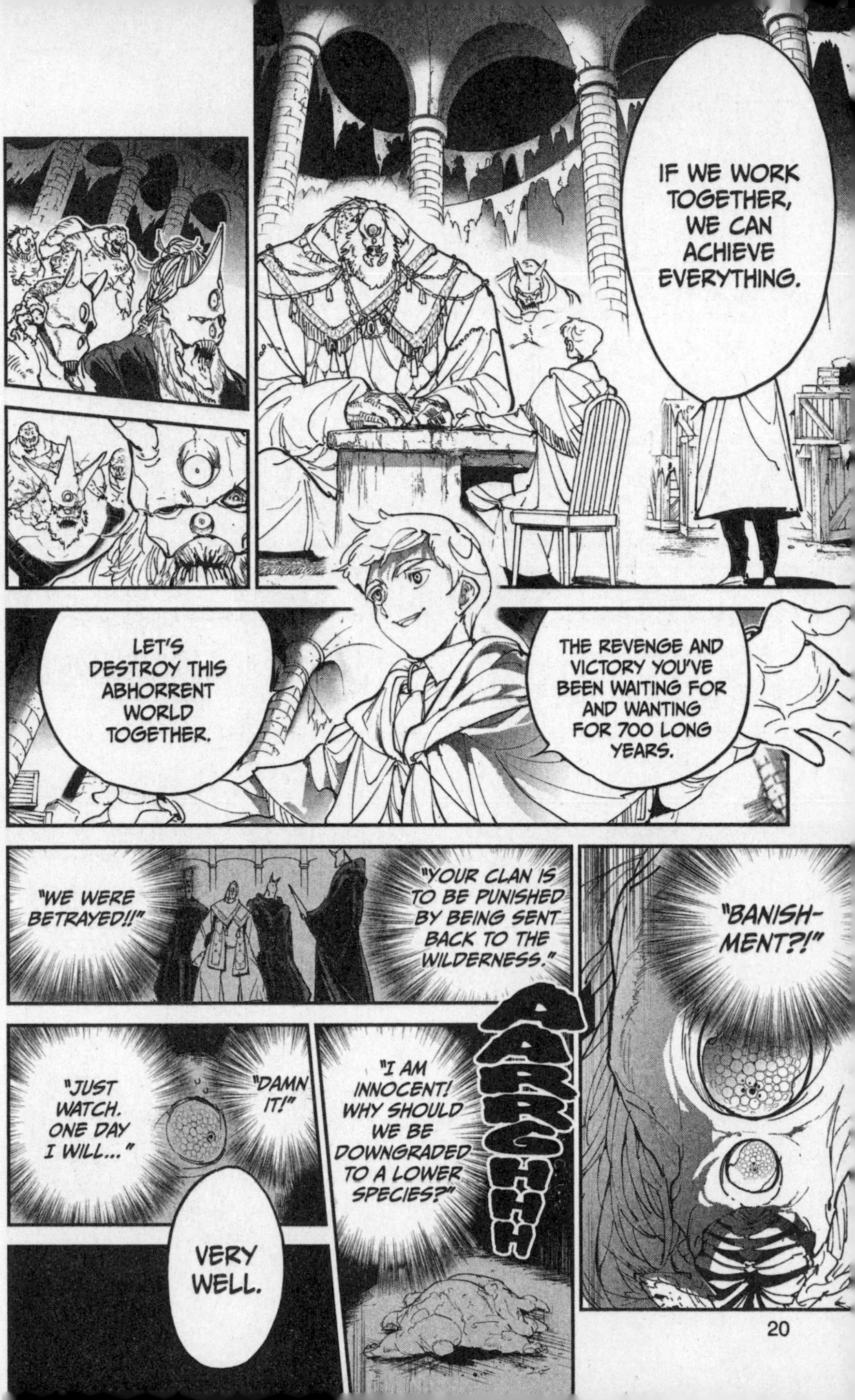
IF WE WORK TOGETHER, WE CAN ACHIEVE EVERYTHING.
THE REVENGE AND VICTORY YOU'VE BEEN WAITING FOR AND WANTING FOR 700 LONG YEARS.
LET'S DESTROY THIS ABHORRENT WORLD TOGETHER.
"BANISHMENT?!"
"YOUR CLAN IS TO BE PUNISHED BY BEING SENT BACK TO THE WILDERNESS."
"WE WERE BETRAYED!!"
AARGHHH
"I AM INNOCENT! WHY SHOULD WE BE DOWNGRADED TO A LOWER SPECIES?"
"DAMN IT!"
"JUST WATCH. ONE DAY I WILL..."
VERY WELL.

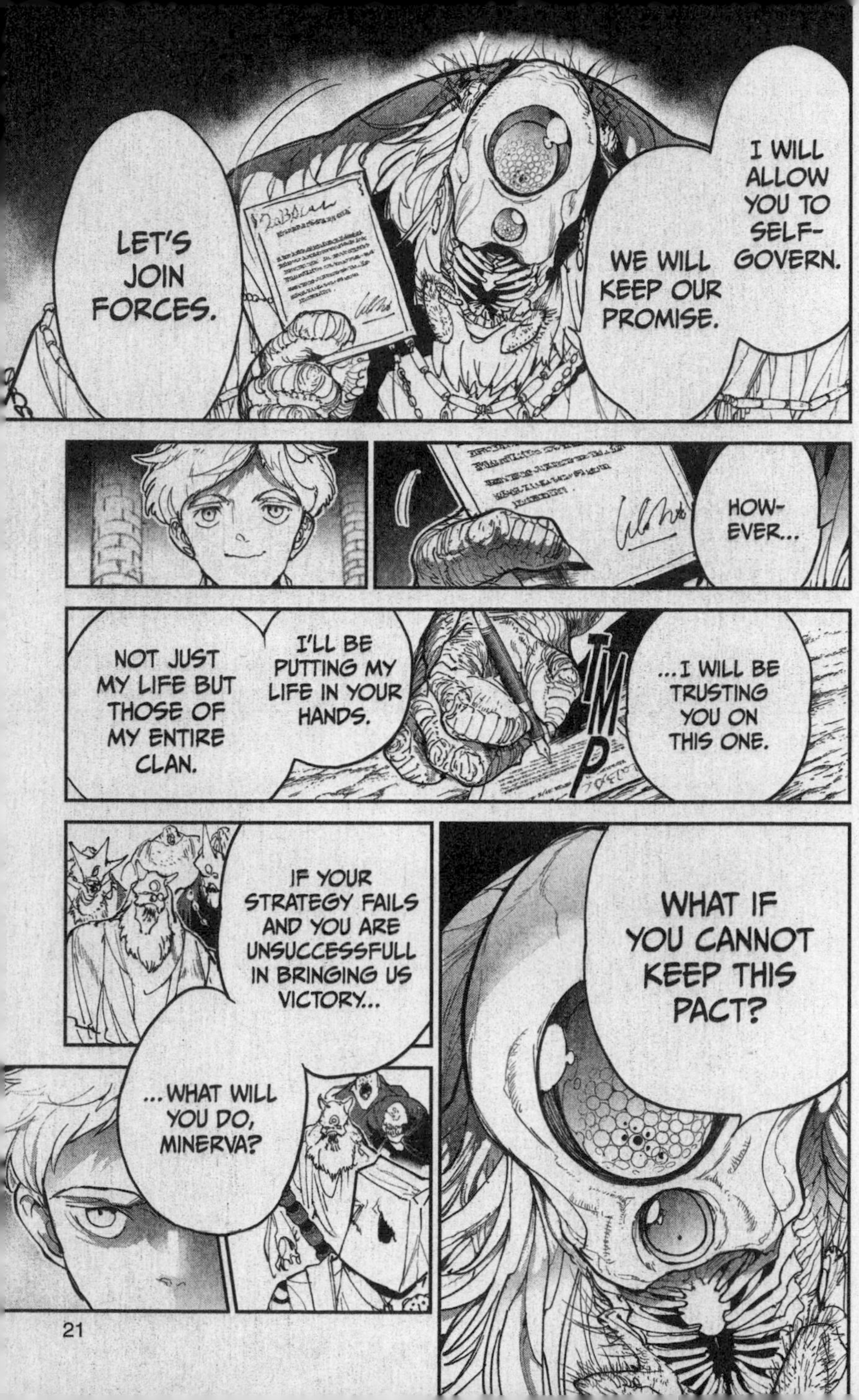
I WILL ALLOW YOU TO SELF-GOVERN.
WE WILL KEEP OUR PROMISE.
LET'S JOIN FORCES.
HOW-EVER...
...I WILL BE TRUSTING YOU ON THIS ONE.
TMP
I'LL BE PUTTING MY LIFE IN YOUR HANDS.
NOT JUST MY LIFE BUT THOSE OF MY ENTIRE CLAN.
WHAT IF YOU CANNOT KEEP THIS PACT?
IF YOUR STRATEGY FAILS AND YOU ARE UNSUCCESSFULL IN BRINGING US VICTORY...
...WHAT WILL YOU DO, MINERVA?

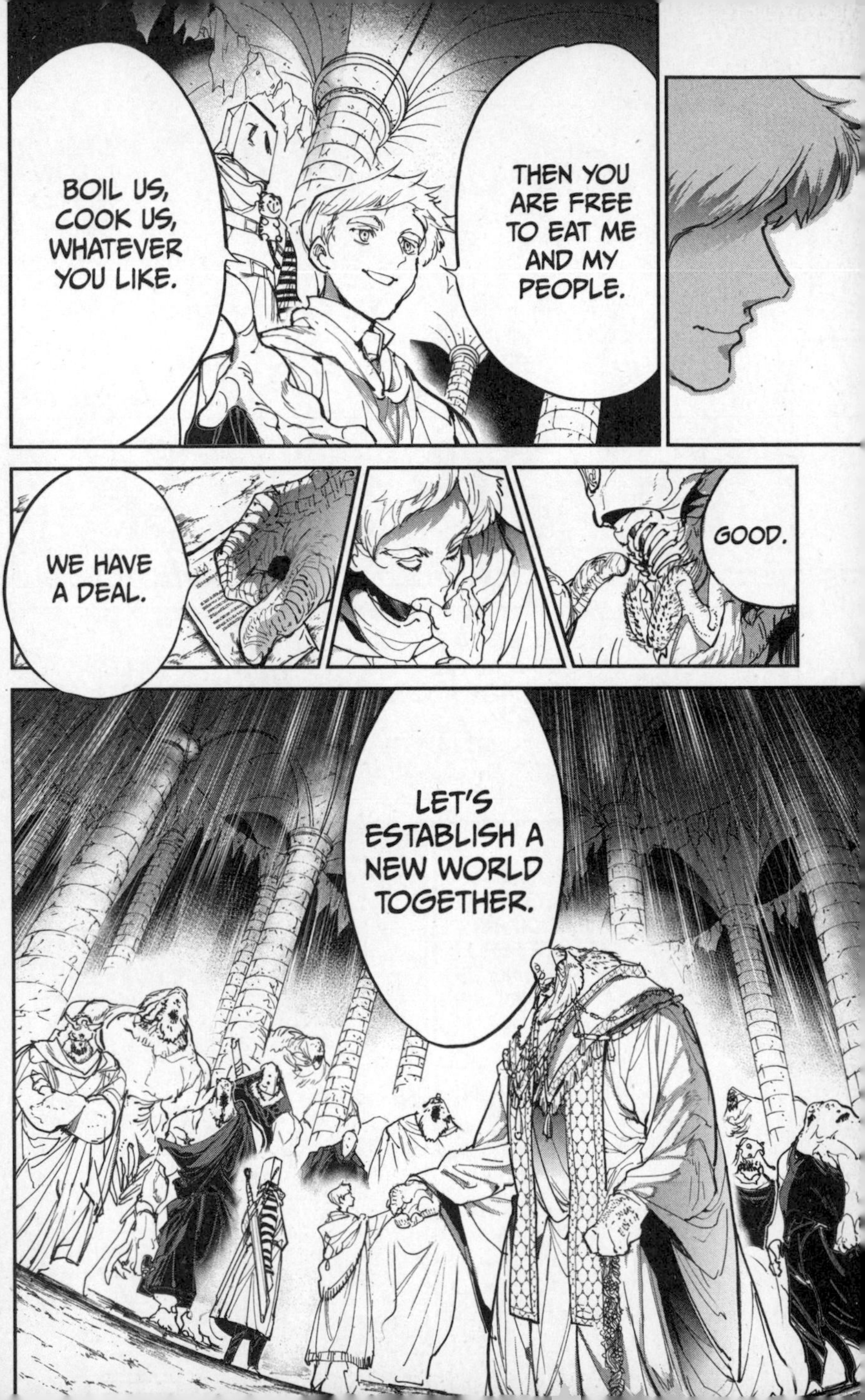
THEN YOU ARE FREE TO EAT ME AND MY PEOPLE.
BOIL US, COOK US, WHATEVER YOU LIKE.
GOOD.
WE HAVE A DEAL.
LET'S ESTABLISH A NEW WORLD TOGETHER.

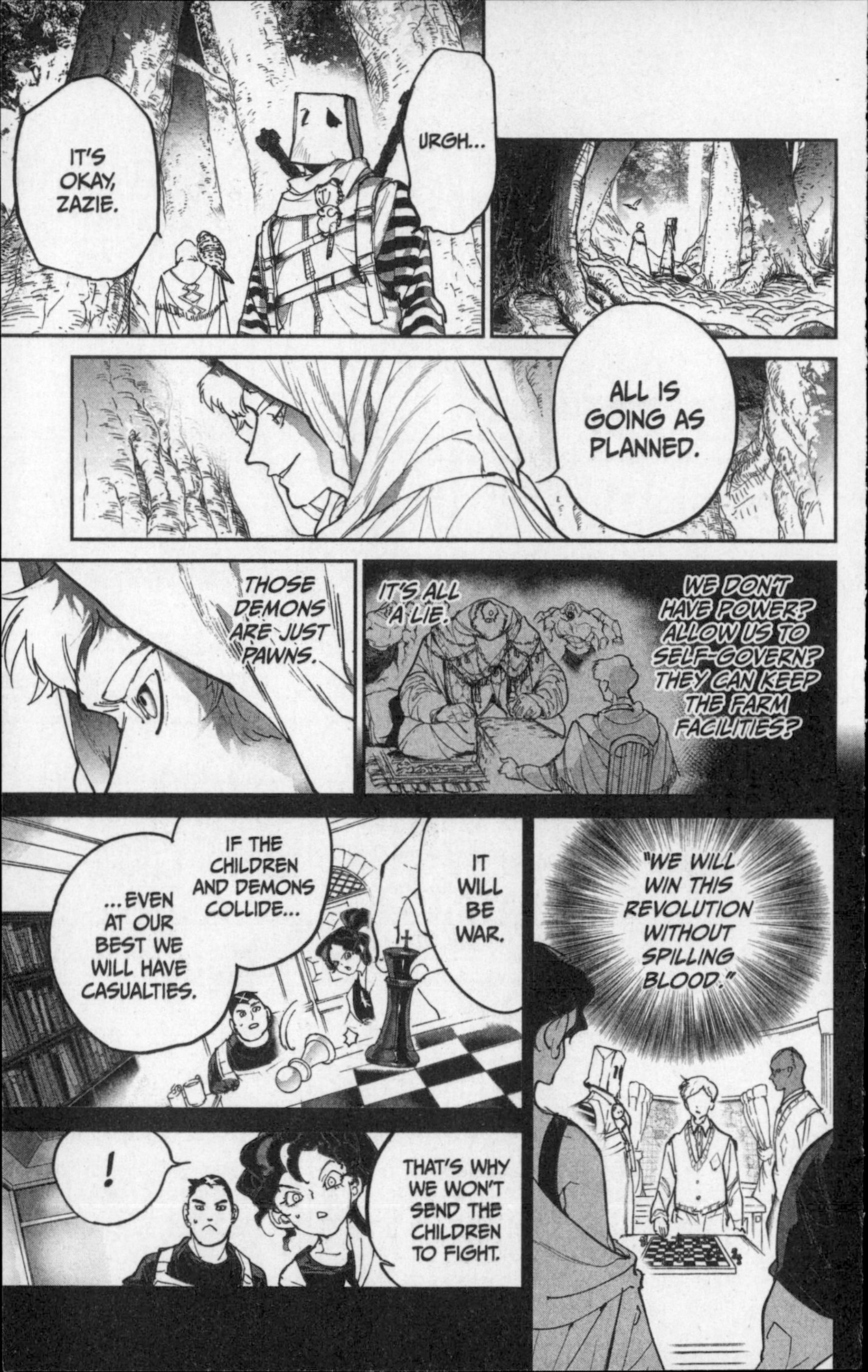
URGH...
IT'S OKAY, ZAZIE.
ALL IS GOING AS PLANNED.
WE DON'T HAVE POWER? ALLOW US TO SELF-GOVERN? THEY CAN KEEP THE FARM FACILITIES?
IT'S ALL A LIE.
THOSE DEMONS ARE JUST PAWNS.
"WE WILL WIN THIS REVOLUTION WITHOUT SPILLING BLOOD."
IT WILL BE WAR.
IF THE CHILDREN AND DEMONS COLLIDE...
...EVEN AT OUR BEST WE WILL HAVE CASUALTIES.
THAT'S WHY WE WON'T SEND THE CHILDREN TO FIGHT.
!

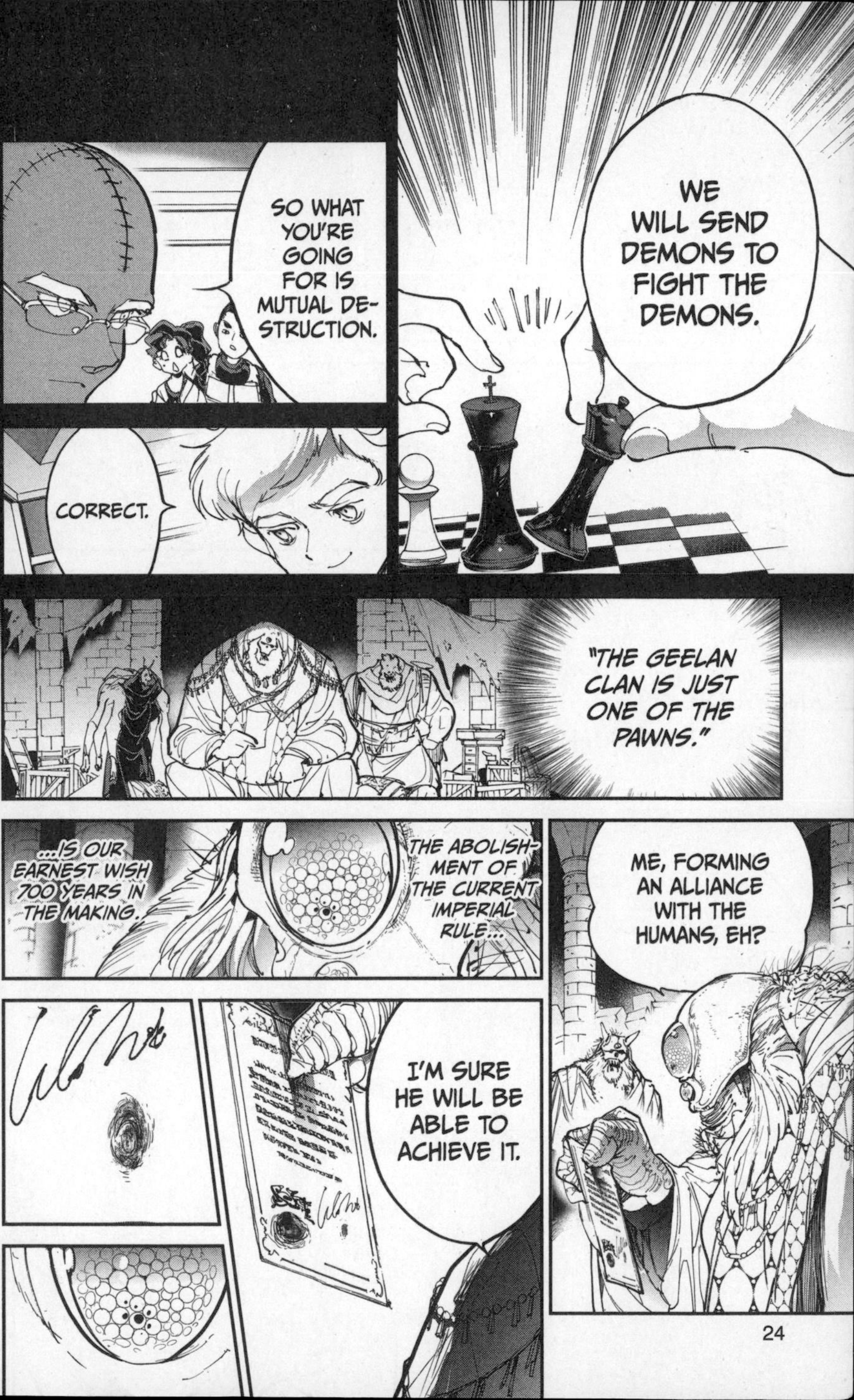
WE WILL SEND DEMONS TO FIGHT THE DEMONS.
SO WHAT YOU'RE GOING FOR IS MUTUAL DE-STRUCTION.
CORRECT.
"THE GEELAN CLAN IS JUST ONE OF THE PAWNS."
ME, FORMING AN ALLIANCE WITH THE HUMANS, EH?
THE ABOLISH-MENT OF THE CURRENT IMPERIAL RULE...
...IS OUR EARNEST WISH 700 YEARS IN THE MAKING.
I'M SURE HE WILL BE ABLE TO ACHIEVE IT.

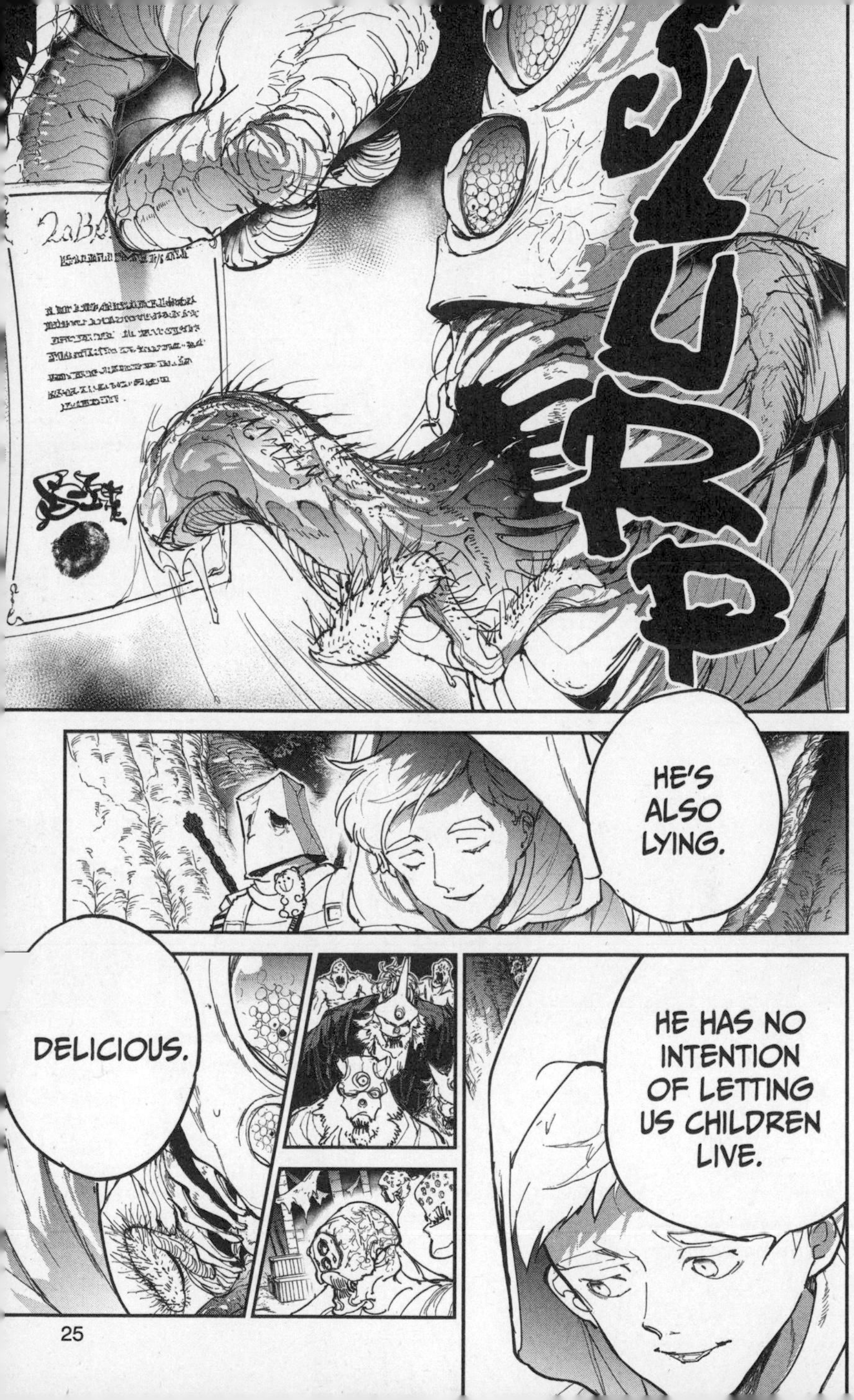
SLURP
HE'S ALSO LYING.
HE HAS NO INTENTION OF LETTING US CHILDREN LIVE.
DELICIOUS.

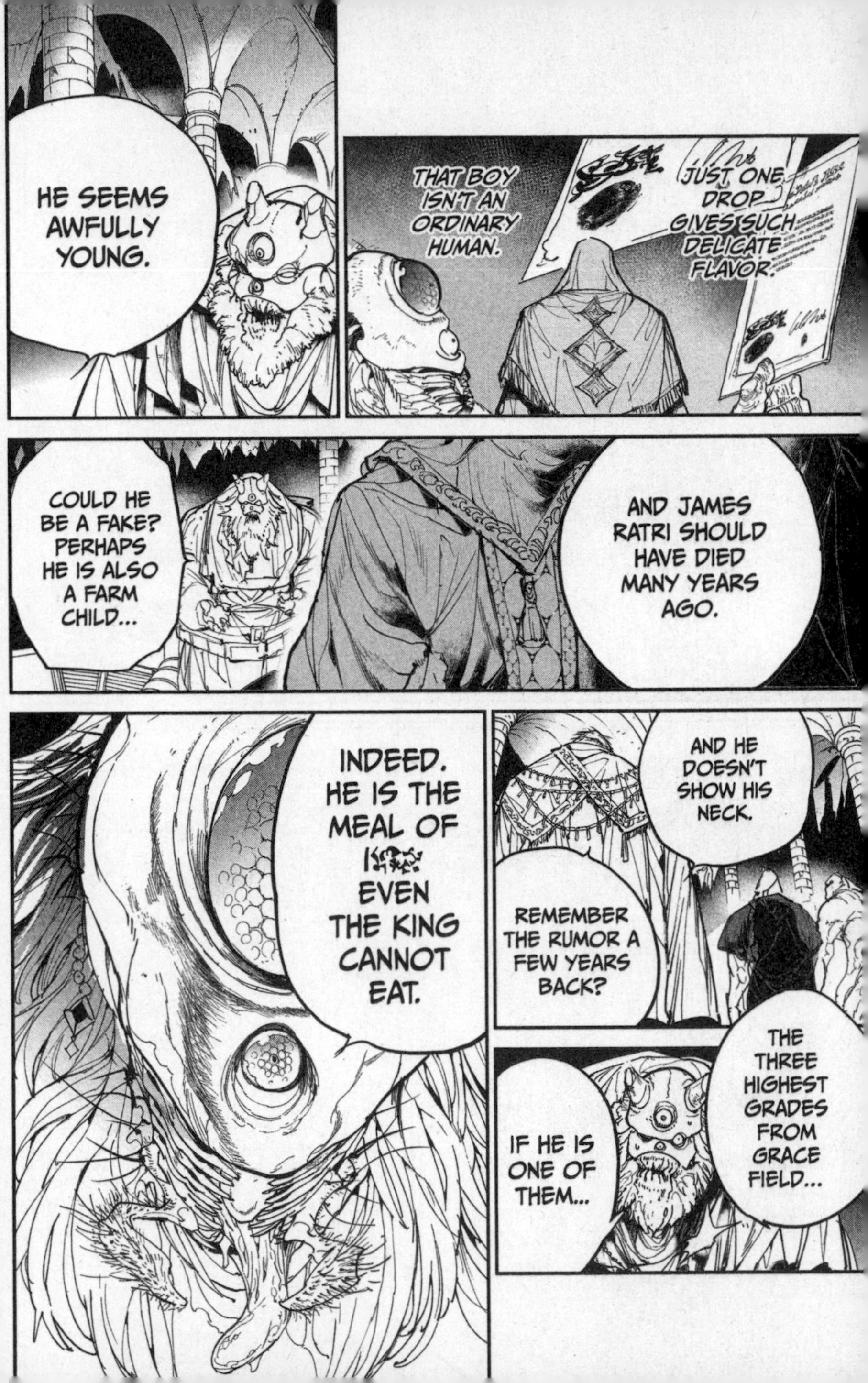
JUST ONE DROP GIVES SUCH DELICATE FLAVOR.
THAT BOY ISN'T AN ORDINARY HUMAN.
HE SEEMS AWFULLY YOUNG.
AND JAMES RATRI SHOULD HAVE DIED MANY YEARS AGO.
COULD HE BE A FAKE? PERHAPS HE IS ALSO A FARM CHILD...
AND HE DOESN'T SHOW HIS NECK.
REMEMBER THE RUMOR A FEW YEARS BACK?
THE THREE HIGHEST GRADES FROM GRACE FIELD...
IF HE IS ONE OF THEM...
INDEED. HE IS THE MEAL OF
EVEN THE KING CANNOT EAT.

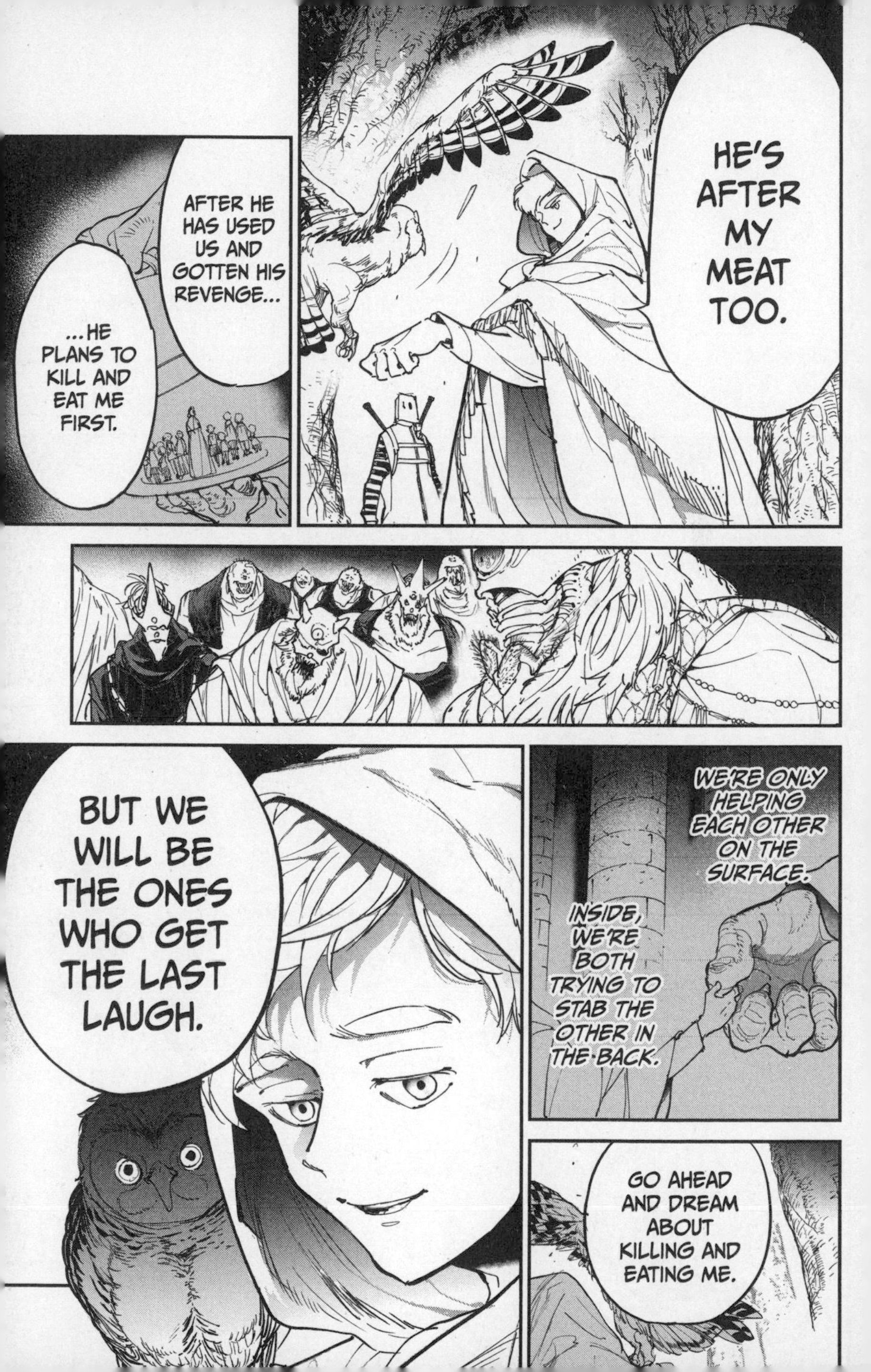
HE'S AFTER MY MEAT TOO.
AFTER HE HAS USED US AND GOTTEN HIS REVENGE...
...HE PLANS TO KILL AND EAT ME FIRST.
WE'RE ONLY HELPING EACH OTHER ON THE SURFACE.
INSIDE, WE'RE BOTH TRYING TO STAB THE OTHER IN THE BACK.
GO AHEAD AND DREAM ABOUT KILLING AND EATING ME.
BUT WE WILL BE THE ONES WHO GET THE LAST LAUGH.

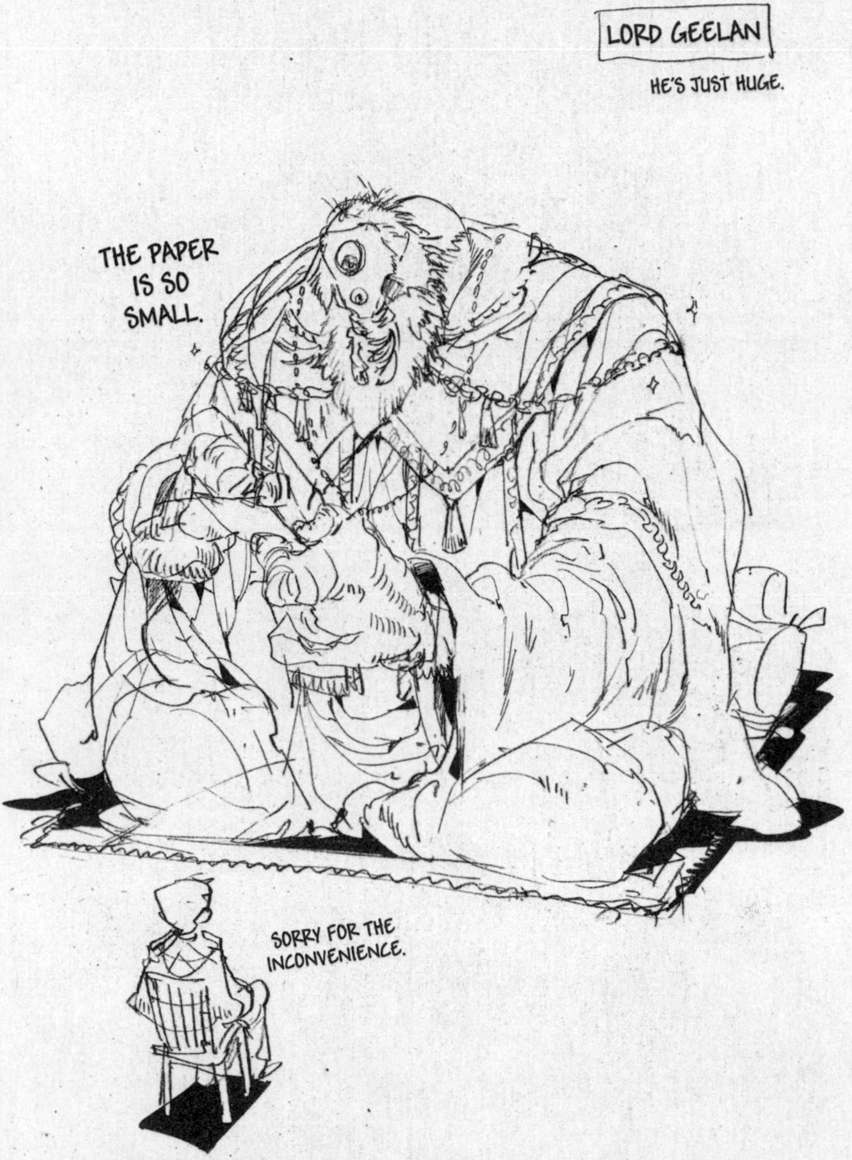
LORD GEELAN
HE'S JUST HUGE.
THE PAPER IS SO SMALL.
SORRY FOR THE INCONVENIENCE.

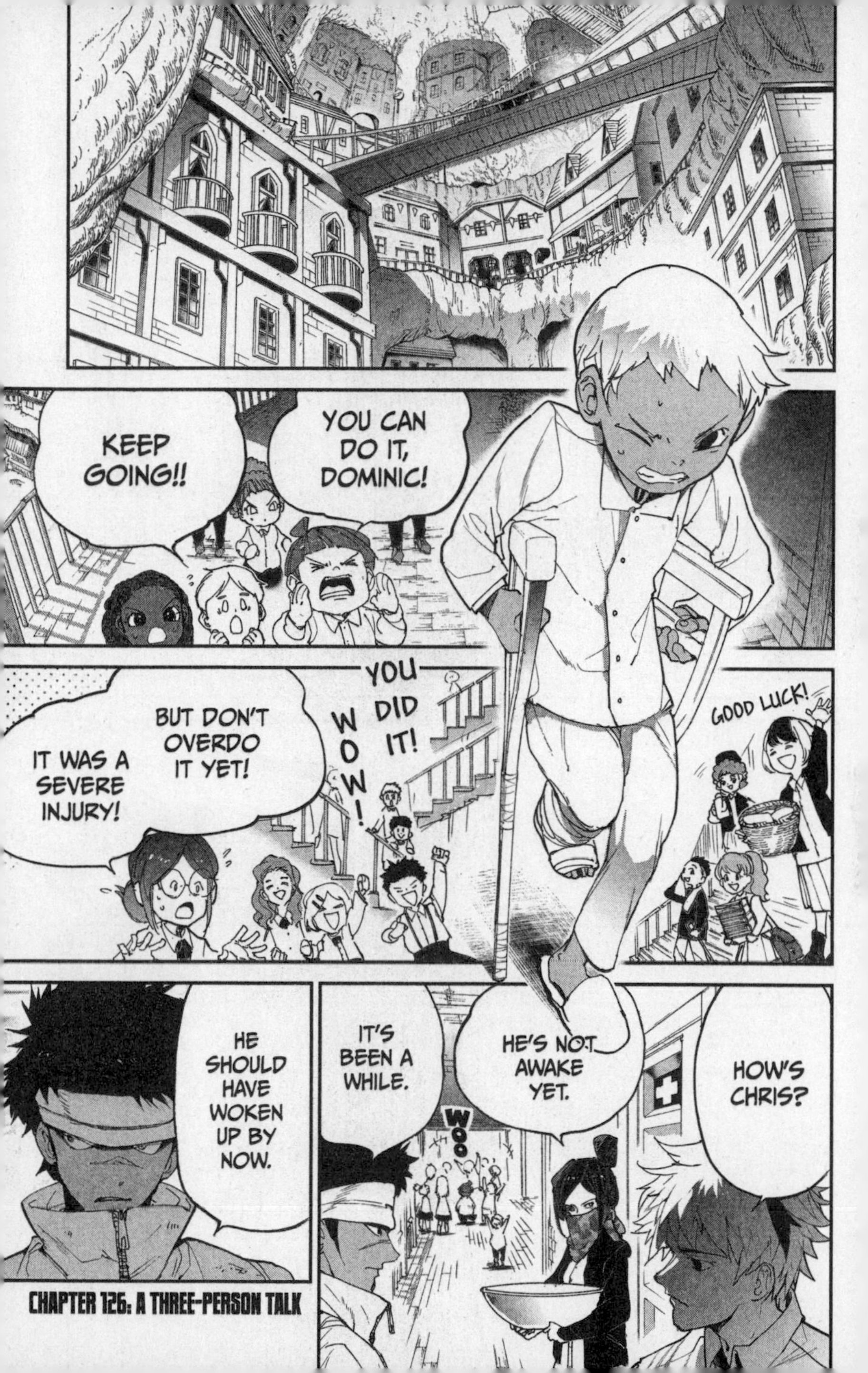
YOU CAN DO IT, DOMINIC!
KEEP GOING!!
GOOD LUCK!
YOU DID IT!
WOW!
BUT DON'T OVERDO IT YET!
IT WAS A SEVERE INJURY!
HOW'S CHRIS?
HE'S NOT AWAKE YET.
IT'S BEEN A WHILE.
WOO
HE SHOULD HAVE WOKEN UP BY NOW.

CHAPTER 126: A THREE-PERSON TALK

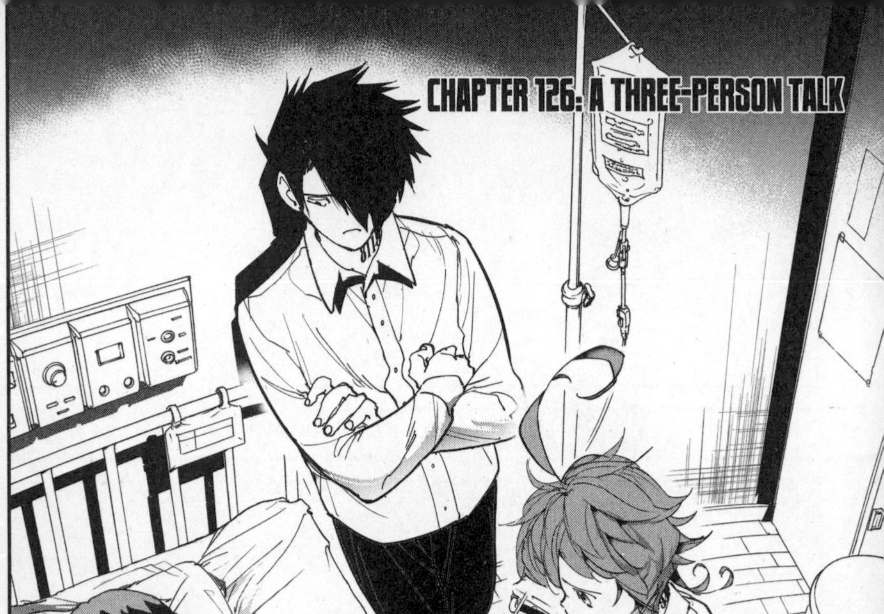
CHAPTER 126: A THREE-PERSON TALK
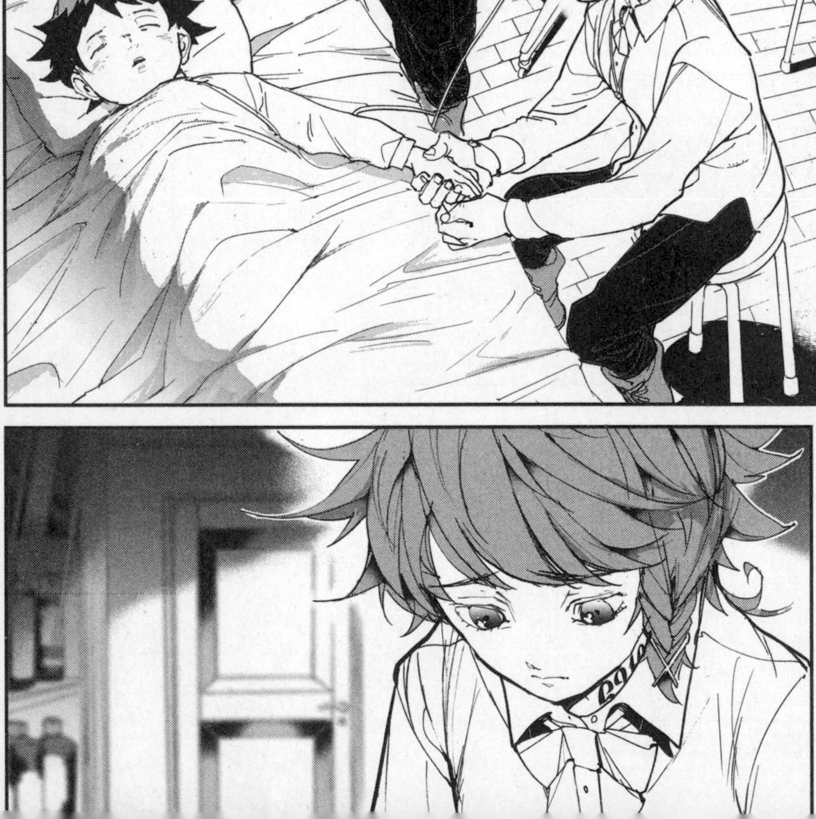

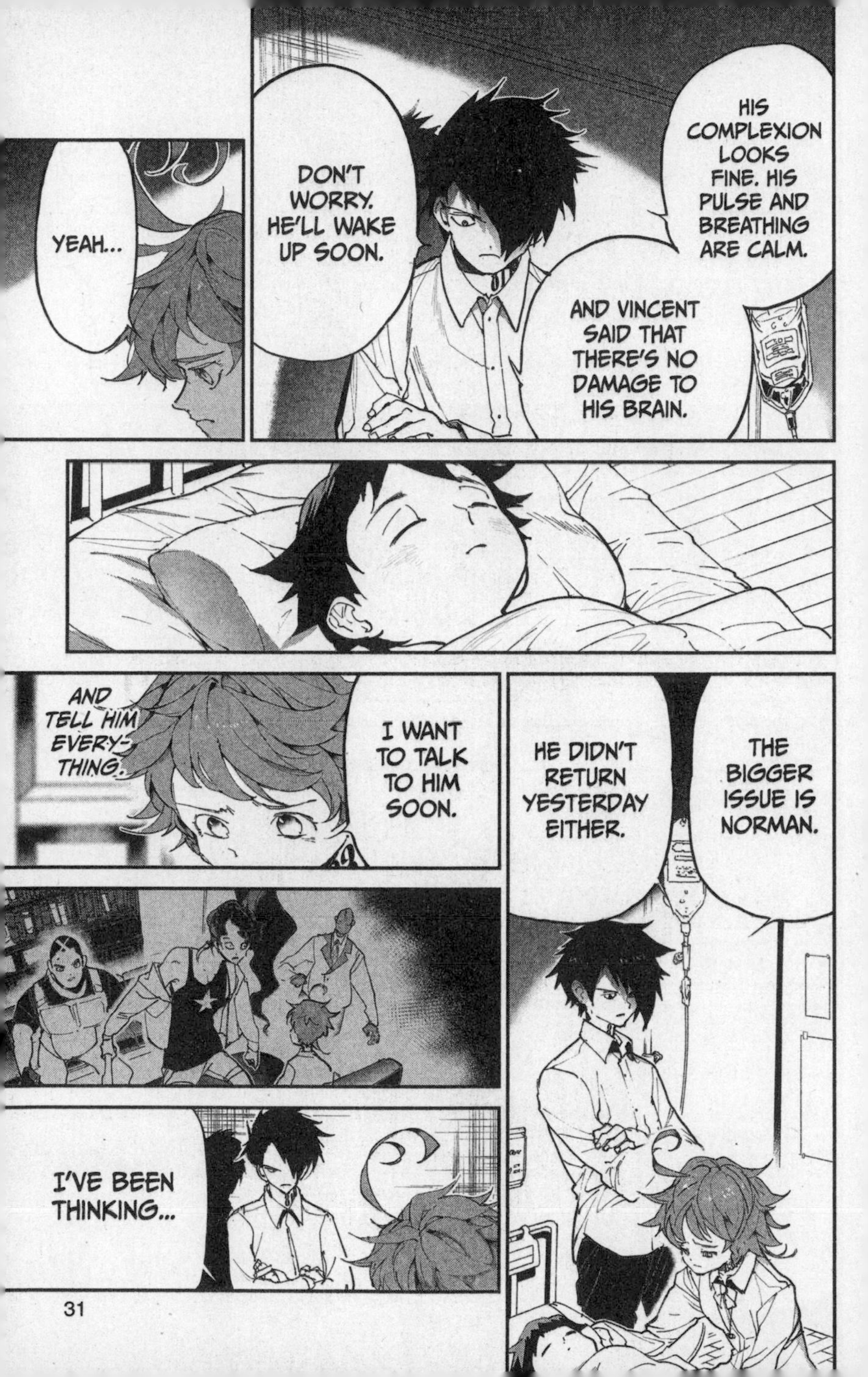
HIS COMPLEXION LOOKS FINE. HIS PULSE AND BREATHING ARE CALM.
AND VINCENT SAID THAT THERE'S NO DAMAGE TO HIS BRAIN.
DON'T WORRY. HE'LL WAKE UP SOON.
YEAH...
THE BIGGER ISSUE IS NORMAN.
HE DIDN'T RETURN YESTERDAY EITHER.
I WANT TO TALK TO HIM SOON.
AND TELL HIM EVERYTHING.
I'VE BEEN THINKING...

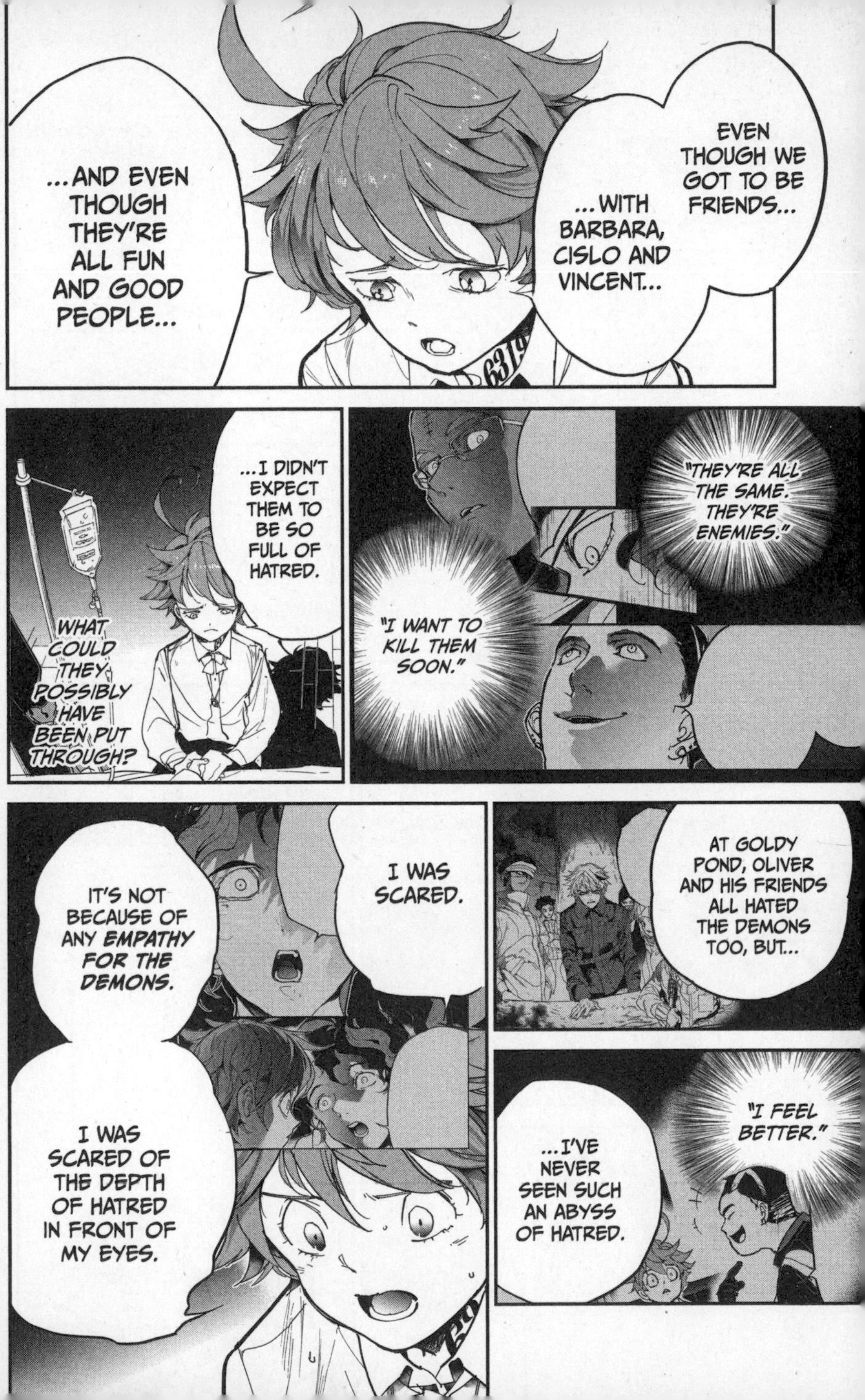
EVEN THOUGH WE GOT TO BE FRIENDS...
...WITH BARBARA, CISLO AND VINCENT...
...AND EVEN THOUGH THEY'RE ALL FUN AND GOOD PEOPLE...
"THEY'RE ALL THE SAME. THEY'RE ENEMIES."
"I WANT TO KILL THEM SOON."
...I DIDN'T EXPECT THEM TO BE SO FULL OF HATRED.
WHAT COULD THEY POSSIBLY HAVE BEEN PUT THROUGH?
AT GOLDY POND, OLIVER AND HIS FRIENDS ALL HATED THE DEMONS TOO, BUT...
"I FEEL BETTER."
...I'VE NEVER SEEN SUCH AN ABYSS OF HATRED.
I WAS SCARED.
IT'S NOT BECAUSE OF ANY *EMPATHY FOR THE DEMONS*.
I WAS SCARED OF THE DEPTH OF HATRED IN FRONT OF MY EYES.

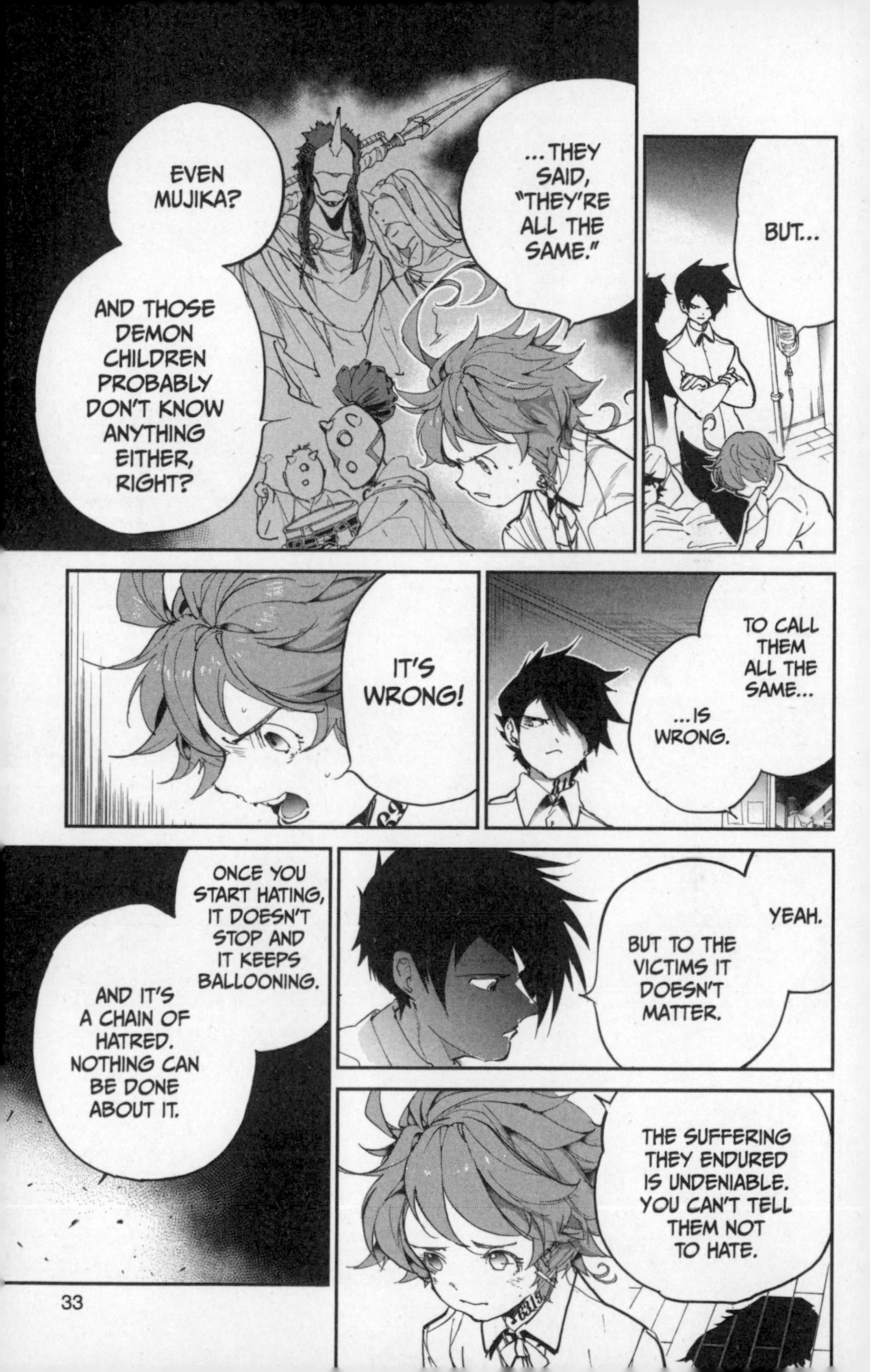
BUT...
...THEY SAID, "THEY'RE ALL THE SAME."
EVEN MUJIKA?
AND THOSE DEMON CHILDREN PROBABLY DON'T KNOW ANYTHING EITHER, RIGHT?
TO CALL THEM ALL THE SAME...
...IS WRONG.
IT'S WRONG!
YEAH.
BUT TO THE VICTIMS IT DOESN'T MATTER.
THE SUFFERING THEY ENDURED IS UNDENIABLE. YOU CAN'T TELL THEM NOT TO HATE.
ONCE YOU START HATING, IT DOESN'T STOP AND IT KEEPS BALLOONING.
AND IT'S A CHAIN OF HATRED. NOTHING CAN BE DONE ABOUT IT.

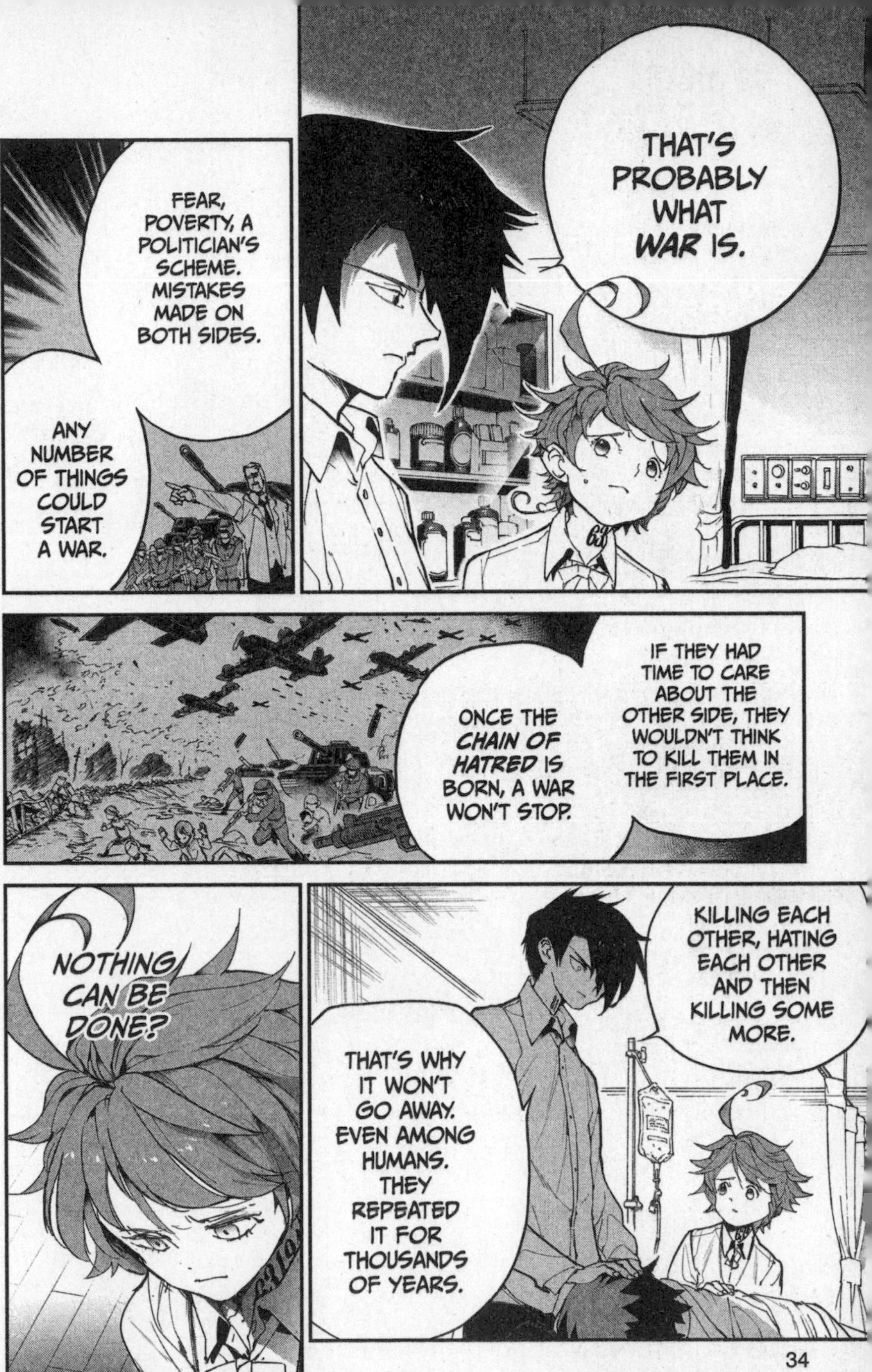
THAT'S PROBABLY WHAT *WAR* IS.
FEAR, POVERTY, A POLITICIAN'S SCHEME. MISTAKES MADE ON BOTH SIDES.
ANY NUMBER OF THINGS COULD START A WAR.
IF THEY HAD TIME TO CARE ABOUT THE OTHER SIDE, THEY WOULDN'T THINK TO KILL THEM IN THE FIRST PLACE.
ONCE THE *CHAIN OF HATRED* IS BORN, A WAR WON'T STOP.
KILLING EACH OTHER, HATING EACH OTHER AND THEN KILLING SOME MORE.
THAT'S WHY IT WON'T GO AWAY. EVEN AMONG HUMANS. THEY REPEATED IT FOR THOUSANDS OF YEARS.
NOTHING CAN BE DONE?

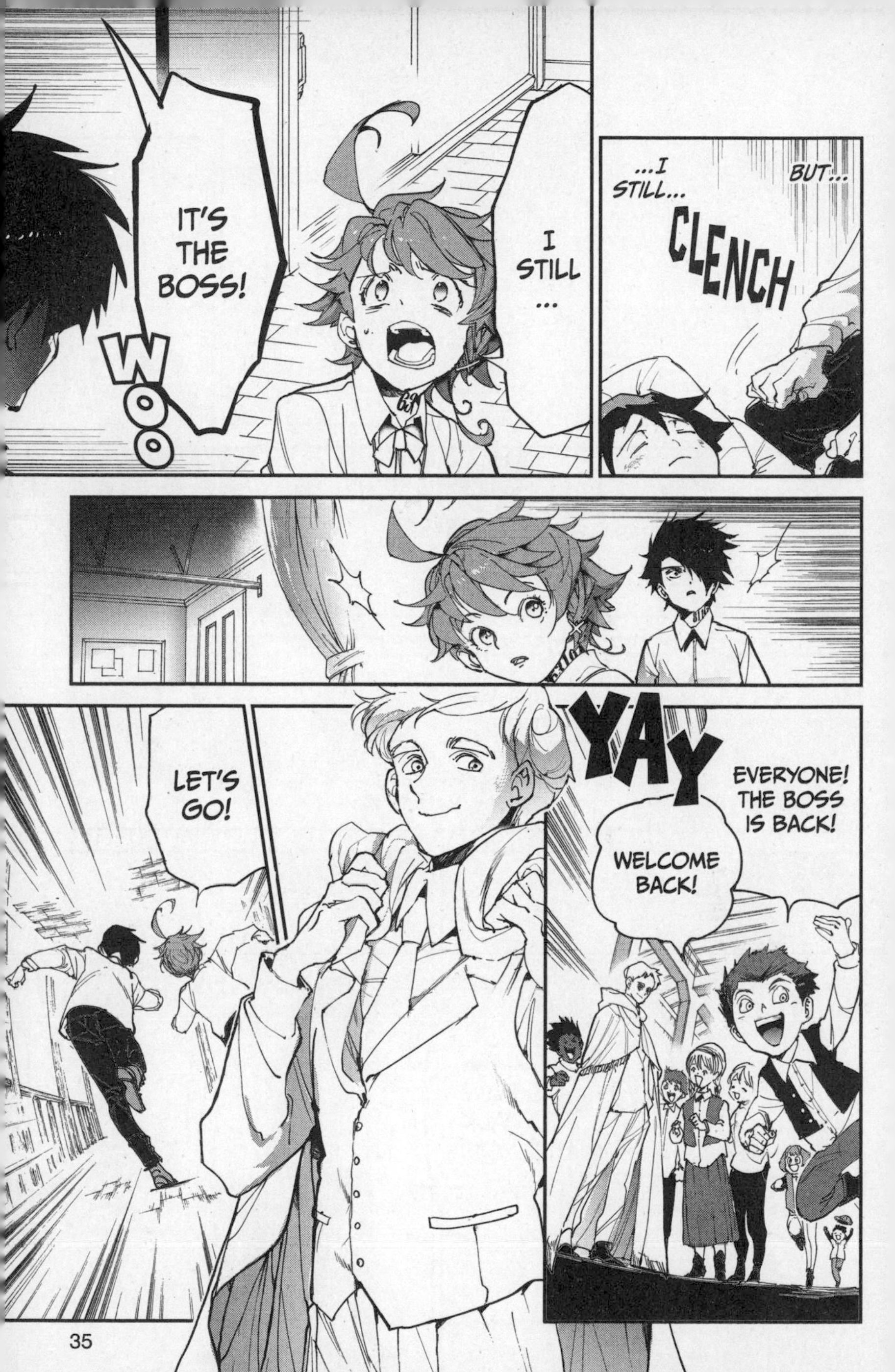
BUT...
...I STILL...
CLENCH
I STILL ...
IT'S THE BOSS!
WOO
YAY
EVERYONE! THE BOSS IS BACK!
WELCOME BACK!
LET'S GO!

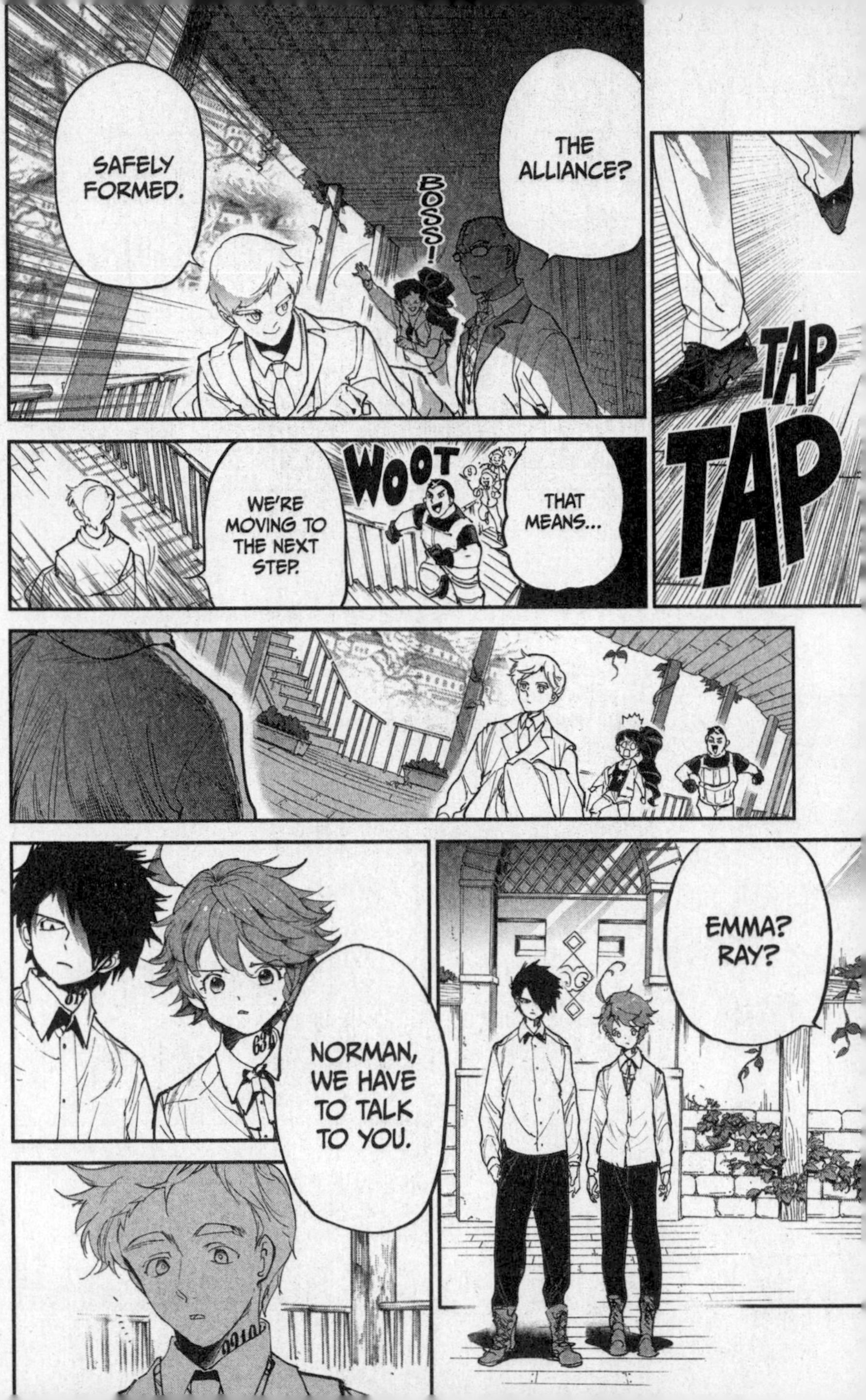
TAP
TAP
THE ALLIANCE?
BOSS!
SAFELY FORMED.
THAT MEANS...
WOOT
WE'RE MOVING TO THE NEXT STEP.
EMMA? RAY?
NORMAN, WE HAVE TO TALK TO YOU.

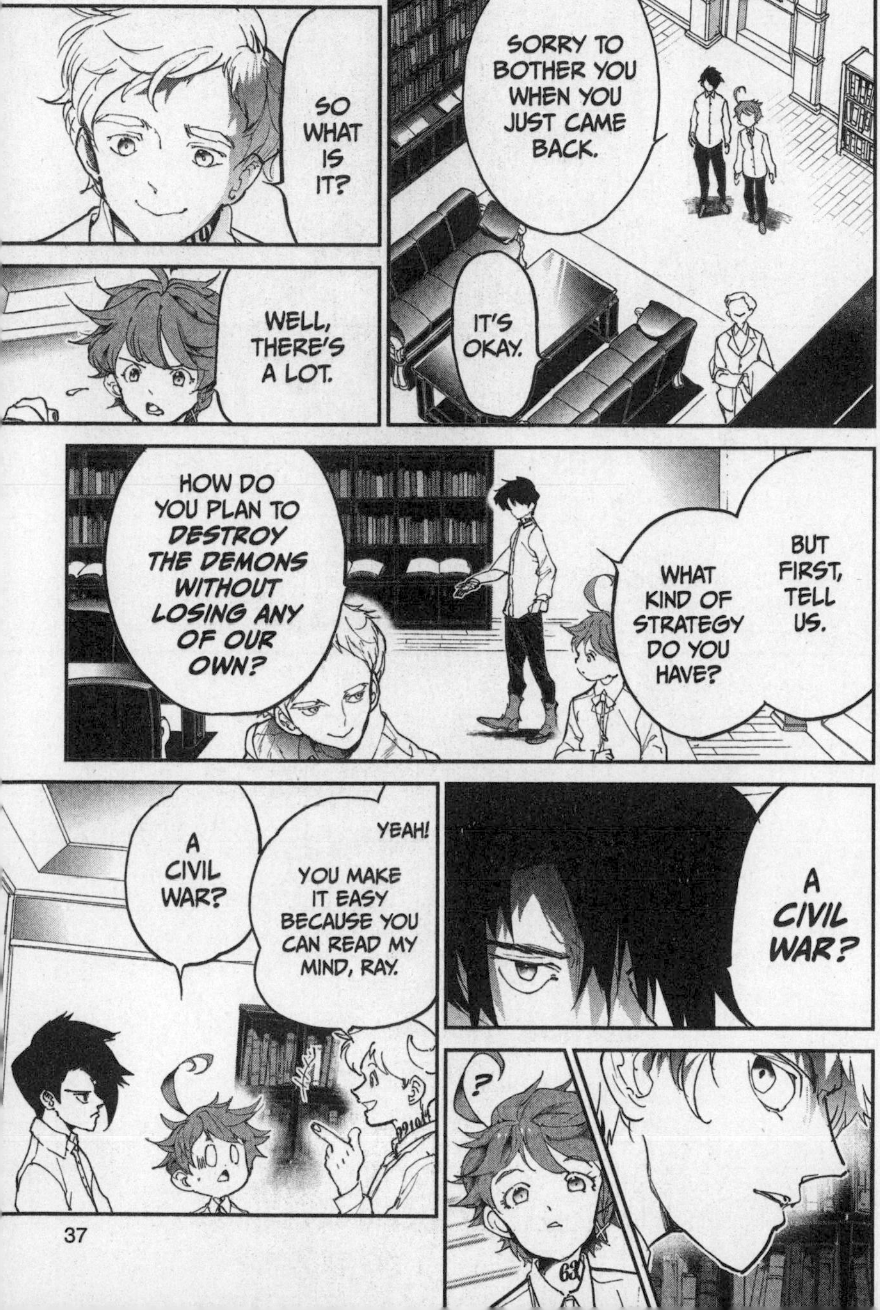
SORRY TO BOTHER YOU WHEN YOU JUST CAME BACK.
IT'S OKAY.
SO WHAT IS IT?
WELL, THERE'S A LOT.
BUT FIRST, TELL US.
WHAT KIND OF STRATEGY DO YOU HAVE?
HOW DO YOU PLAN TO *DESTROY THE DEMONS WITHOUT LOSING ANY OF OUR OWN?*
A *CIVIL WAR?*
?
A CIVIL WAR?
YEAH!
YOU MAKE IT EASY BECAUSE YOU CAN READ MY MIND, RAY.

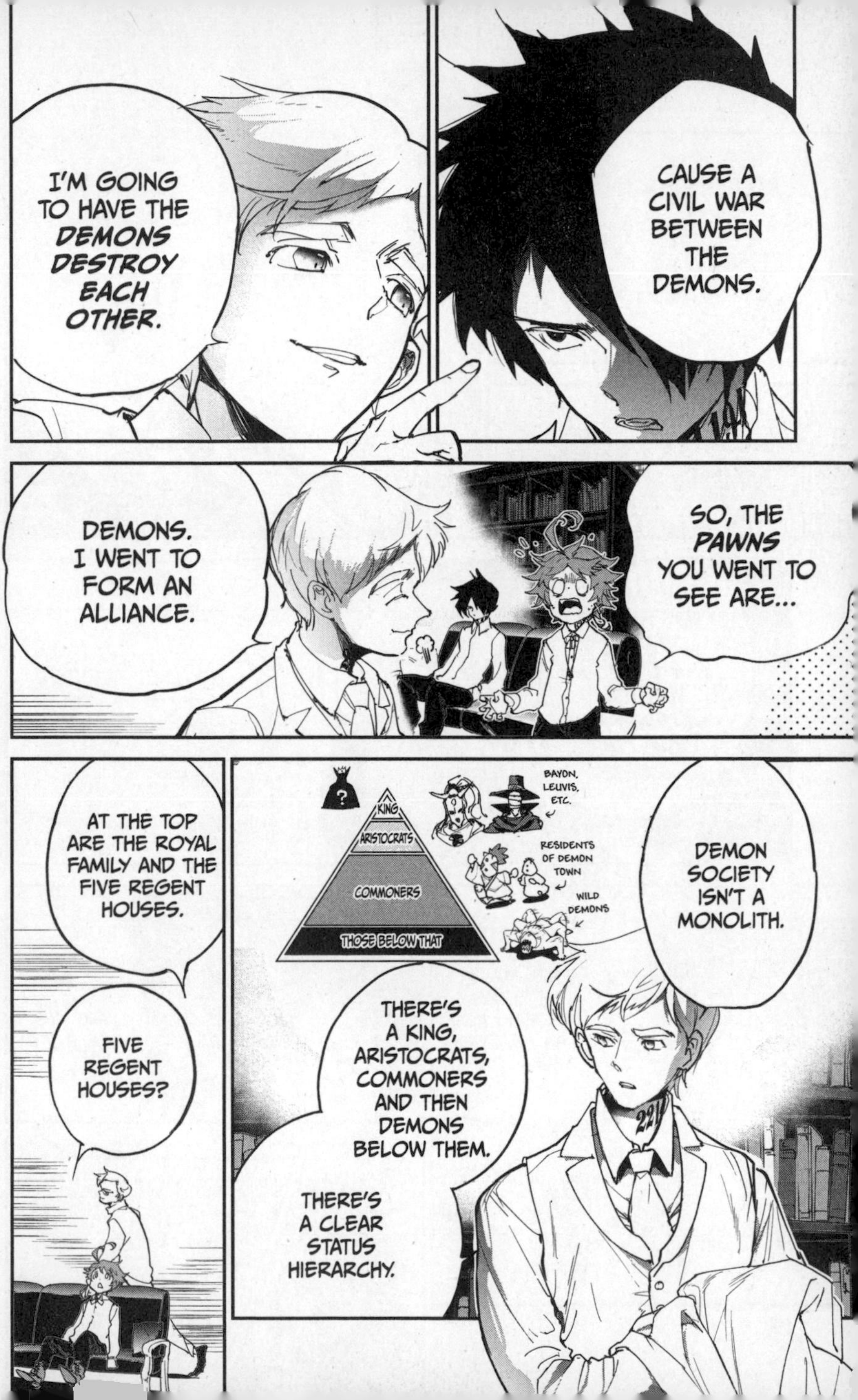
CAUSE A CIVIL WAR BETWEEN THE DEMONS.
I'M GOING TO HAVE THE *DEMONS DESTROY EACH OTHER.*
SO, THE *PAWNS* YOU WENT TO SEE ARE...
DEMONS. I WENT TO FORM AN ALLIANCE.
DEMON SOCIETY ISN'T A MONOLITH.
KING
ARISTOCRATS
COMMONERS
THOSE BELOW THAT
BAYON, LEUVIS, ETC.
RESIDENTS OF DEMON TOWN
WILD DEMONS
THERE'S A KING, ARISTOCRATS, COMMONERS AND THEN DEMONS BELOW THEM.
THERE'S A CLEAR STATUS HIERARCHY.
AT THE TOP ARE THE ROYAL FAMILY AND THE FIVE REGENT HOUSES.
FIVE REGENT HOUSES?

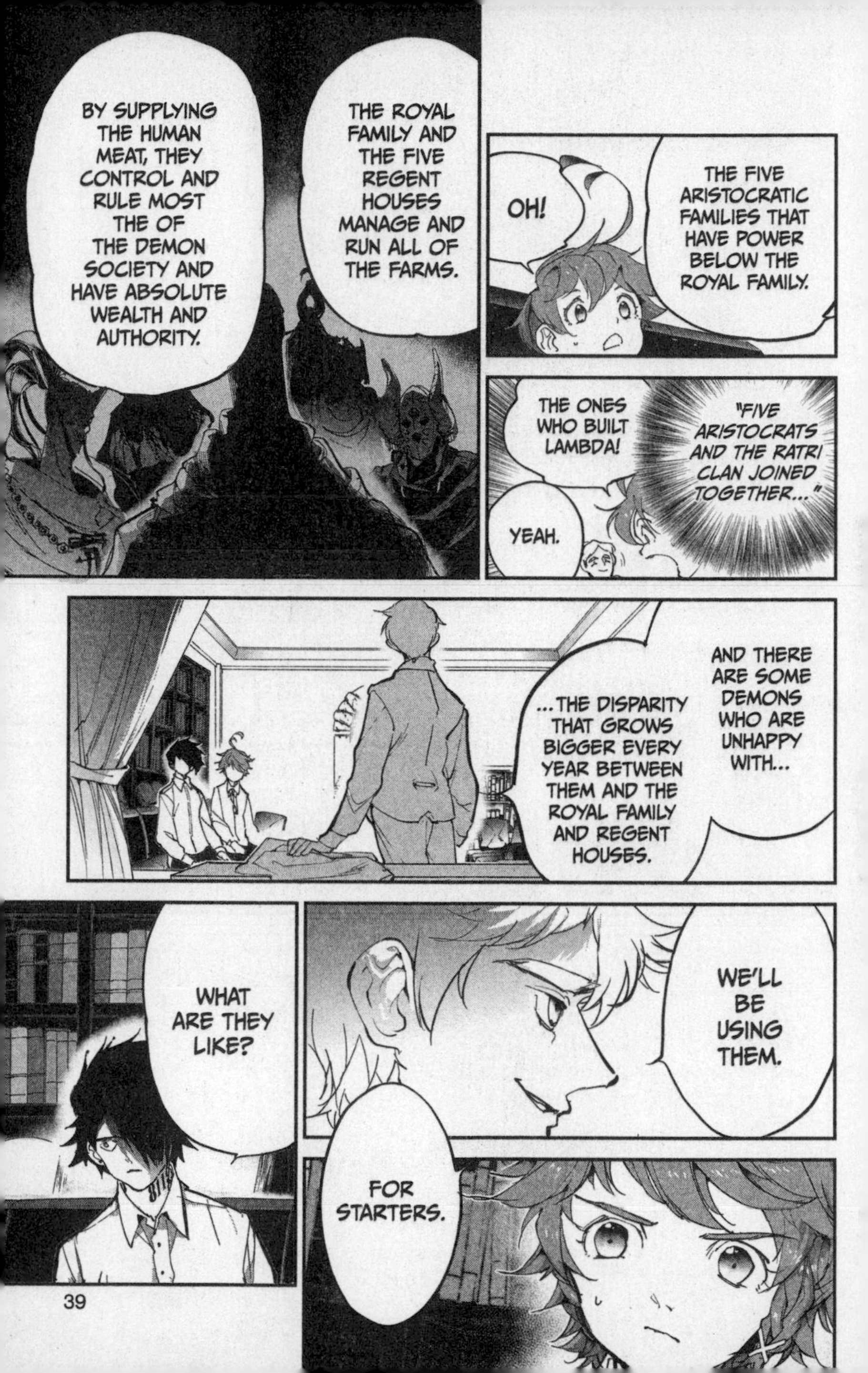
THE FIVE ARISTOCRATIC FAMILIES THAT HAVE POWER BELOW THE ROYAL FAMILY.
OH!
"FIVE ARISTOCRATS AND THE RATRI CLAN JOINED TOGETHER..."
THE ONES WHO BUILT LAMBDA!
YEAH.
THE ROYAL FAMILY AND THE FIVE REGENT HOUSES MANAGE AND RUN ALL OF THE FARMS.
BY SUPPLYING THE HUMAN MEAT, THEY CONTROL AND RULE MOST THE OF THE DEMON SOCIETY AND HAVE ABSOLUTE WEALTH AND AUTHORITY.
AND THERE ARE SOME DEMONS WHO ARE UNHAPPY WITH...
...THE DISPARITY THAT GROWS BIGGER EVERY YEAR BETWEEN THEM AND THE ROYAL FAMILY AND REGENT HOUSES.
WE'LL BE USING THEM.
FOR STARTERS.
WHAT ARE THEY LIKE?

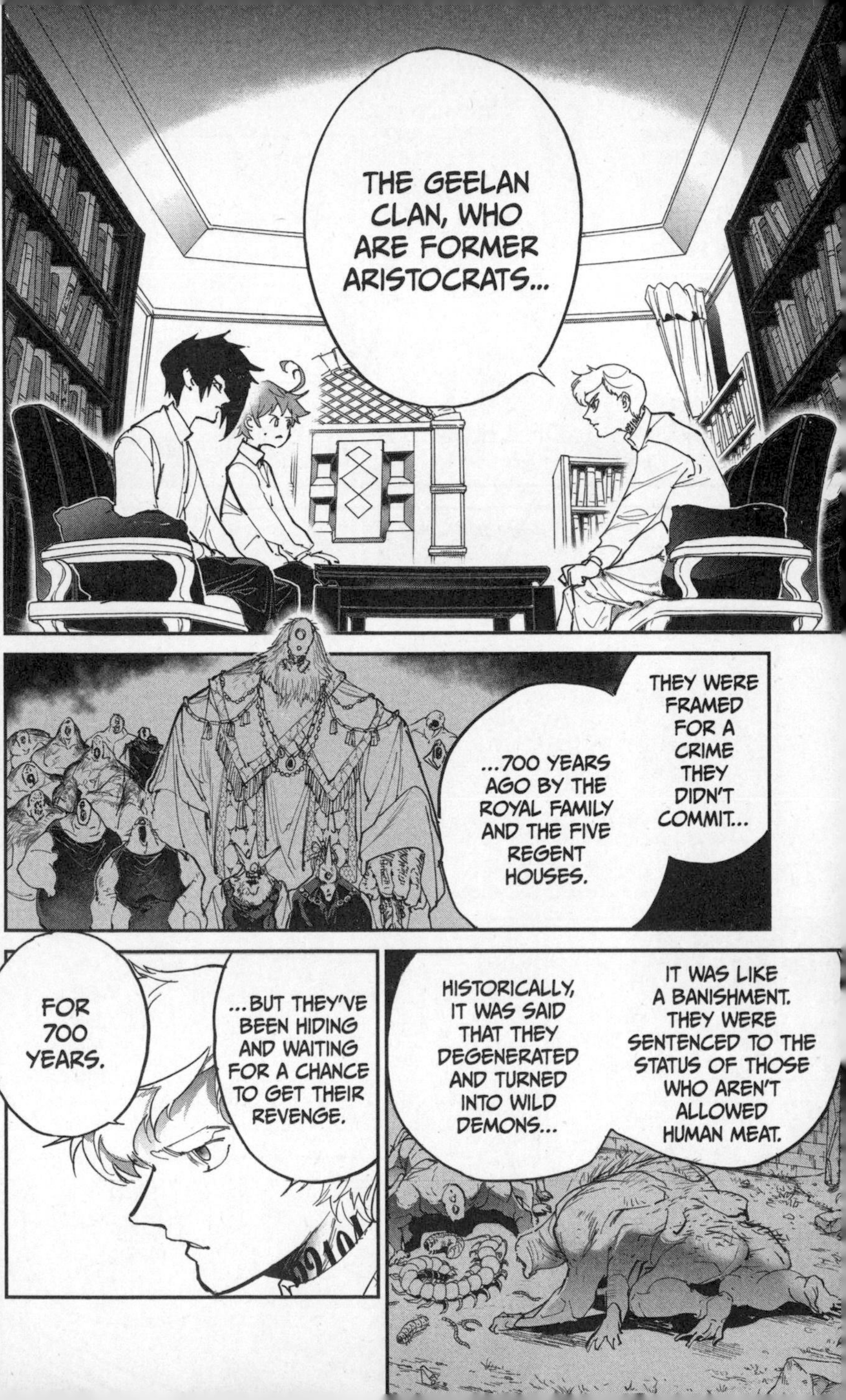
THE GEELAN CLAN, WHO ARE FORMER ARISTOCRATS...
THEY WERE FRAMED FOR A CRIME THEY DIDN'T COMMIT...
...700 YEARS AGO BY THE ROYAL FAMILY AND THE FIVE REGENT HOUSES.
IT WAS LIKE A BANISHMENT. THEY WERE SENTENCED TO THE STATUS OF THOSE WHO AREN'T ALLOWED HUMAN MEAT.
HISTORICALLY, IT WAS SAID THAT THEY DEGENERATED AND TURNED INTO WILD DEMONS...
...BUT THEY'VE BEEN HIDING AND WAITING FOR A CHANCE TO GET THEIR REVENGE.
FOR 700 YEARS.

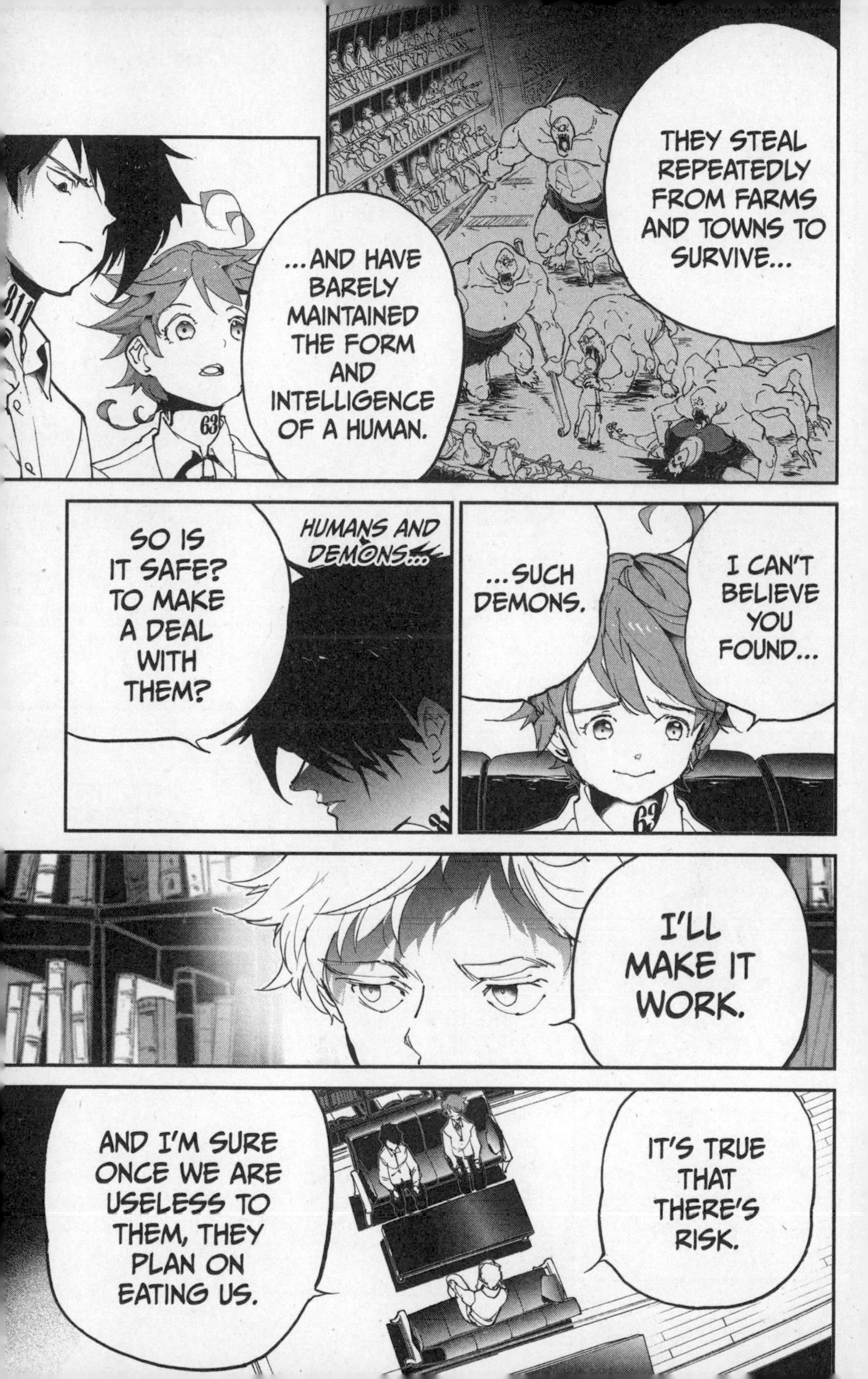
THEY STEAL REPEATEDLY FROM FARMS AND TOWNS TO SURVIVE...
...AND HAVE BARELY MAINTAINED THE FORM AND INTELLIGENCE OF A HUMAN.
I CAN'T BELIEVE YOU FOUND...
...SUCH DEMONS.
HUMANS AND DEMONS...
SO IS IT SAFE? TO MAKE A DEAL WITH THEM?
I'LL MAKE IT WORK.
IT'S TRUE THAT THERE'S RISK.
AND I'M SURE ONCE WE ARE USELESS TO THEM, THEY PLAN ON EATING US.

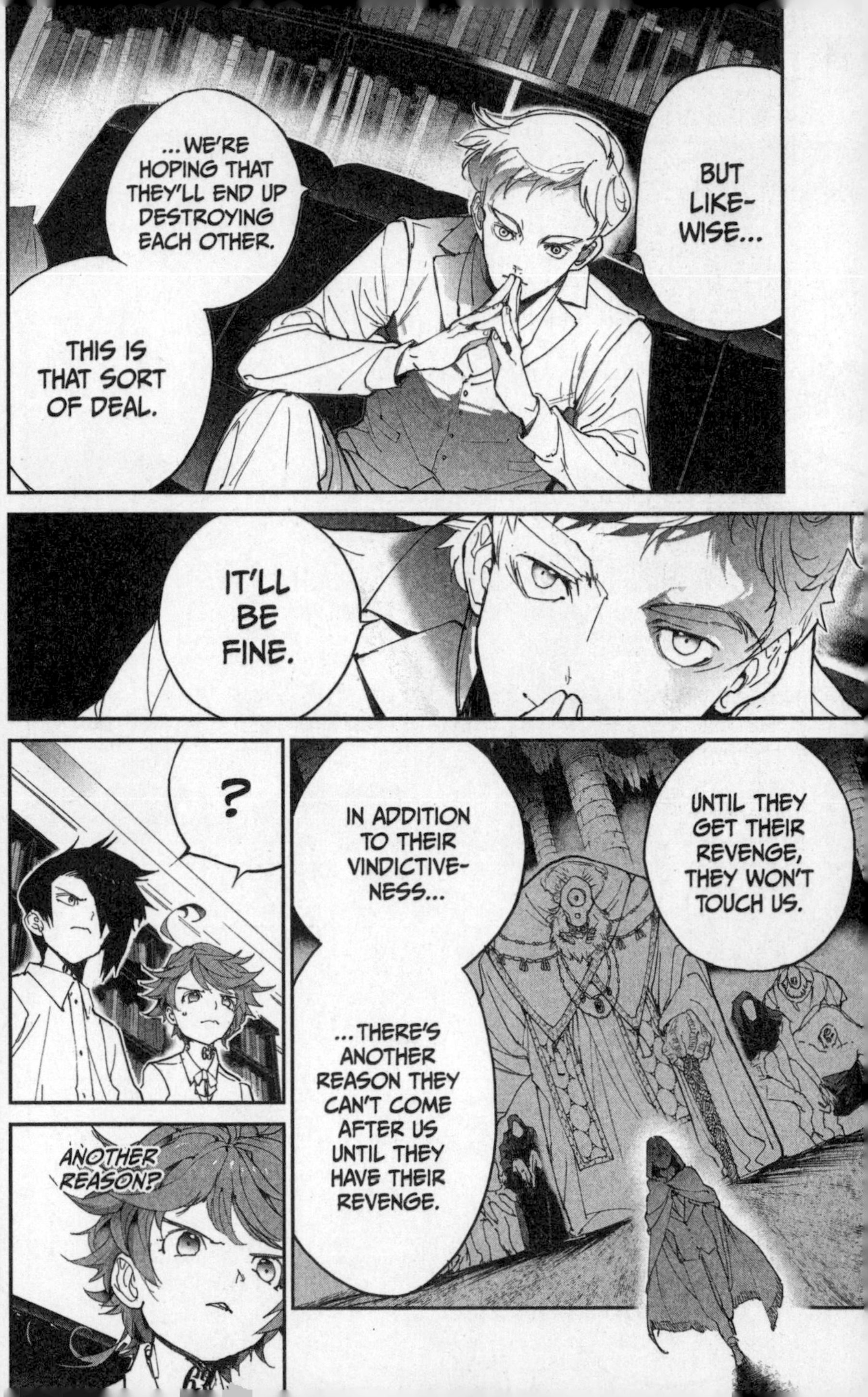
BUT LIKEWISE...
...WE'RE HOPING THAT THEY'LL END UP DESTROYING EACH OTHER.
THIS IS THAT SORT OF DEAL.
IT'LL BE FINE.
UNTIL THEY GET THEIR REVENGE, THEY WON'T TOUCH US.
IN ADDITION TO THEIR VINDICTIVENESS...
...THERE'S ANOTHER REASON THEY CAN'T COME AFTER US UNTIL THEY HAVE THEIR REVENGE.
?
ANOTHER REASON?

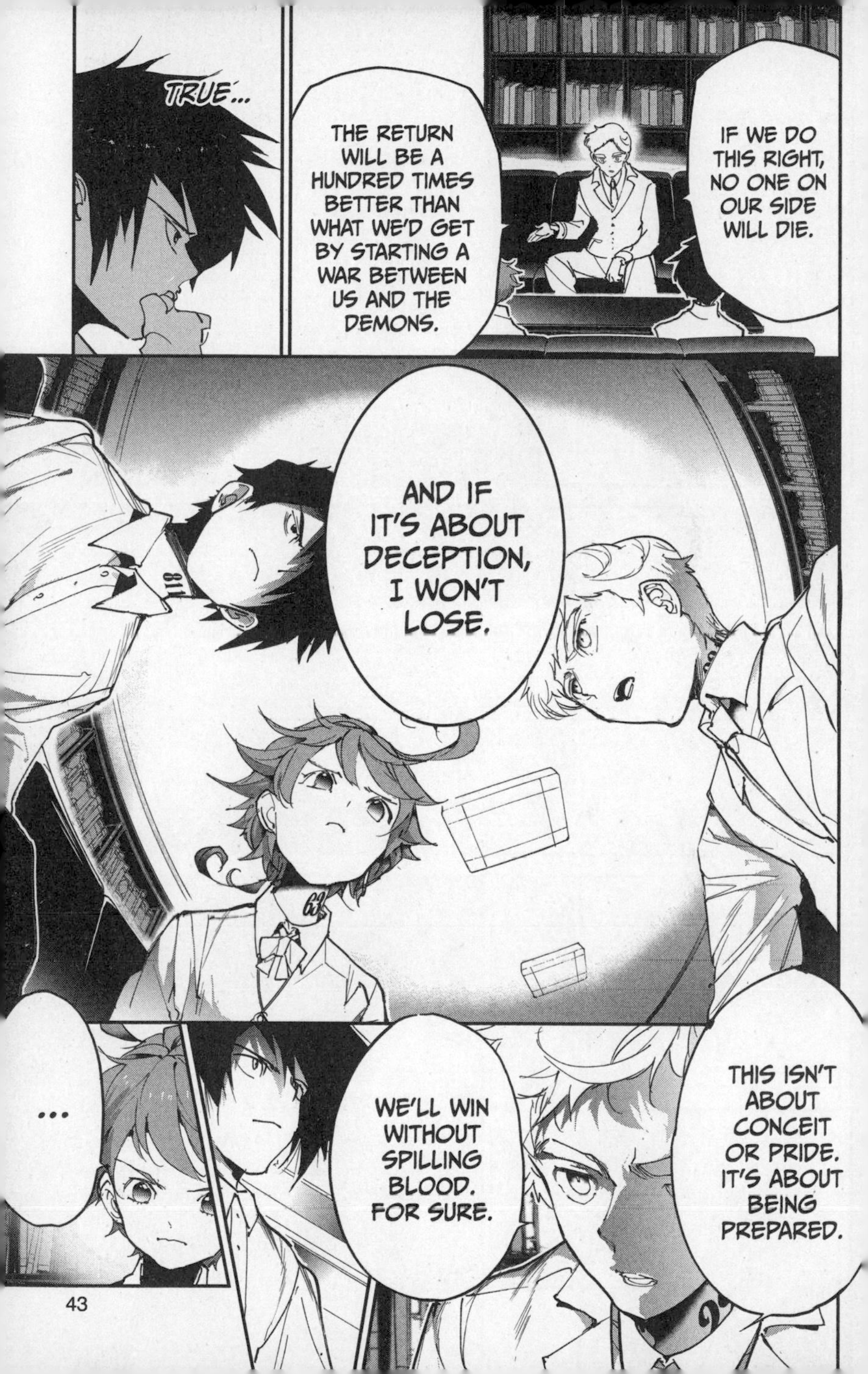
IF WE DO THIS RIGHT, NO ONE ON OUR SIDE WILL DIE.
THE RETURN WILL BE A HUNDRED TIMES BETTER THAN WHAT WE'D GET BY STARTING A WAR BETWEEN US AND THE DEMONS.
TRUE...
AND IF IT'S ABOUT DECEPTION, I WON'T LOSE.
THIS ISN'T ABOUT CONCEIT OR PRIDE. IT'S ABOUT BEING PREPARED.
WE'LL WIN WITHOUT SPILLING BLOOD. FOR SURE.
...

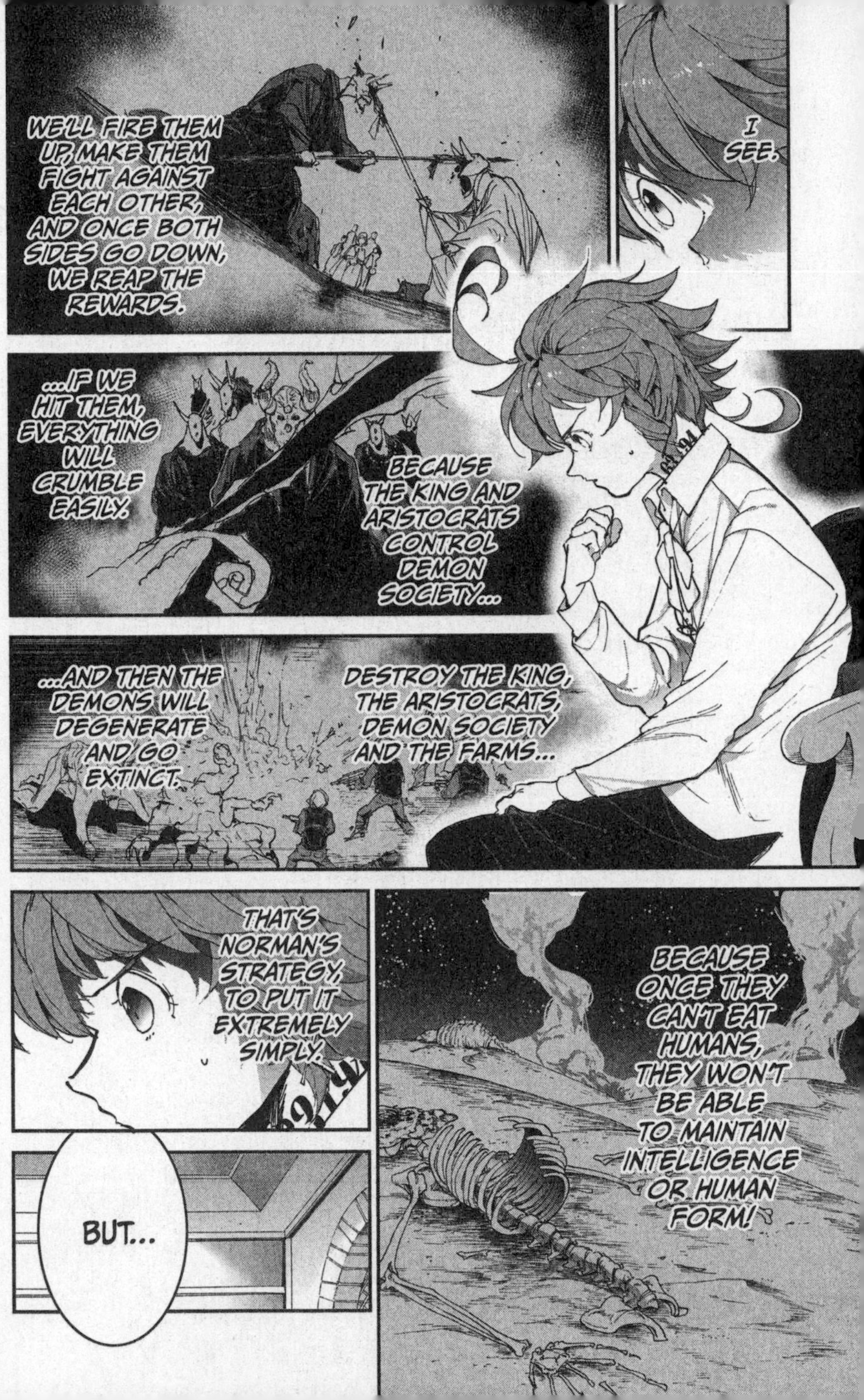
I SEE.
WE'LL FIRE THEM UP, MAKE THEM FIGHT AGAINST EACH OTHER, AND ONCE BOTH SIDES GO DOWN, WE REAP THE REWARDS.
BECAUSE THE KING AND ARISTOCRATS CONTROL DEMON SOCIETY...
...IF WE HIT THEM, EVERYTHING WILL CRUMBLE EASILY.
DESTROY THE KING, THE ARISTOCRATS, DEMON SOCIETY AND THE FARMS...
...AND THEN THE DEMONS WILL DEGENERATE AND GO EXTINCT.
BECAUSE ONCE THEY CAN'T EAT HUMANS, THEY WON'T BE ABLE TO MAINTAIN INTELLIGENCE OR HUMAN FORM!
THAT'S NORMAN'S STRATEGY, TO PUT IT EXTREMELY SIMPLY.
BUT...

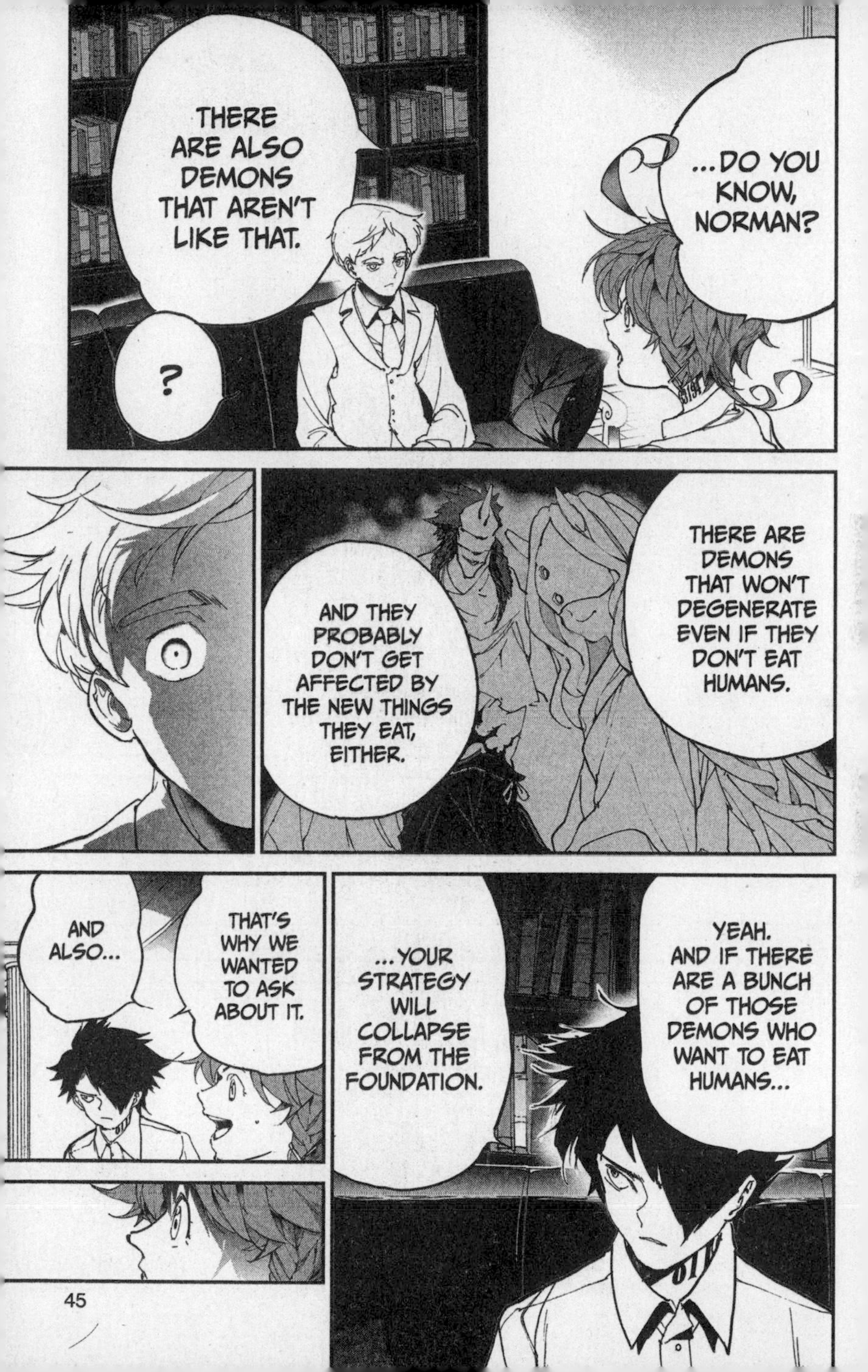
...DO YOU KNOW, NORMAN?
THERE ARE ALSO DEMONS THAT AREN'T LIKE THAT.
?
THERE ARE DEMONS THAT WON'T DEGENERATE EVEN IF THEY DON'T EAT HUMANS.
AND THEY PROBABLY DON'T GET AFFECTED BY THE NEW THINGS THEY EAT, EITHER.
YEAH. AND IF THERE ARE A BUNCH OF THOSE DEMONS WHO WANT TO EAT HUMANS...
...YOUR STRATEGY WILL COLLAPSE FROM THE FOUNDATION.
THAT'S WHY WE WANTED TO ASK ABOUT IT.
AND ALSO...

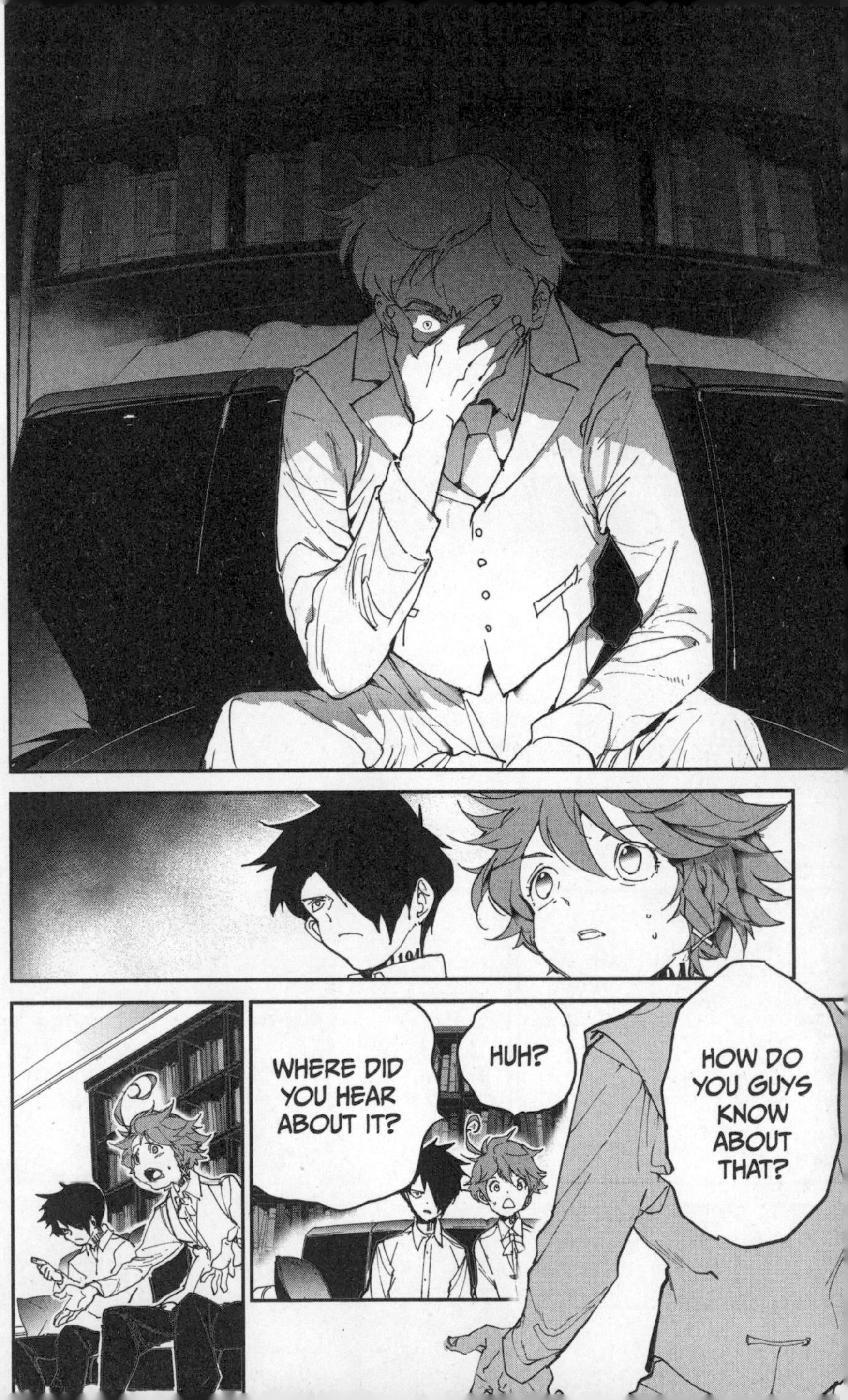
HOW DO YOU GUYS KNOW ABOUT THAT?
HUH?
WHERE DID YOU HEAR ABOUT IT?

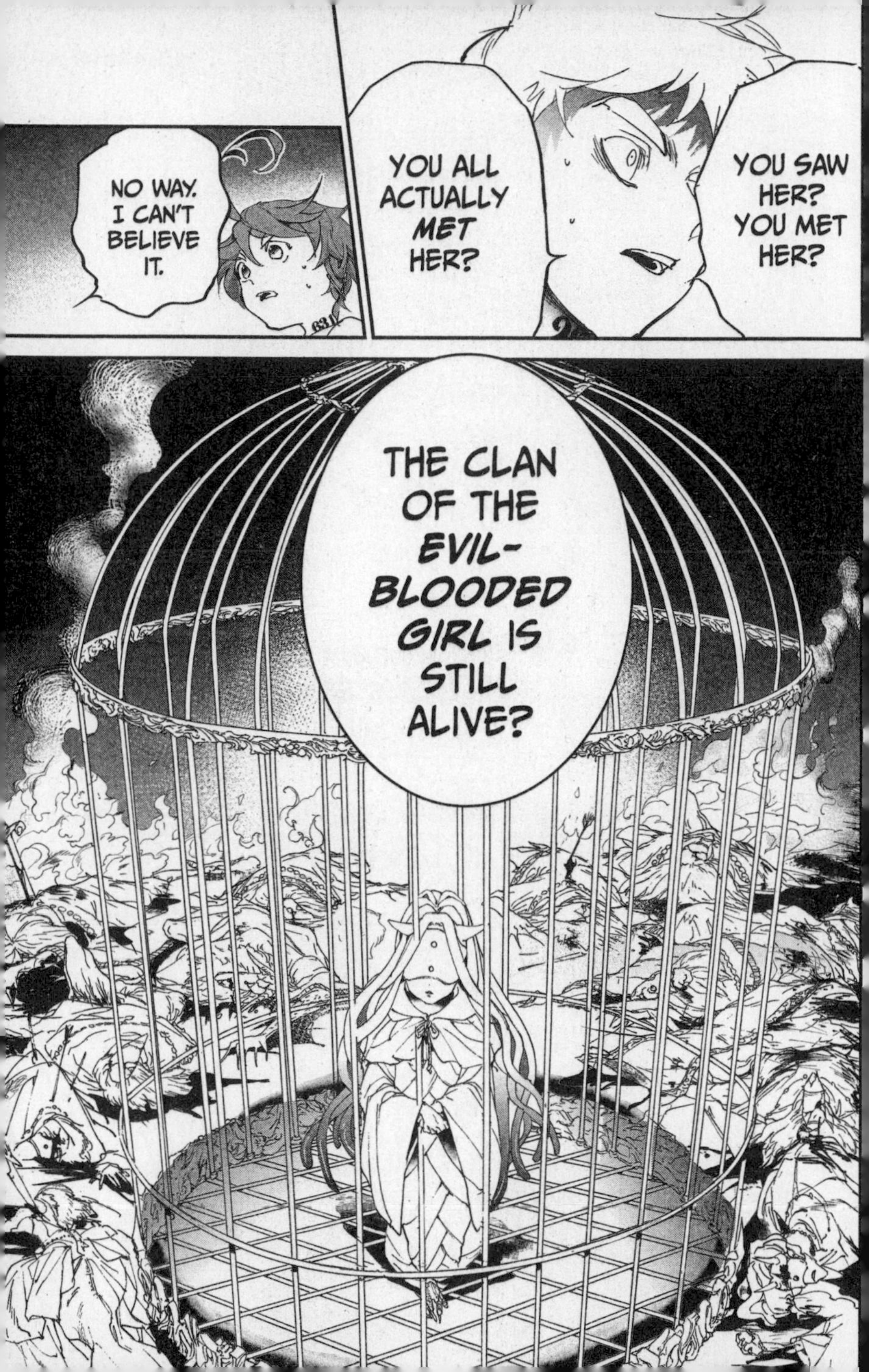
YOU SAW HER? YOU MET HER?
YOU ALL ACTUALLY MET HER?
NO WAY. I CAN'T BELIEVE IT.
THE CLAN OF THE EVIL-BLOODED GIRL IS STILL ALIVE?

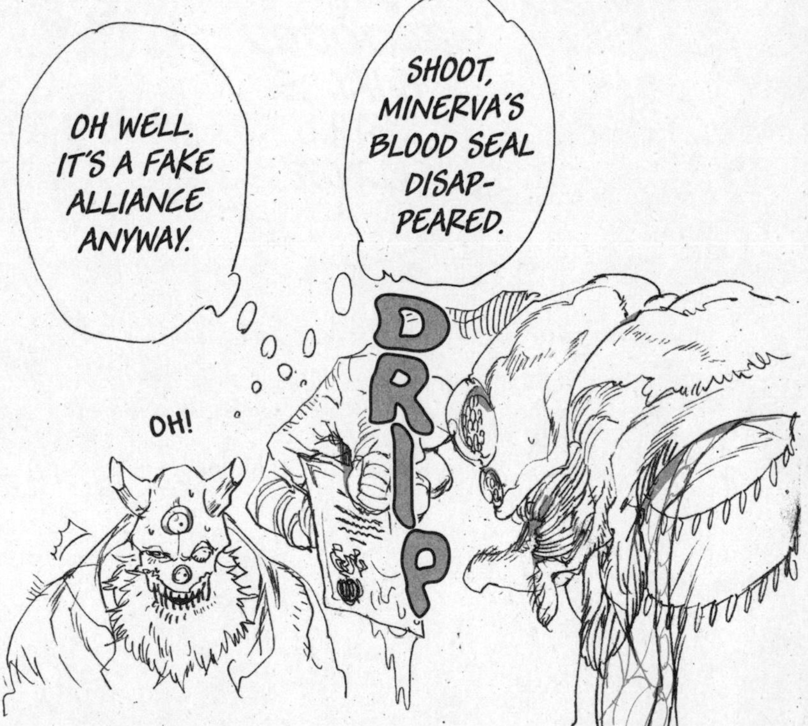
SHOOT, MINERVA'S BLOOD SEAL DISAP-PEARED.
OH WELL. IT'S A FAKE ALLIANCE ANYWAY.
DRIP
OH!

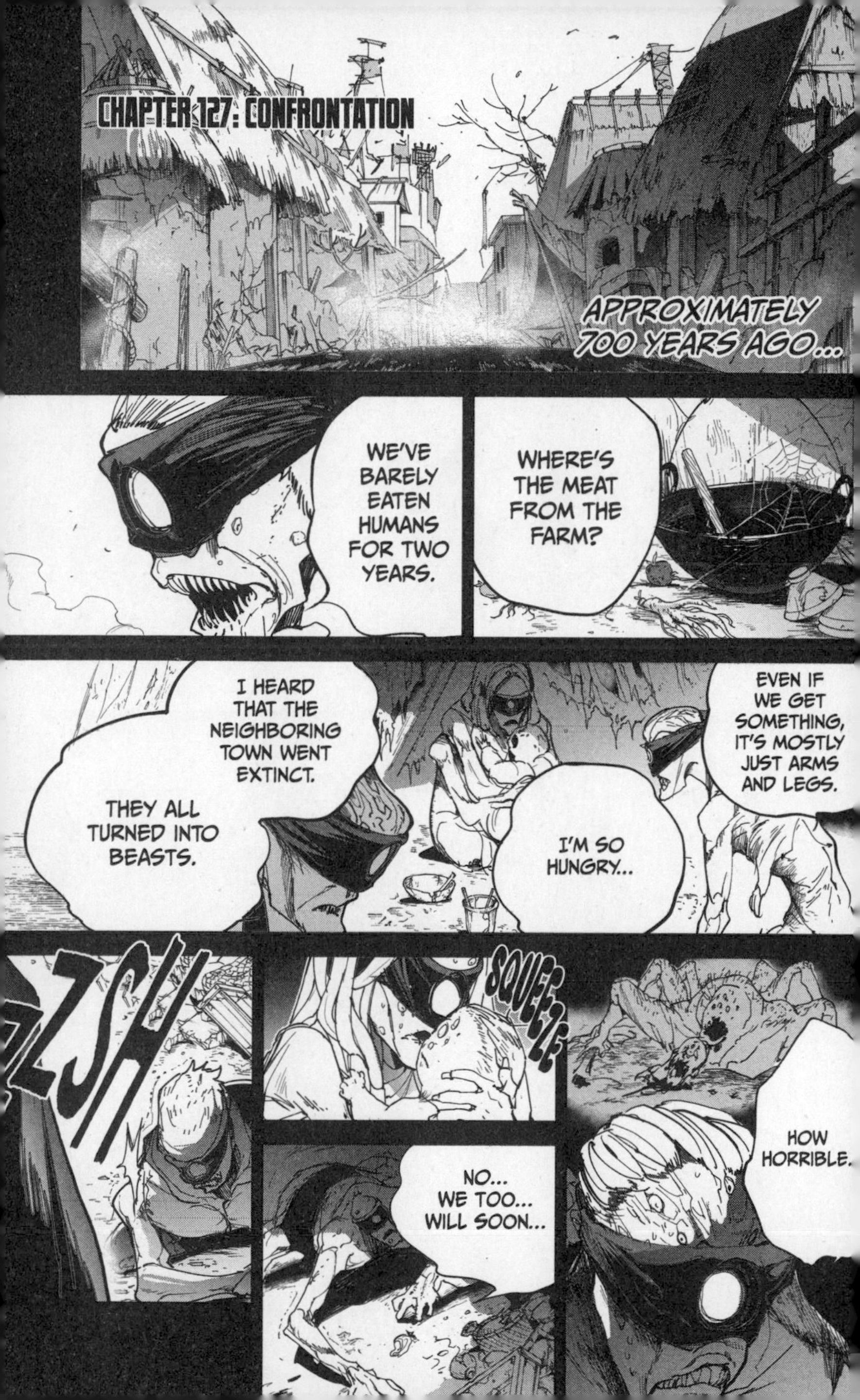
CHAPTER 127: CONFRONTATION
APPROXIMATELY 700 YEARS AGO...
WHERE'S THE MEAT FROM THE FARM?
WE'VE BARELY EATEN HUMANS FOR TWO YEARS.
EVEN IF WE GET SOMETHING, IT'S MOSTLY JUST ARMS AND LEGS.
I'M SO HUNGRY...
I HEARD THAT THE NEIGHBORING TOWN WENT EXTINCT.
THEY ALL TURNED INTO BEASTS.
HOW HORRIBLE.
SQUEEZE
NO... WE TOO... WILL SOON...
ZSH

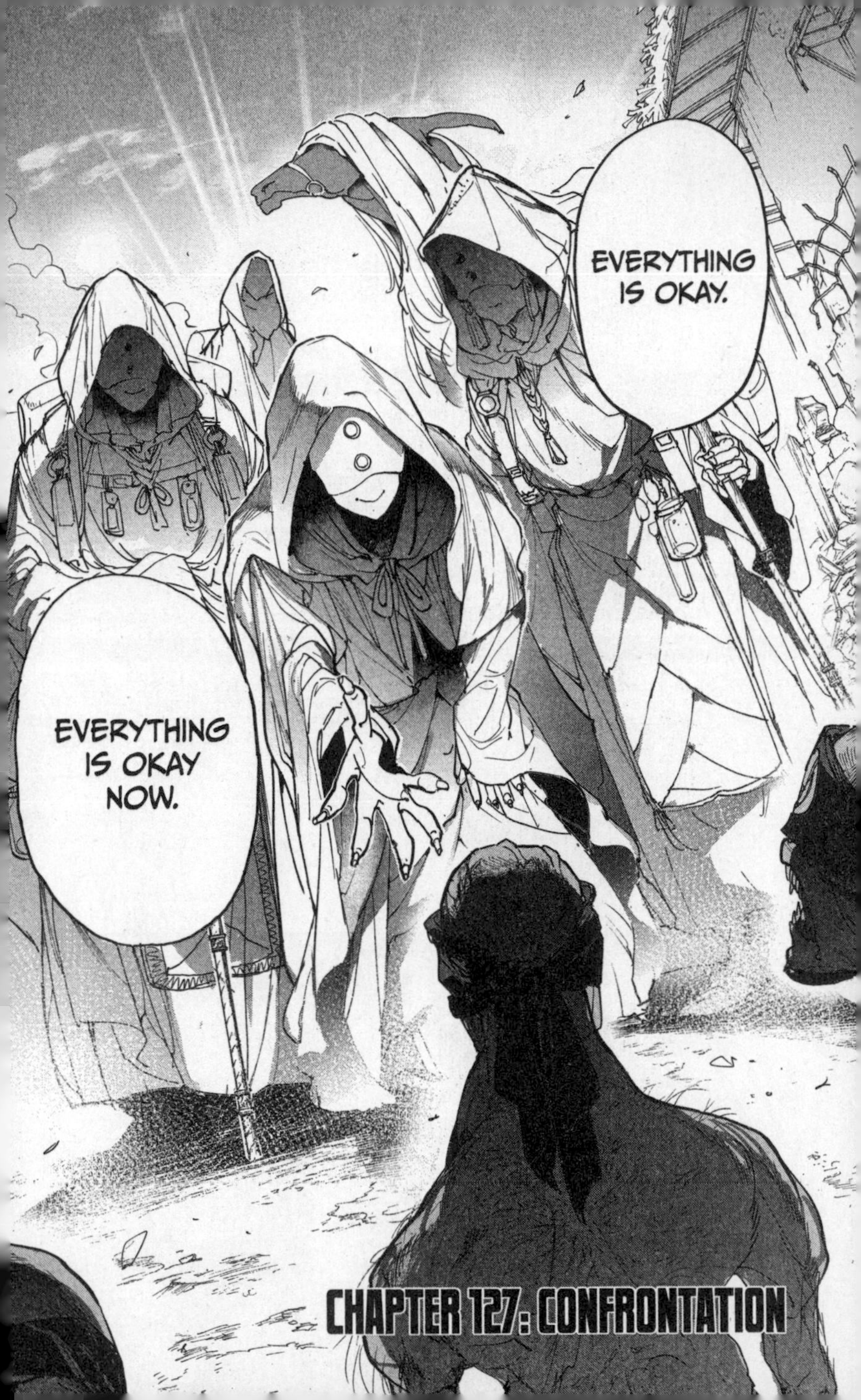
EVERYTHING IS OKAY.
EVERYTHING IS OKAY NOW.
CHAPTER 127: CONFRONTATION

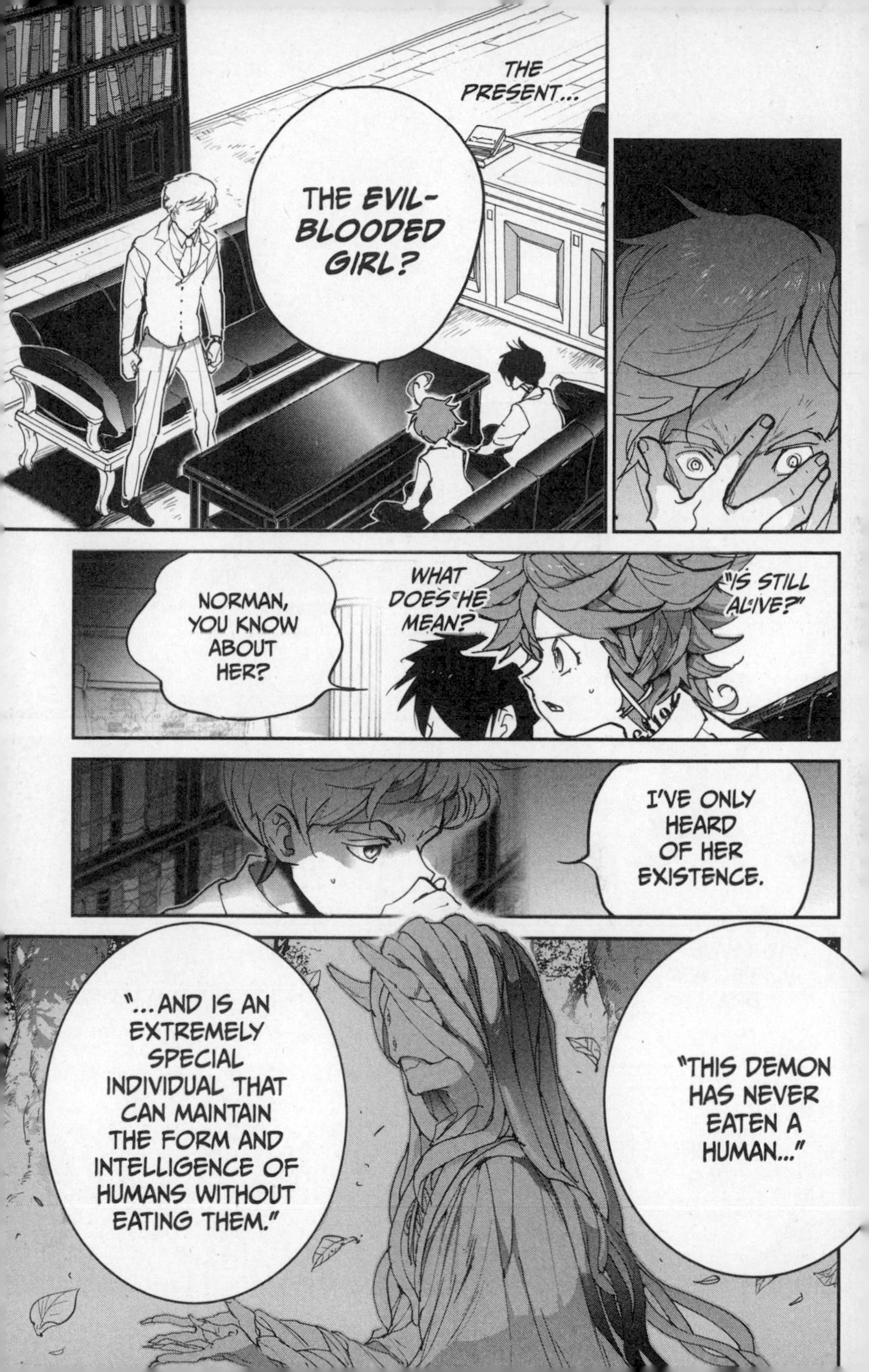
THE PRESENT...
THE EVIL-BLOODED GIRL?
"IS STILL ALIVE?"
WHAT DOES HE MEAN?
NORMAN, YOU KNOW ABOUT HER?
I'VE ONLY HEARD OF HER EXISTENCE.
"THIS DEMON HAS NEVER EATEN A HUMAN..."
"...AND IS AN EXTREMELY SPECIAL INDIVIDUAL THAT CAN MAINTAIN THE FORM AND INTELLIGENCE OF HUMANS WITHOUT EATING THEM."

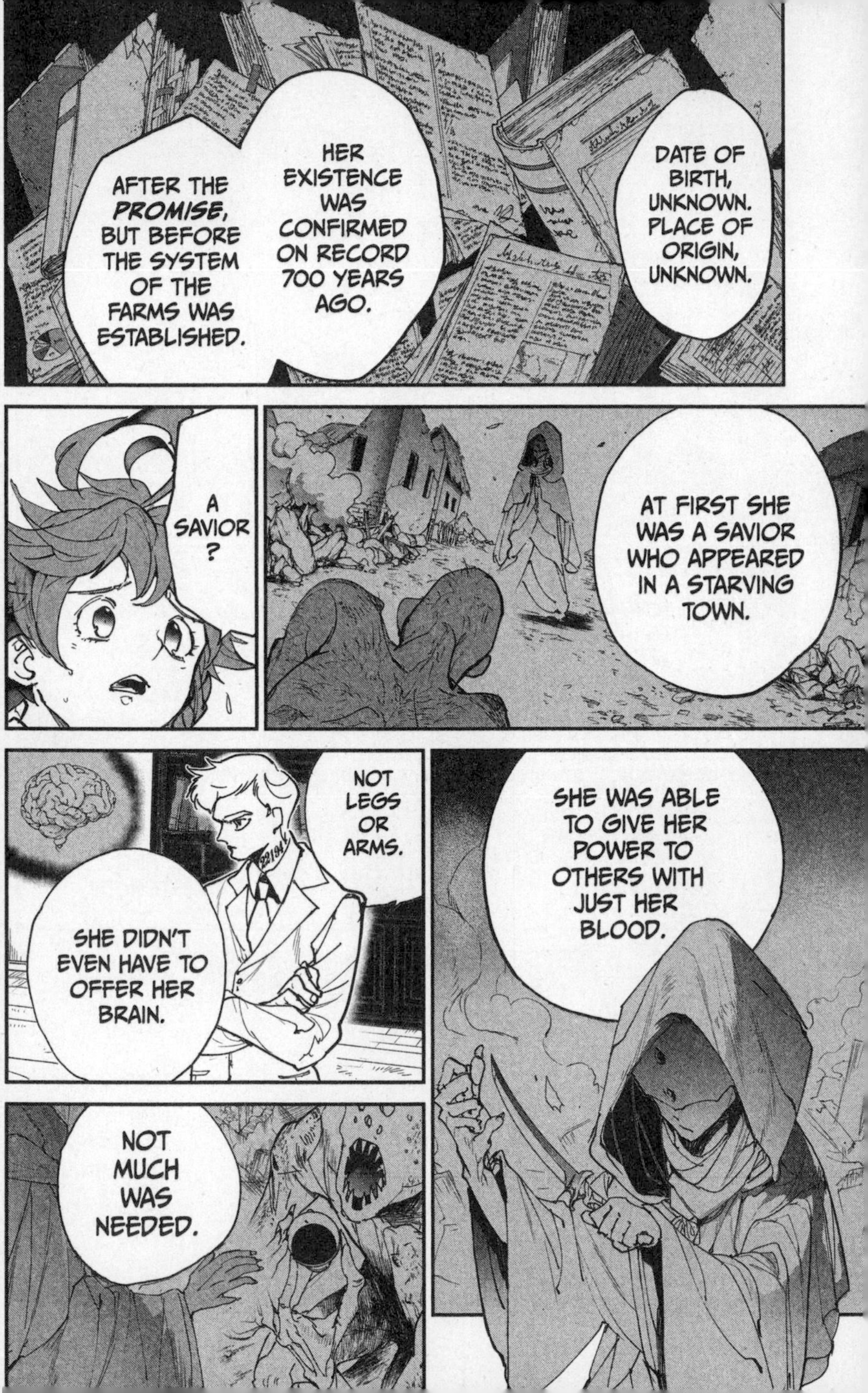
DATE OF BIRTH, UNKNOWN. PLACE OF ORIGIN, UNKNOWN.
HER EXISTENCE WAS CONFIRMED ON RECORD 700 YEARS AGO.
AFTER THE *PROMISE*, BUT BEFORE THE SYSTEM OF THE FARMS WAS ESTABLISHED.
AT FIRST SHE WAS A SAVIOR WHO APPEARED IN A STARVING TOWN.
A SAVIOR?
SHE WAS ABLE TO GIVE HER POWER TO OTHERS WITH JUST HER BLOOD.
NOT LEGS OR ARMS.
SHE DIDN'T EVEN HAVE TO OFFER HER BRAIN.
NOT MUCH WAS NEEDED.

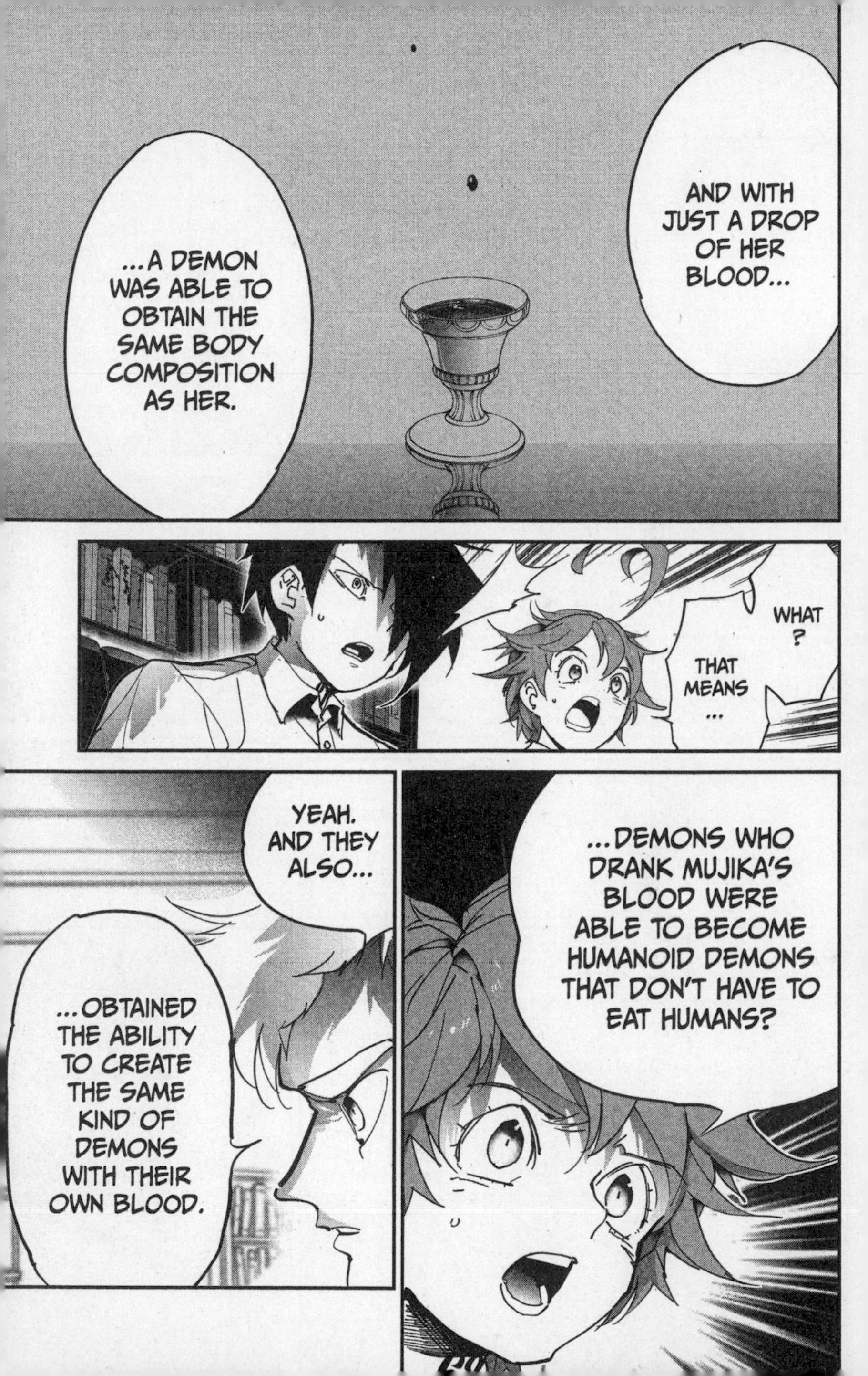
AND WITH JUST A DROP OF HER BLOOD...
...A DEMON WAS ABLE TO OBTAIN THE SAME BODY COMPOSITION AS HER.
WHAT?
THAT MEANS...
...DEMONS WHO DRANK MUJIKA'S BLOOD WERE ABLE TO BECOME HUMANOID DEMONS THAT DON'T HAVE TO EAT HUMANS?
YEAH. AND THEY ALSO...
...OBTAINED THE ABILITY TO CREATE THE SAME KIND OF DEMONS WITH THEIR OWN BLOOD.

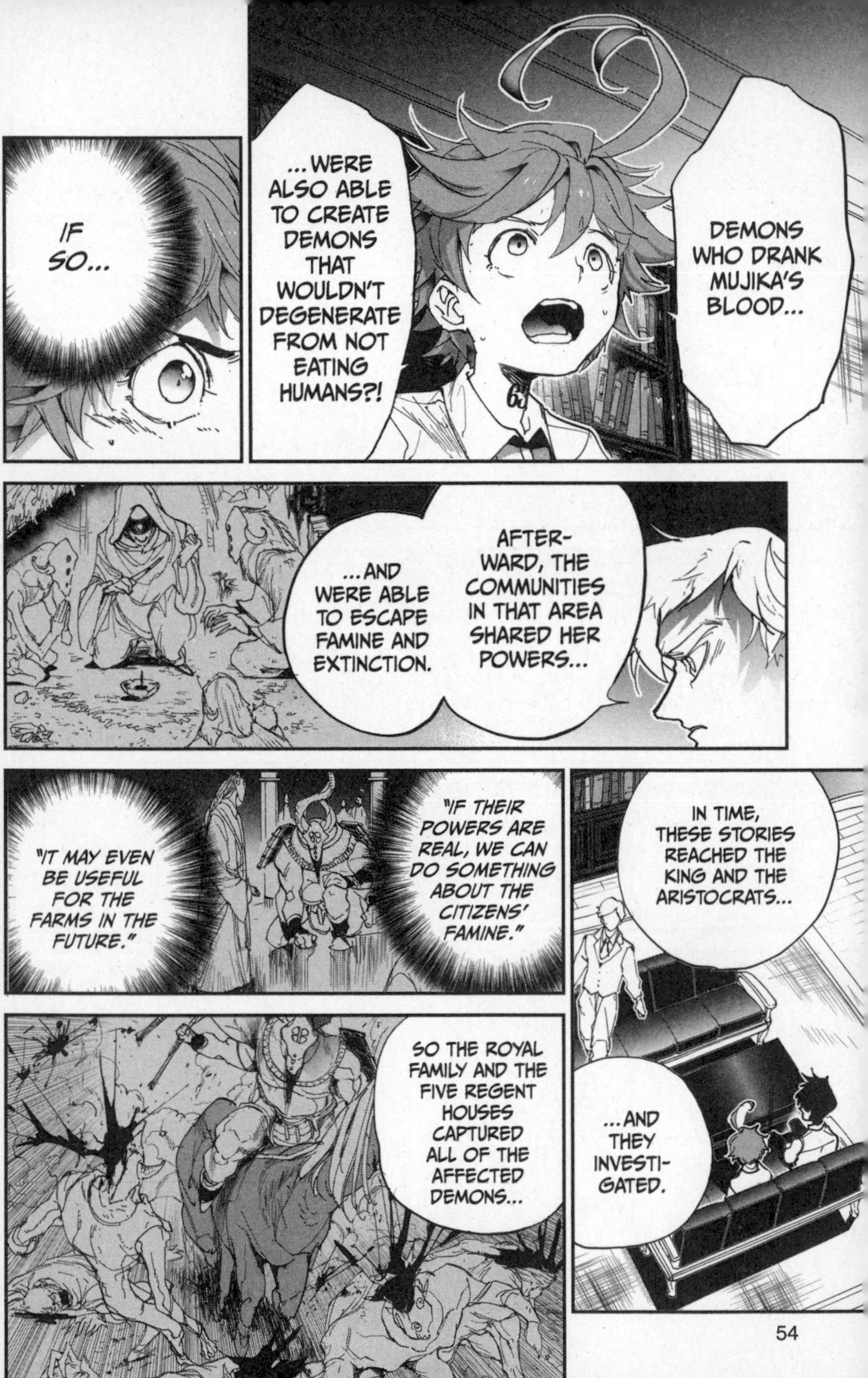
DEMONS WHO DRANK MUJIKA'S BLOOD...
...WERE ALSO ABLE TO CREATE DEMONS THAT WOULDN'T DEGENERATE FROM NOT EATING HUMANS?!
IF SO...
AFTERWARD, THE COMMUNITIES IN THAT AREA SHARED HER POWERS...
...AND WERE ABLE TO ESCAPE FAMINE AND EXTINCTION.
IN TIME, THESE STORIES REACHED THE KING AND THE ARISTOCRATS...
...AND THEY INVESTIGATED.
"IF THEIR POWERS ARE REAL, WE CAN DO SOMETHING ABOUT THE CITIZENS' FAMINE."
"IT MAY EVEN BE USEFUL FOR THE FARMS IN THE FUTURE."
SO THE ROYAL FAMILY AND THE FIVE REGENT HOUSES CAPTURED ALL OF THE AFFECTED DEMONS...

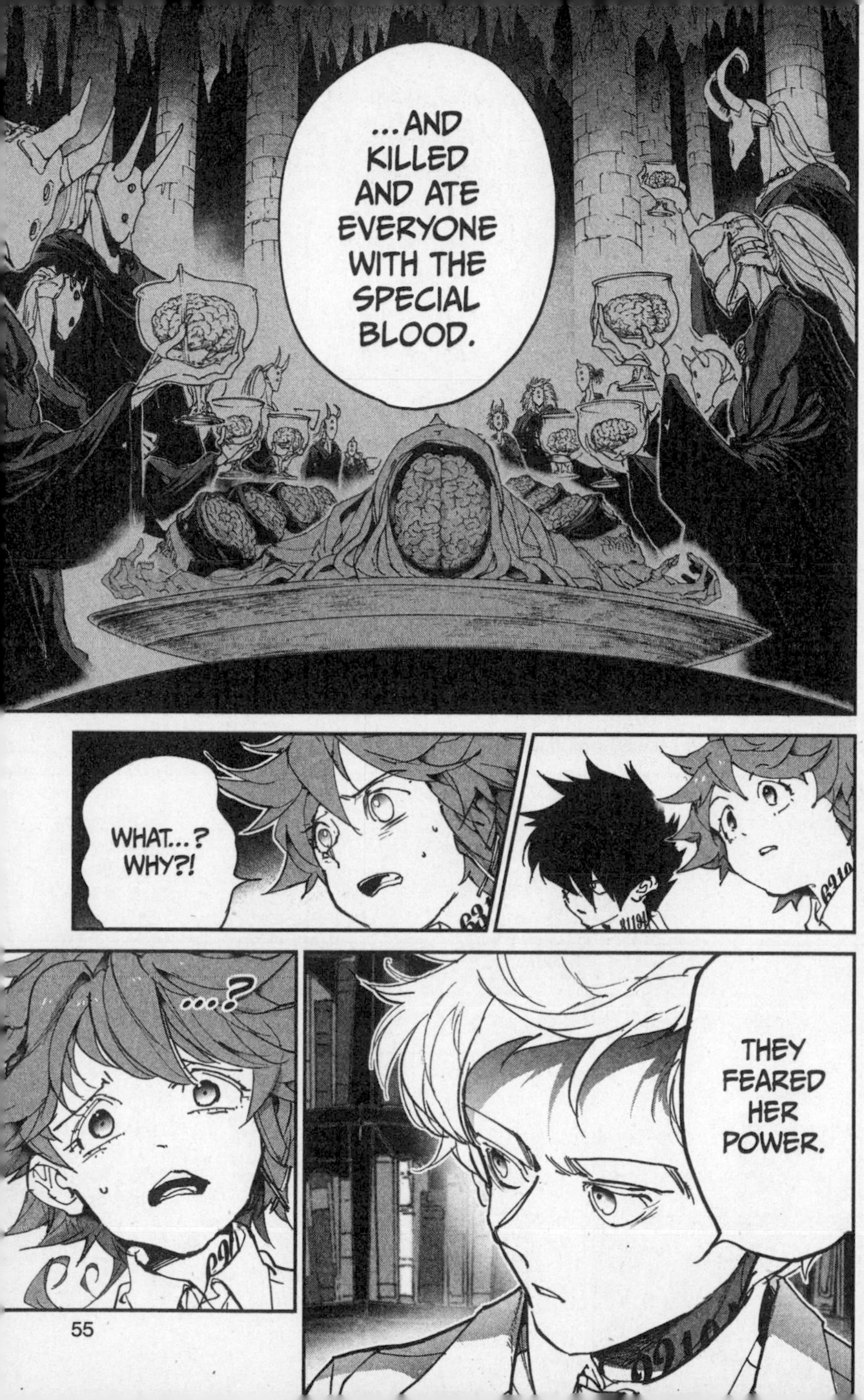
...AND KILLED AND ATE EVERYONE WITH THE SPECIAL BLOOD.
WHAT...? WHY?!
THEY FEARED HER POWER.
...?

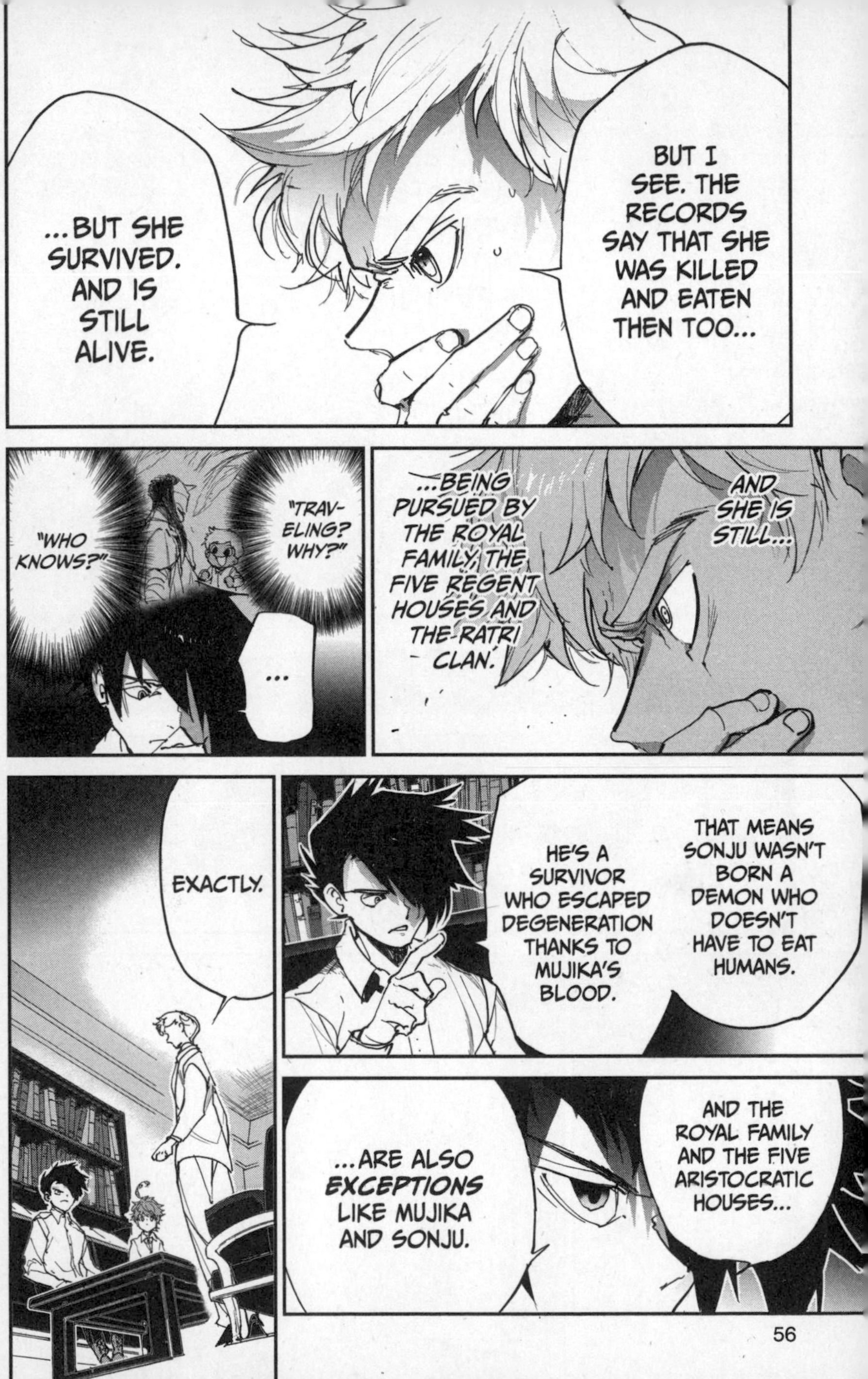
BUT I SEE. THE RECORDS SAY THAT SHE WAS KILLED AND EATEN THEN TOO...
...BUT SHE SURVIVED. AND IS STILL ALIVE.
AND SHE IS STILL...
...BEING PURSUED BY THE ROYAL FAMILY, THE FIVE REGENT HOUSES AND THE RATRI CLAN.
"TRAV-ELING? WHY?"
"WHO KNOWS?"
...
THAT MEANS SONJU WASN'T BORN A DEMON WHO DOESN'T HAVE TO EAT HUMANS.
HE'S A SURVIVOR WHO ESCAPED DEGENERATION THANKS TO MUJIKA'S BLOOD.
AND THE ROYAL FAMILY AND THE FIVE ARISTOCRATIC HOUSES...
...ARE ALSO ***EXCEPTIONS*** LIKE MUJIKA AND SONJU.
EXACTLY.

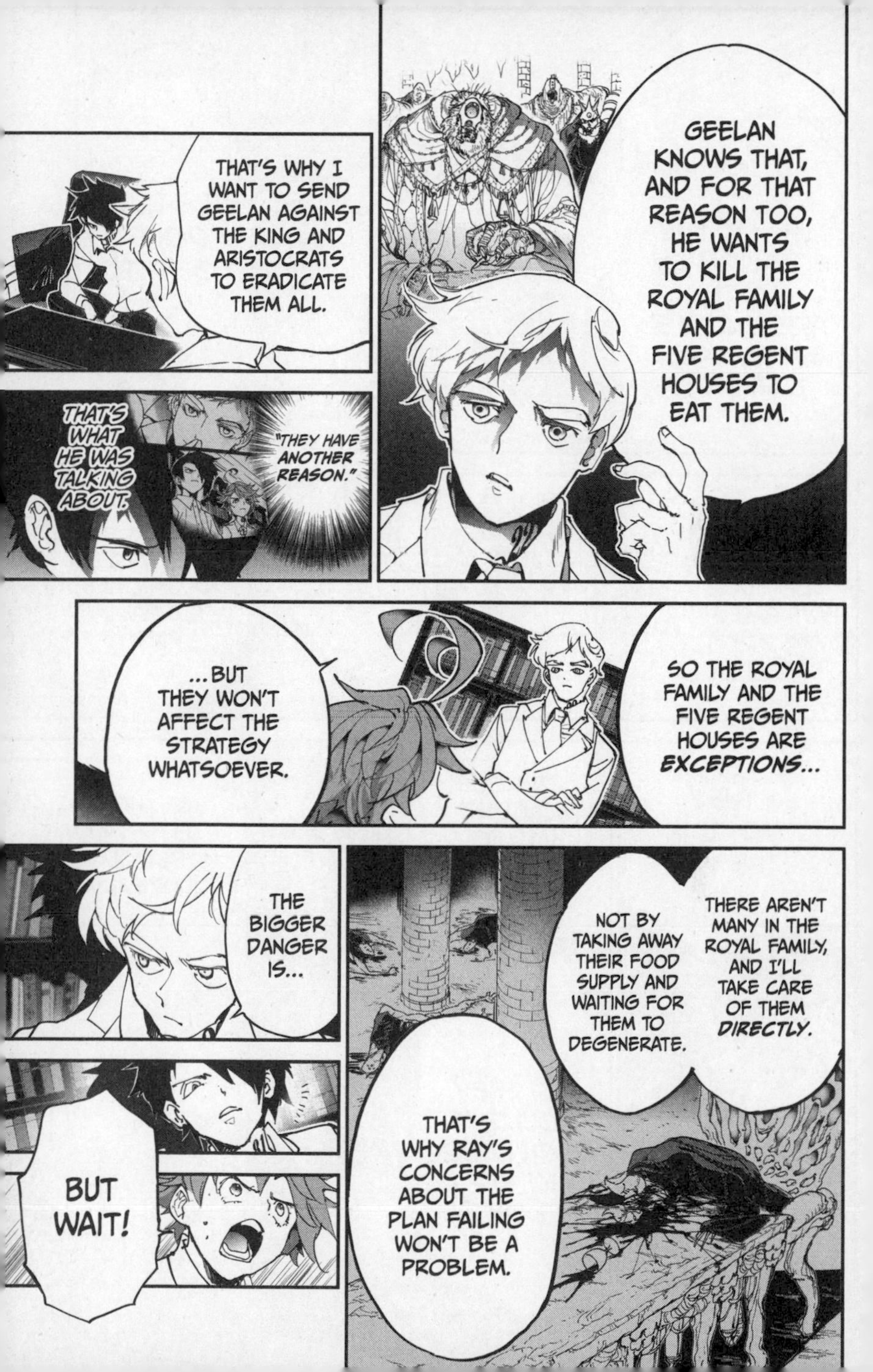
GEELAN KNOWS THAT, AND FOR THAT REASON TOO, HE WANTS TO KILL THE ROYAL FAMILY AND THE FIVE REGENT HOUSES TO EAT THEM.
THAT'S WHY I WANT TO SEND GEELAN AGAINST THE KING AND ARISTOCRATS TO ERADICATE THEM ALL.
"THEY HAVE ANOTHER REASON."
THAT'S WHAT HE WAS TALKING ABOUT.
SO THE ROYAL FAMILY AND THE FIVE REGENT HOUSES ARE *EXCEPTIONS*...
...BUT THEY WON'T AFFECT THE STRATEGY WHATSOEVER.
THERE AREN'T MANY IN THE ROYAL FAMILY, AND I'LL TAKE CARE OF THEM *DIRECTLY*.
NOT BY TAKING AWAY THEIR FOOD SUPPLY AND WAITING FOR THEM TO DEGENERATE.
THAT'S WHY RAY'S CONCERNS ABOUT THE PLAN FAILING WON'T BE A PROBLEM.
THE BIGGER DANGER IS...
BUT WAIT!

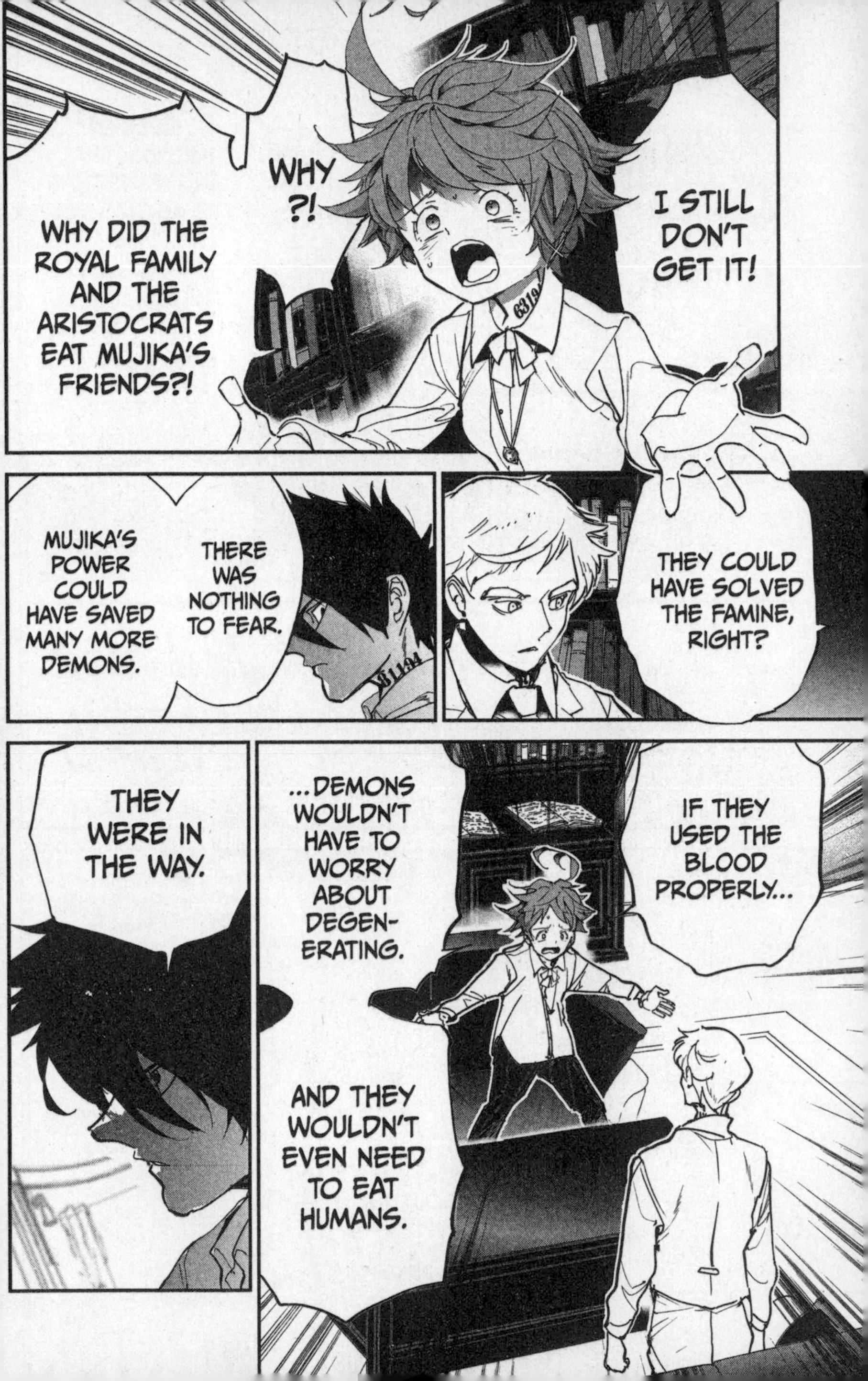
I STILL DON'T GET IT!
WHY ?!
WHY DID THE ROYAL FAMILY AND THE ARISTOCRATS EAT MUJIKA'S FRIENDS?!
THEY COULD HAVE SOLVED THE FAMINE, RIGHT?
THERE WAS NOTHING TO FEAR.
MUJIKA'S POWER COULD HAVE SAVED MANY MORE DEMONS.
IF THEY USED THE BLOOD PROPERLY...
...DEMONS WOULDN'T HAVE TO WORRY ABOUT DEGEN-ERATING.
AND THEY WOULDN'T EVEN NEED TO EAT HUMANS.
THEY WERE IN THE WAY.

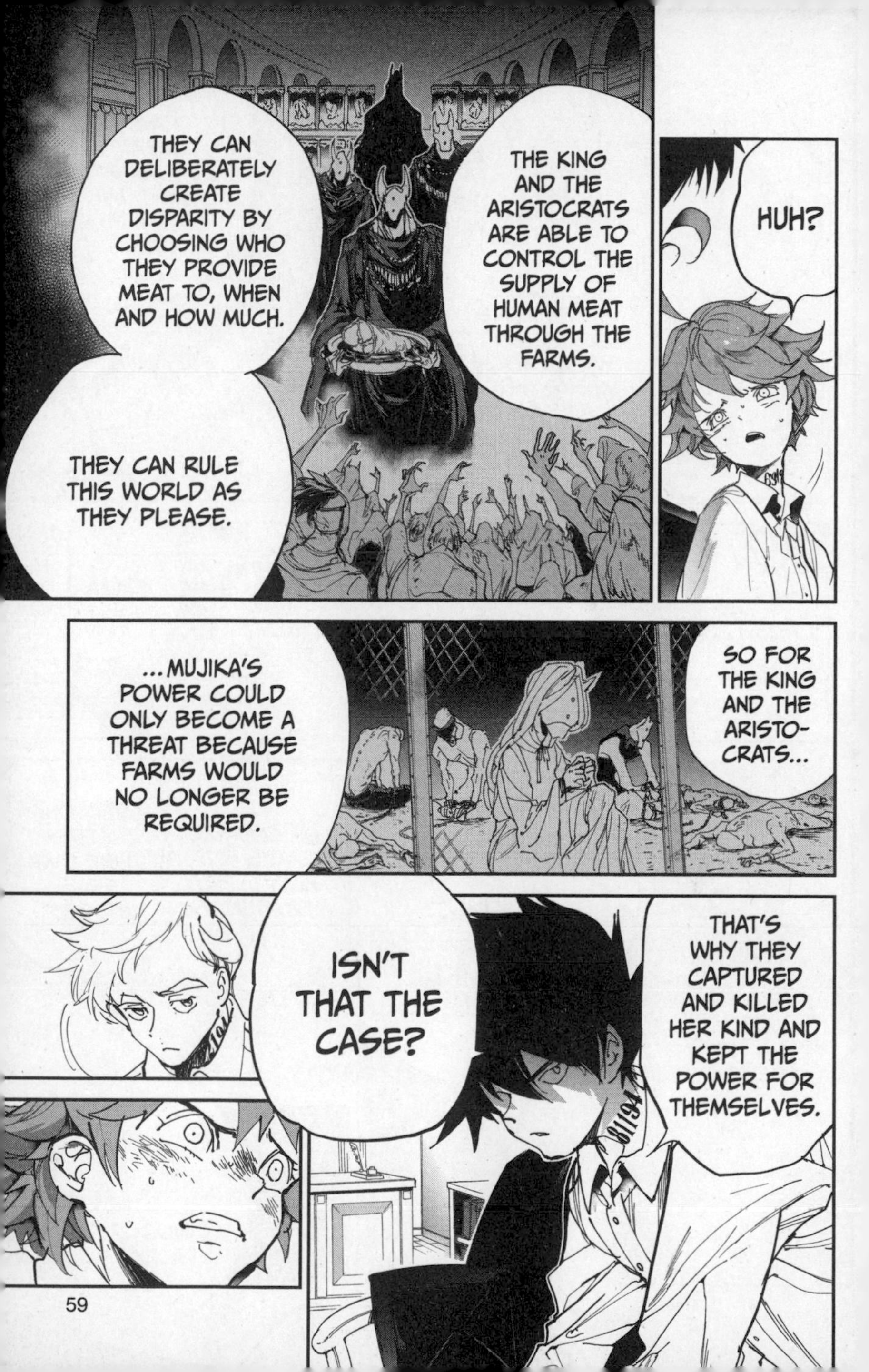
HUH?
THE KING AND THE ARISTOCRATS ARE ABLE TO CONTROL THE SUPPLY OF HUMAN MEAT THROUGH THE FARMS.
THEY CAN DELIBERATELY CREATE DISPARITY BY CHOOSING WHO THEY PROVIDE MEAT TO, WHEN AND HOW MUCH.
THEY CAN RULE THIS WORLD AS THEY PLEASE.
SO FOR THE KING AND THE ARISTO-CRATS...
...MUJIKA'S POWER COULD ONLY BECOME A THREAT BECAUSE FARMS WOULD NO LONGER BE REQUIRED.
THAT'S WHY THEY CAPTURED AND KILLED HER KIND AND KEPT THE POWER FOR THEMSELVES.
ISN'T THAT THE CASE?

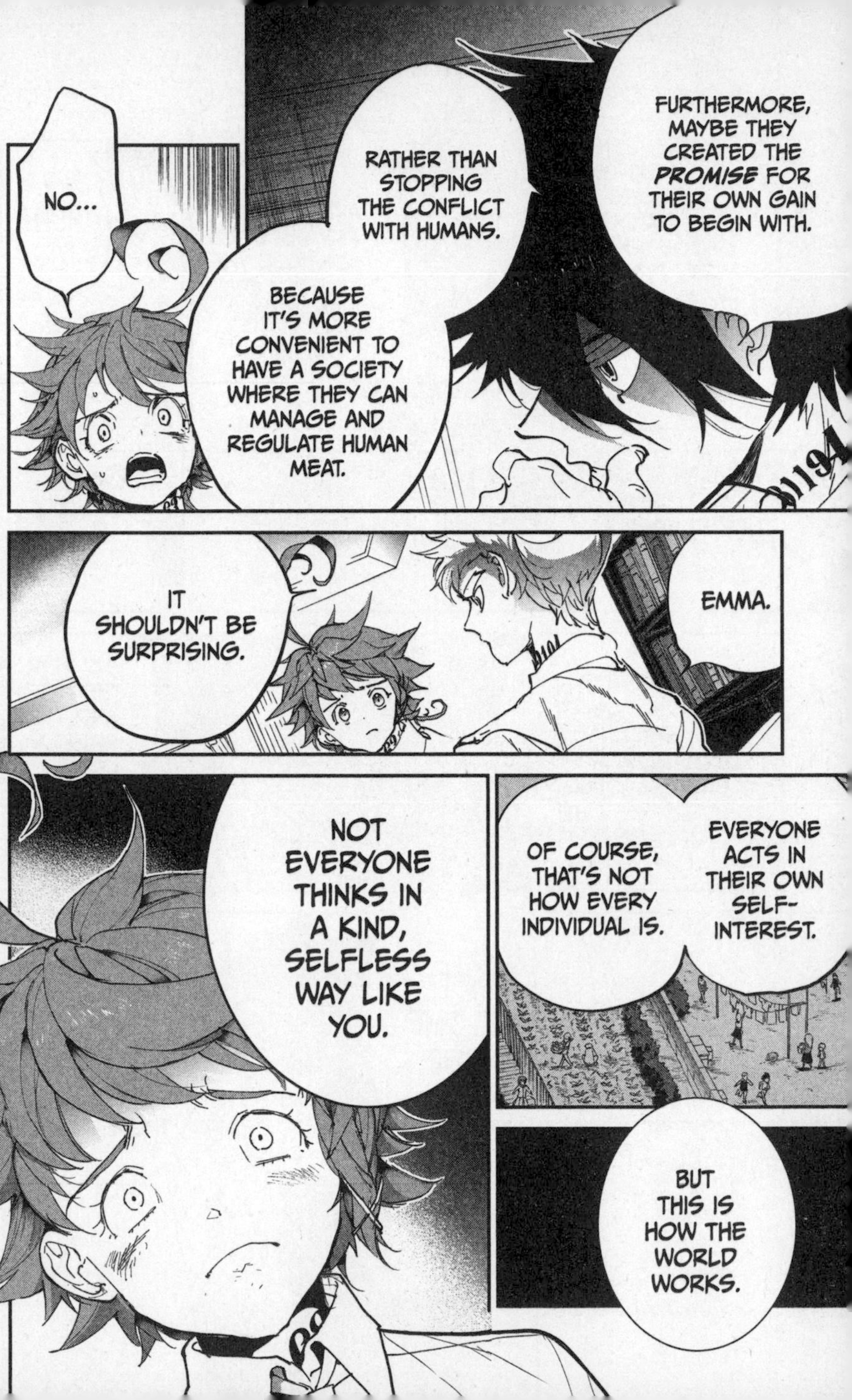
FURTHERMORE, MAYBE THEY CREATED THE *PROMISE* FOR THEIR OWN GAIN TO BEGIN WITH.
RATHER THAN STOPPING THE CONFLICT WITH HUMANS.
BECAUSE IT'S MORE CONVENIENT TO HAVE A SOCIETY WHERE THEY CAN MANAGE AND REGULATE HUMAN MEAT.
NO...
EMMA.
IT SHOULDN'T BE SURPRISING.
EVERYONE ACTS IN THEIR OWN SELF-INTEREST.
OF COURSE, THAT'S NOT HOW EVERY INDIVIDUAL IS.
BUT THIS IS HOW THE WORLD WORKS.
NOT EVERYONE THINKS IN A KIND, SELFLESS WAY LIKE YOU.

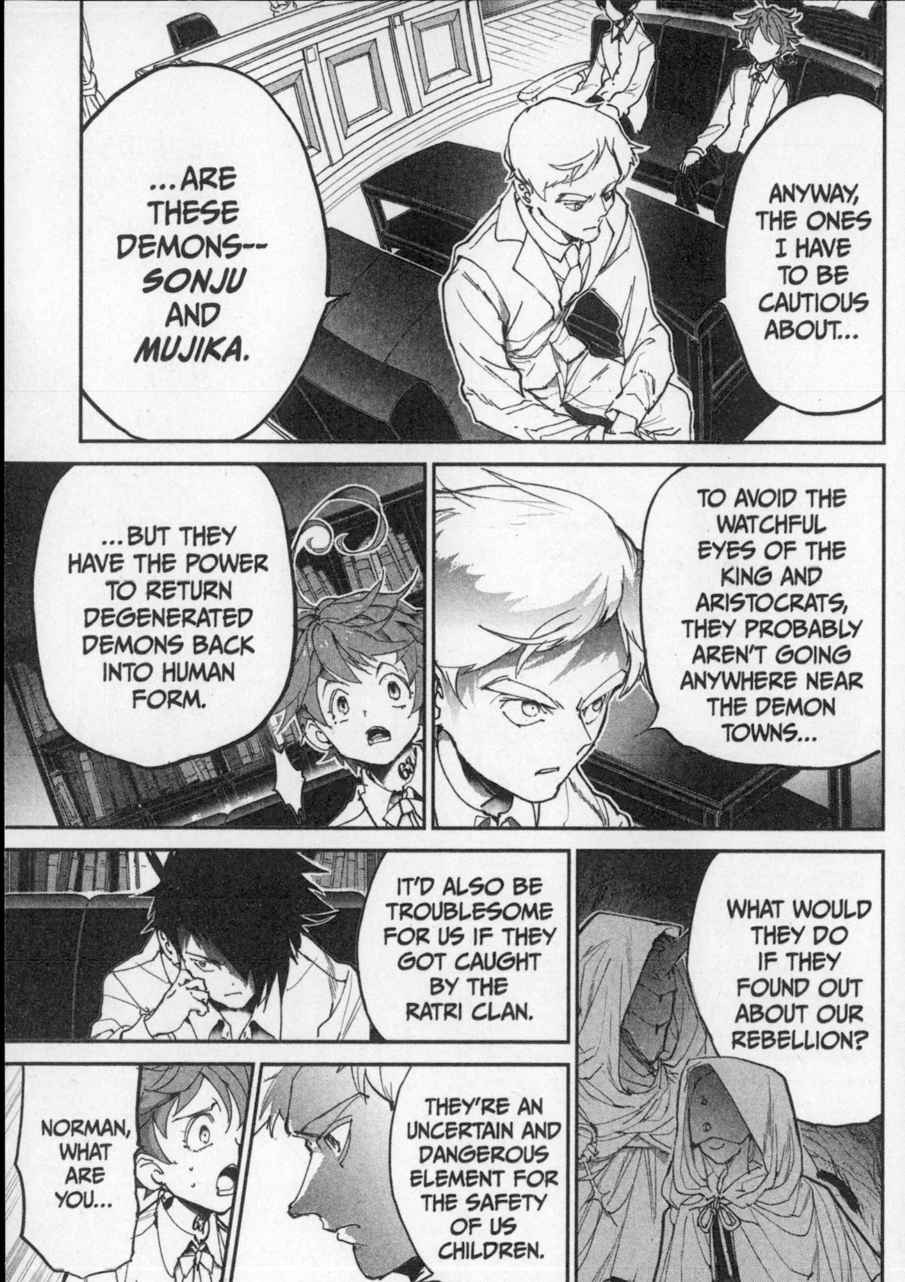
ANYWAY, THE ONES I HAVE TO BE CAUTIOUS ABOUT...
...ARE THESE DEMONS-- *SONJU* AND *MUJIKA*.
TO AVOID THE WATCHFUL EYES OF THE KING AND ARISTOCRATS, THEY PROBABLY AREN'T GOING ANYWHERE NEAR THE DEMON TOWNS...
...BUT THEY HAVE THE POWER TO RETURN DEGENERATED DEMONS BACK INTO HUMAN FORM.
WHAT WOULD THEY DO IF THEY FOUND OUT ABOUT OUR REBELLION?
IT'D ALSO BE TROUBLESOME FOR US IF THEY GOT CAUGHT BY THE RATRI CLAN.
THEY'RE AN UNCERTAIN AND DANGEROUS ELEMENT FOR THE SAFETY OF US CHILDREN.
NORMAN, WHAT ARE YOU...

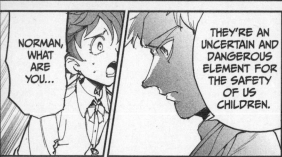

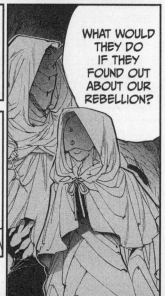

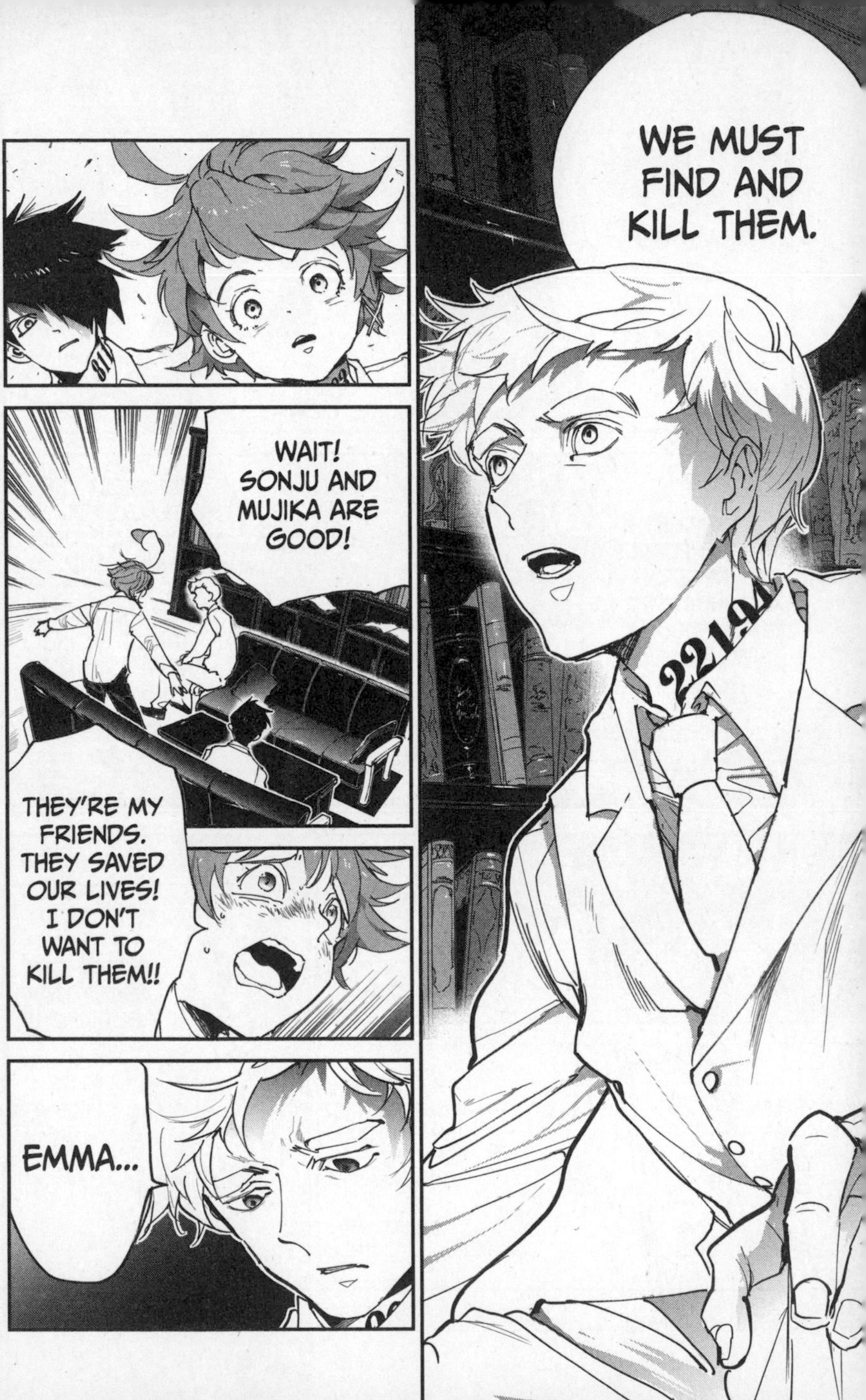
WE MUST FIND AND KILL THEM.
WAIT! SONJU AND MUJIKA ARE GOOD!
THEY'RE MY FRIENDS. THEY SAVED OUR LIVES! I DON'T WANT TO KILL THEM!!
EMMA...

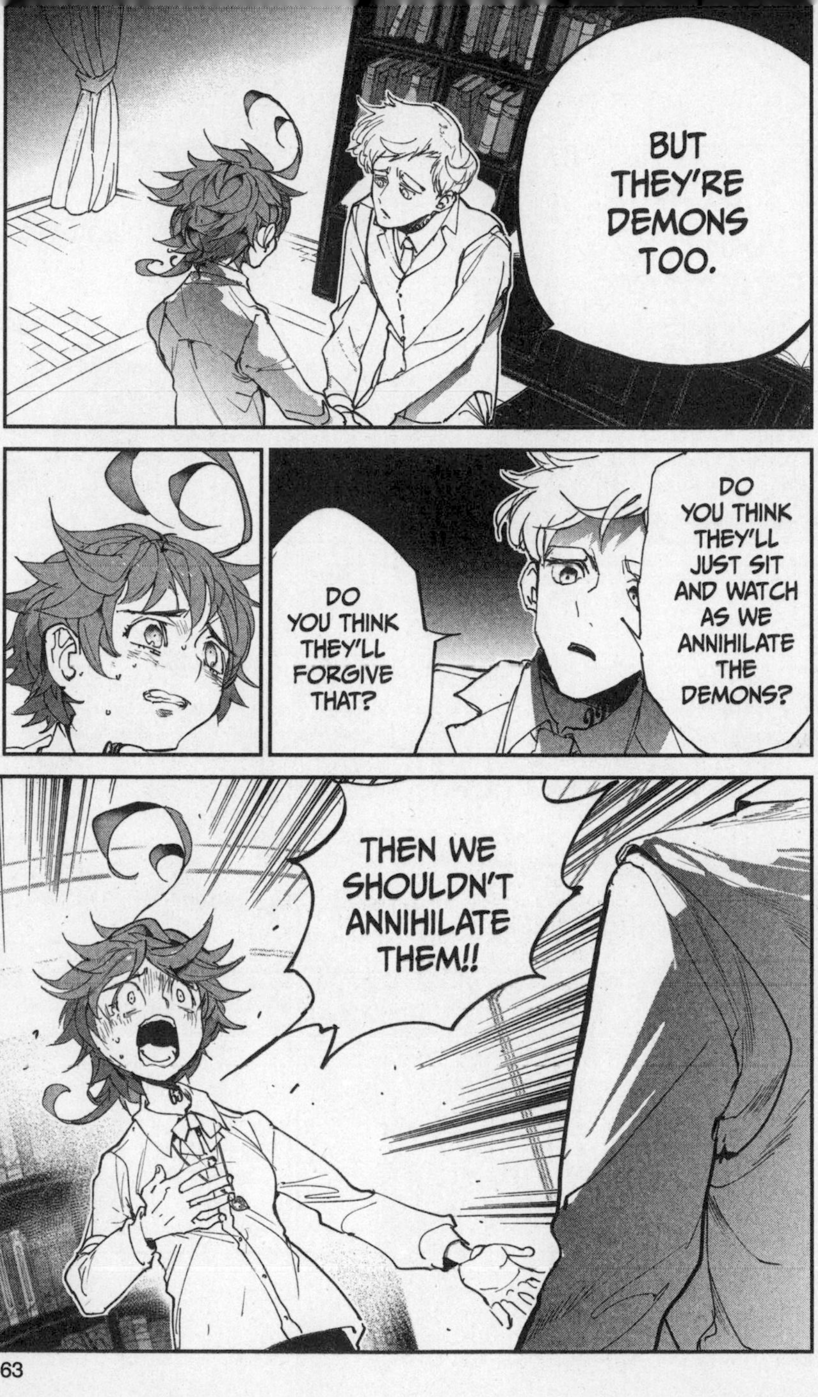
BUT THEY'RE DEMONS TOO.
DO YOU THINK THEY'LL JUST SIT AND WATCH AS WE ANNIHILATE THE DEMONS?
DO YOU THINK THEY'LL FORGIVE THAT?
THEN WE SHOULDN'T ANNIHILATE THEM!!

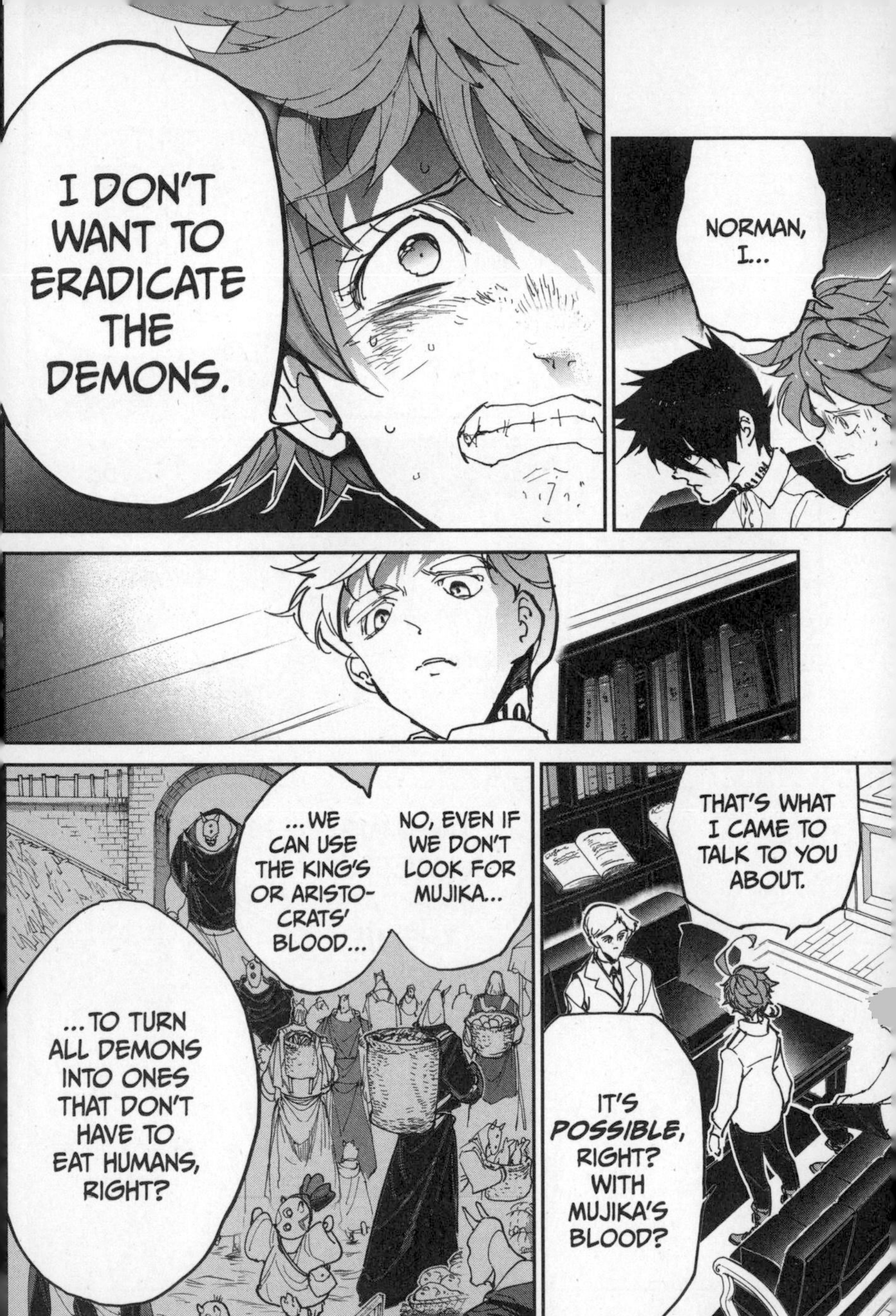
NORMAN, I...
I DON'T WANT TO ERADICATE THE DEMONS.
THAT'S WHAT I CAME TO TALK TO YOU ABOUT.
IT'S *POSSIBLE*, RIGHT? WITH MUJIKA'S BLOOD?
NO, EVEN IF WE DON'T LOOK FOR MUJIKA...
...WE CAN USE THE KING'S OR ARISTO-CRATS' BLOOD...
...TO TURN ALL DEMONS INTO ONES THAT DON'T HAVE TO EAT HUMANS, RIGHT?

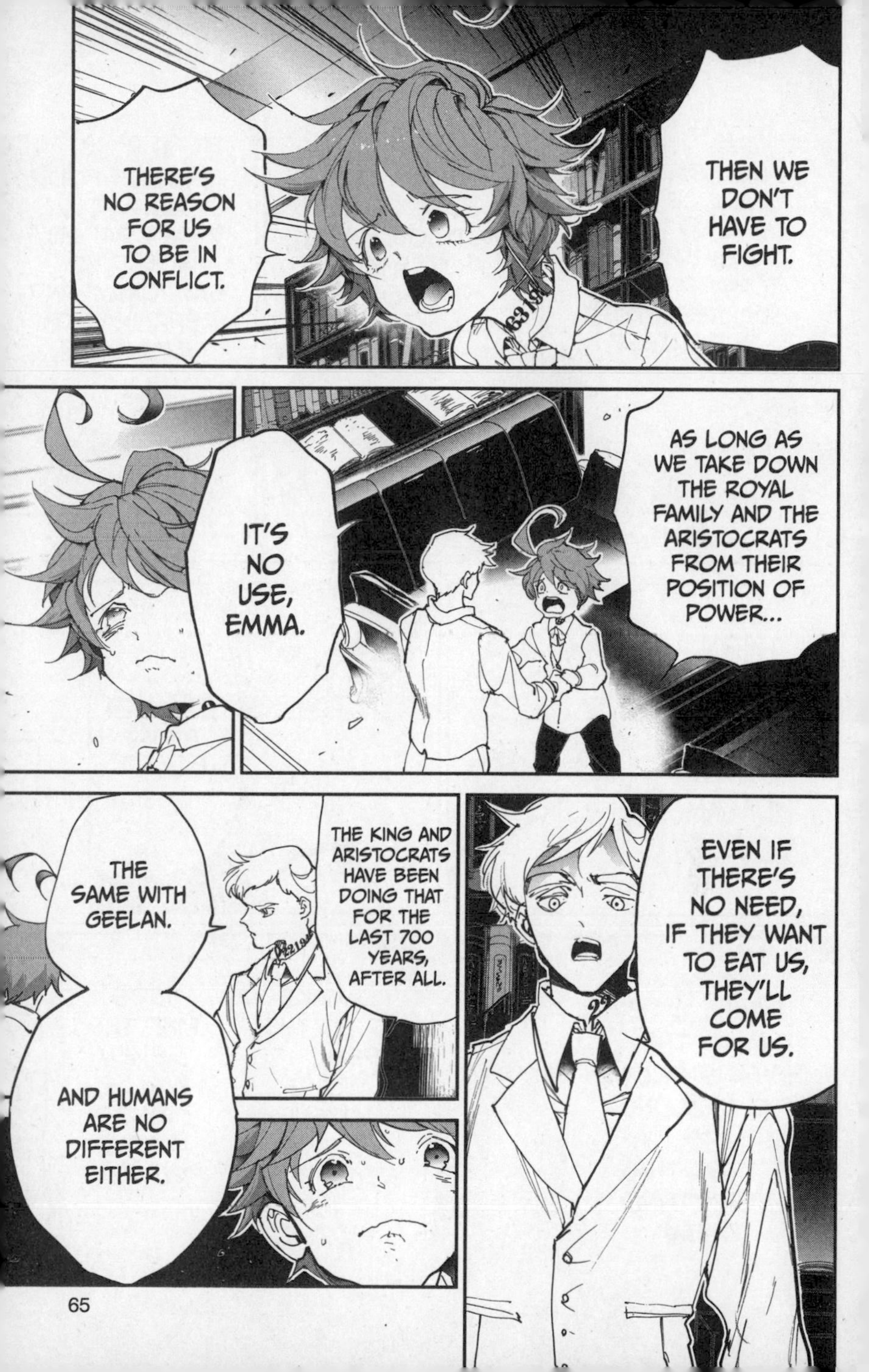
THEN WE DON'T HAVE TO FIGHT.
THERE'S NO REASON FOR US TO BE IN CONFLICT.
AS LONG AS WE TAKE DOWN THE ROYAL FAMILY AND THE ARISTOCRATS FROM THEIR POSITION OF POWER...
IT'S NO USE, EMMA.
EVEN IF THERE'S NO NEED, IF THEY WANT TO EAT US, THEY'LL COME FOR US.
THE KING AND ARISTOCRATS HAVE BEEN DOING THAT FOR THE LAST 700 YEARS, AFTER ALL.
THE SAME WITH GEELAN.
AND HUMANS ARE NO DIFFERENT EITHER.

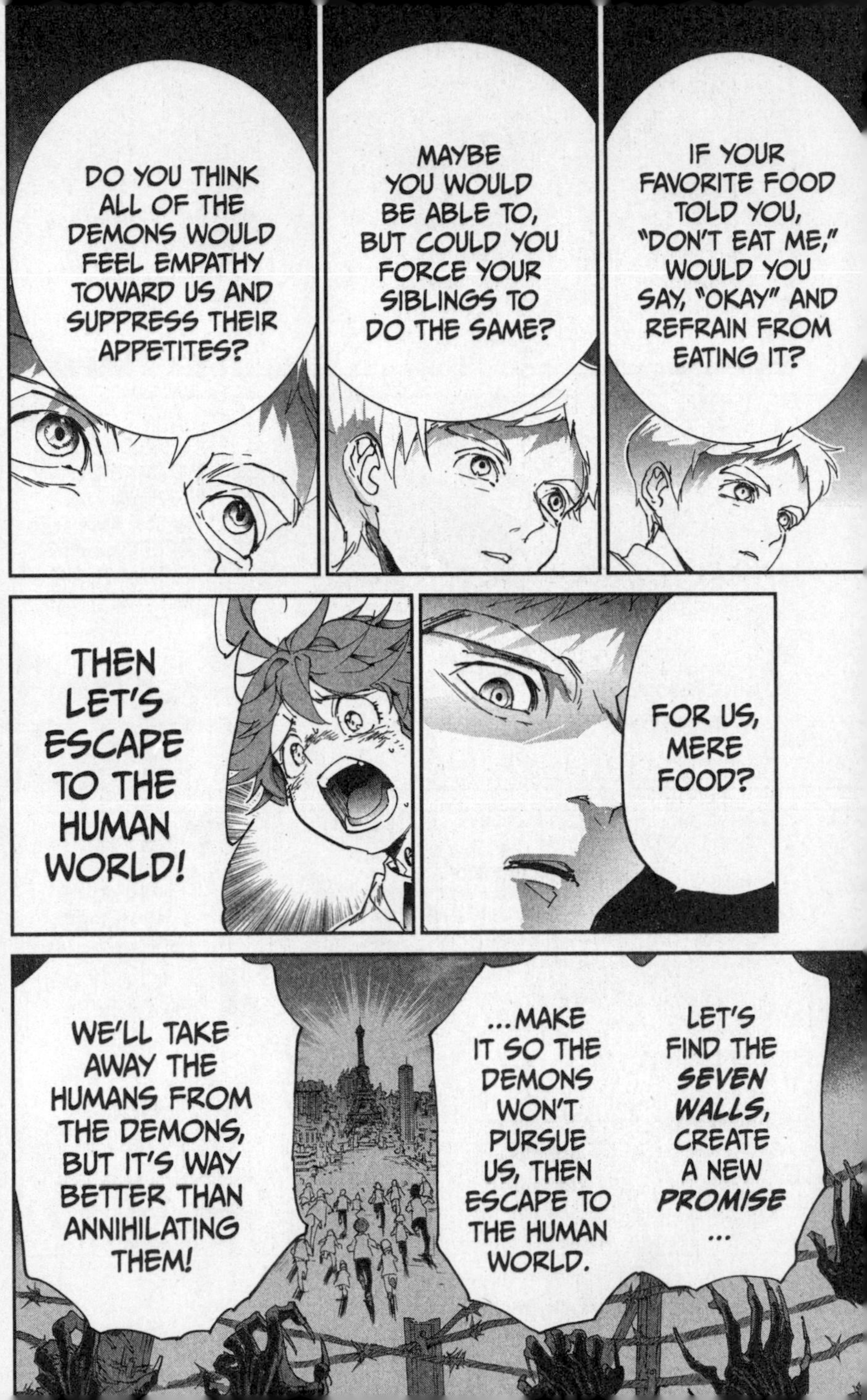
IF YOUR FAVORITE FOOD TOLD YOU, "DON'T EAT ME," WOULD YOU SAY, "OKAY" AND REFRAIN FROM EATING IT?
MAYBE YOU WOULD BE ABLE TO, BUT COULD YOU FORCE YOUR SIBLINGS TO DO THE SAME?
DO YOU THINK ALL OF THE DEMONS WOULD FEEL EMPATHY TOWARD US AND SUPPRESS THEIR APPETITES?
FOR US, MERE FOOD?
THEN LET'S ESCAPE TO THE HUMAN WORLD!
LET'S FIND THE *SEVEN WALLS*, CREATE A NEW *PROMISE* ...
...MAKE IT SO THE DEMONS WON'T PURSUE US, THEN ESCAPE TO THE HUMAN WORLD.
WE'LL TAKE AWAY THE HUMANS FROM THE DEMONS, BUT IT'S WAY BETTER THAN ANNIHILATING THEM!

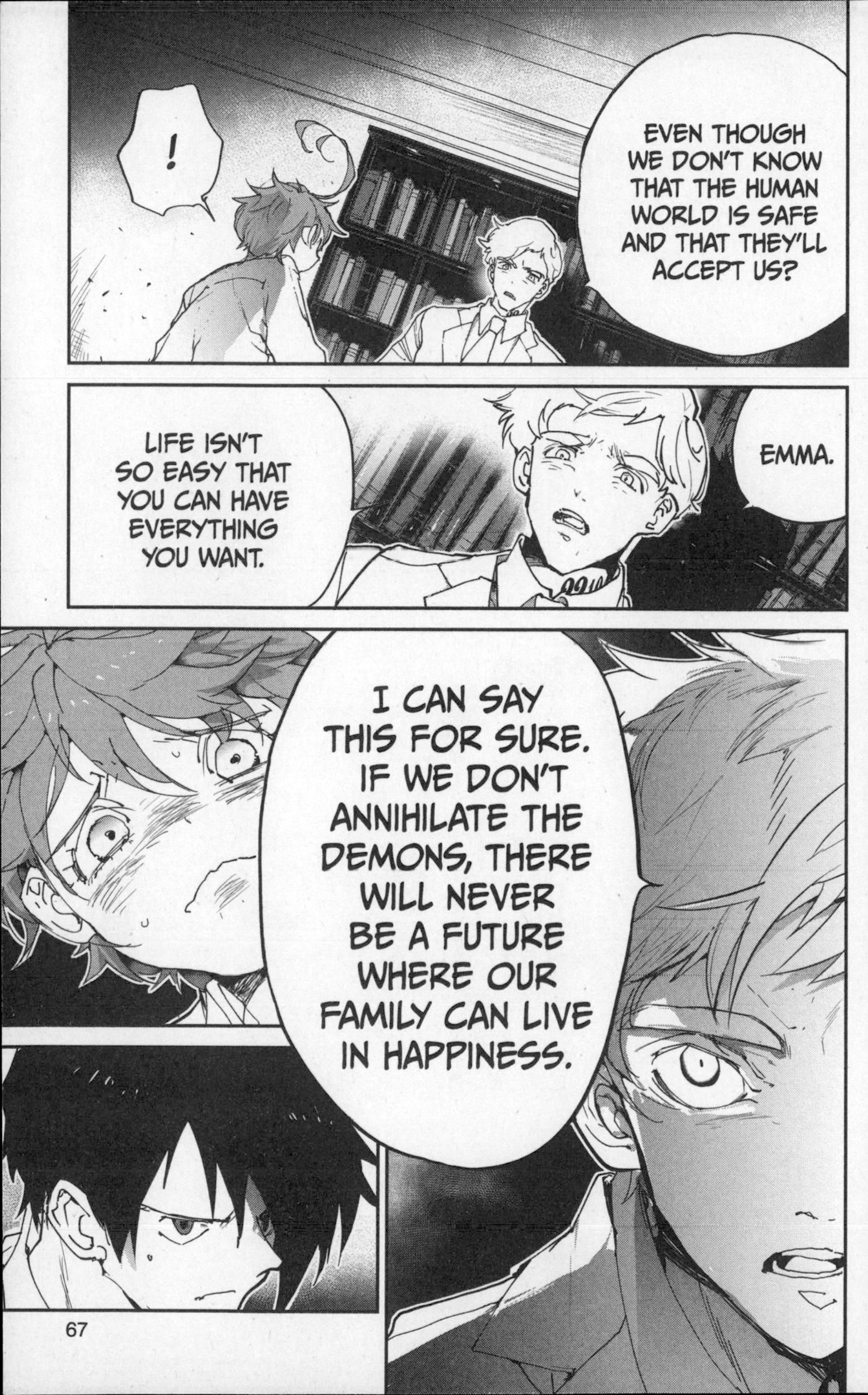
EVEN THOUGH WE DON'T KNOW THAT THE HUMAN WORLD IS SAFE AND THAT THEY'LL ACCEPT US?
!
EMMA.
LIFE ISN'T SO EASY THAT YOU CAN HAVE EVERYTHING YOU WANT.
I CAN SAY THIS FOR SURE. IF WE DON'T ANNIHILATE THE DEMONS, THERE WILL NEVER BE A FUTURE WHERE OUR FAMILY CAN LIVE IN HAPPINESS.

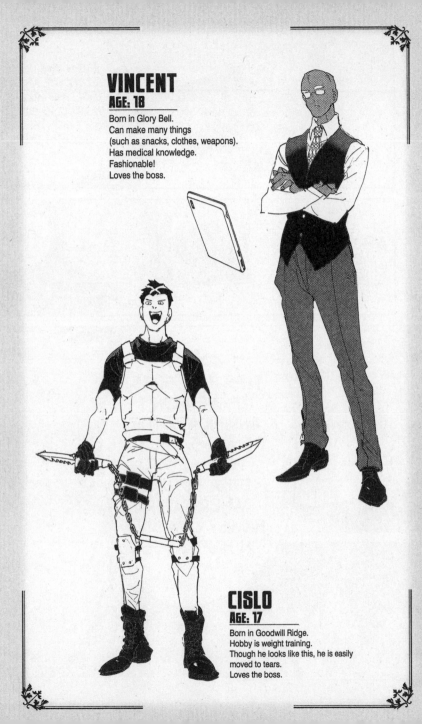

VINCENT

AGE: 18

Born in Glory Bell.
Can make many things
(such as snacks, clothes, weapons).
Has medical knowledge.
Fashionable!
Loves the boss.

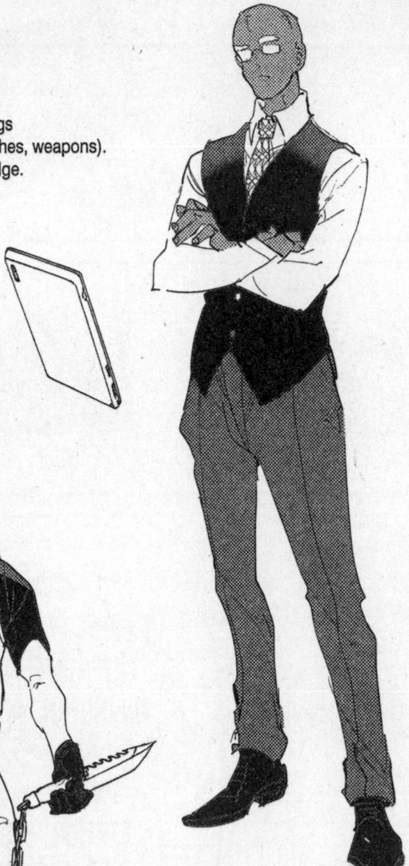

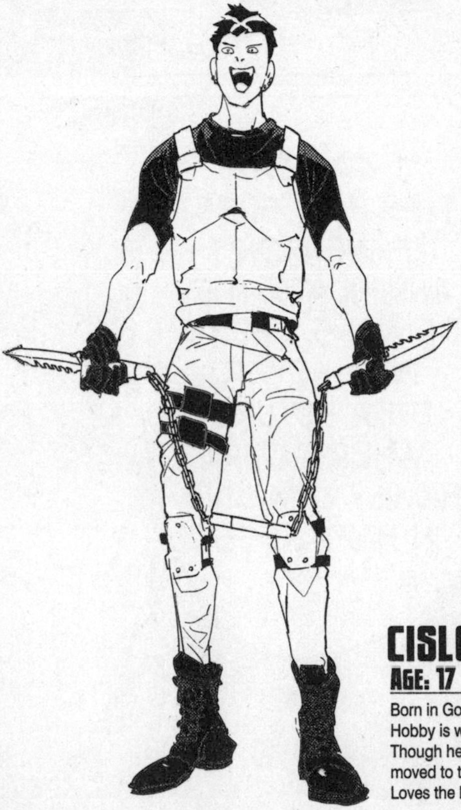

CISLO

AGE: 17

Born in Goodwill Ridge.
Hobby is weight training.
Though he looks like this, he is easily
moved to tears.
Loves the boss.

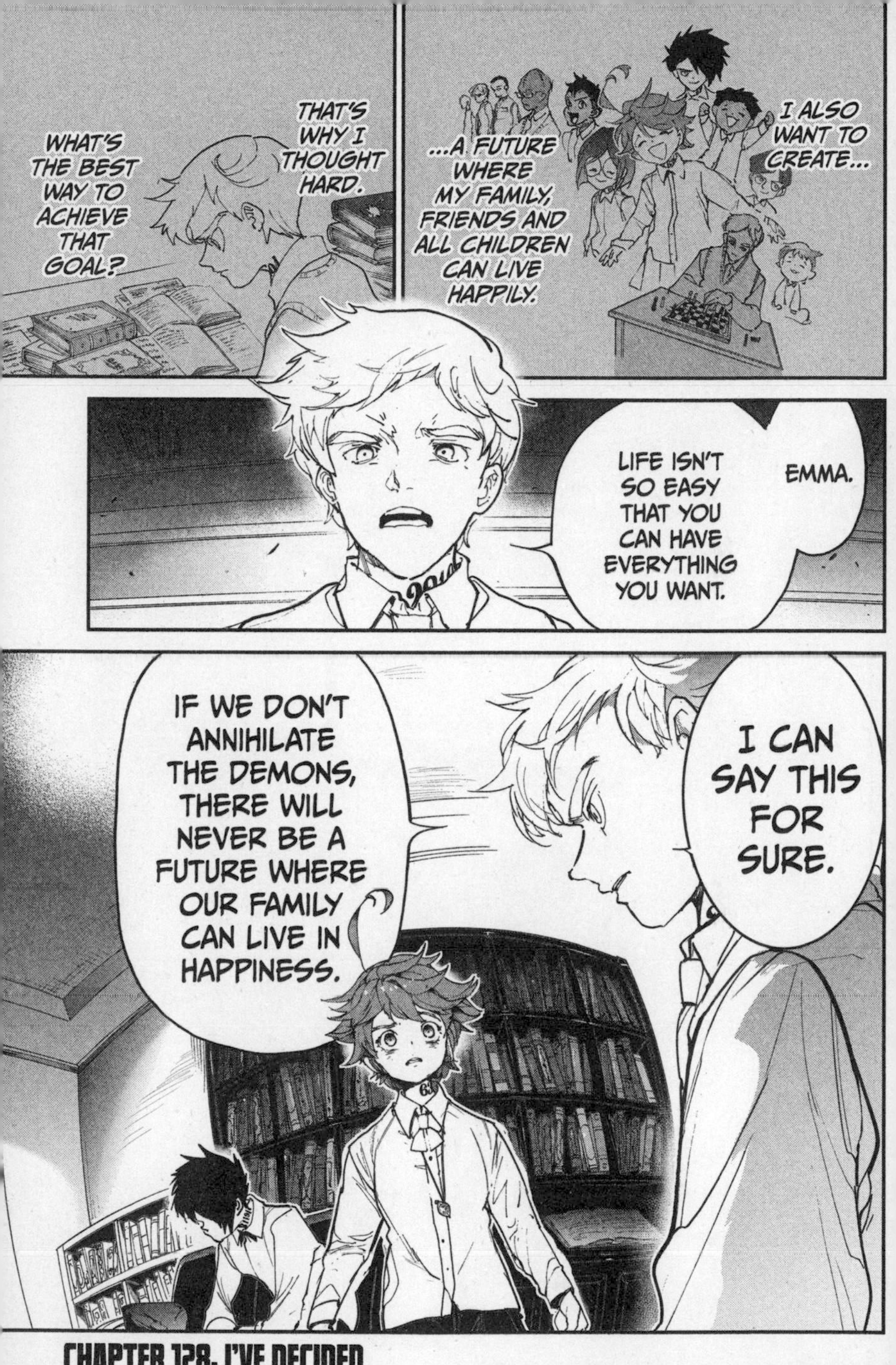
I ALSO WANT TO CREATE...
...A FUTURE WHERE MY FAMILY, FRIENDS AND ALL CHILDREN CAN LIVE HAPPILY.
THAT'S WHY I THOUGHT HARD.
WHAT'S THE BEST WAY TO ACHIEVE THAT GOAL?
EMMA.
LIFE ISN'T SO EASY THAT YOU CAN HAVE EVERYTHING YOU WANT.
I CAN SAY THIS FOR SURE.
IF WE DON'T ANNIHILATE THE DEMONS, THERE WILL NEVER BE A FUTURE WHERE OUR FAMILY CAN LIVE IN HAPPINESS.

CHAPTER 128: I'VE DECIDED

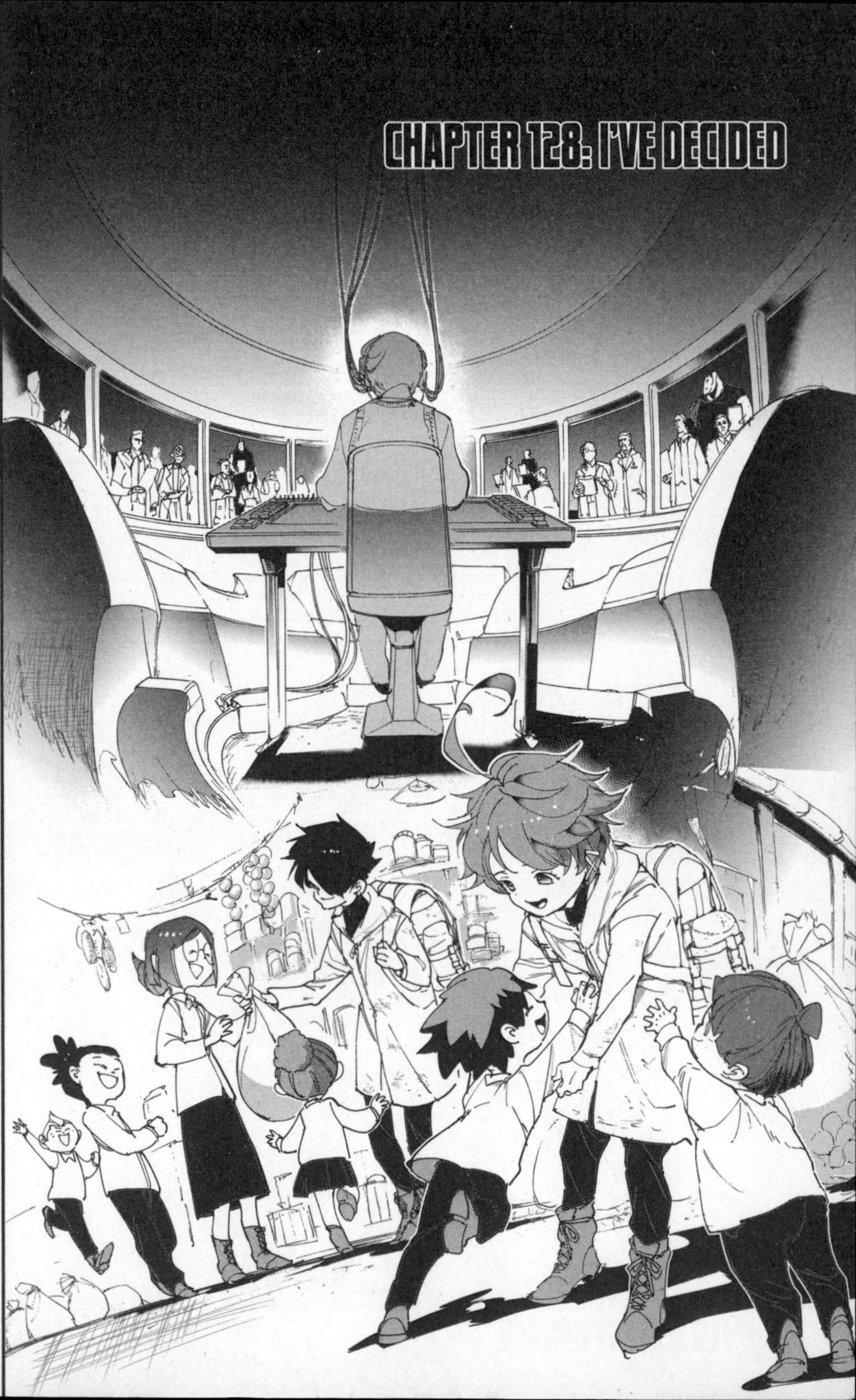
CHAPTER 128: I'VE DECIDED

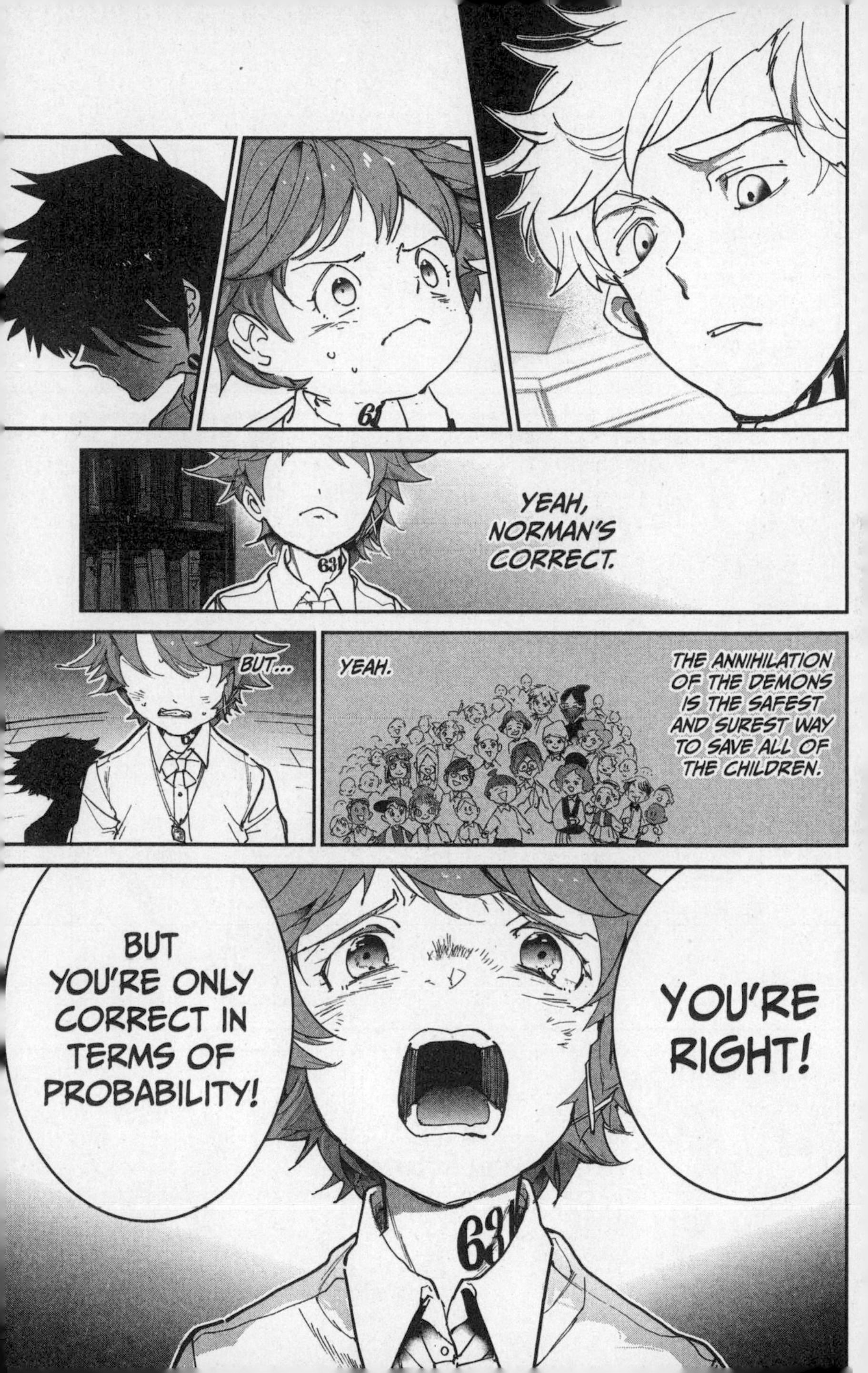
YEAH, NORMAN'S CORRECT.
THE ANNIHILATION OF THE DEMONS IS THE SAFEST AND SUREST WAY TO SAVE ALL OF THE CHILDREN.
YEAH.
BUT...
YOU'RE RIGHT!
BUT YOU'RE ONLY CORRECT IN TERMS OF PROBABILITY!

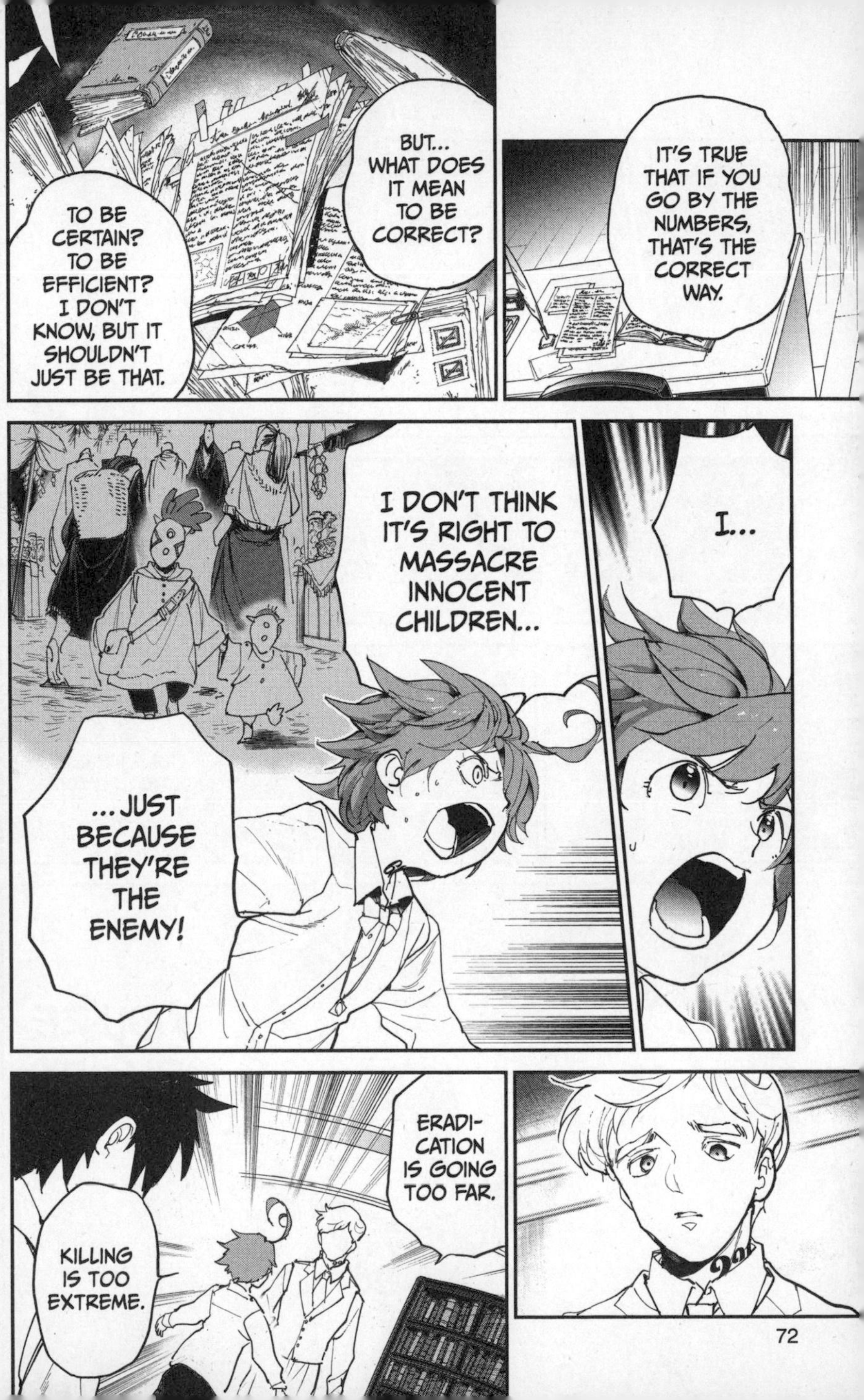
IT'S TRUE THAT IF YOU GO BY THE NUMBERS, THAT'S THE CORRECT WAY.
BUT... WHAT DOES IT MEAN TO BE CORRECT?
TO BE CERTAIN? TO BE EFFICIENT? I DON'T KNOW, BUT IT SHOULDN'T JUST BE THAT.
I...
I DON'T THINK IT'S RIGHT TO MASSACRE INNOCENT CHILDREN...
...JUST BECAUSE THEY'RE THE ENEMY!
ERADI-CATION IS GOING TOO FAR.
KILLING IS TOO EXTREME.

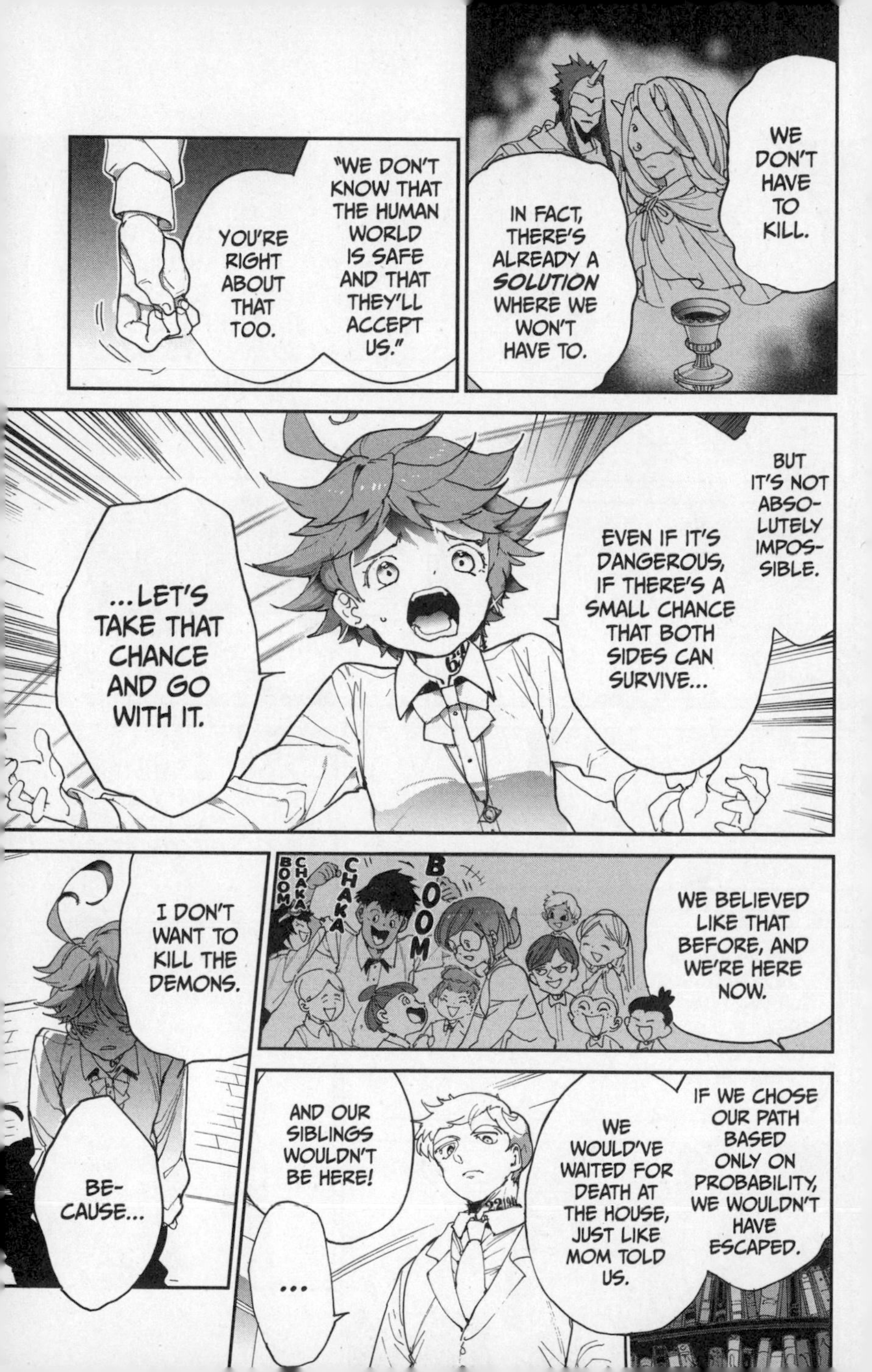
WE DON'T HAVE TO KILL.
IN FACT, THERE'S ALREADY A *SOLUTION* WHERE WE WON'T HAVE TO.
"WE DON'T KNOW THAT THE HUMAN WORLD IS SAFE AND THAT THEY'LL ACCEPT US."
YOU'RE RIGHT ABOUT THAT TOO.
BUT IT'S NOT ABSO-LUTELY IMPOS-SIBLE.
EVEN IF IT'S DANGEROUS, IF THERE'S A SMALL CHANCE THAT BOTH SIDES CAN SURVIVE...
...LET'S TAKE THAT CHANCE AND GO WITH IT.
WE BELIEVED LIKE THAT BEFORE, AND WE'RE HERE NOW.
BOOM
CHAKA
CHAKA
BOOM
IF WE CHOSE OUR PATH BASED ONLY ON PROBABILITY, WE WOULDN'T HAVE ESCAPED.
WE WOULD'VE WAITED FOR DEATH AT THE HOUSE, JUST LIKE MOM TOLD US.
AND OUR SIBLINGS WOULDN'T BE HERE!
...
I DON'T WANT TO KILL THE DEMONS.
BE-CAUSE...

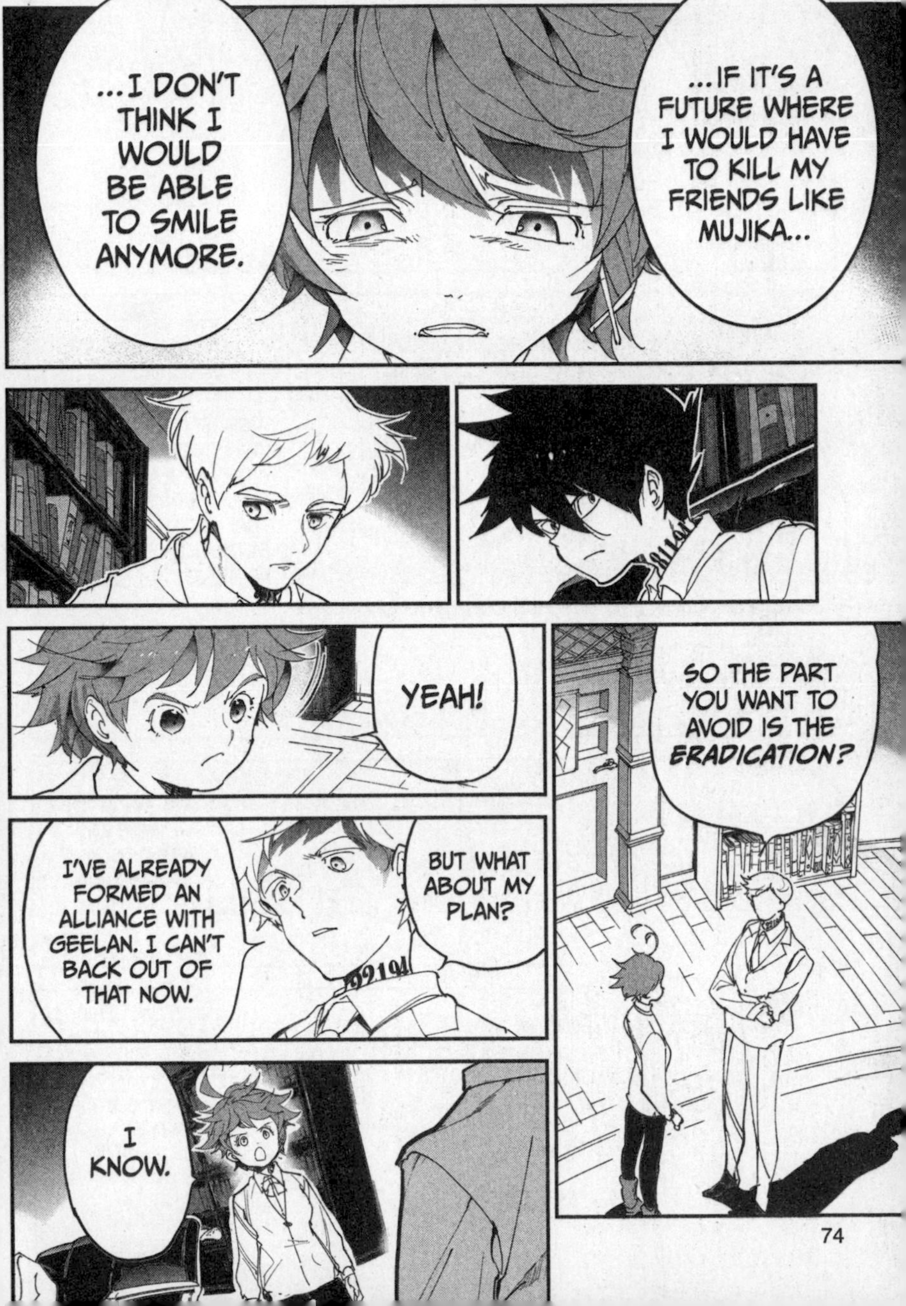
...IF IT'S A FUTURE WHERE I WOULD HAVE TO KILL MY FRIENDS LIKE MUJIKA...
...I DON'T THINK I WOULD BE ABLE TO SMILE ANYMORE.
SO THE PART YOU WANT TO AVOID IS THE *ERADICATION?*
YEAH!
BUT WHAT ABOUT MY PLAN?
I'VE ALREADY FORMED AN ALLIANCE WITH GEELAN. I CAN'T BACK OUT OF THAT NOW.
I KNOW.

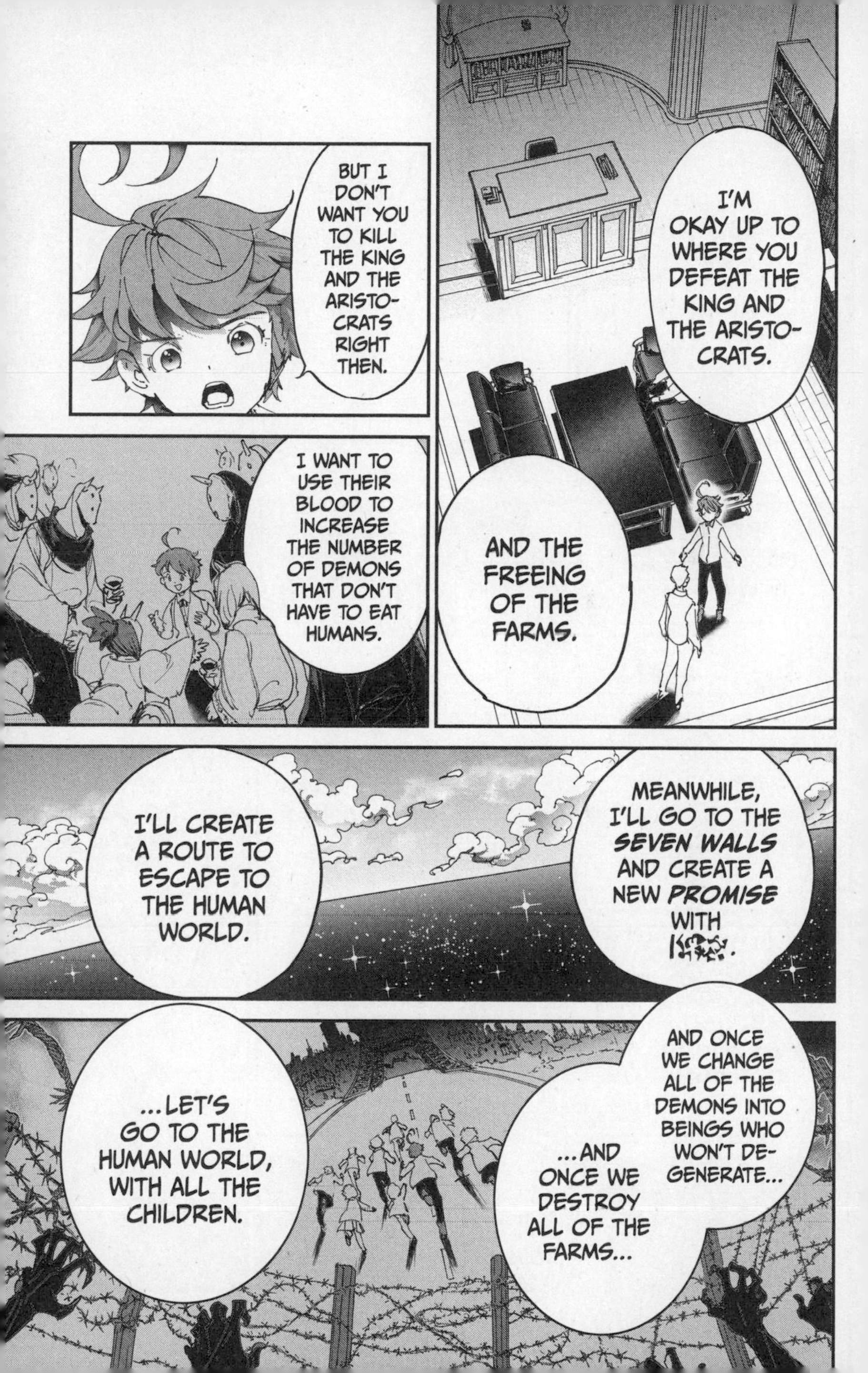
I'M OKAY UP TO WHERE YOU DEFEAT THE KING AND THE ARISTO-CRATS.
AND THE FREEING OF THE FARMS.
BUT I DON'T WANT YOU TO KILL THE KING AND THE ARISTO-CRATS RIGHT THEN.
I WANT TO USE THEIR BLOOD TO INCREASE THE NUMBER OF DEMONS THAT DON'T HAVE TO EAT HUMANS.
MEANWHILE, I'LL GO TO THE *SEVEN WALLS* AND CREATE A NEW *PROMISE* WITH
I'LL CREATE A ROUTE TO ESCAPE TO THE HUMAN WORLD.
AND ONCE WE CHANGE ALL OF THE DEMONS INTO BEINGS WHO WON'T DE-GENERATE...
...AND ONCE WE DESTROY ALL OF THE FARMS...
...LET'S GO TO THE HUMAN WORLD, WITH ALL THE CHILDREN.

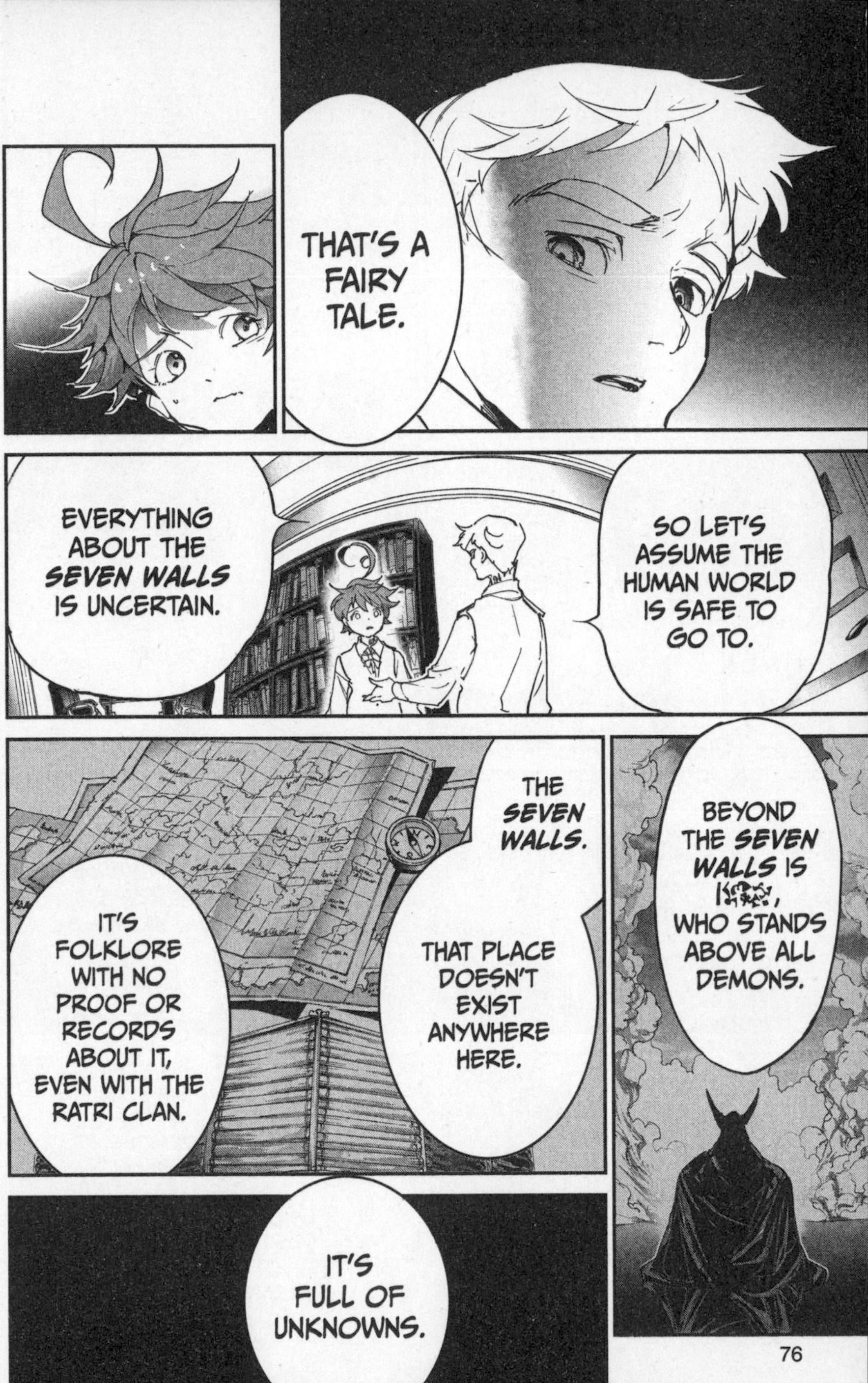
THAT'S A FAIRY TALE.
SO LET'S ASSUME THE HUMAN WORLD IS SAFE TO GO TO.
EVERYTHING ABOUT THE SEVEN WALLS IS UNCERTAIN.
BEYOND THE SEVEN WALLS IS
, WHO STANDS ABOVE ALL DEMONS.
THE SEVEN WALLS.
THAT PLACE DOESN'T EXIST ANYWHERE HERE.
IT'S FOLKLORE WITH NO PROOF OR RECORDS ABOUT IT, EVEN WITH THE RATRI CLAN.
IT'S FULL OF UNKNOWNS.

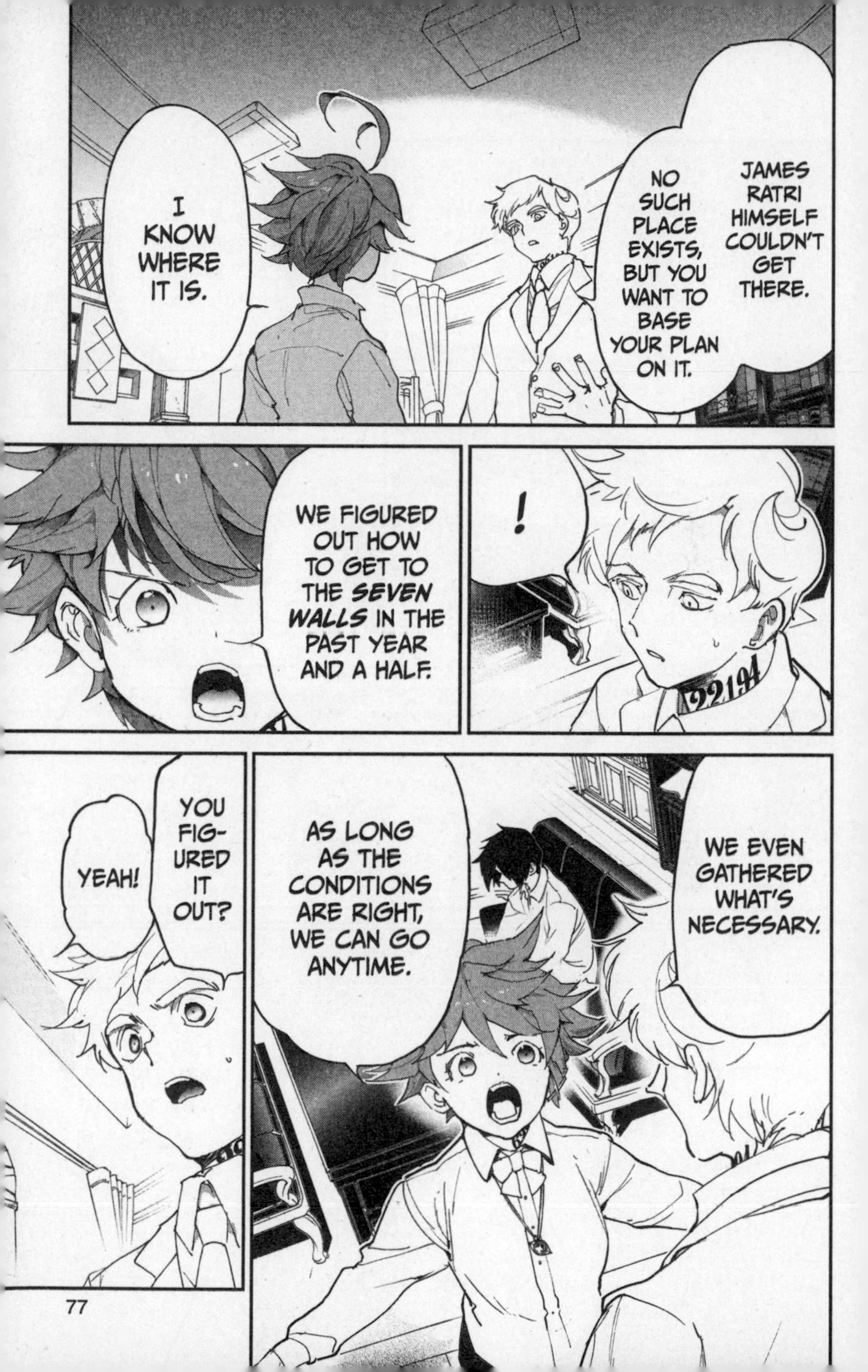
JAMES RATRI HIMSELF COULDN'T GET THERE.
NO SUCH PLACE EXISTS, BUT YOU WANT TO BASE YOUR PLAN ON IT.
I KNOW WHERE IT IS.
!
22194
WE FIGURED OUT HOW TO GET TO THE *SEVEN WALLS* IN THE PAST YEAR AND A HALF.
WE EVEN GATHERED WHAT'S NECESSARY.
AS LONG AS THE CONDITIONS ARE RIGHT, WE CAN GO ANYTIME.
YOU FIG-URED IT OUT?
YEAH!

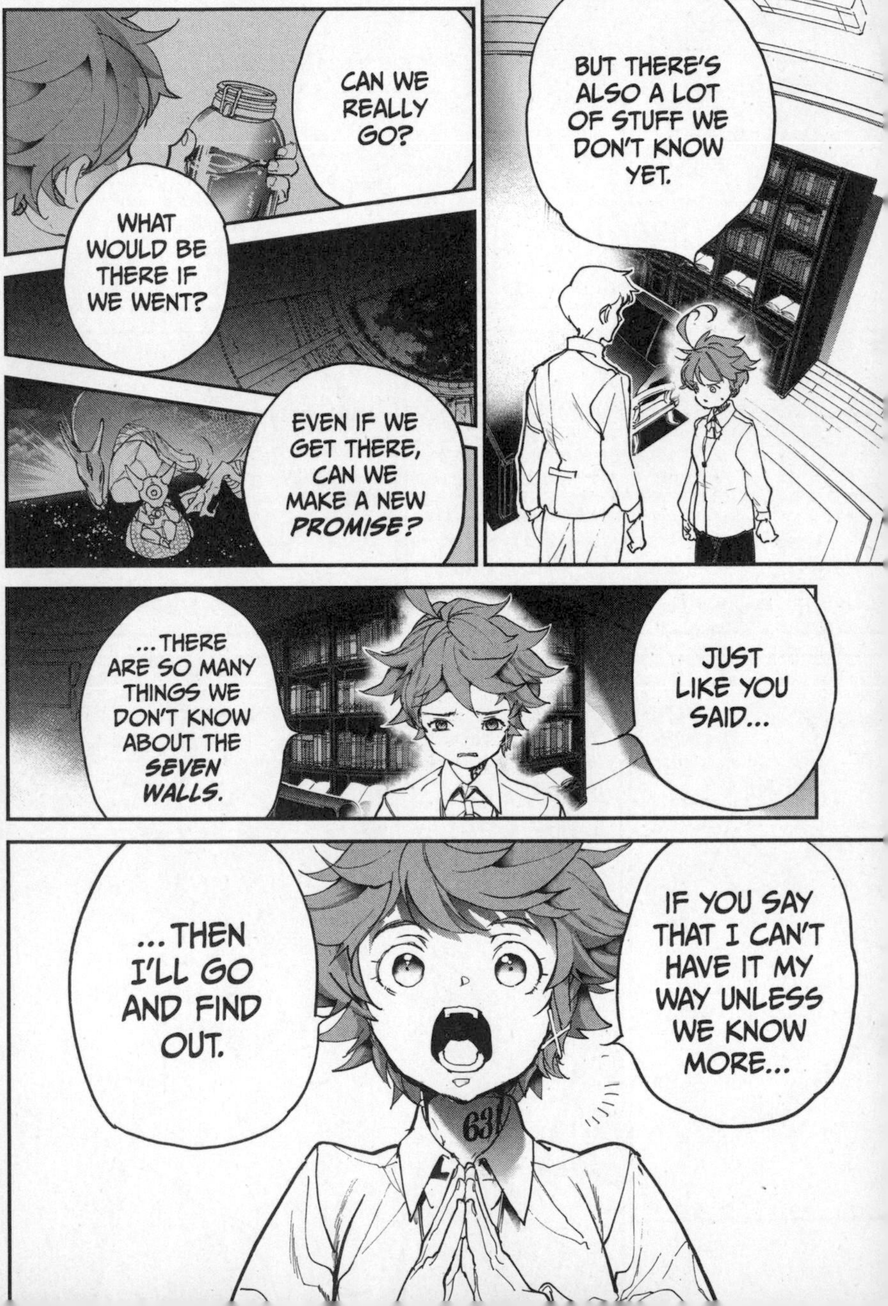
BUT THERE'S ALSO A LOT OF STUFF WE DON'T KNOW YET.
CAN WE REALLY GO?
WHAT WOULD BE THERE IF WE WENT?
EVEN IF WE GET THERE, CAN WE MAKE A NEW *PROMISE?*
JUST LIKE YOU SAID...
...THERE ARE SO MANY THINGS WE DON'T KNOW ABOUT THE *SEVEN WALLS.*
IF YOU SAY THAT I CAN'T HAVE IT MY WAY UNLESS WE KNOW MORE...
...THEN I'LL GO AND FIND OUT.
631

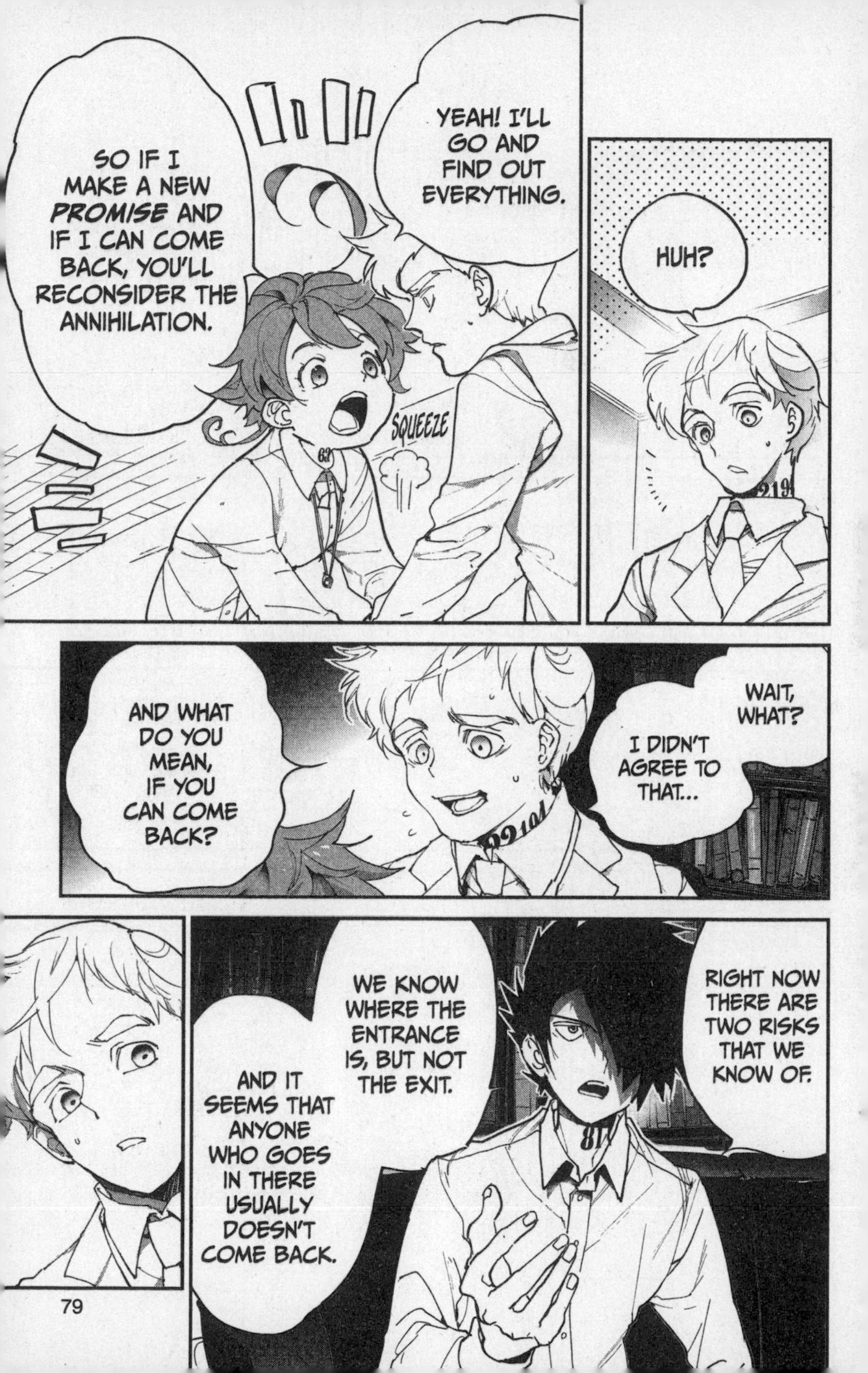
YEAH! I'LL GO AND FIND OUT EVERYTHING.
SO IF I MAKE A NEW *PROMISE* AND IF I CAN COME BACK, YOU'LL RECONSIDER THE ANNIHILATION.
SQUEEZE
HUH?
WAIT, WHAT?
I DIDN'T AGREE TO THAT...
AND WHAT DO YOU MEAN, IF YOU CAN COME BACK?
RIGHT NOW THERE ARE TWO RISKS THAT WE KNOW OF.
WE KNOW WHERE THE ENTRANCE IS, BUT NOT THE EXIT.
AND IT SEEMS THAT ANYONE WHO GOES IN THERE USUALLY DOESN'T COME BACK.

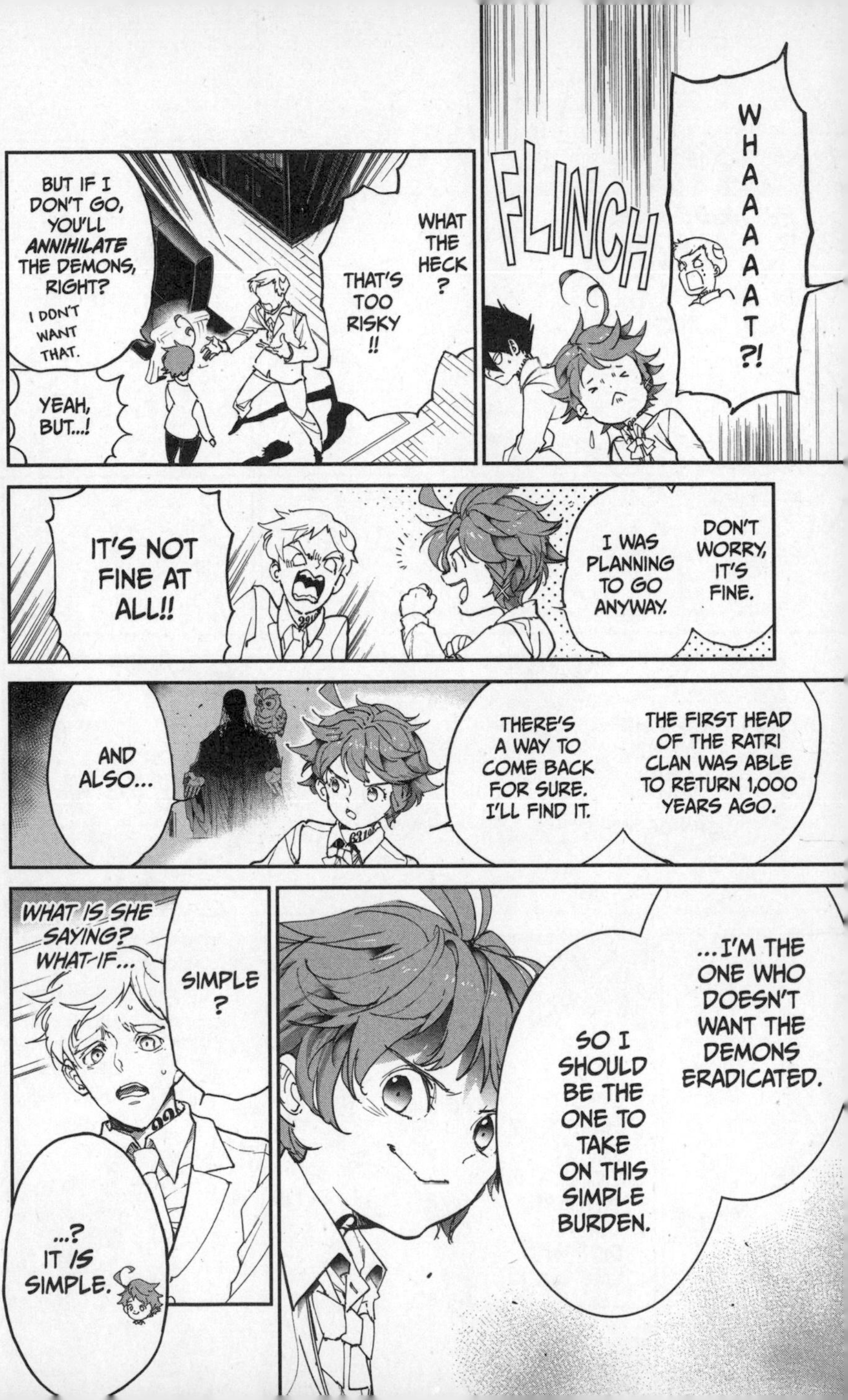
WHAAAAAT?!
FLINCH
WHAT THE HECK?
THAT'S TOO RISKY!!
BUT IF I DON'T GO, YOU'LL *ANNIHILATE* THE DEMONS, RIGHT?
I DON'T WANT THAT.
YEAH, BUT...!
DON'T WORRY, IT'S FINE.
I WAS PLANNING TO GO ANYWAY.
IT'S NOT FINE AT ALL!!
THE FIRST HEAD OF THE RATRI CLAN WAS ABLE TO RETURN 1,000 YEARS AGO.
THERE'S A WAY TO COME BACK FOR SURE. I'LL FIND IT.
AND ALSO...
...I'M THE ONE WHO DOESN'T WANT THE DEMONS ERADICATED.
SO I SHOULD BE THE ONE TO TAKE ON THIS SIMPLE BURDEN.
SIMPLE?
WHAT IS SHE SAYING? WHAT-IF...
...? IT *IS* SIMPLE.

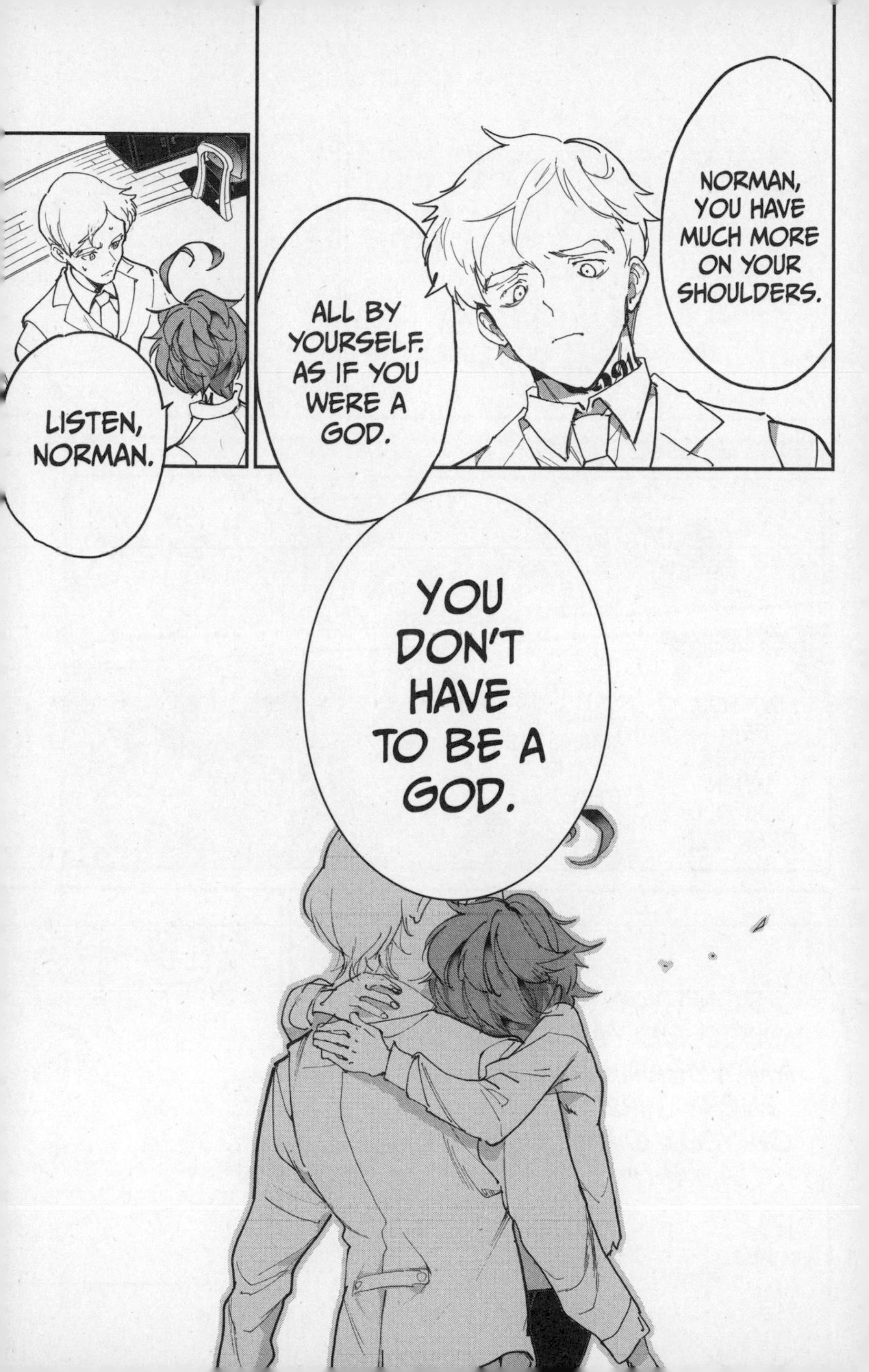
NORMAN, YOU HAVE MUCH MORE ON YOUR SHOULDERS.
ALL BY YOURSELF. AS IF YOU WERE A GOD.
LISTEN, NORMAN.
YOU DON'T HAVE TO BE A GOD.

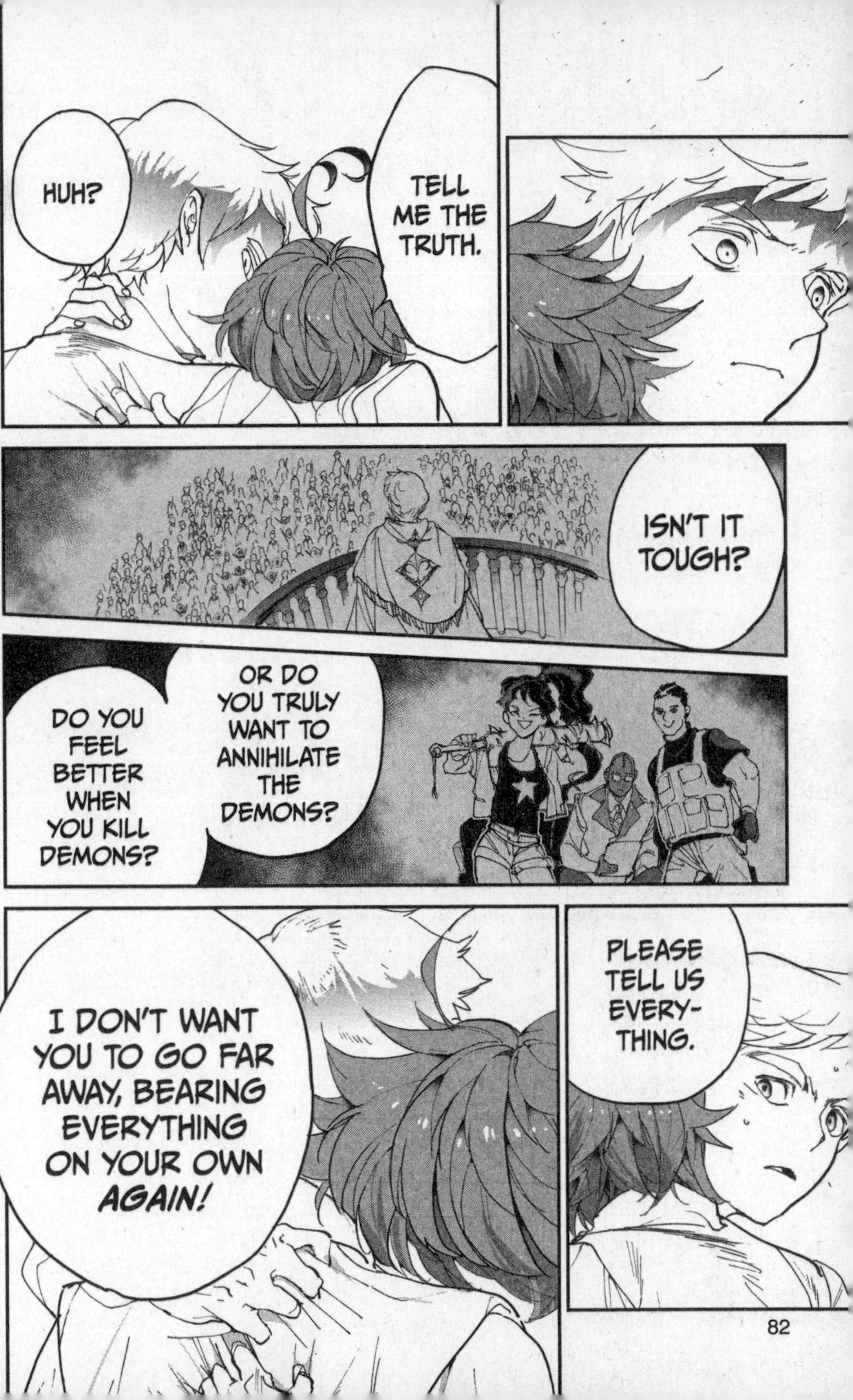
TELL ME THE TRUTH.
HUH?
ISN'T IT TOUGH?
DO YOU FEEL BETTER WHEN YOU KILL DEMONS?
OR DO YOU TRULY WANT TO ANNIHILATE THE DEMONS?
PLEASE TELL US EVERY-THING.
I DON'T WANT YOU TO GO FAR AWAY, BEARING EVERYTHING ON YOUR OWN *AGAIN!*

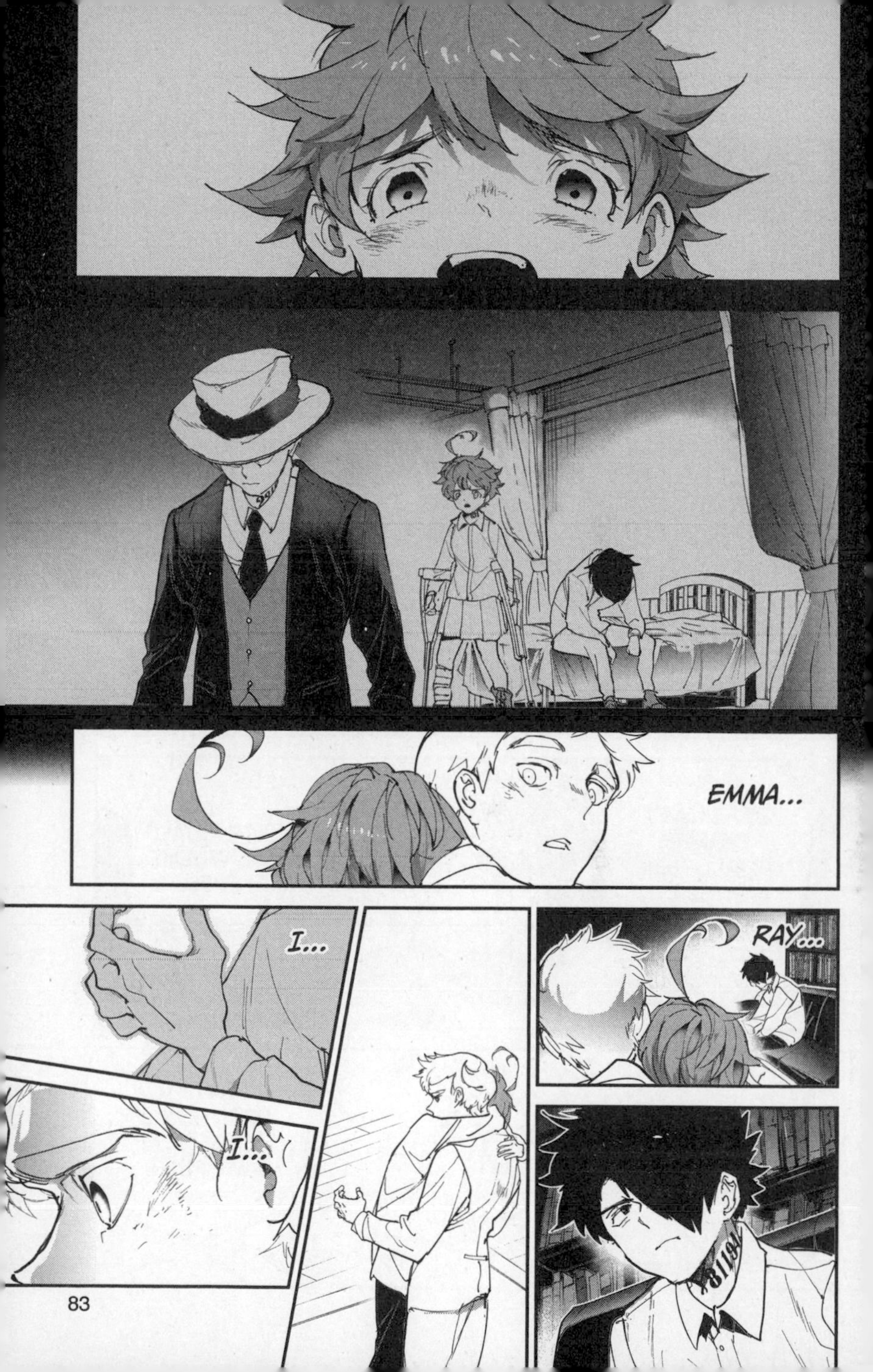
EMMA...
RAY...
I...
I...

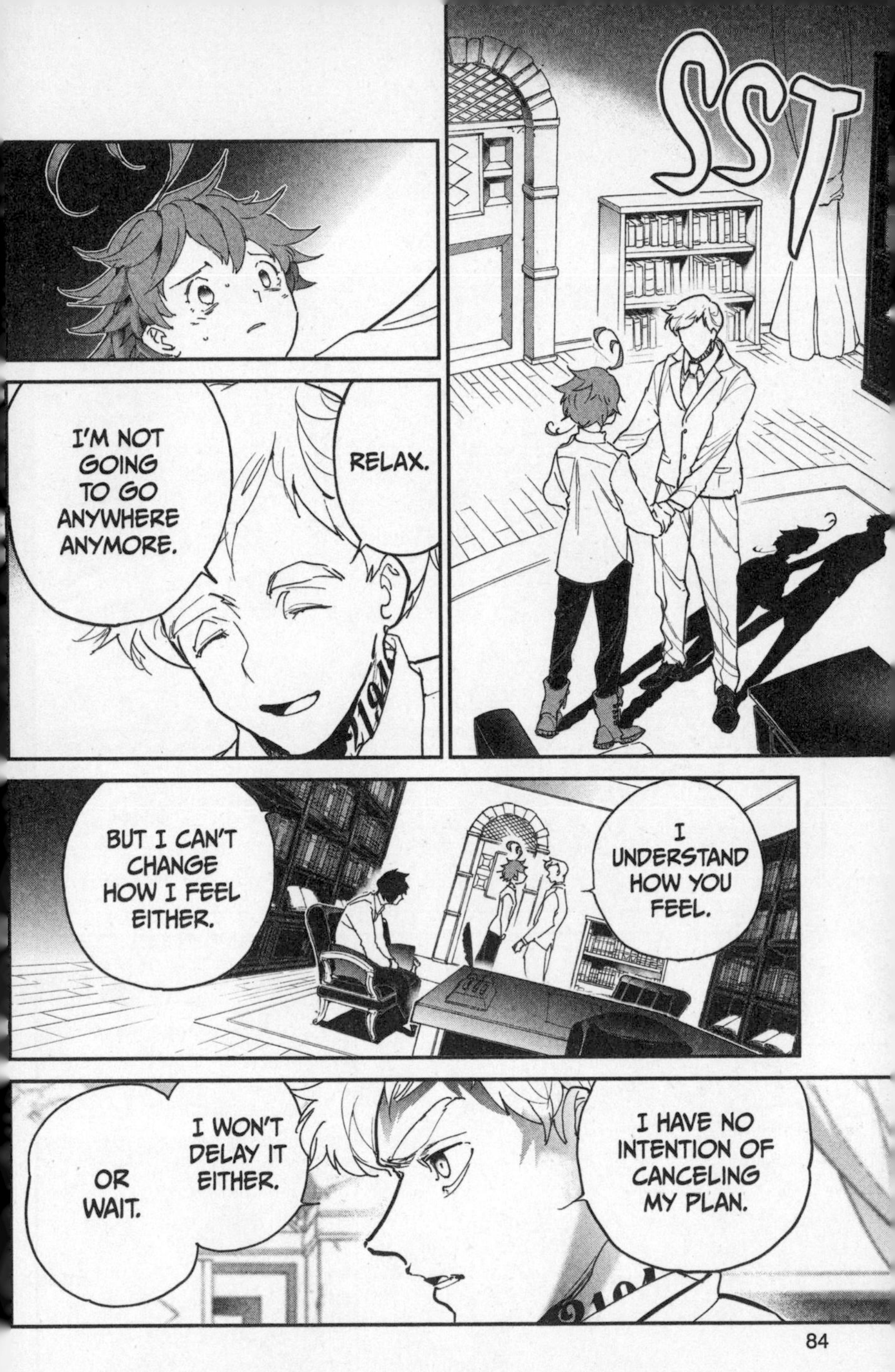
SST
RELAX.
I'M NOT GOING TO GO ANYWHERE ANYMORE.
I UNDERSTAND HOW YOU FEEL.
BUT I CAN'T CHANGE HOW I FEEL EITHER.
I HAVE NO INTENTION OF CANCELING MY PLAN.
I WON'T DELAY IT EITHER.
OR WAIT.

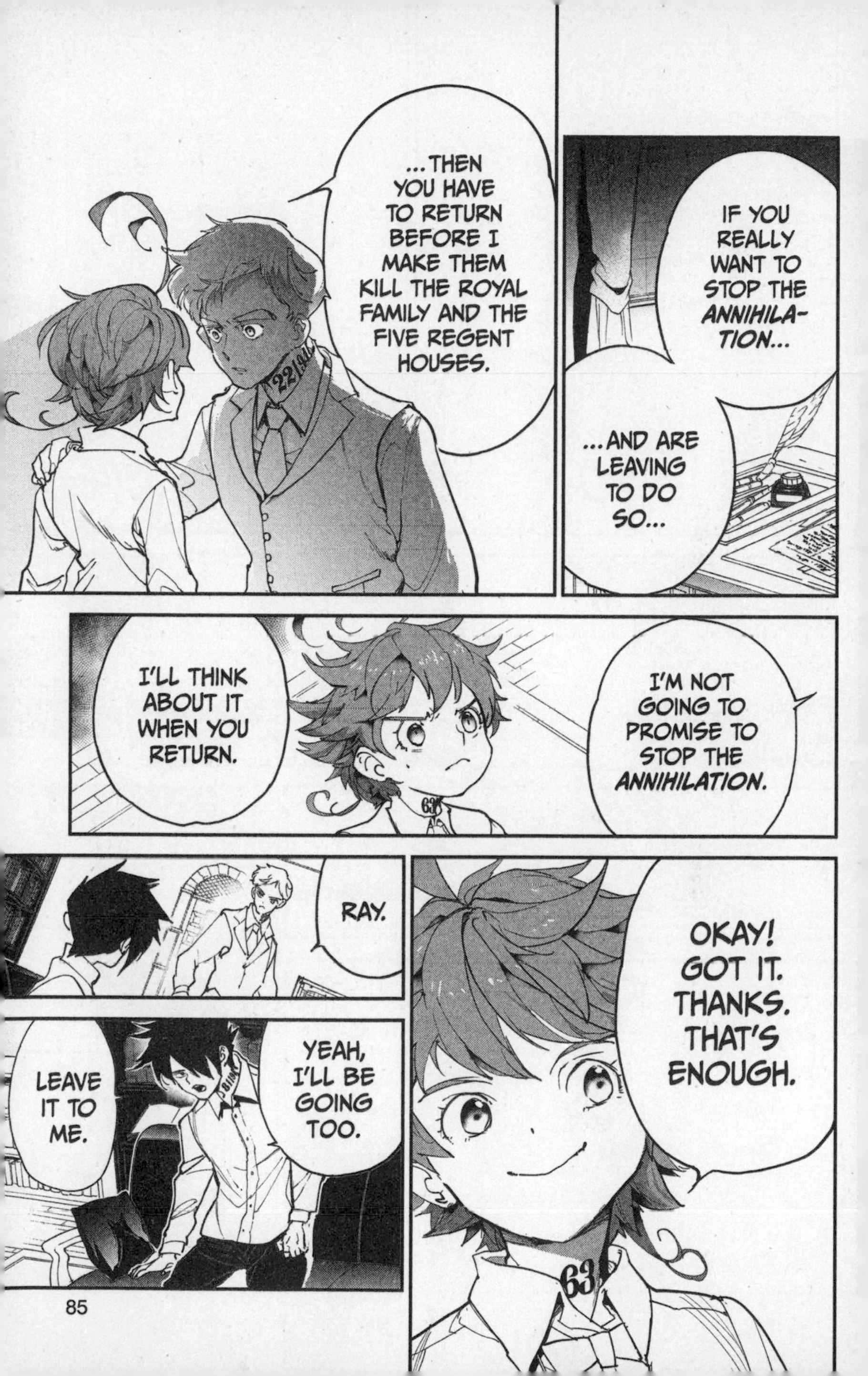
IF YOU REALLY WANT TO STOP THE *ANNIHILATION*...
...AND ARE LEAVING TO DO SO...
...THEN YOU HAVE TO RETURN BEFORE I MAKE THEM KILL THE ROYAL FAMILY AND THE FIVE REGENT HOUSES.
I'M NOT GOING TO PROMISE TO STOP THE *ANNIHILATION*.
I'LL THINK ABOUT IT WHEN YOU RETURN.
OKAY! GOT IT. THANKS. THAT'S ENOUGH.
RAY.
YEAH, I'LL BE GOING TOO.
LEAVE IT TO ME.

OKAY!

MAKE SURE YOU BOTH COME BACK SAFELY.

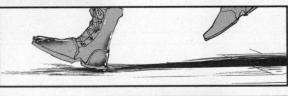

YEAH?

RAY.

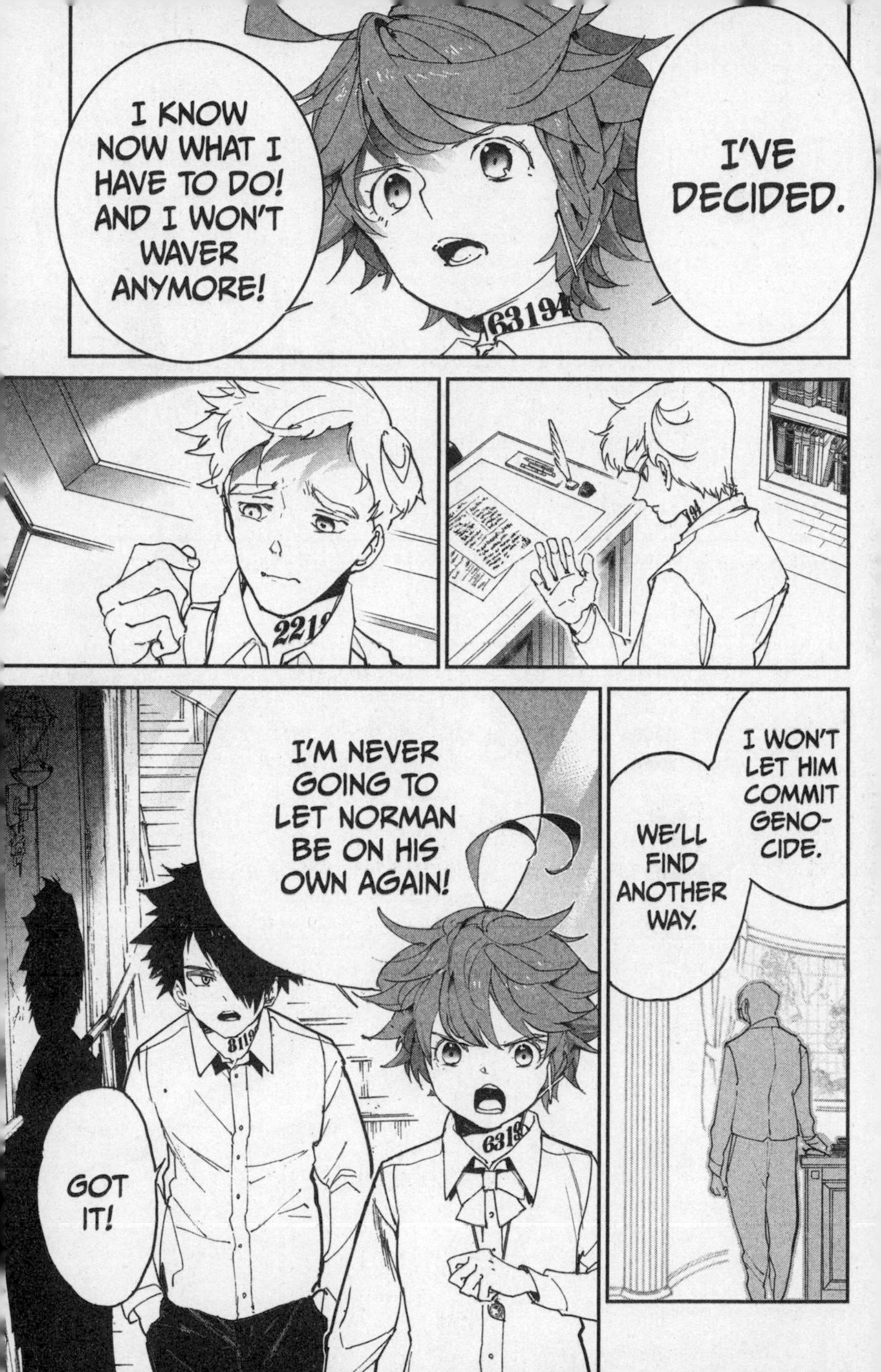
I'VE DECIDED.
I KNOW NOW WHAT I HAVE TO DO! AND I WON'T WAVER ANYMORE!
I WON'T LET HIM COMMIT GENO-CIDE.
WE'LL FIND ANOTHER WAY.
I'M NEVER GOING TO LET NORMAN BE ON HIS OWN AGAIN!
GOT IT!

BARBARA

AGE: 16

Born in Goodwill Ridge.
Has superhuman power.
Eats a lot.
She doesn't really understand what Momotaro is.
Loves the boss.

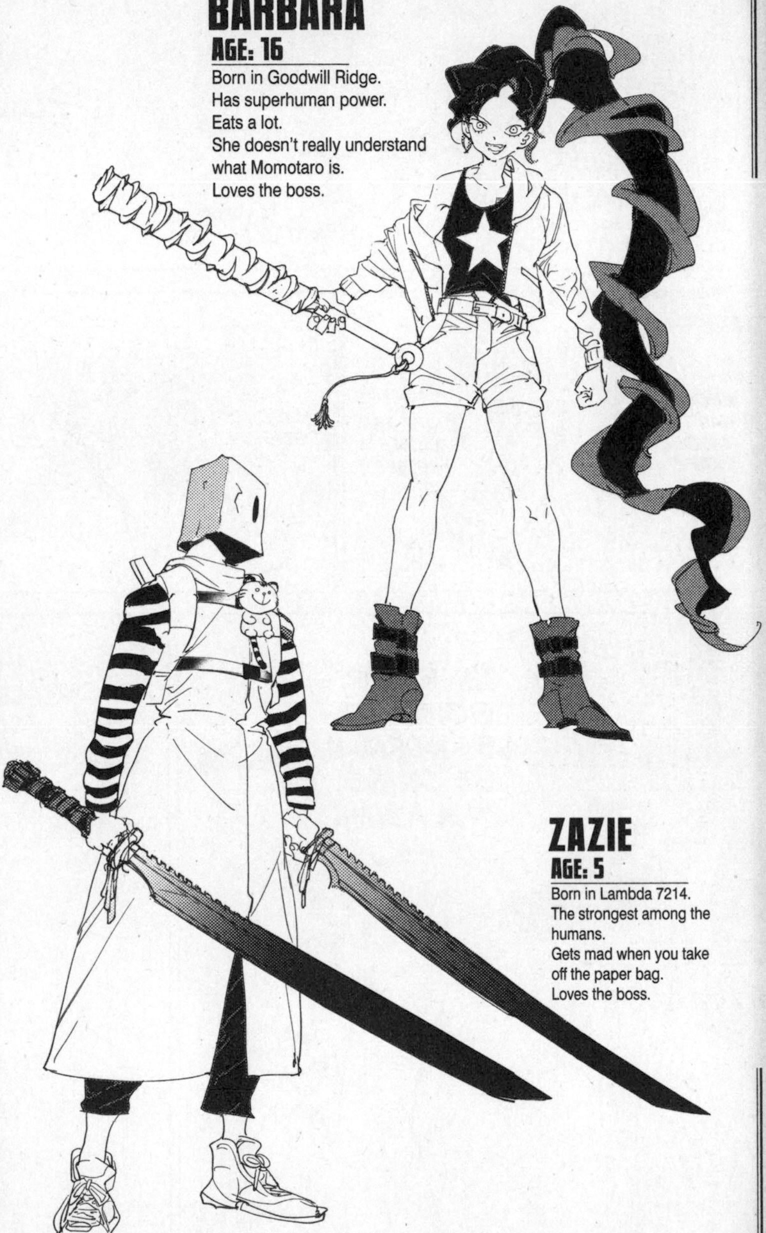

ZAZIE

AGE: 5

Born in Lambda 7214.
The strongest among the humans.
Gets mad when you take off the paper bag.
Loves the boss.

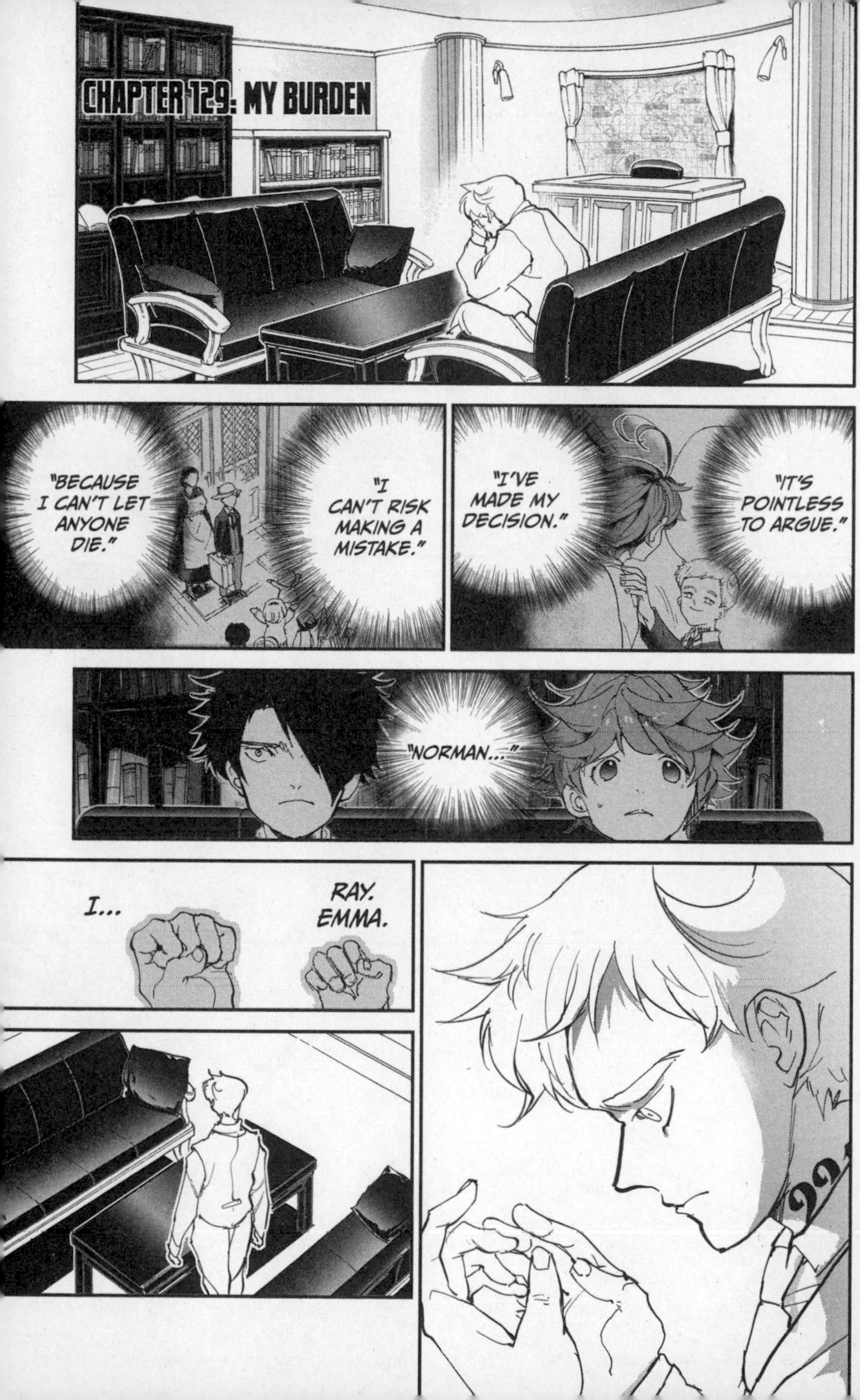
CHAPTER 129: MY BURDEN
"IT'S POINTLESS TO ARGUE."
"I'VE MADE MY DECISION."
"I CAN'T RISK MAKING A MISTAKE."
"BECAUSE I CAN'T LET ANYONE DIE."
"NORMAN..."
RAY. EMMA.
I...

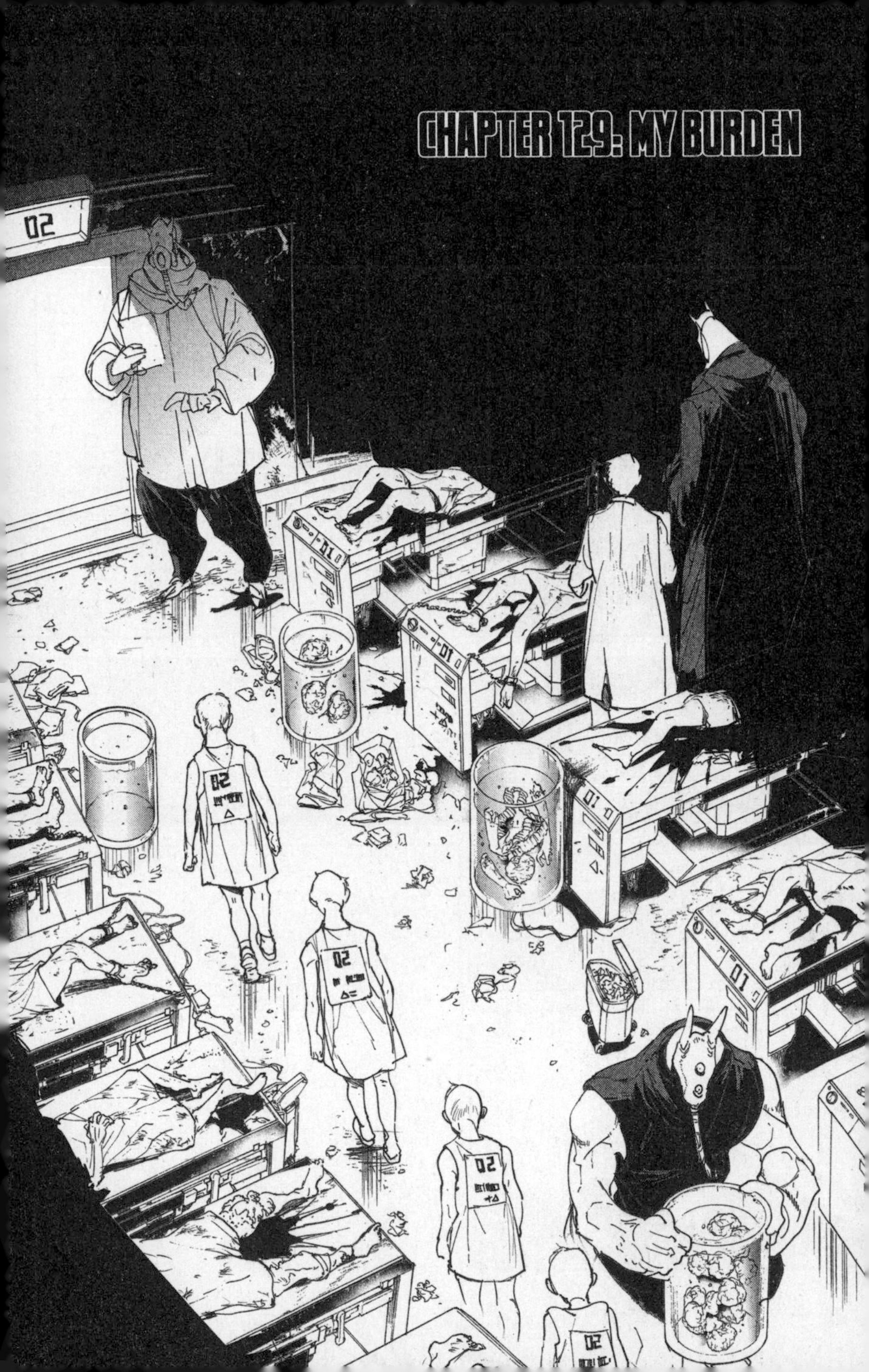
CHAPTER 129: MY BURDEN

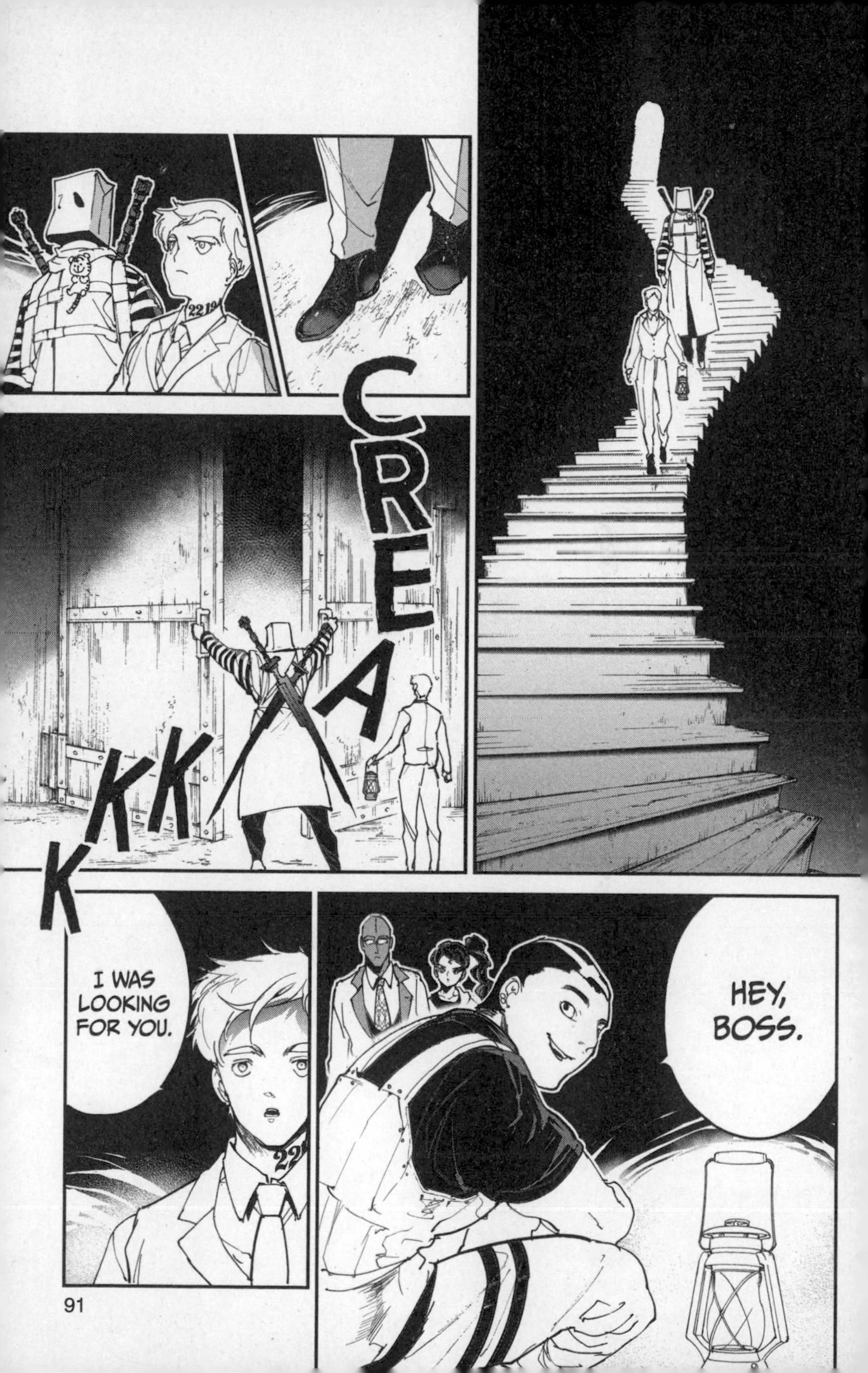
CREAKKK
HEY, BOSS.
I WAS LOOKING FOR YOU.

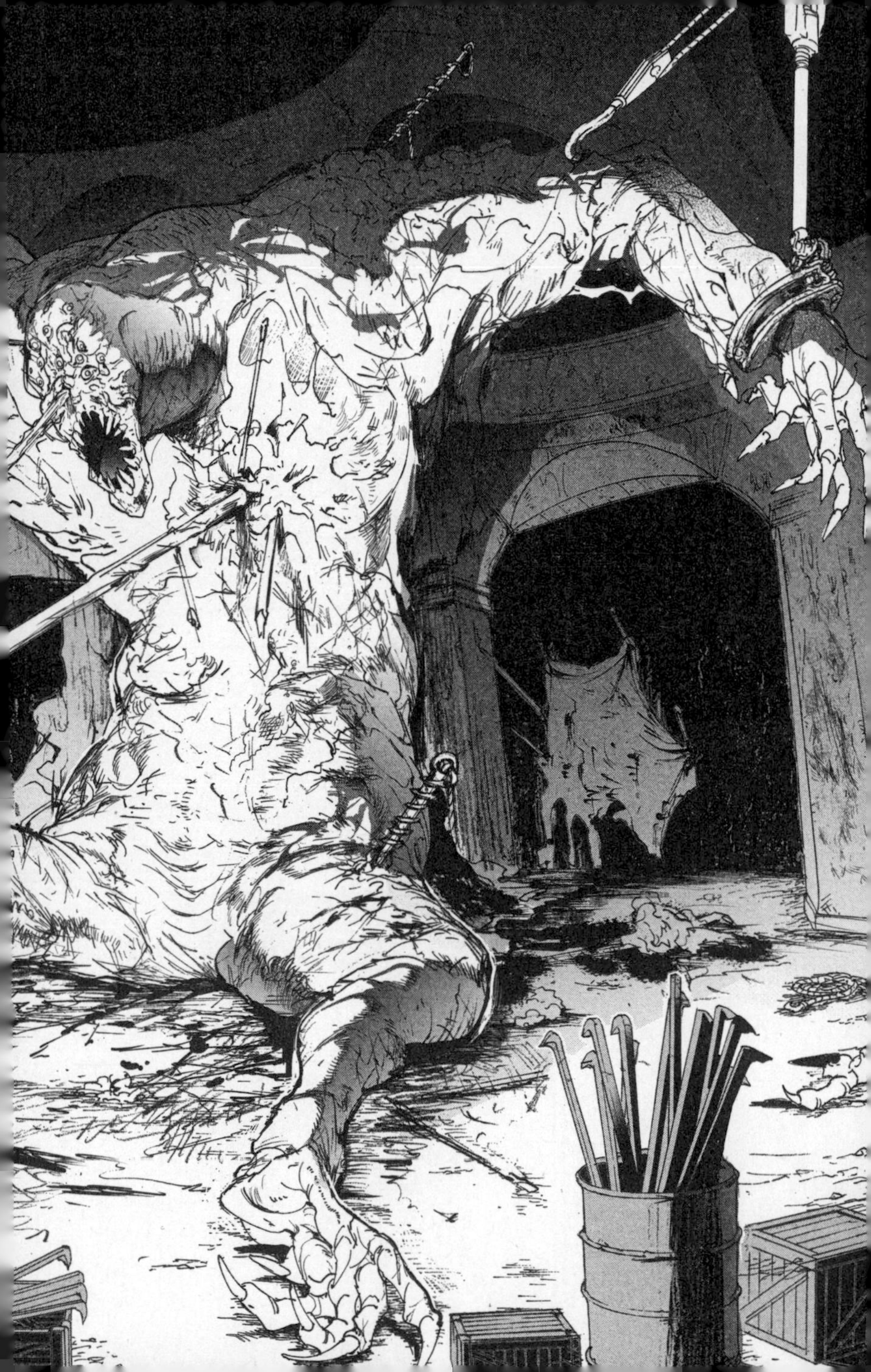

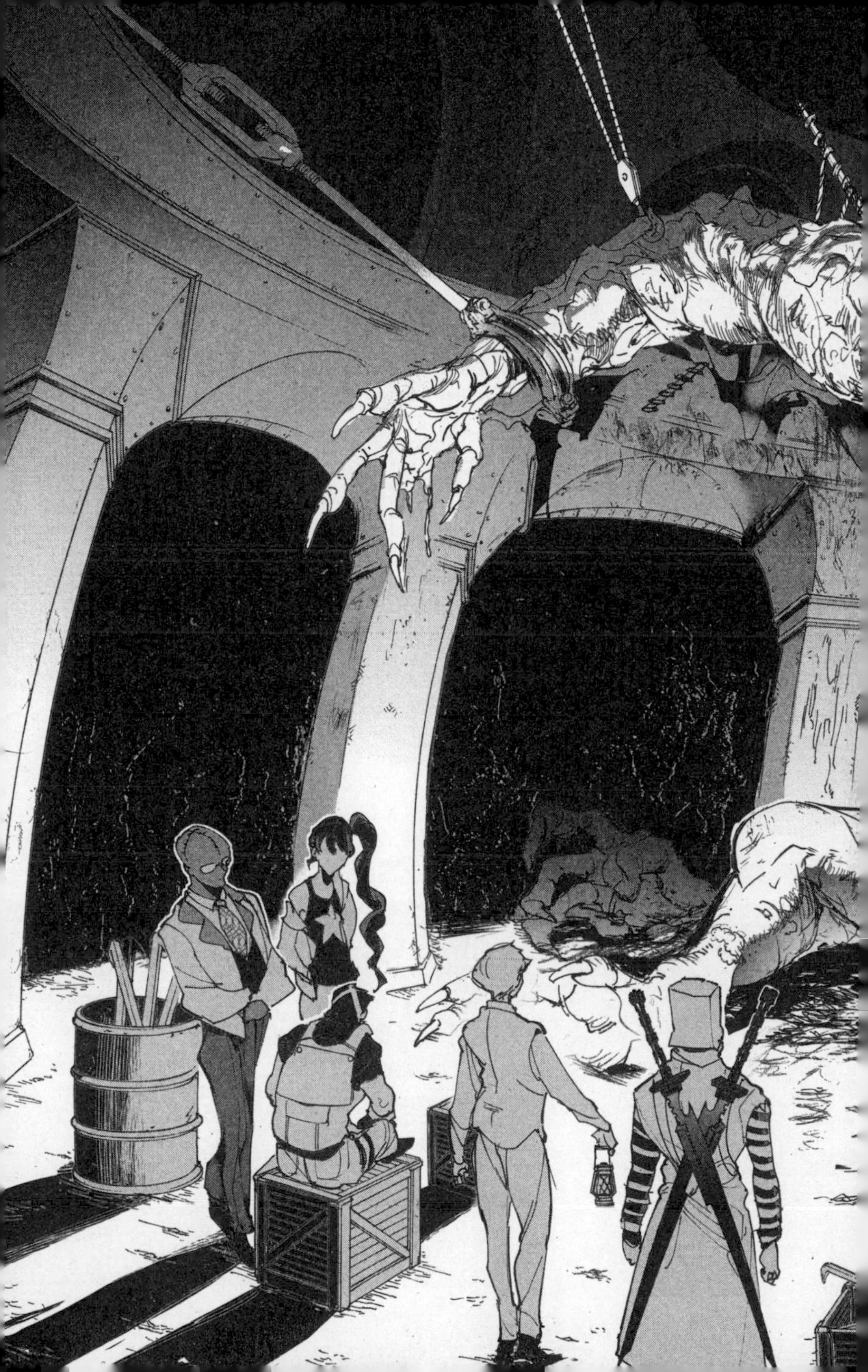

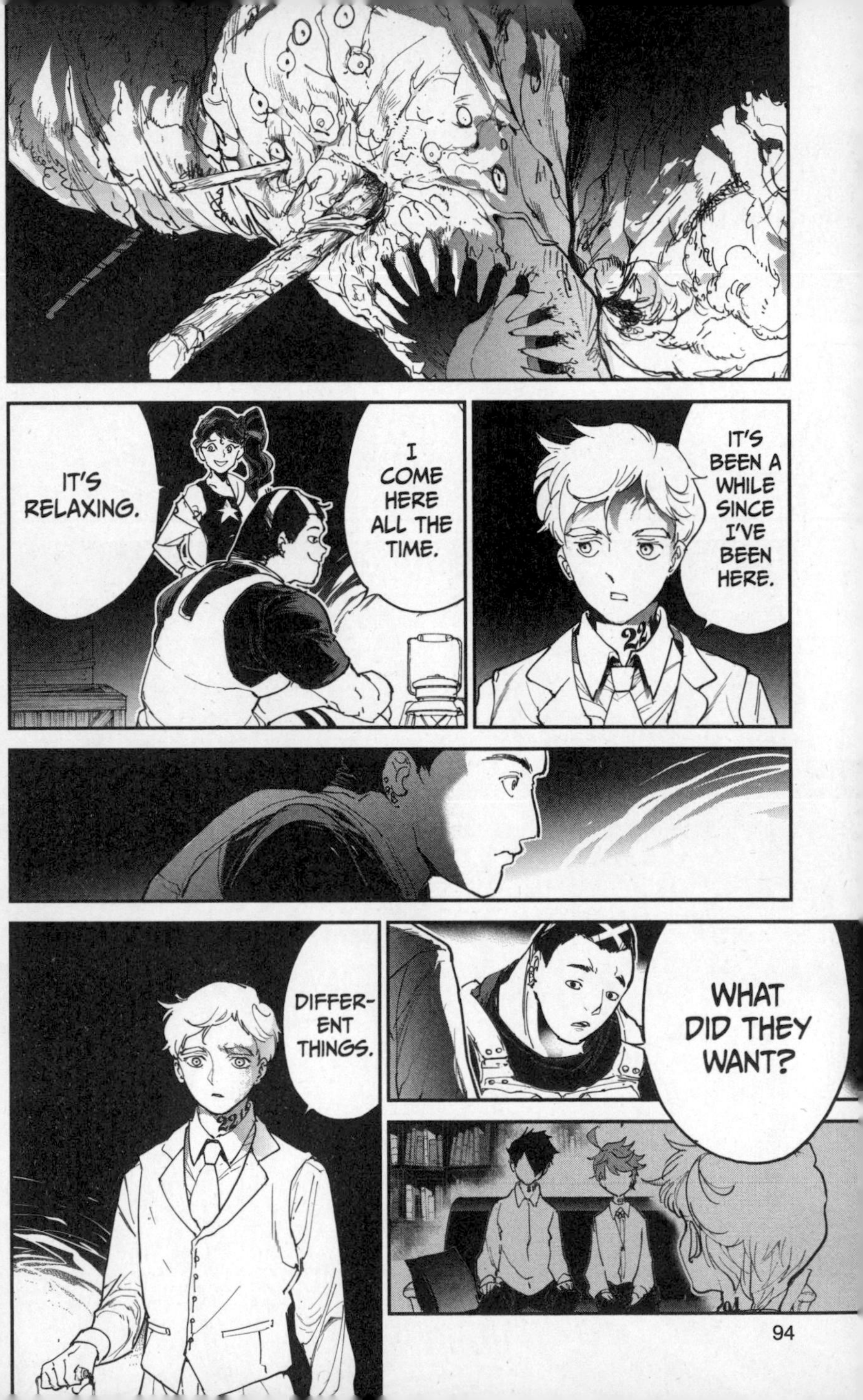
IT'S BEEN A WHILE SINCE I'VE BEEN HERE.
I COME HERE ALL THE TIME.
IT'S RELAXING.
WHAT DID THEY WANT?
DIFFER-ENT THINGS.

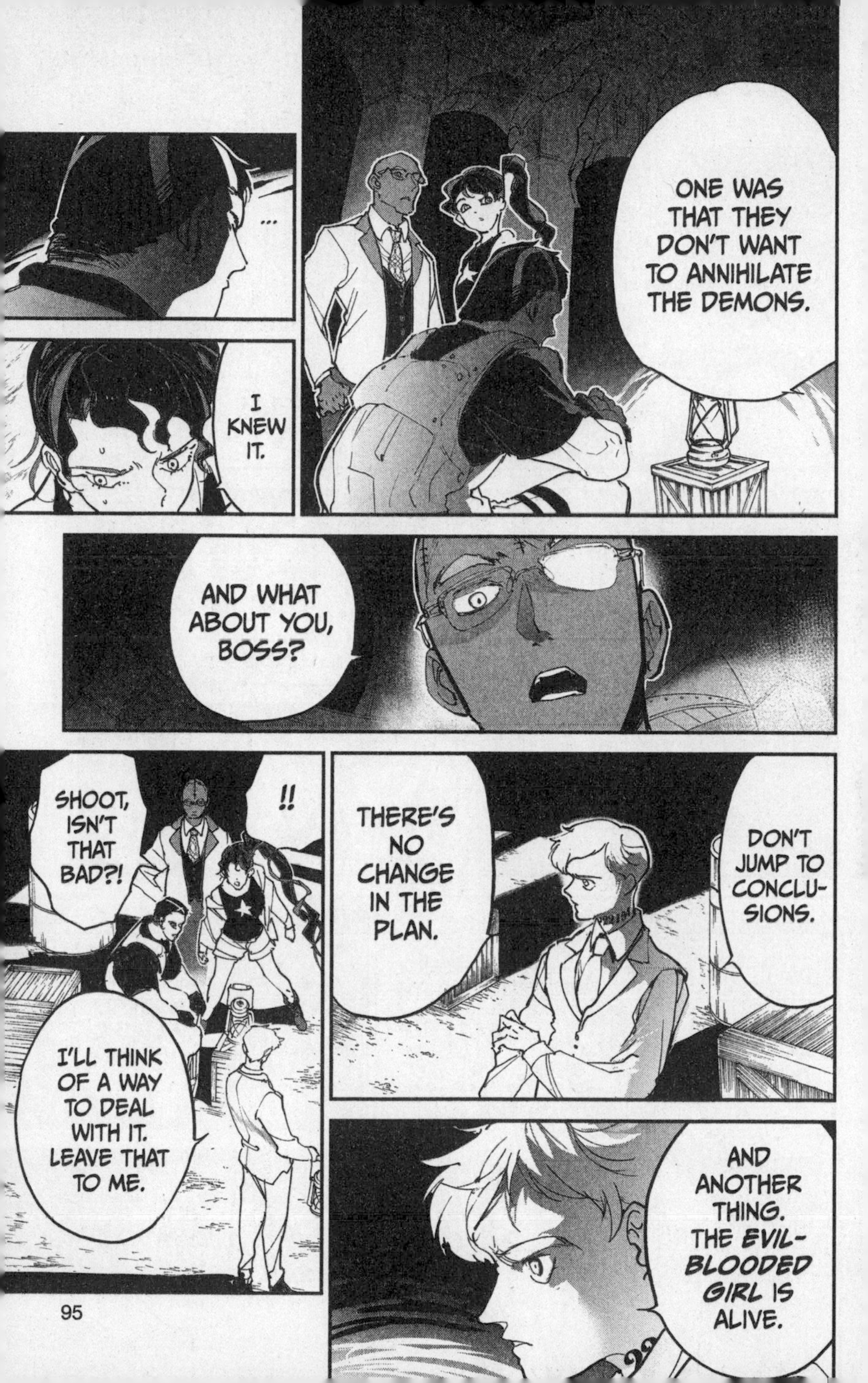
ONE WAS THAT THEY DON'T WANT TO ANNIHILATE THE DEMONS.
...
I KNEW IT.
AND WHAT ABOUT YOU, BOSS?
DON'T JUMP TO CONCLUSIONS.
THERE'S NO CHANGE IN THE PLAN.
AND ANOTHER THING. THE *EVIL-BLOODED GIRL* IS ALIVE.
!!
SHOOT, ISN'T THAT BAD?!
I'LL THINK OF A WAY TO DEAL WITH IT. LEAVE THAT TO ME.

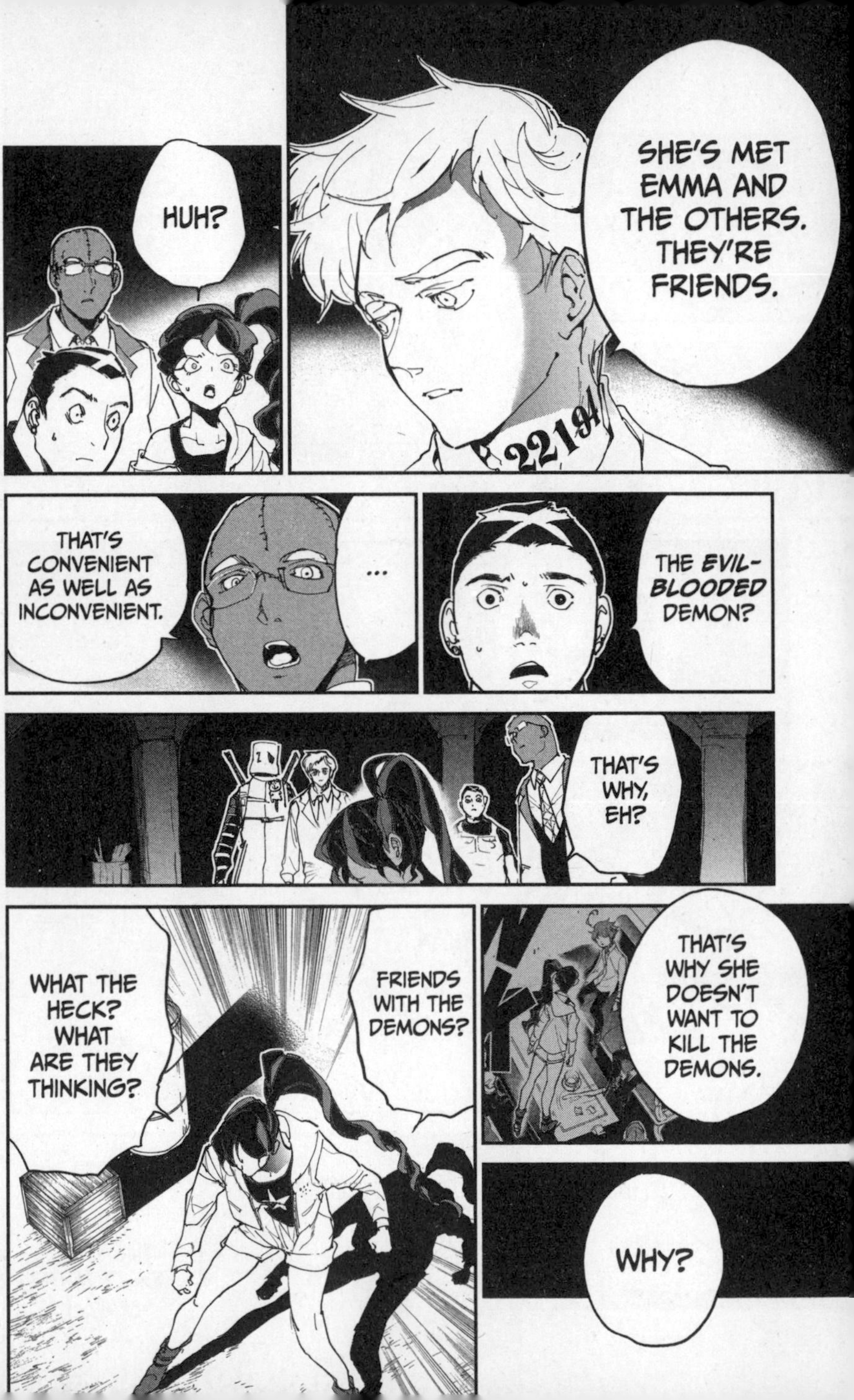
SHE'S MET EMMA AND THE OTHERS. THEY'RE FRIENDS.
22194
HUH?
THE EVIL-BLOODED DEMON?
...
THAT'S CONVENIENT AS WELL AS INCONVENIENT.
THAT'S WHY, EH?
THAT'S WHY SHE DOESN'T WANT TO KILL THE DEMONS.
WHY?
FRIENDS WITH THE DEMONS?
WHAT THE HECK? WHAT ARE THEY THINKING?

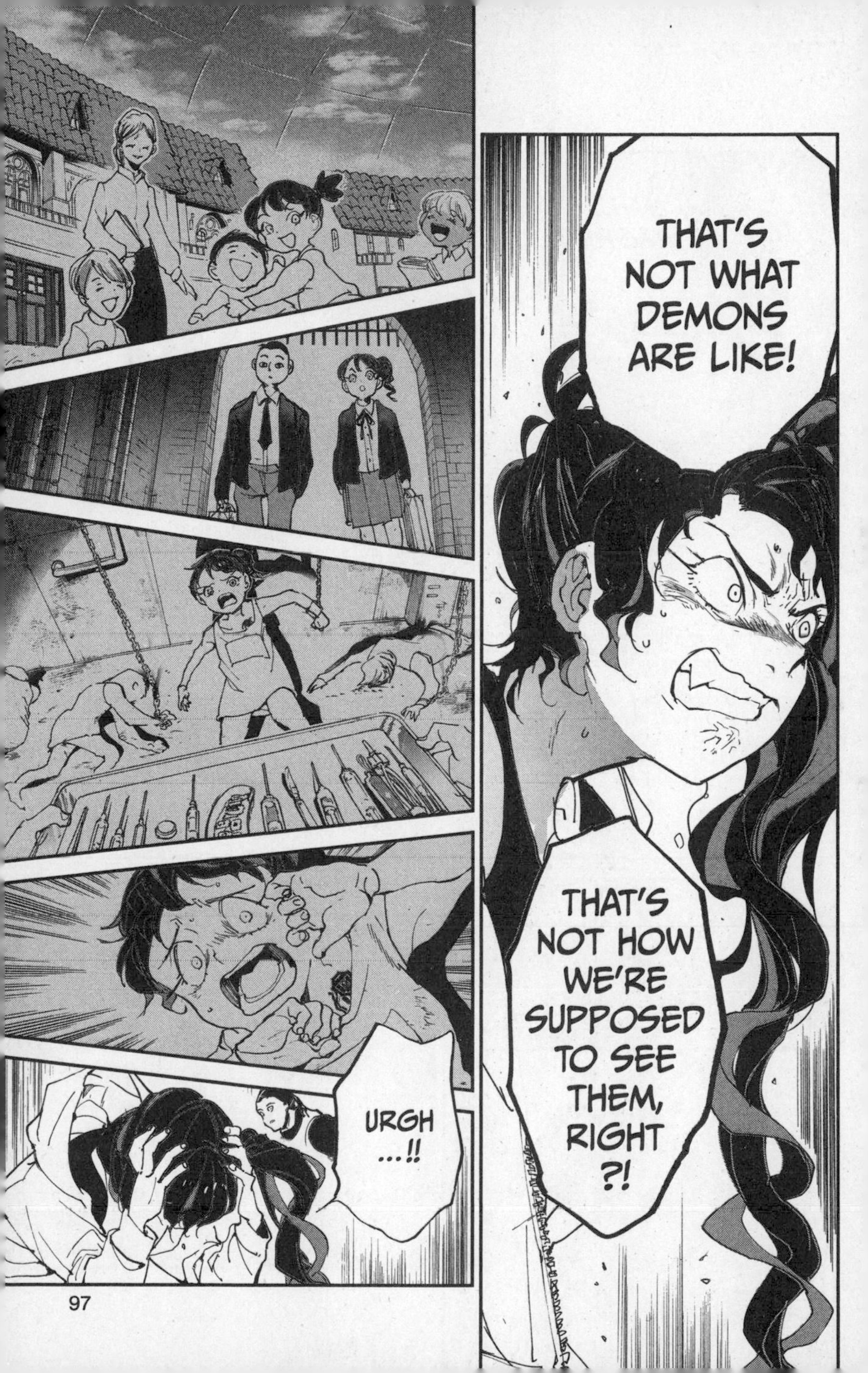
THAT'S NOT WHAT DEMONS ARE LIKE!
THAT'S NOT HOW WE'RE SUPPOSED TO SEE THEM, RIGHT?!
URGH ...!!

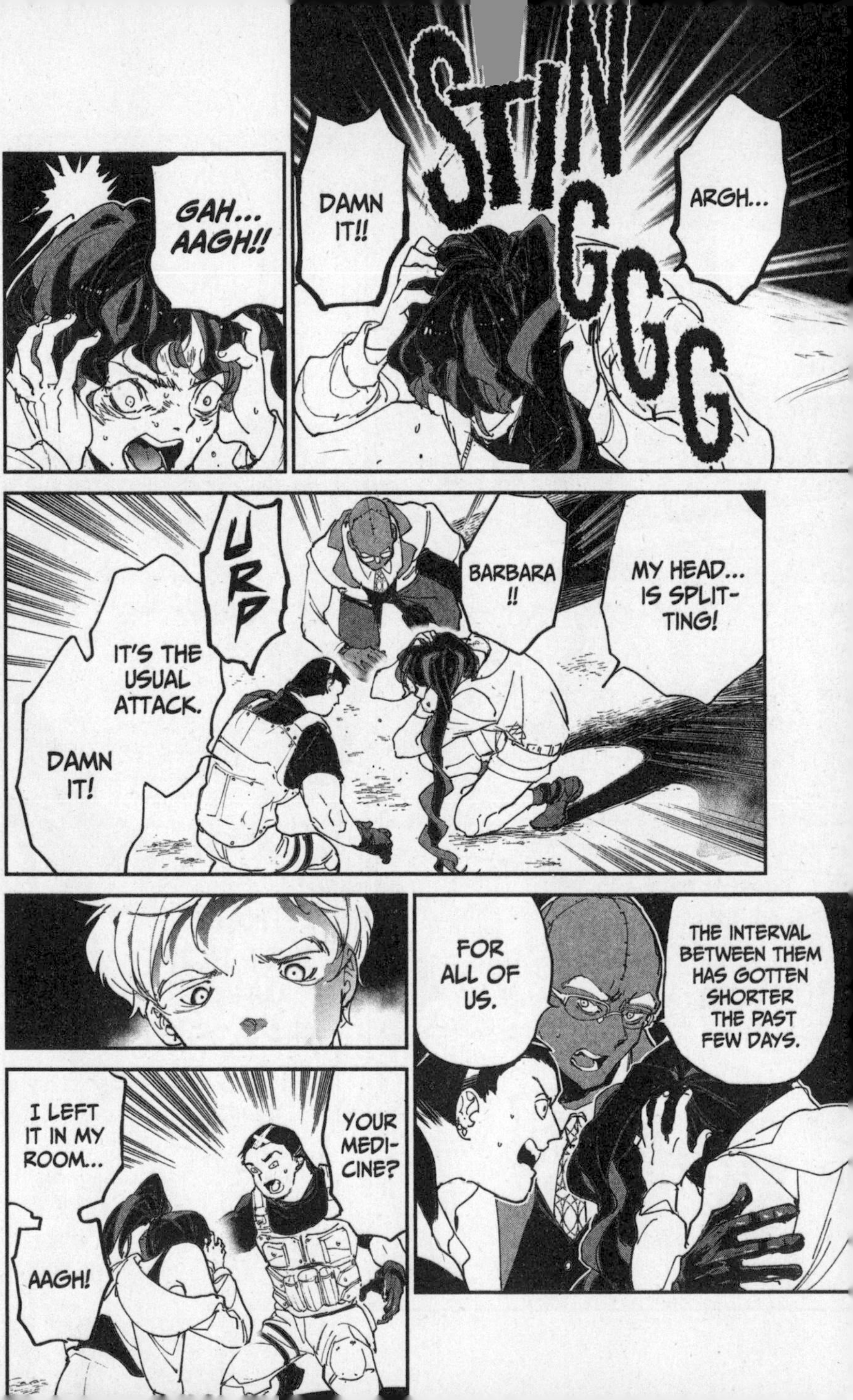
ARGH...
STINGGG
DAMN IT!!
GAH... AAGH!!
MY HEAD... IS SPLIT-TING!
BARBARA!!
URP
IT'S THE USUAL ATTACK.
DAMN IT!
THE INTERVAL BETWEEN THEM HAS GOTTEN SHORTER THE PAST FEW DAYS.
FOR ALL OF US.
YOUR MEDI-CINE?
I LEFT IT IN MY ROOM...
AAGH!

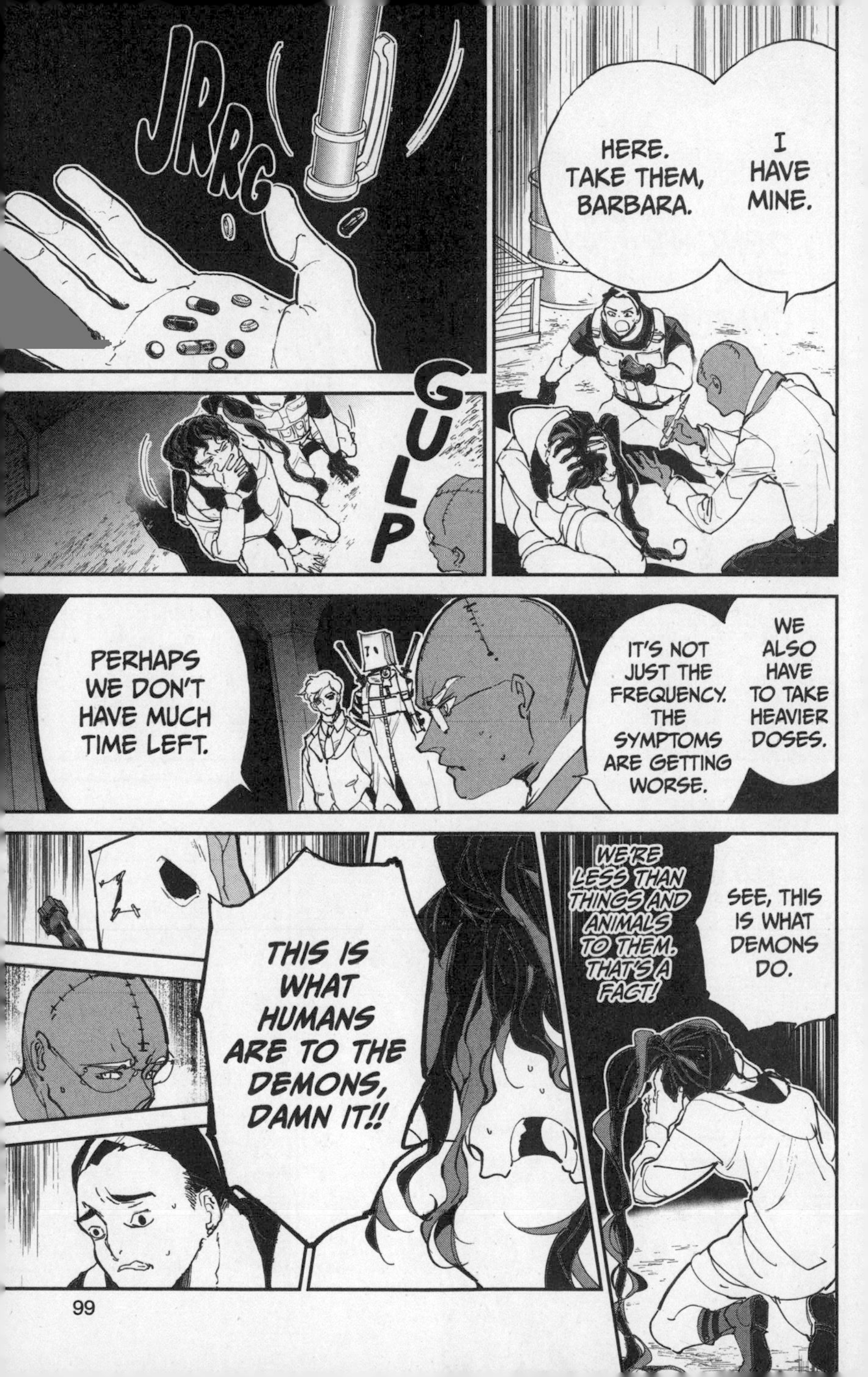
I HAVE MINE.
HERE. TAKE THEM, BARBARA.
JRRG
GULP
WE ALSO HAVE TO TAKE HEAVIER DOSES.
IT'S NOT JUST THE FREQUENCY. THE SYMPTOMS ARE GETTING WORSE.
PERHAPS WE DON'T HAVE MUCH TIME LEFT.
SEE, THIS IS WHAT DEMONS DO.
WE'RE LESS THAN THINGS AND ANIMALS TO THEM. THAT'S A FACT!
THIS IS WHAT HUMANS ARE TO THE DEMONS, DAMN IT!!

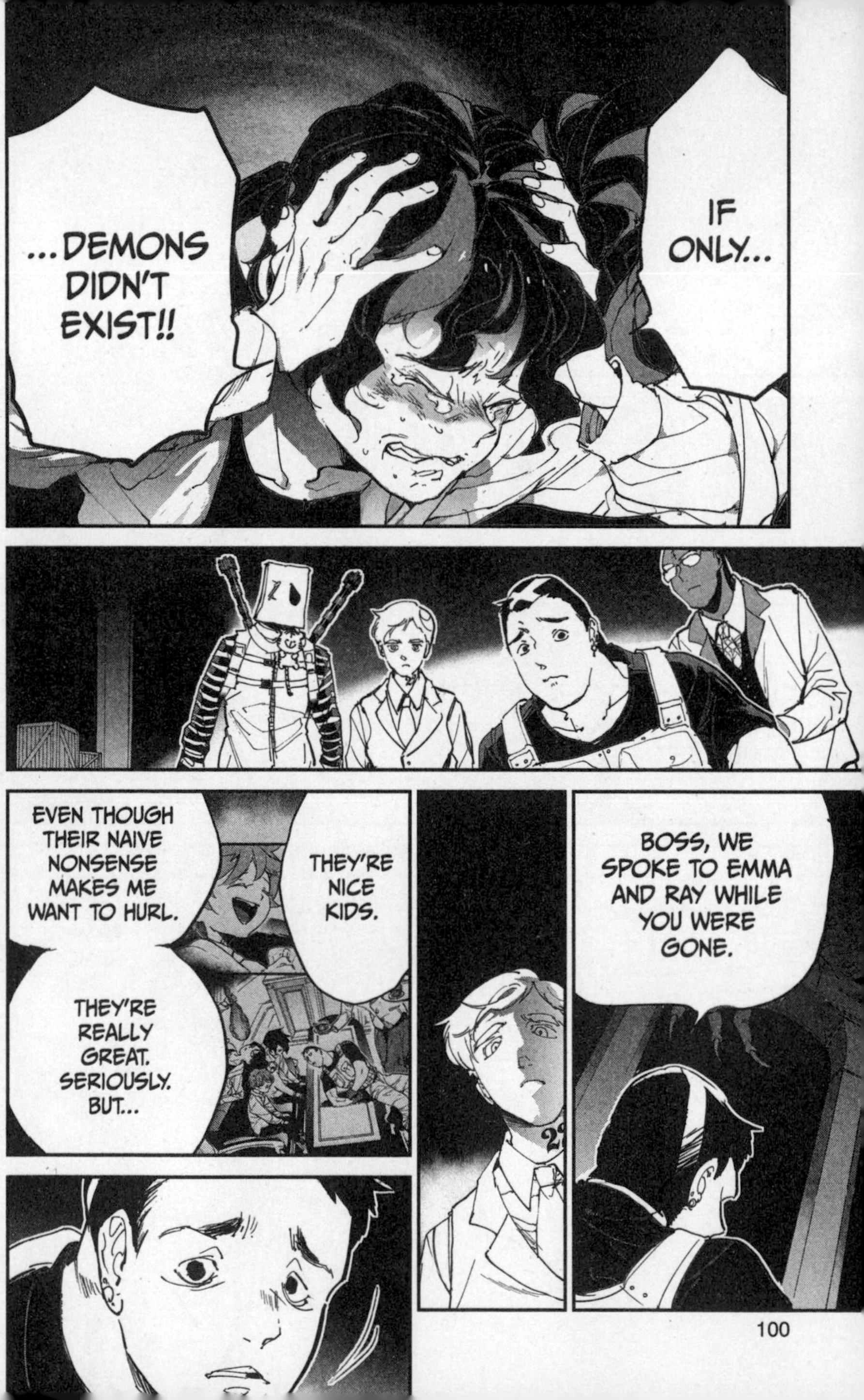
IF ONLY...
...DEMONS DIDN'T EXIST!!
BOSS, WE SPOKE TO EMMA AND RAY WHILE YOU WERE GONE.
THEY'RE NICE KIDS.
EVEN THOUGH THEIR NAIVE NONSENSE MAKES ME WANT TO HURL.
THEY'RE REALLY GREAT. SERIOUSLY. BUT...

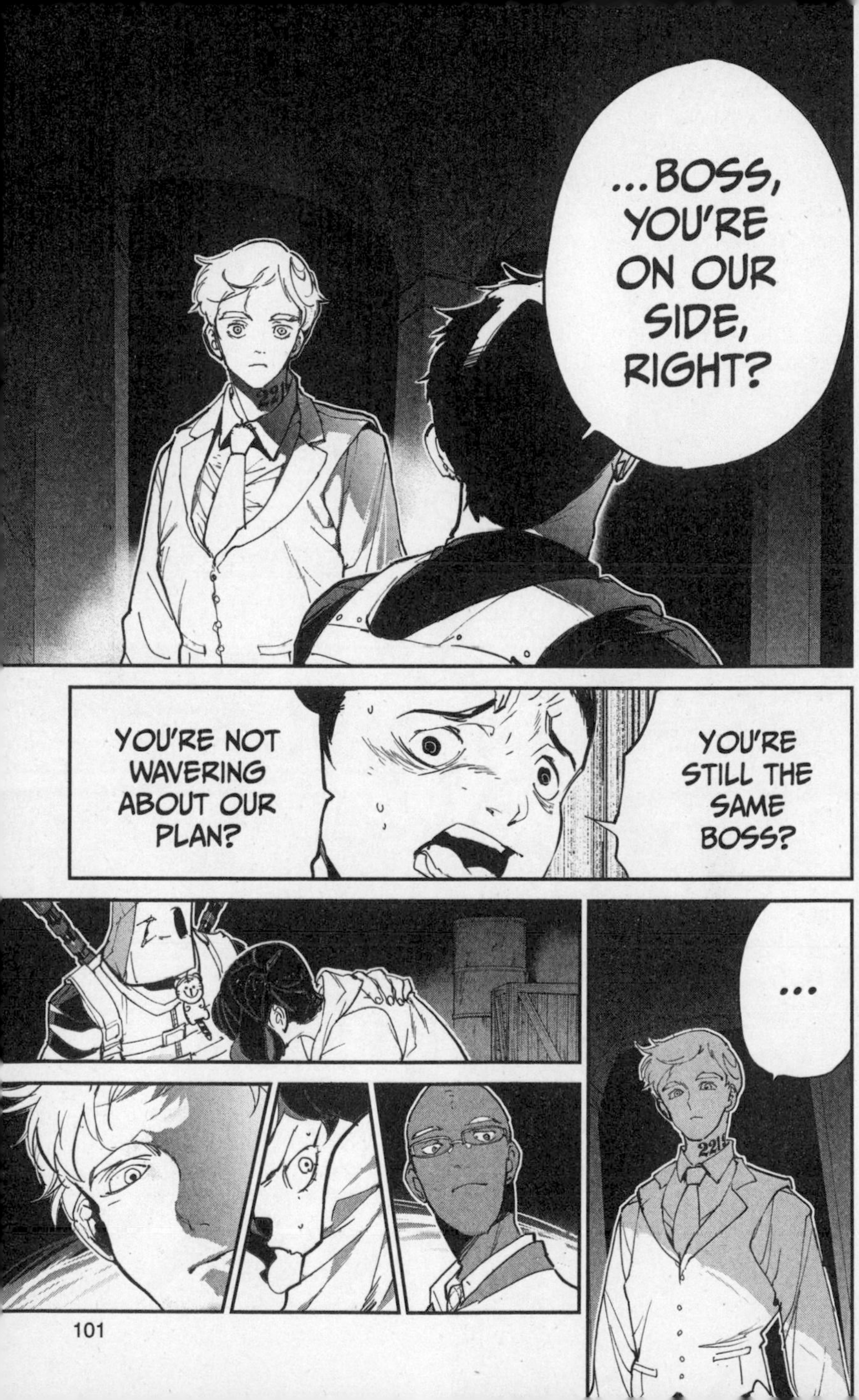
...BOSS, YOU'RE ON OUR SIDE, RIGHT?
YOU'RE STILL THE SAME BOSS?
YOU'RE NOT WAVERING ABOUT OUR PLAN?
...

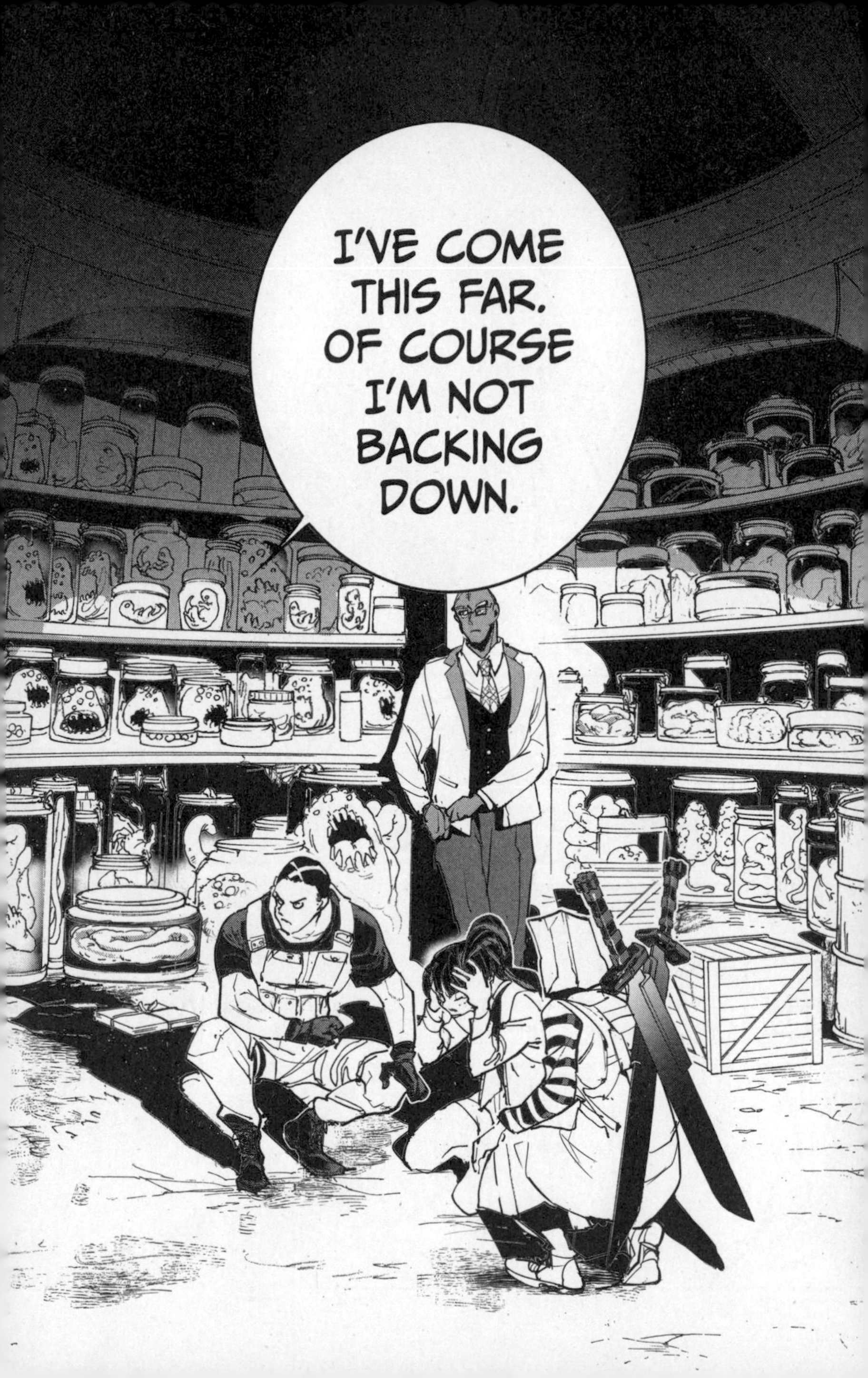
I'VE COME THIS FAR. OF COURSE I'M NOT BACKING DOWN.

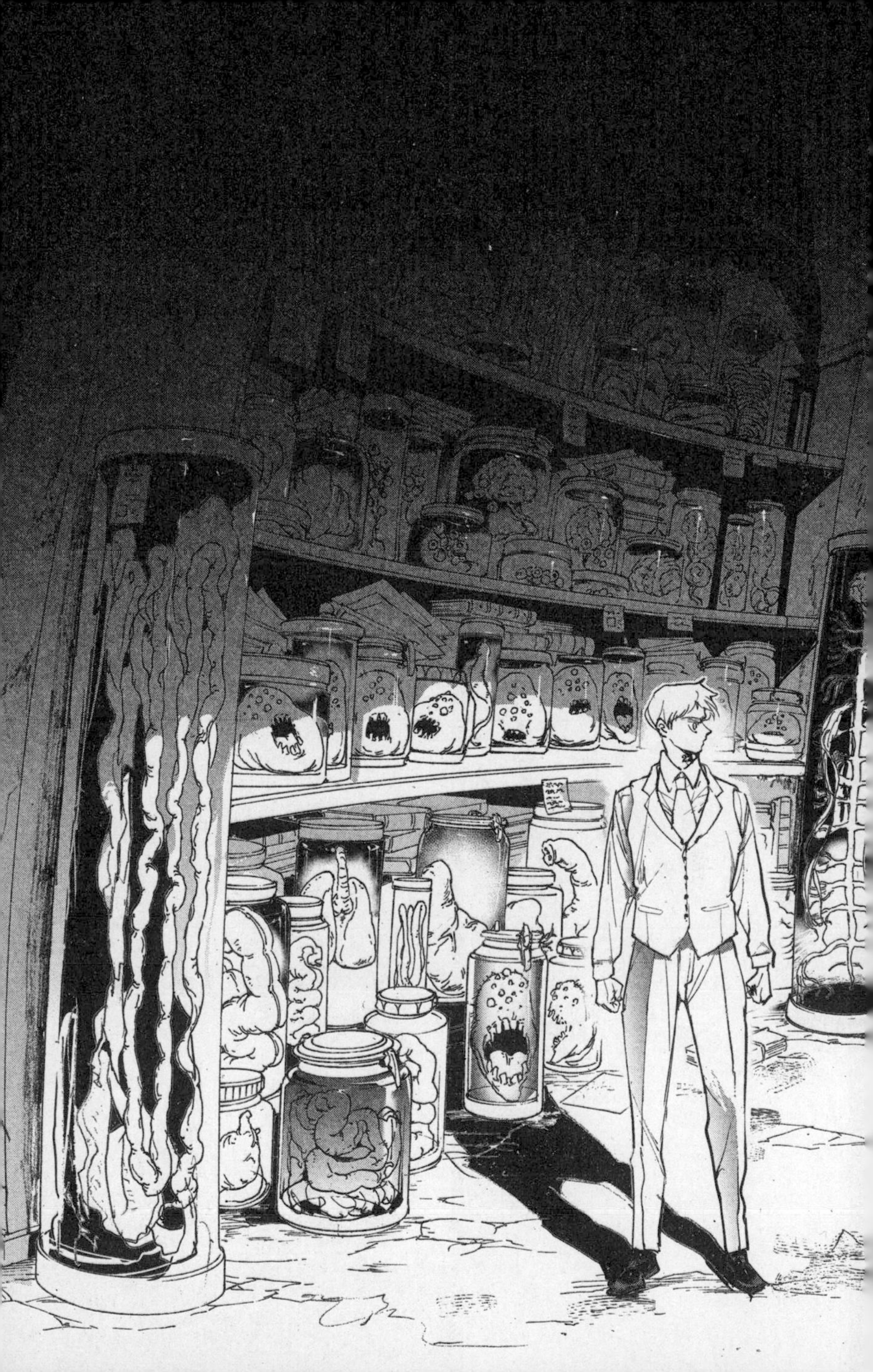

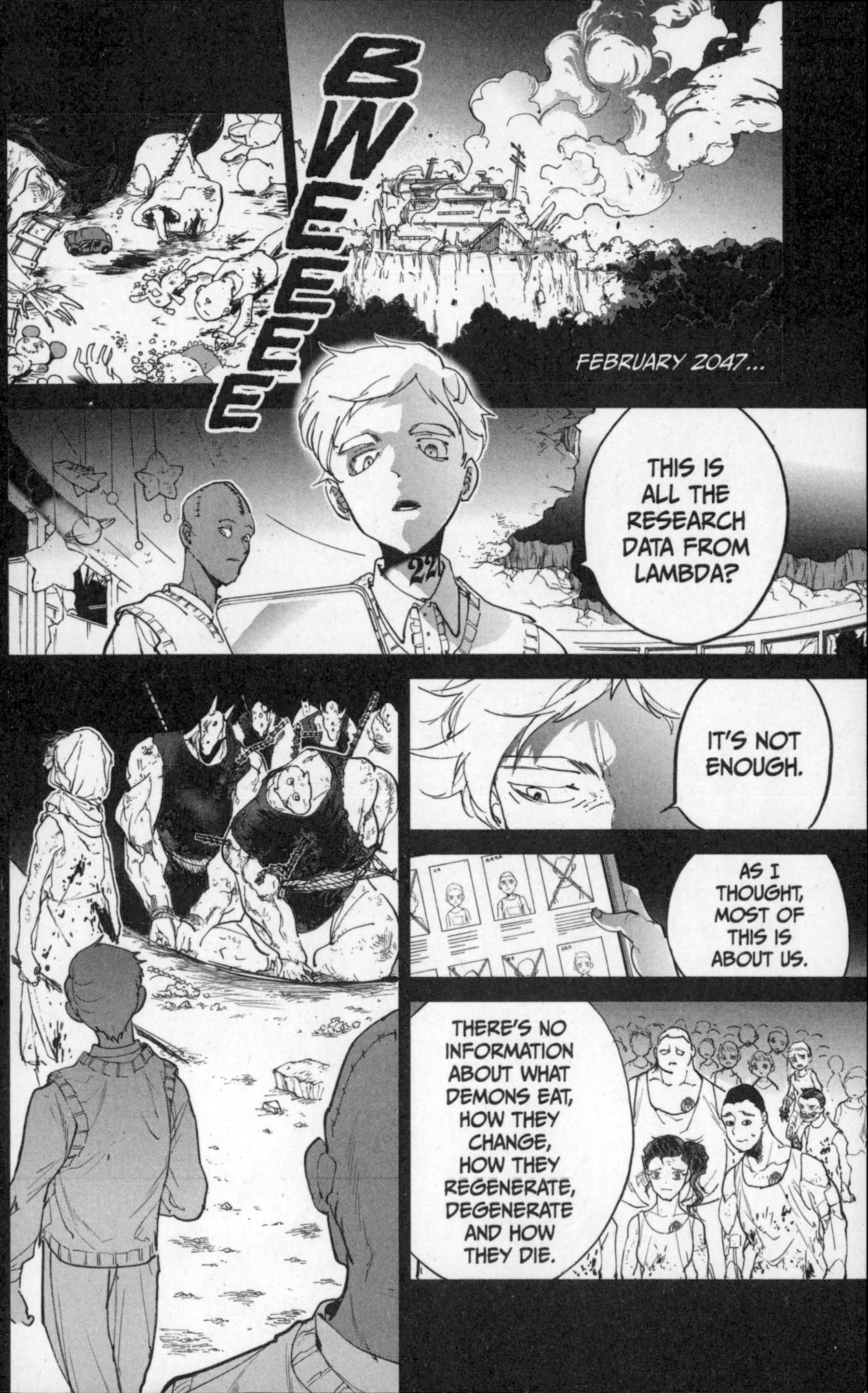
BWEEEEEE
FEBRUARY 2047...
THIS IS ALL THE RESEARCH DATA FROM LAMBDA?
IT'S NOT ENOUGH.
AS I THOUGHT, MOST OF THIS IS ABOUT US.
THERE'S NO INFORMATION ABOUT WHAT DEMONS EAT, HOW THEY CHANGE, HOW THEY REGENERATE, DEGENERATE AND HOW THEY DIE.

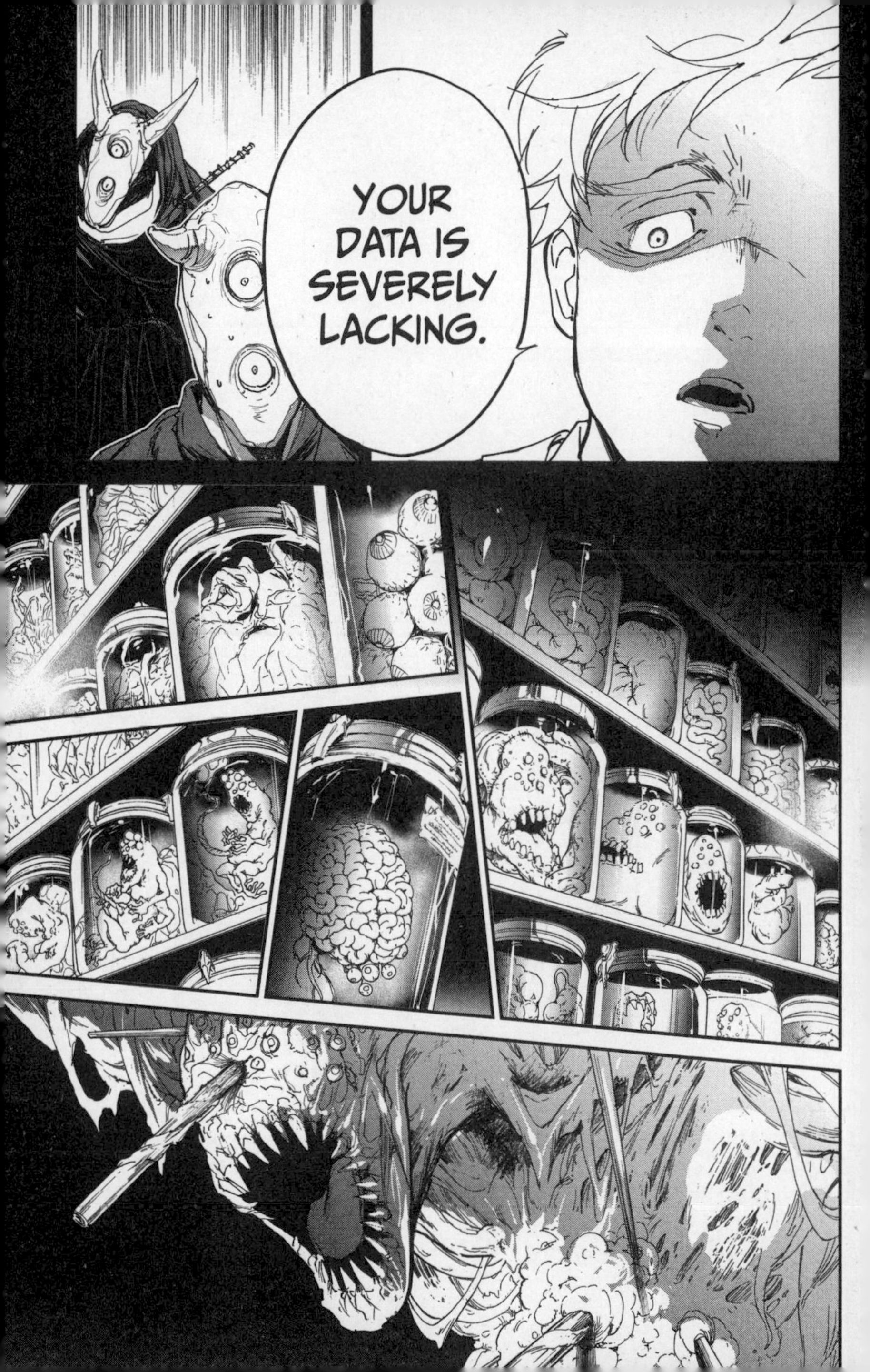
YOUR DATA IS SEVERELY LACKING.

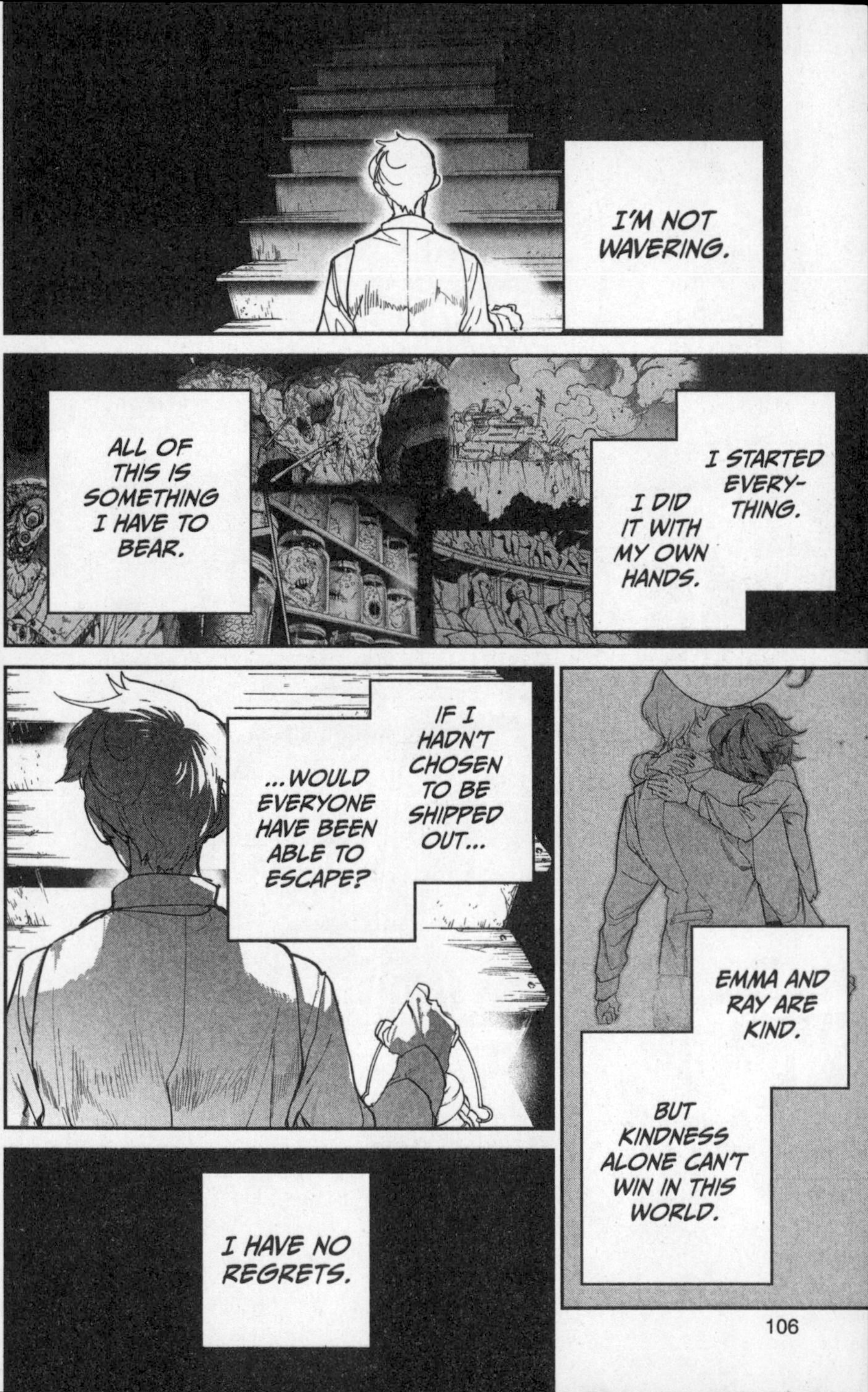
I'M NOT WAVERING.
I STARTED EVERYTHING.
I DID IT WITH MY OWN HANDS.
ALL OF THIS IS SOMETHING I HAVE TO BEAR.
EMMA AND RAY ARE KIND.
BUT KINDNESS ALONE CAN'T WIN IN THIS WORLD.
IF I HADN'T CHOSEN TO BE SHIPPED OUT...
...WOULD EVERYONE HAVE BEEN ABLE TO ESCAPE?
I HAVE NO REGRETS.

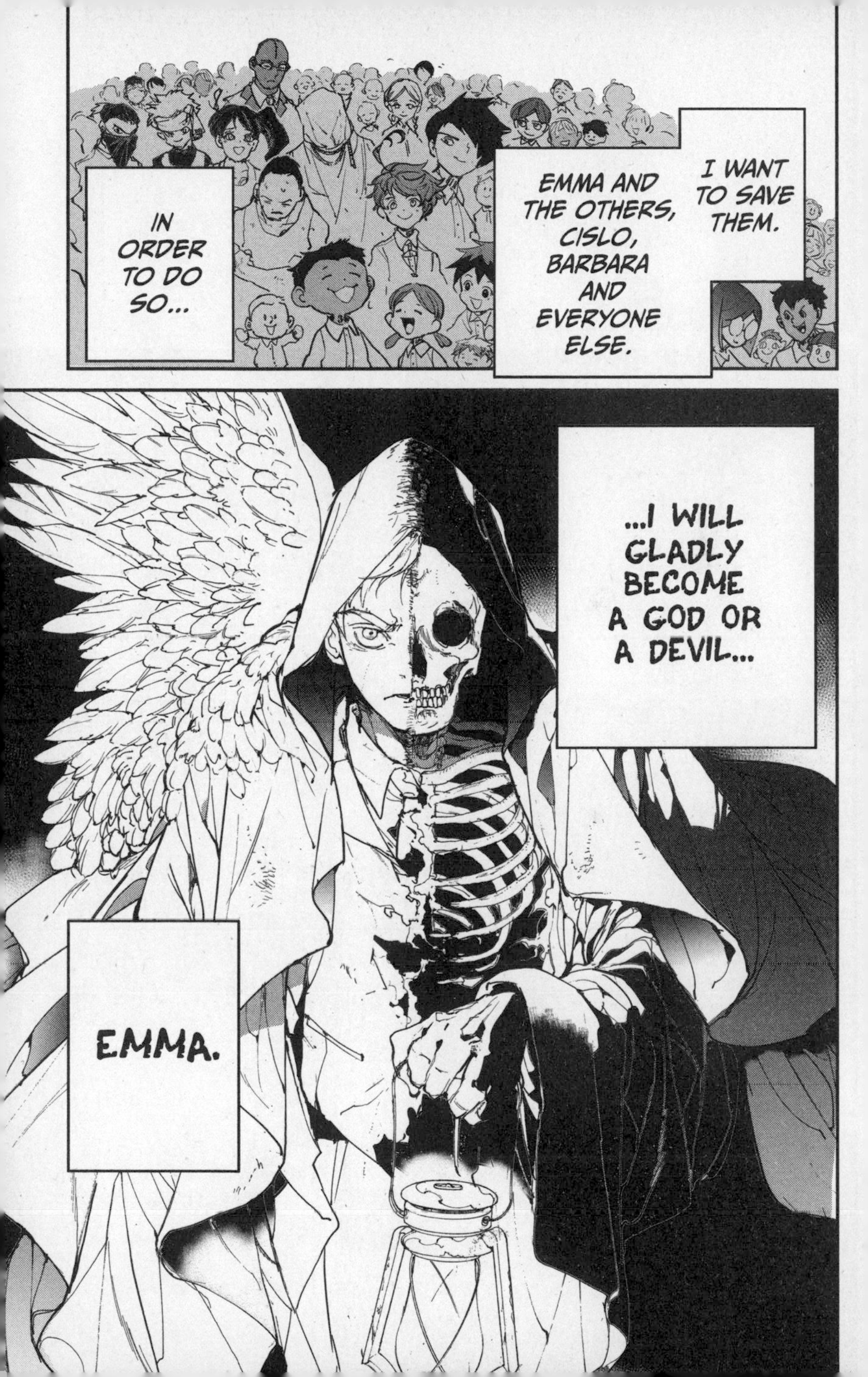
I WANT TO SAVE THEM.
EMMA AND THE OTHERS, CISLO, BARBARA AND EVERYONE ELSE.
IN ORDER TO DO SO...
...I WILL GLADLY BECOME A GOD OR A DEVIL...
EMMA.

A SPECIAL EXTRA PART 2

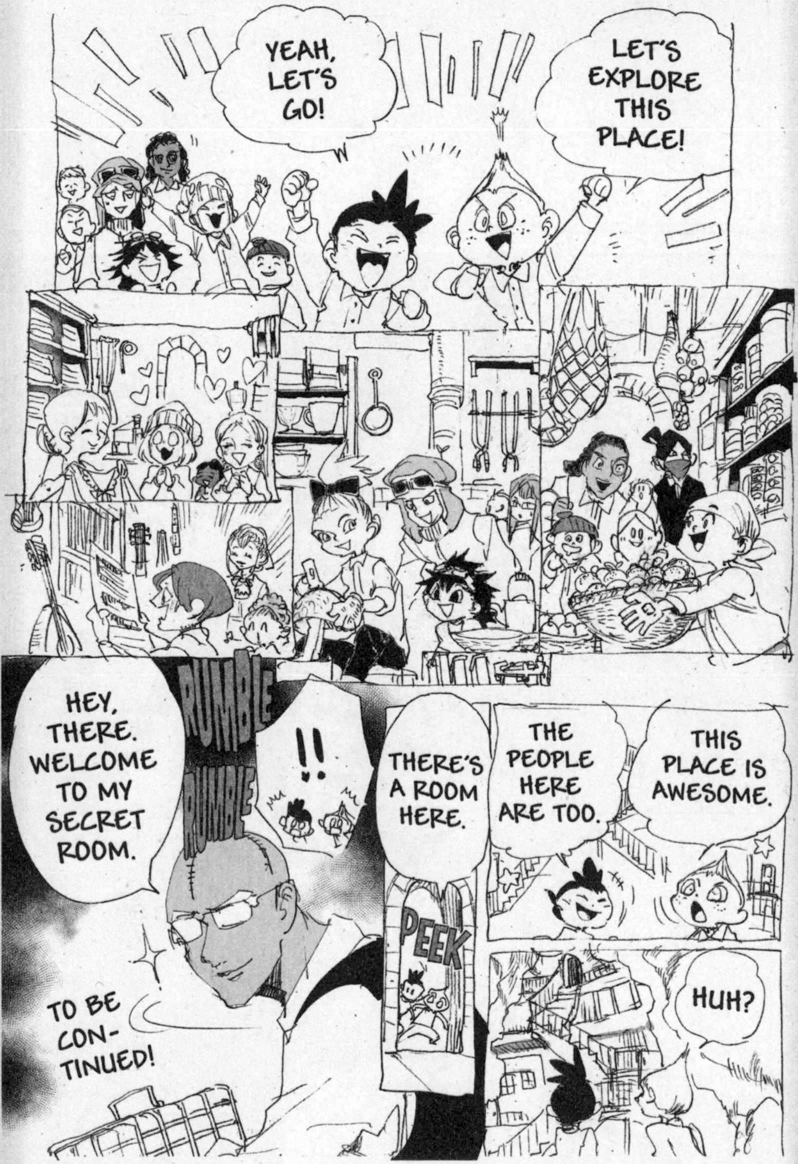
LET'S EXPLORE THIS PLACE!
YEAH, LET'S GO!
THIS PLACE IS AWESOME.
THE PEOPLE HERE ARE TOO.
HUH?
THERE'S A ROOM HERE.
PEEK
!!
RUMBLE
RUMBLE
HEY, THERE. WELCOME TO MY SECRET ROOM.
TO BE CON-TINUED!

CHAPTER 130: SOMETHING TO REPORT

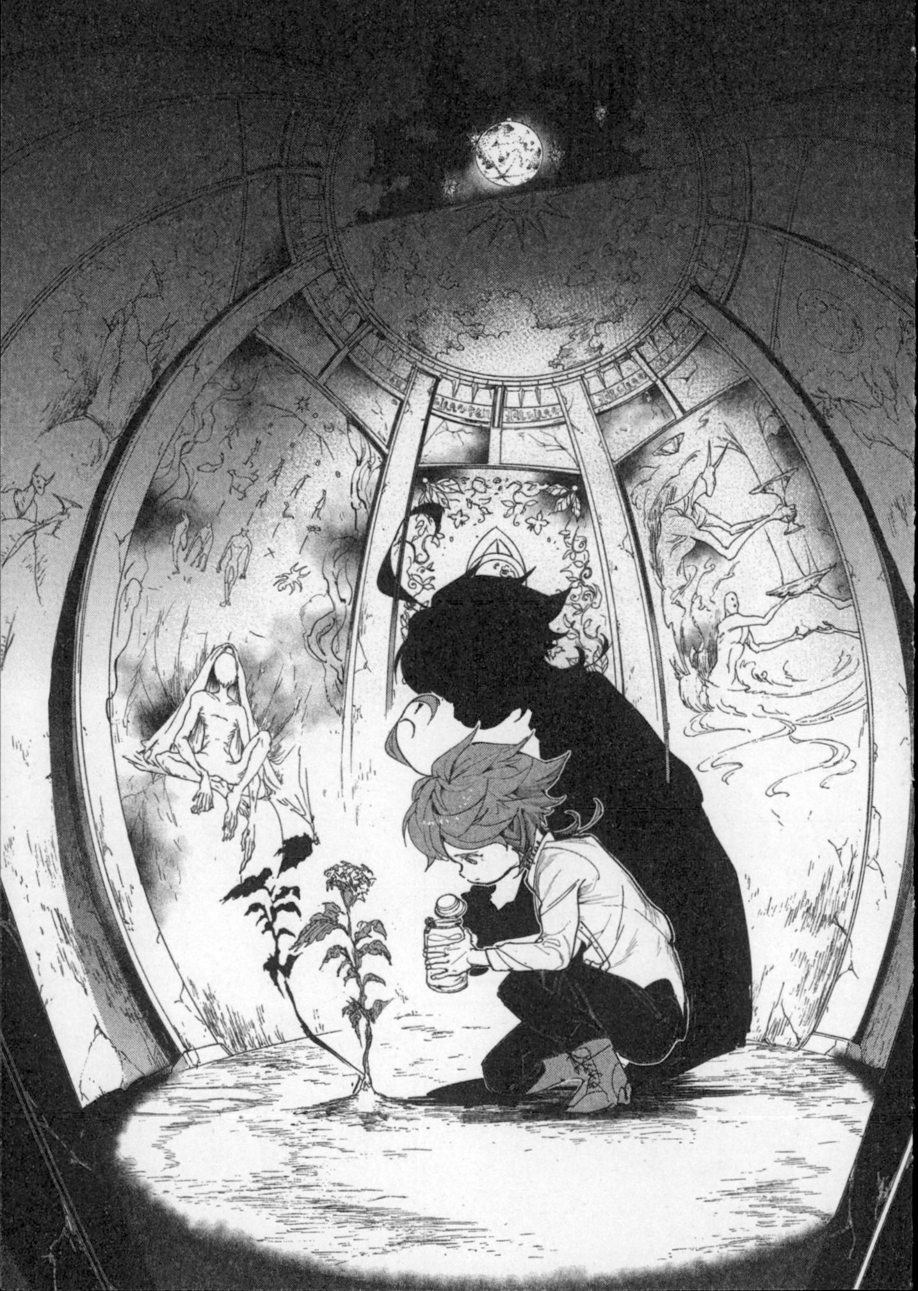

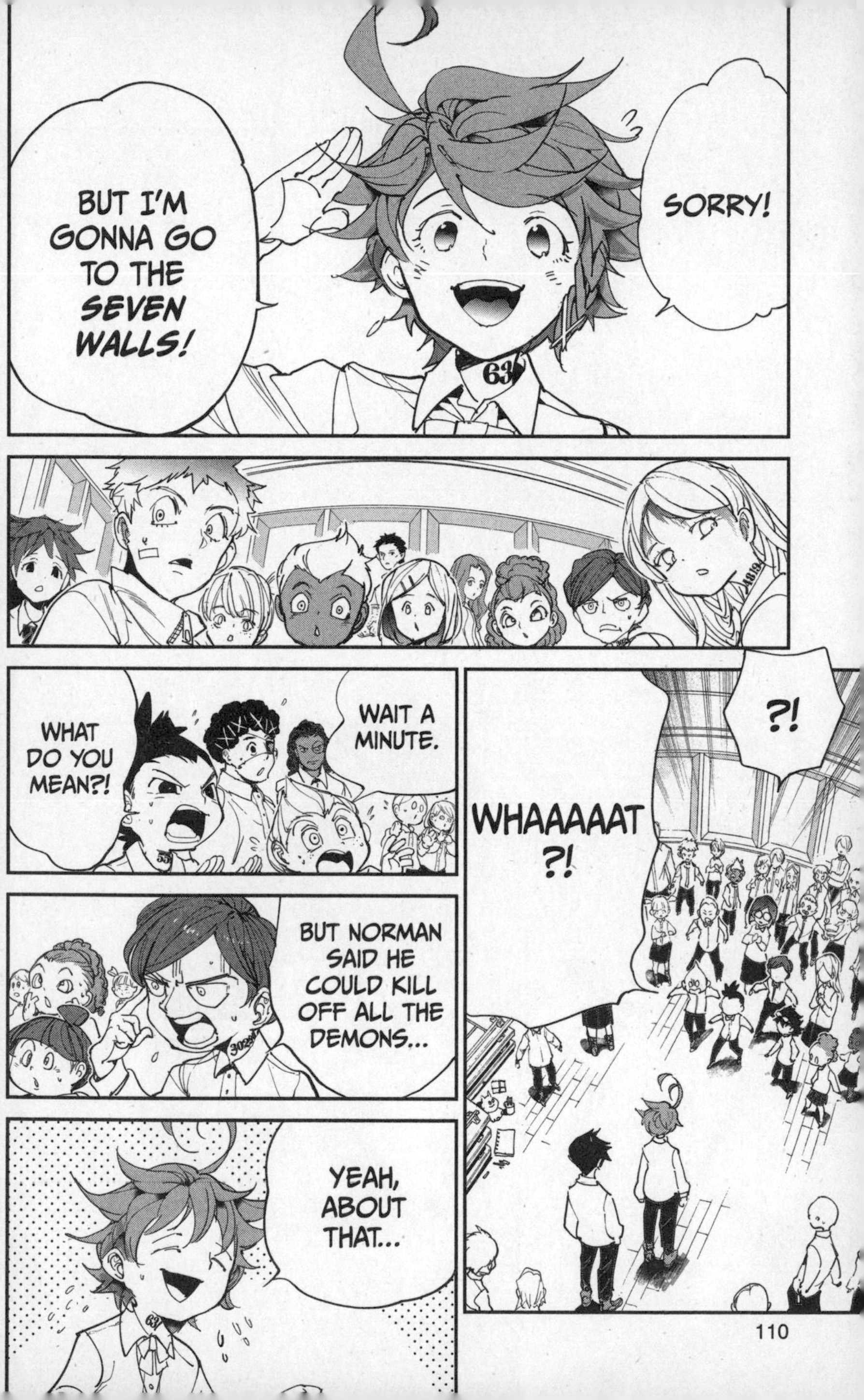
SORRY!
BUT I'M GONNA GO TO THE SEVEN WALLS!
?!
WHAAAAAT ?!
WAIT A MINUTE.
WHAT DO YOU MEAN?!
BUT NORMAN SAID HE COULD KILL OFF ALL THE DEMONS...
YEAH, ABOUT THAT...

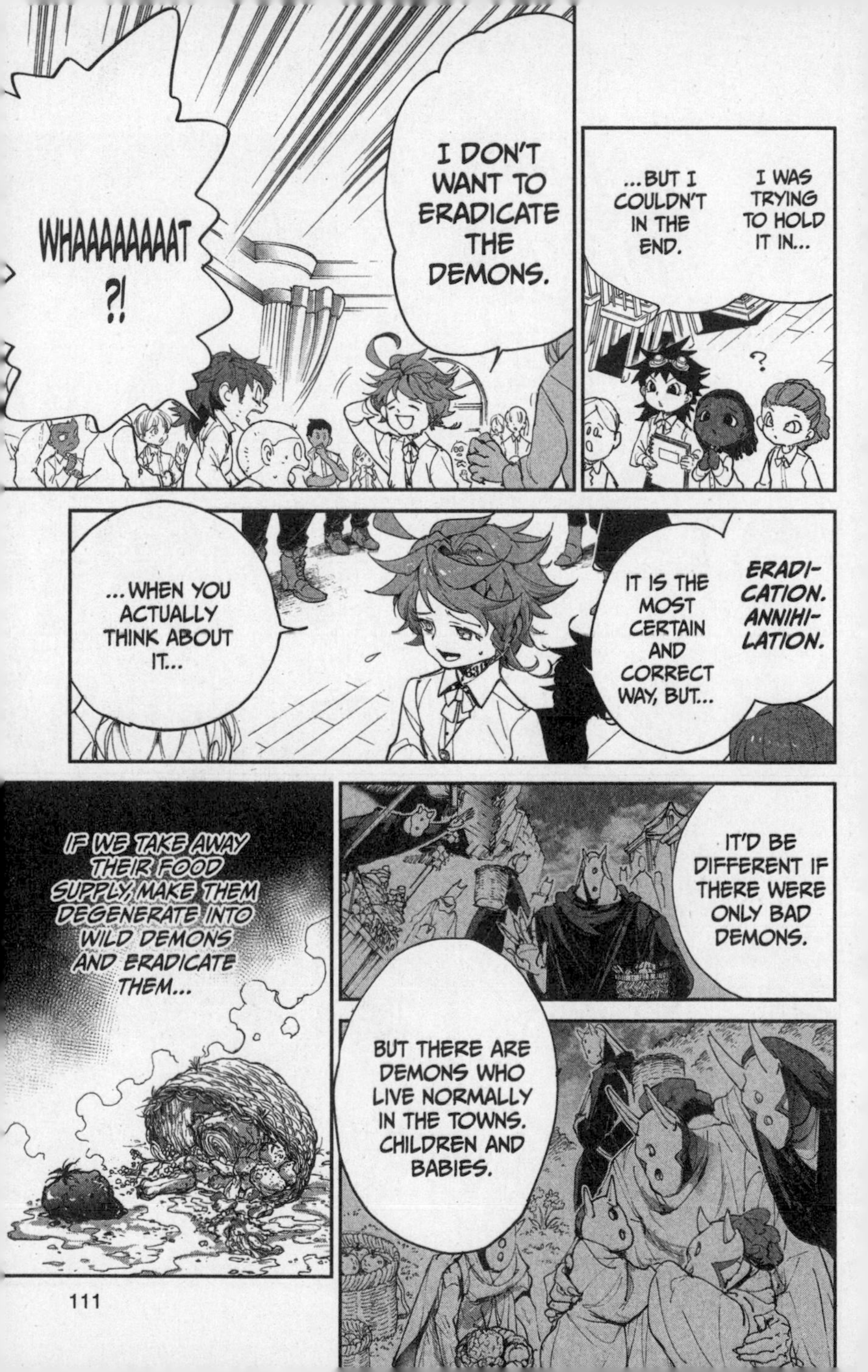
I WAS TRYING TO HOLD IT IN...
...BUT I COULDN'T IN THE END.
?
I DON'T WANT TO ERADICATE THE DEMONS.
WHAAAAAAAAT ?!
ERADICATION. ANNIHILATION.
IT IS THE MOST CERTAIN AND CORRECT WAY, BUT...
...WHEN YOU ACTUALLY THINK ABOUT IT...
IT'D BE DIFFERENT IF THERE WERE ONLY BAD DEMONS.
BUT THERE ARE DEMONS WHO LIVE NORMALLY IN THE TOWNS. CHILDREN AND BABIES.
IF WE TAKE AWAY THEIR FOOD SUPPLY, MAKE THEM DEGENERATE INTO WILD DEMONS AND ERADICATE THEM...

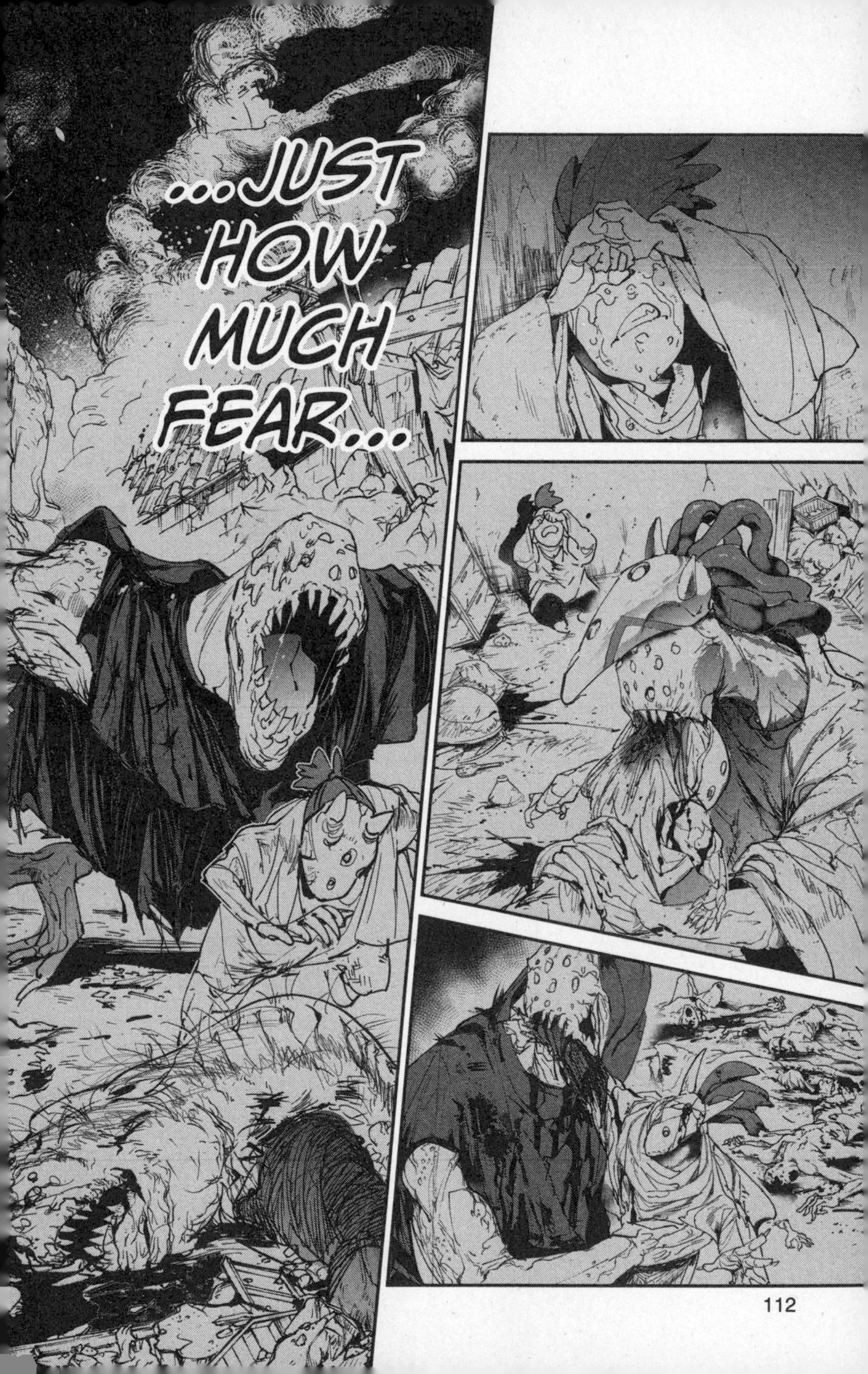
...JUST HOW MUCH FEAR...

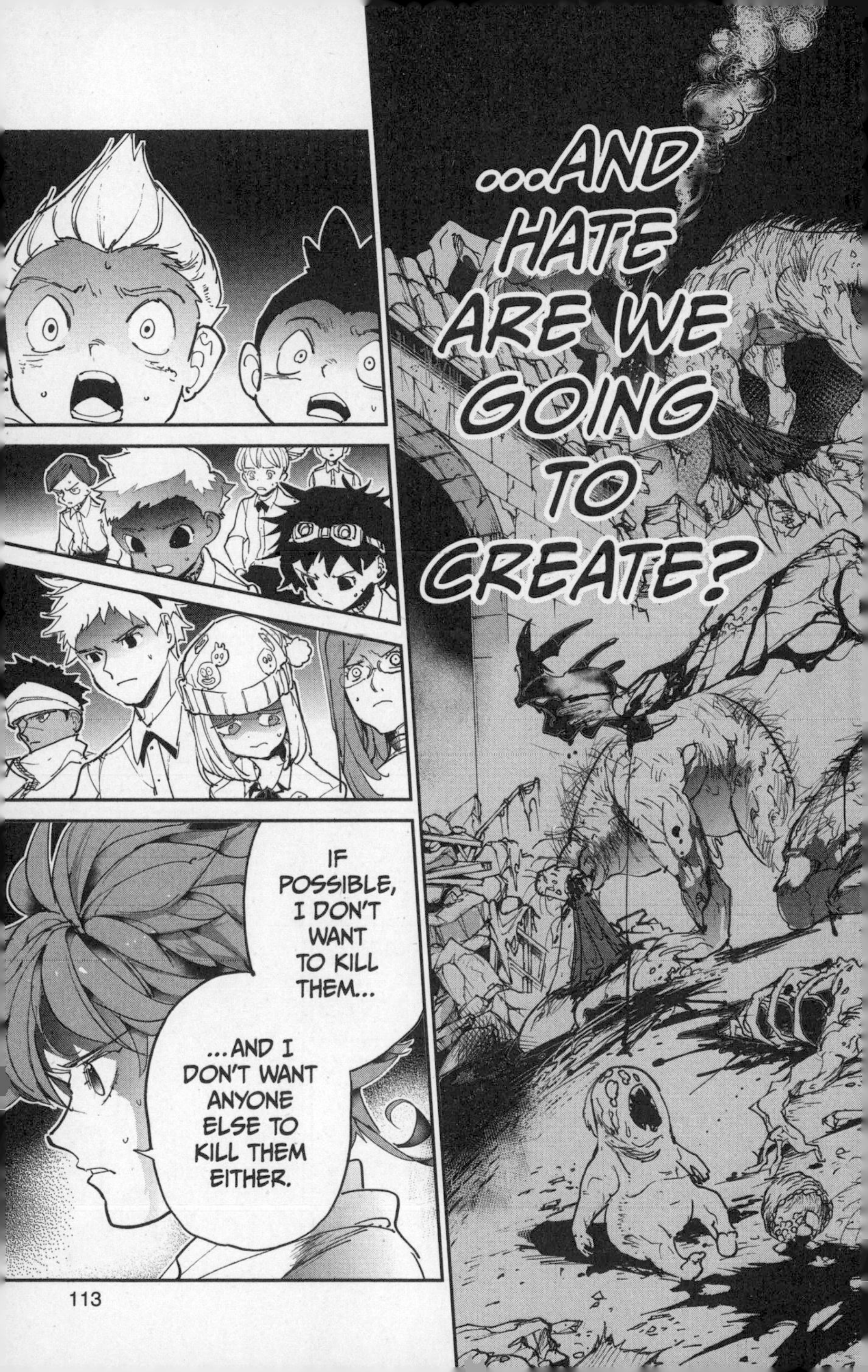
...AND HATE ARE WE GOING TO CREATE?
IF POSSIBLE, I DON'T WANT TO KILL THEM...
...AND I DON'T WANT ANYONE ELSE TO KILL THEM EITHER.

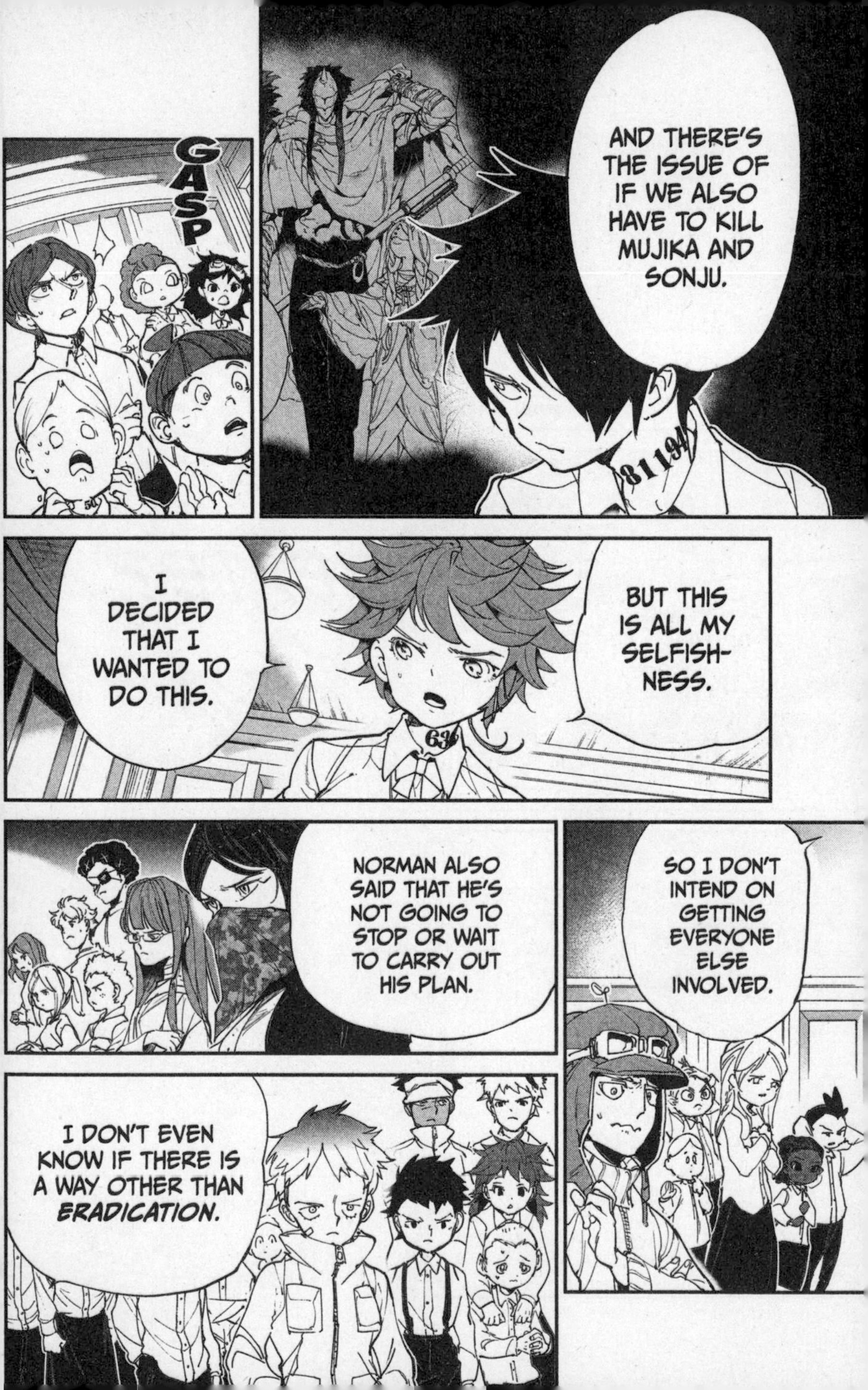
AND THERE'S THE ISSUE OF IF WE ALSO HAVE TO KILL MUJIKA AND SONJU.
81194
GASP
BUT THIS IS ALL MY SELFISH-NESS.
I DECIDED THAT I WANTED TO DO THIS.
63
SO I DON'T INTEND ON GETTING EVERYONE ELSE INVOLVED.
NORMAN ALSO SAID THAT HE'S NOT GOING TO STOP OR WAIT TO CARRY OUT HIS PLAN.
I DON'T EVEN KNOW IF THERE IS A WAY OTHER THAN *ERADICATION*.

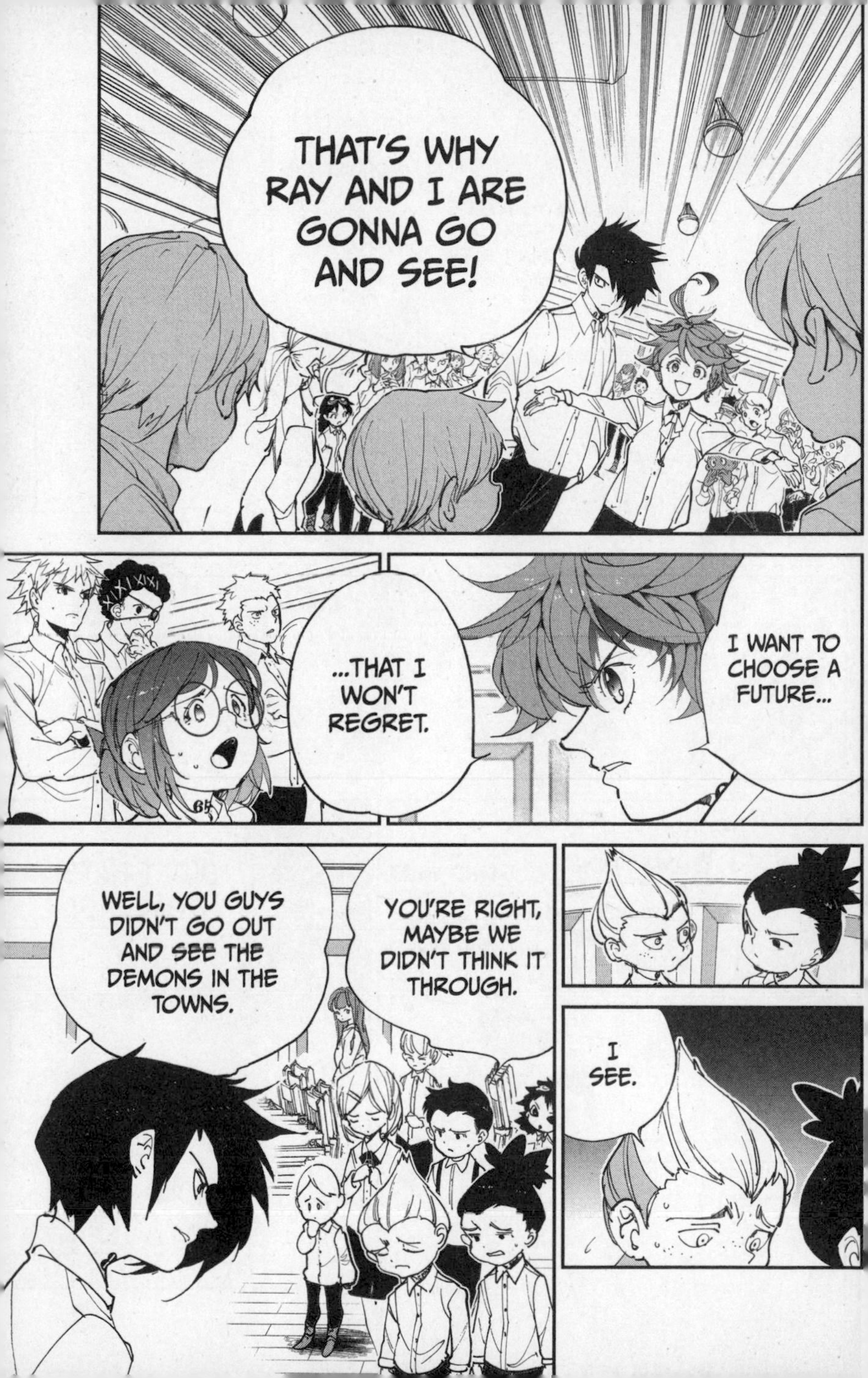
THAT'S WHY RAY AND I ARE GONNA GO AND SEE!
I WANT TO CHOOSE A FUTURE...
...THAT I WON'T REGRET.
I SEE.
YOU'RE RIGHT, MAYBE WE DIDN'T THINK IT THROUGH.
WELL, YOU GUYS DIDN'T GO OUT AND SEE THE DEMONS IN THE TOWNS.

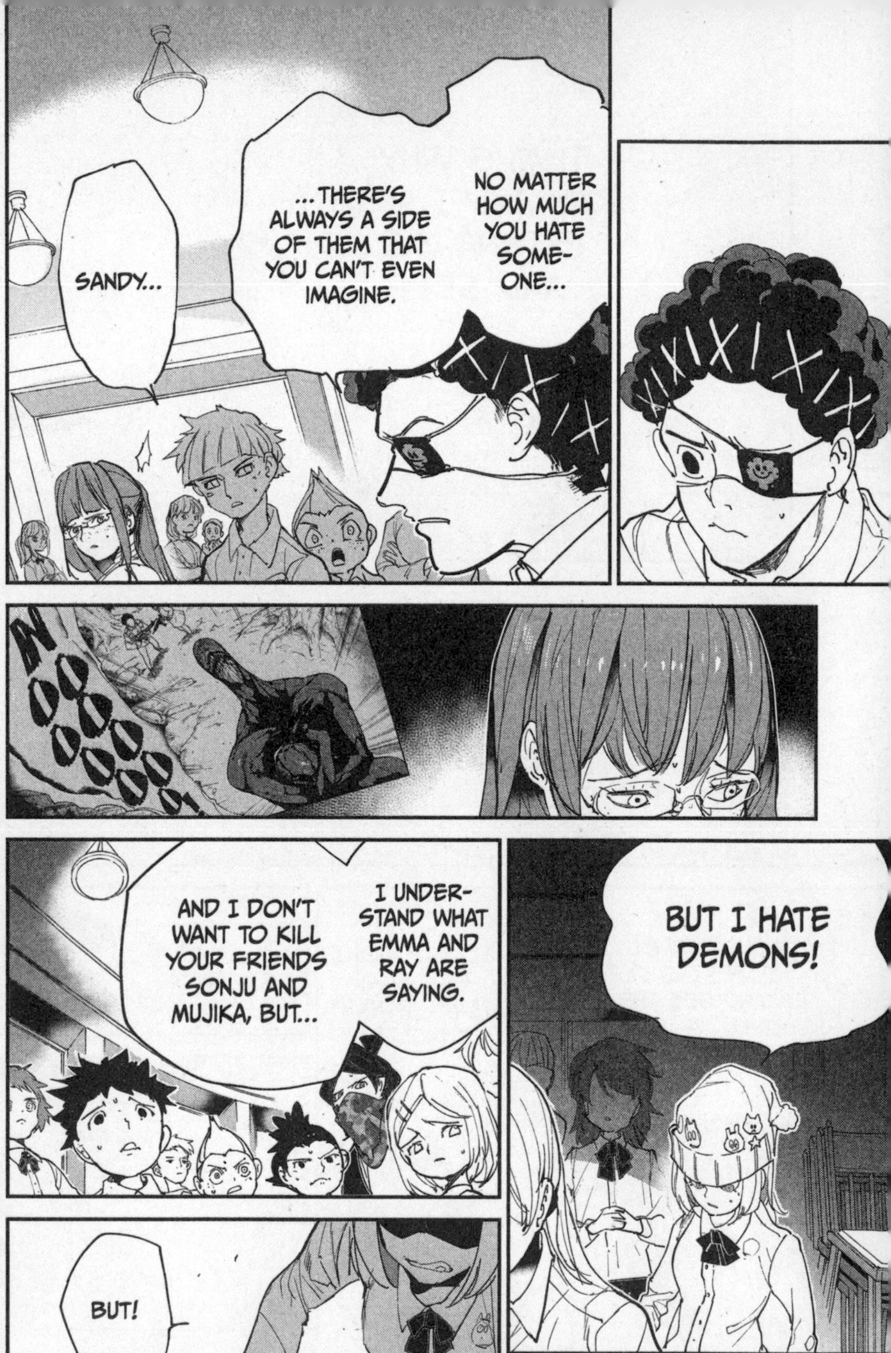

NO MATTER HOW MUCH YOU HATE SOME-ONE...
...THERE'S ALWAYS A SIDE OF THEM THAT YOU CAN'T EVEN IMAGINE.
SANDY...
BUT I HATE DEMONS!
I UNDER-STAND WHAT EMMA AND RAY ARE SAYING.
AND I DON'T WANT TO KILL YOUR FRIENDS SONJU AND MUJIKA, BUT...
BUT!

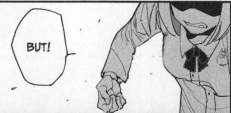

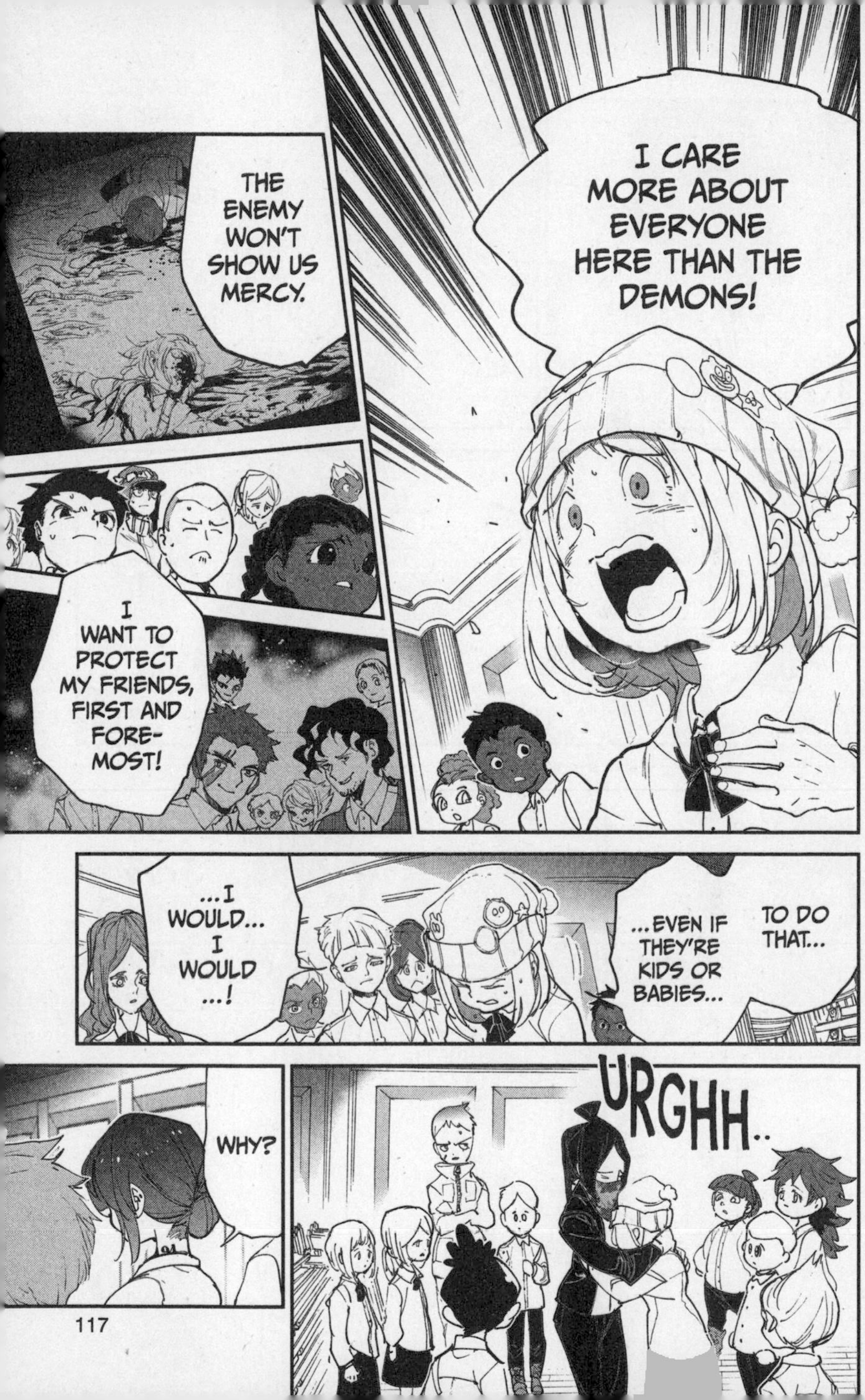
I CARE MORE ABOUT EVERYONE HERE THAN THE DEMONS!
THE ENEMY WON'T SHOW US MERCY.
I WANT TO PROTECT MY FRIENDS, FIRST AND FORE-MOST!
TO DO THAT...
...EVEN IF THEY'RE KIDS OR BABIES...
...I WOULD... I WOULD ...!
URGHH..
WHY?

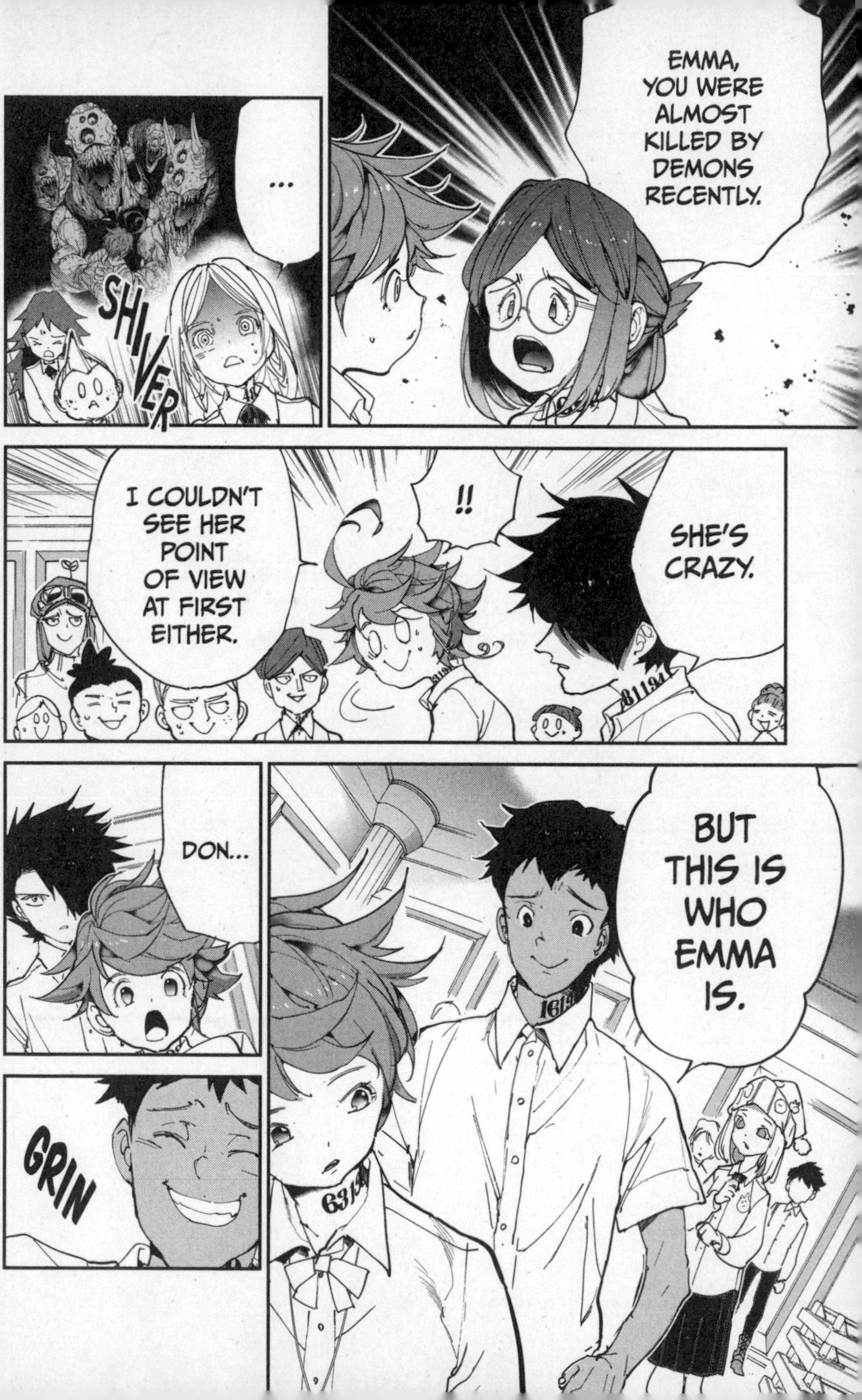
EMMA, YOU WERE ALMOST KILLED BY DEMONS RECENTLY.
...
SHIVER
SHE'S CRAZY.
!!
I COULDN'T SEE HER POINT OF VIEW AT FIRST EITHER.
BUT THIS IS WHO EMMA IS.
DON...
GRIN

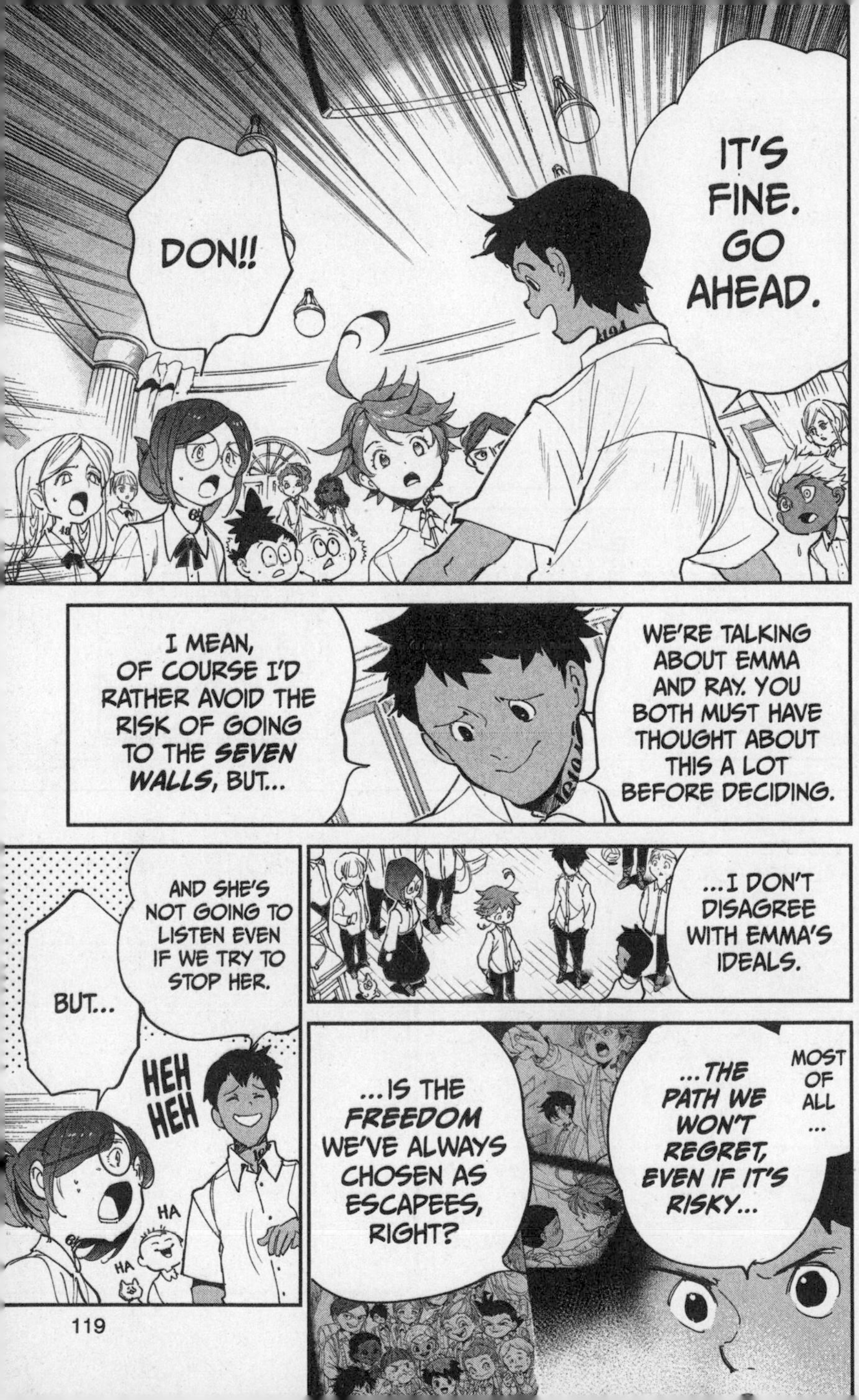
IT'S FINE. GO AHEAD.
DON!!
WE'RE TALKING ABOUT EMMA AND RAY. YOU BOTH MUST HAVE THOUGHT ABOUT THIS A LOT BEFORE DECIDING.
I MEAN, OF COURSE I'D RATHER AVOID THE RISK OF GOING TO THE *SEVEN WALLS*, BUT...
...I DON'T DISAGREE WITH EMMA'S IDEALS.
MOST OF ALL...
...THE PATH WE WON'T REGRET, EVEN IF IT'S RISKY...
...IS THE *FREEDOM* WE'VE ALWAYS CHOSEN AS ESCAPEES, RIGHT?
AND SHE'S NOT GOING TO LISTEN EVEN IF WE TRY TO STOP HER.
BUT...
HEH HEH
HA
HA

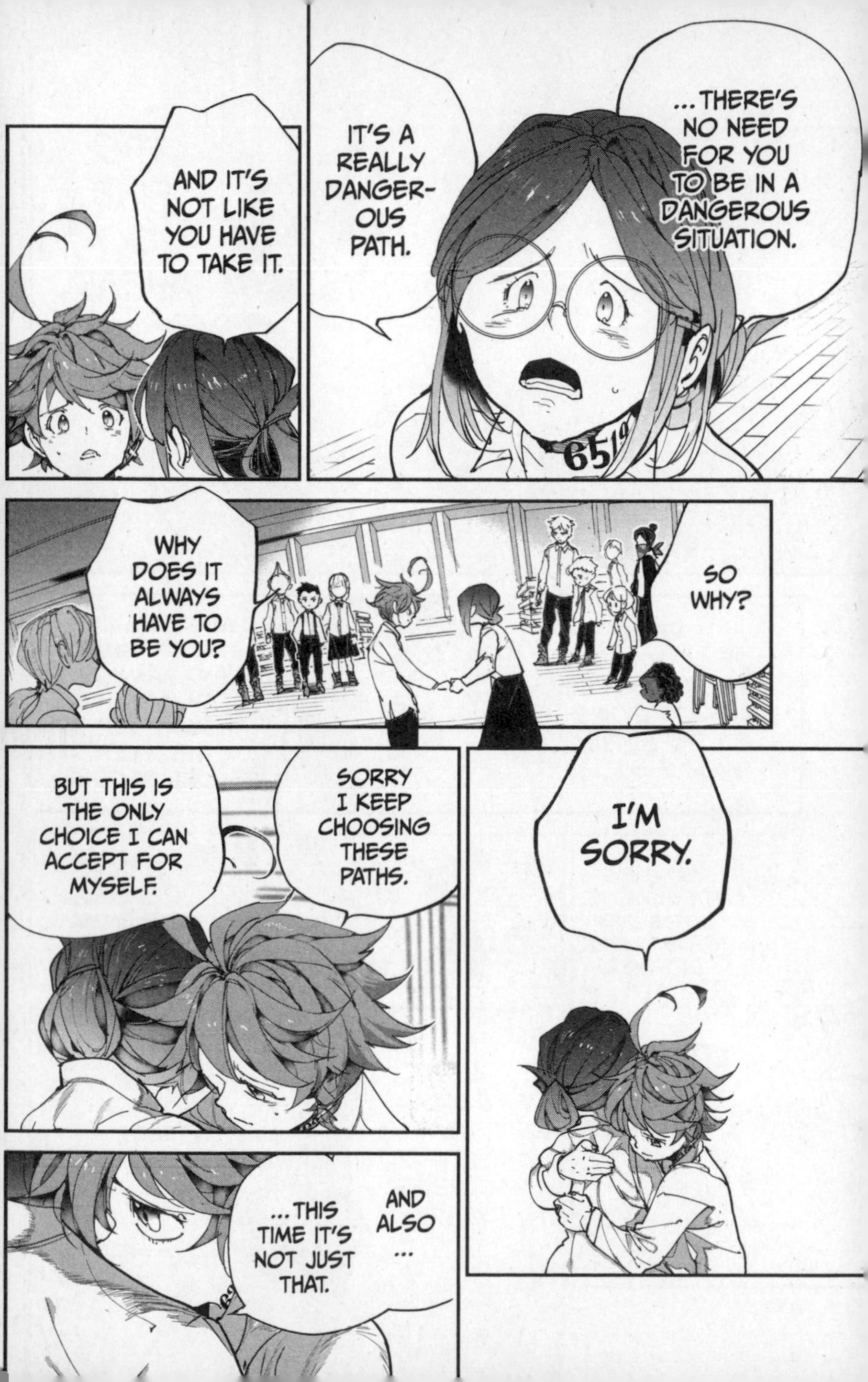
...THERE'S NO NEED FOR YOU TO BE IN A DANGEROUS SITUATION.
IT'S A REALLY DANGER-OUS PATH.
AND IT'S NOT LIKE YOU HAVE TO TAKE IT.
SO WHY?
WHY DOES IT ALWAYS HAVE TO BE YOU?
I'M SORRY.
SORRY I KEEP CHOOSING THESE PATHS.
BUT THIS IS THE ONLY CHOICE I CAN ACCEPT FOR MYSELF.
AND ALSO...
...THIS TIME IT'S NOT JUST THAT.

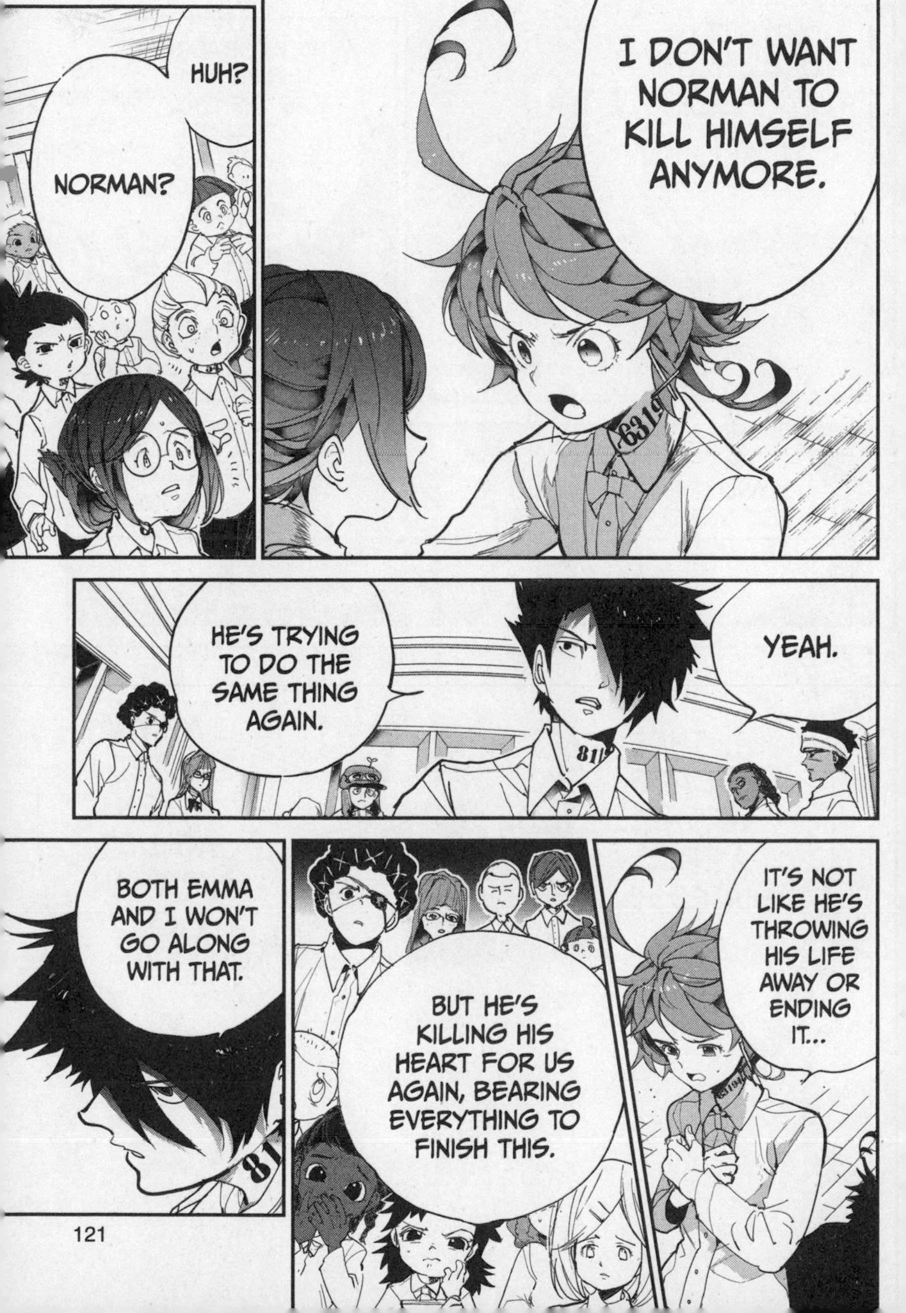
I DON'T WANT NORMAN TO KILL HIMSELF ANYMORE.
HUH?
NORMAN?
YEAH.
HE'S TRYING TO DO THE SAME THING AGAIN.
IT'S NOT LIKE HE'S THROWING HIS LIFE AWAY OR ENDING IT...
BUT HE'S KILLING HIS HEART FOR US AGAIN, BEARING EVERYTHING TO FINISH THIS.
BOTH EMMA AND I WON'T GO ALONG WITH THAT.

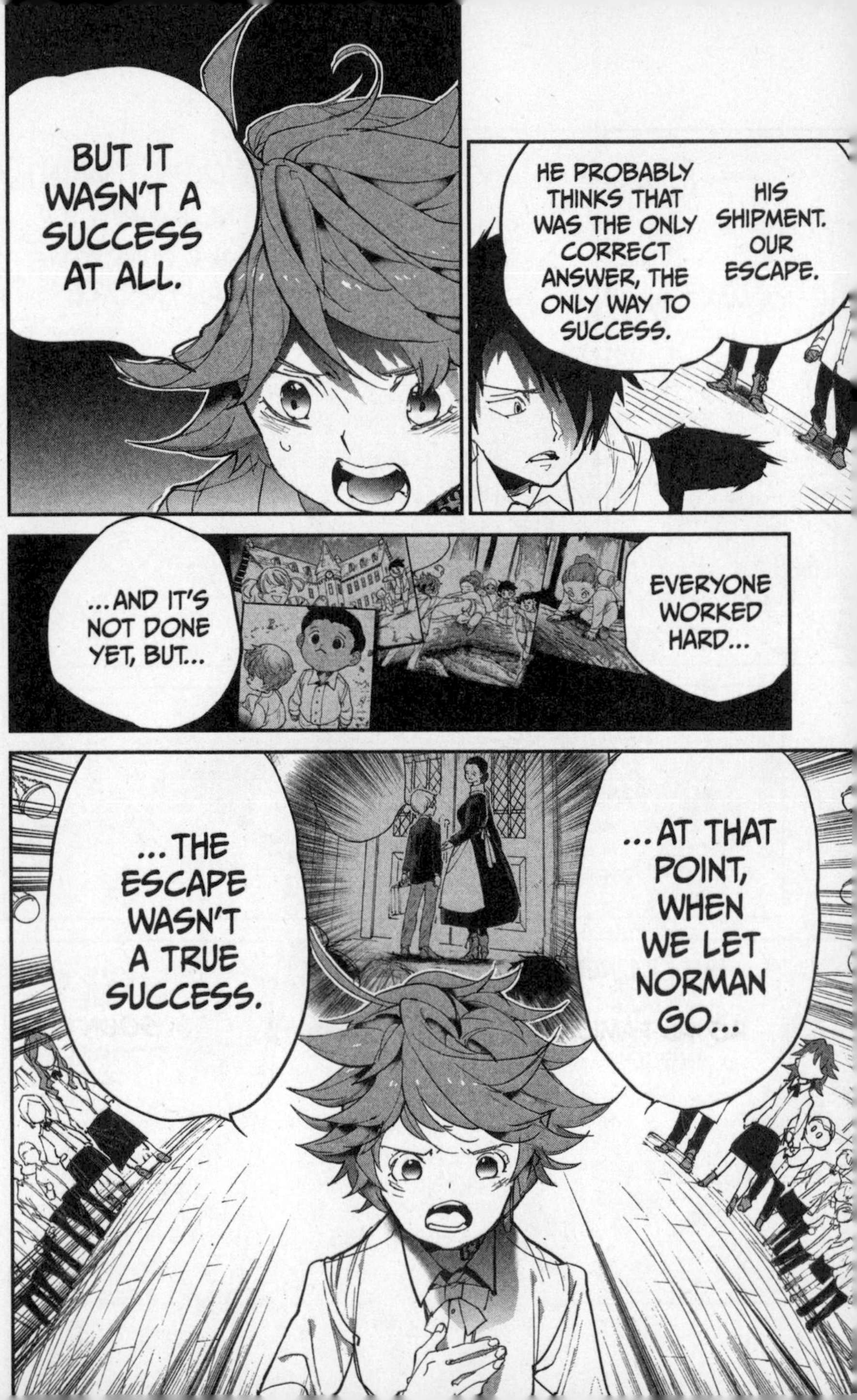
HE PROBABLY THINKS THAT WAS THE ONLY CORRECT ANSWER, THE ONLY WAY TO SUCCESS.
HIS SHIPMENT. OUR ESCAPE.
BUT IT WASN'T A SUCCESS AT ALL.
EVERYONE WORKED HARD...
...AND IT'S NOT DONE YET, BUT...
...AT THAT POINT, WHEN WE LET NORMAN GO...
...THE ESCAPE WASN'T A TRUE SUCCESS.

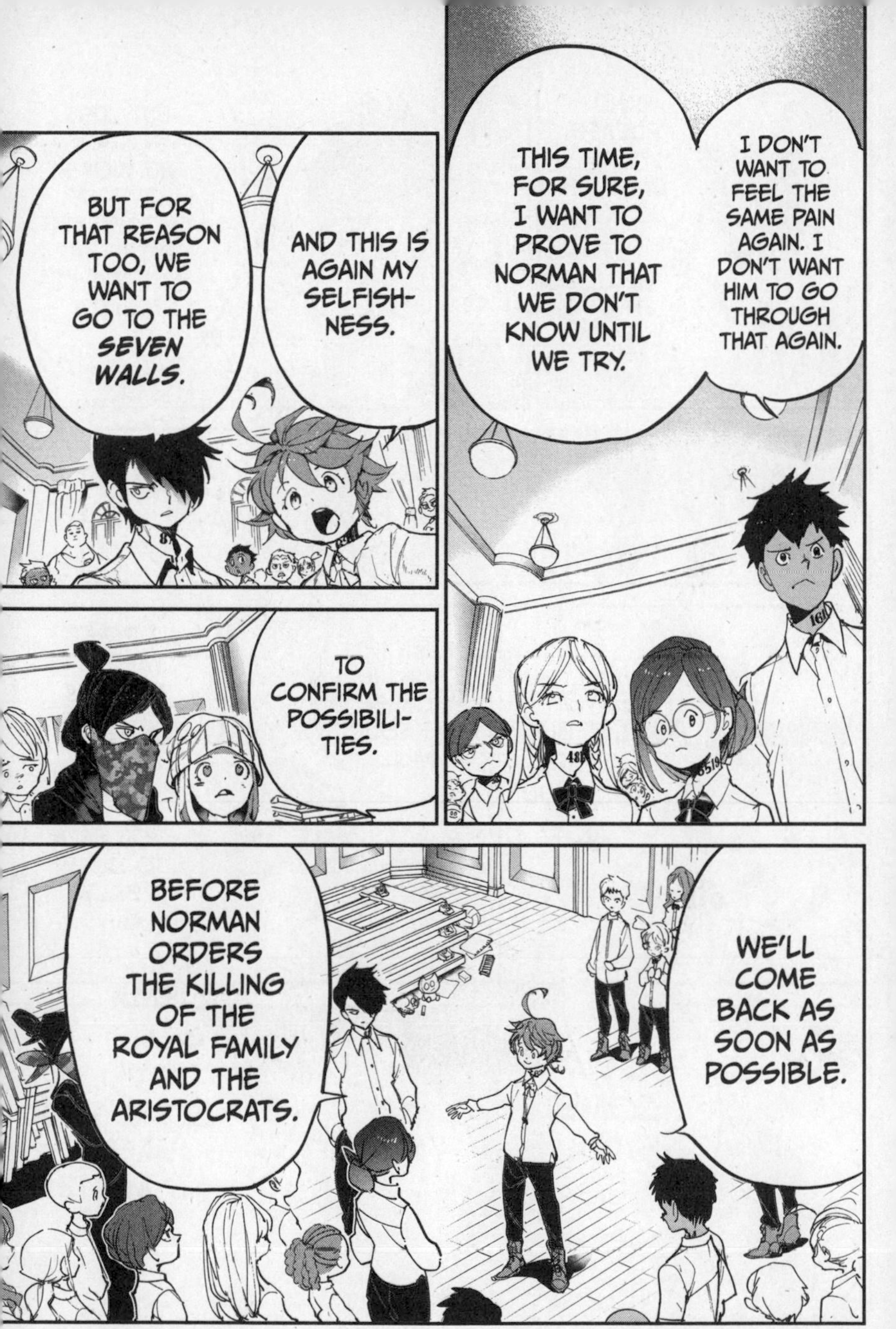
I DON'T WANT TO FEEL THE SAME PAIN AGAIN. I DON'T WANT HIM TO GO THROUGH THAT AGAIN.
THIS TIME, FOR SURE, I WANT TO PROVE TO NORMAN THAT WE DON'T KNOW UNTIL WE TRY.
AND THIS IS AGAIN MY SELFISH-NESS.
BUT FOR THAT REASON TOO, WE WANT TO GO TO THE SEVEN WALLS.
TO CONFIRM THE POSSIBILI-TIES.
WE'LL COME BACK AS SOON AS POSSIBLE.
BEFORE NORMAN ORDERS THE KILLING OF THE ROYAL FAMILY AND THE ARISTOCRATS.

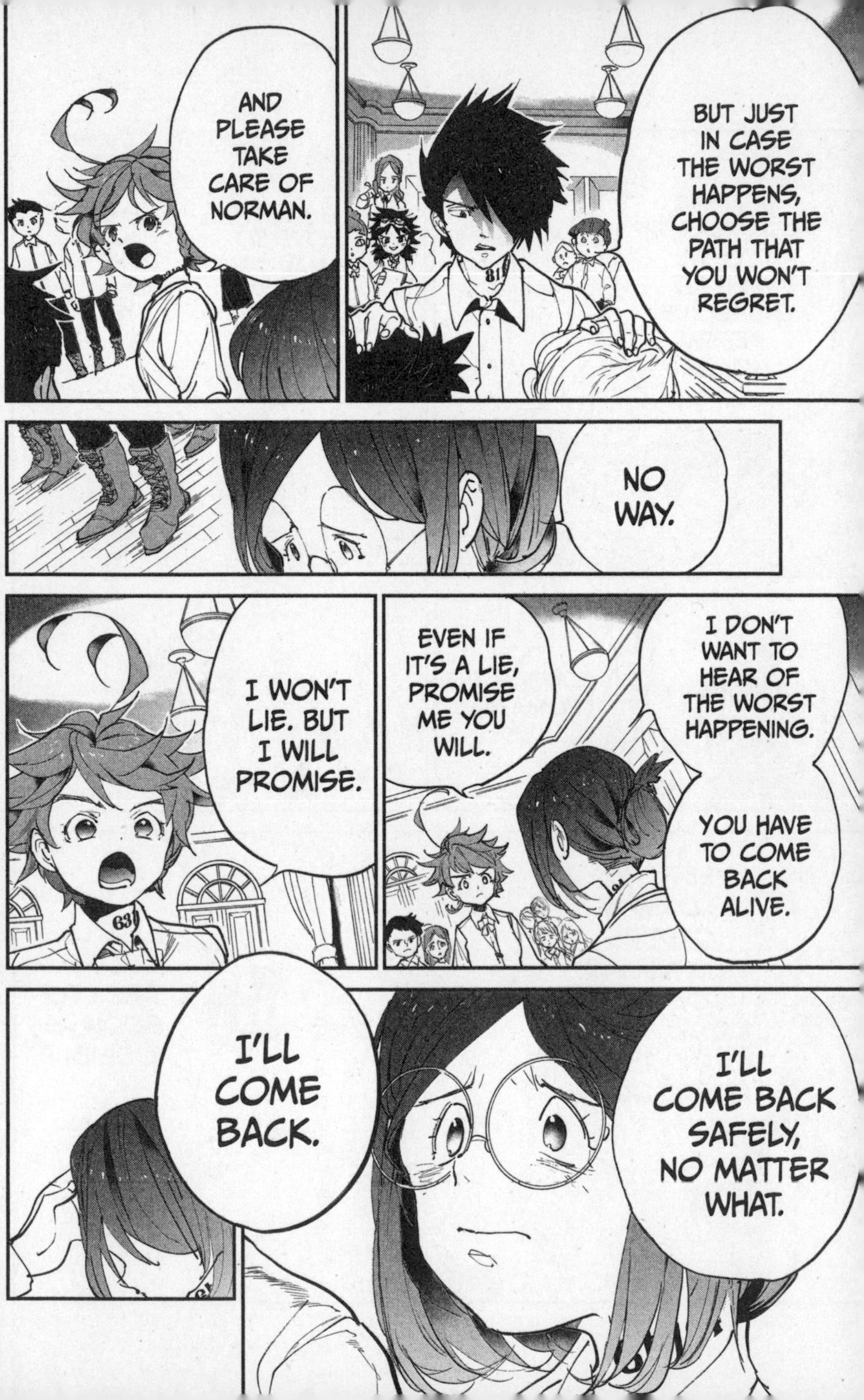
BUT JUST IN CASE THE WORST HAPPENS, CHOOSE THE PATH THAT YOU WON'T REGRET.
AND PLEASE TAKE CARE OF NORMAN.
NO WAY.
I DON'T WANT TO HEAR OF THE WORST HAPPENING.
YOU HAVE TO COME BACK ALIVE.
EVEN IF IT'S A LIE, PROMISE ME YOU WILL.
I WON'T LIE. BUT I WILL PROMISE.
I'LL COME BACK SAFELY, NO MATTER WHAT.
I'LL COME BACK.

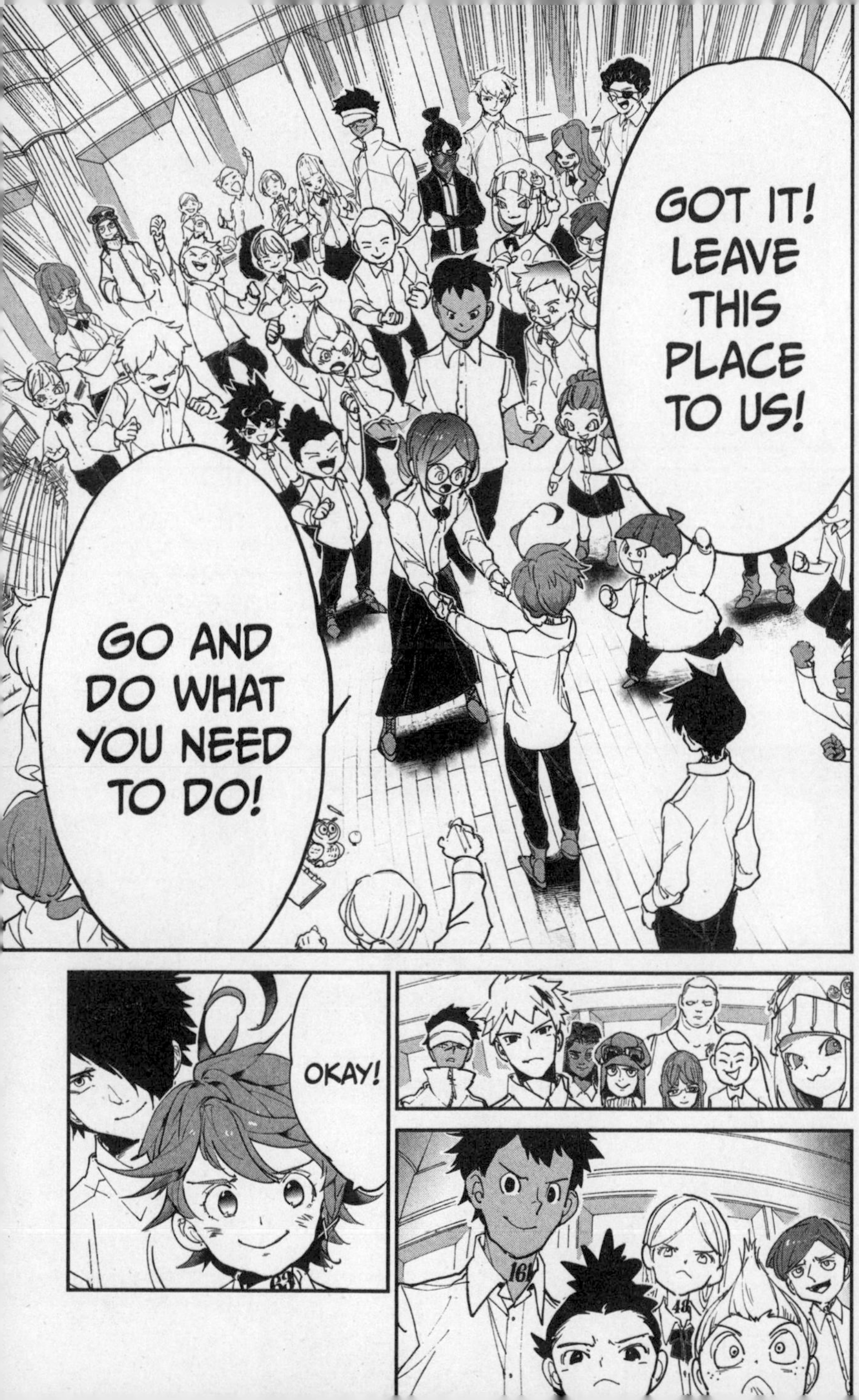
GOT IT! LEAVE THIS PLACE TO US!
GO AND DO WHAT YOU NEED TO DO!
OKAY!

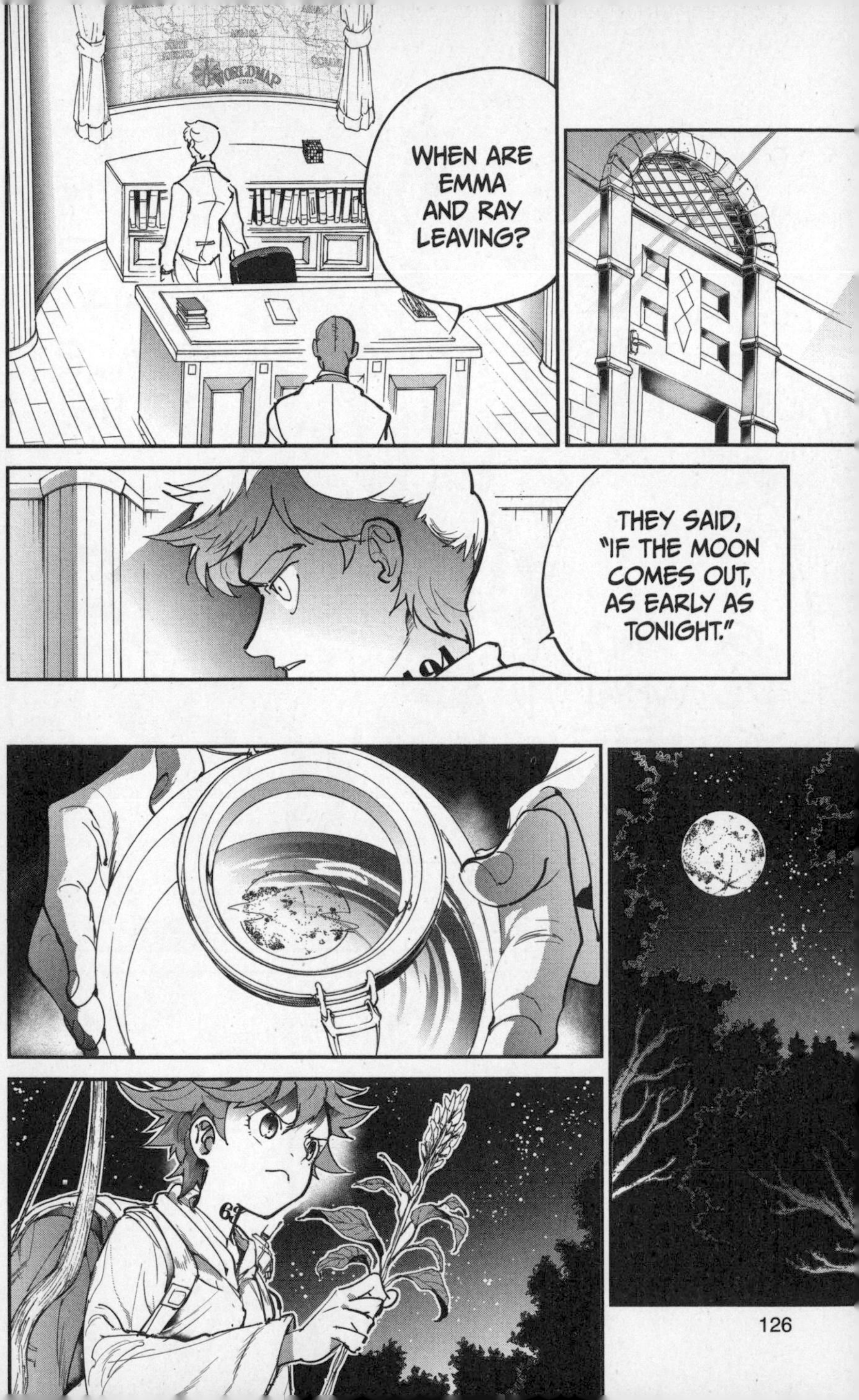
WHEN ARE EMMA AND RAY LEAVING?
THEY SAID, "IF THE MOON COMES OUT, AS EARLY AS TONIGHT."

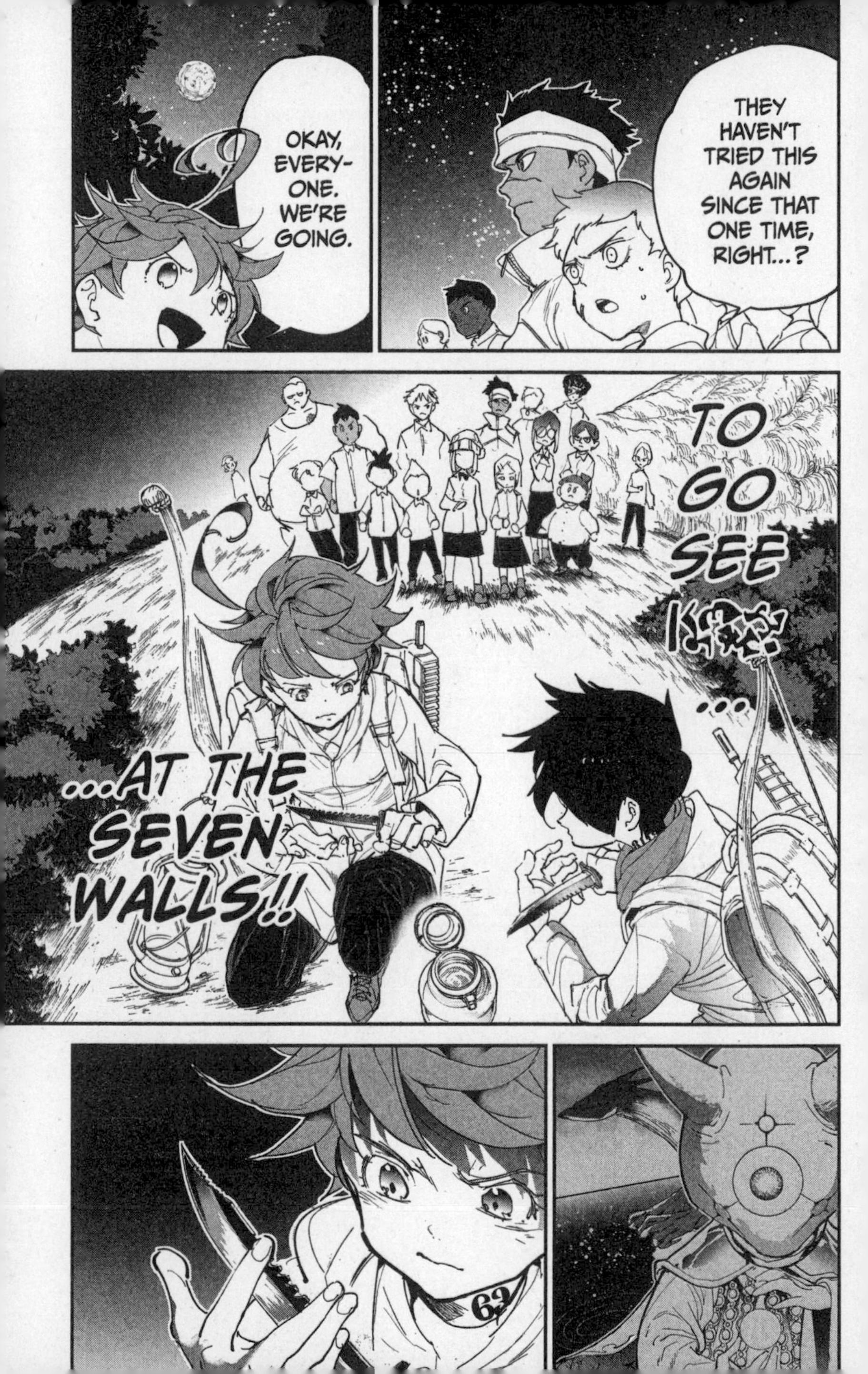
THEY HAVEN'T TRIED THIS AGAIN SINCE THAT ONE TIME, RIGHT...?
OKAY, EVERY-ONE. WE'RE GOING.
TO GO SEE
...
...AT THE SEVEN WALLS!!

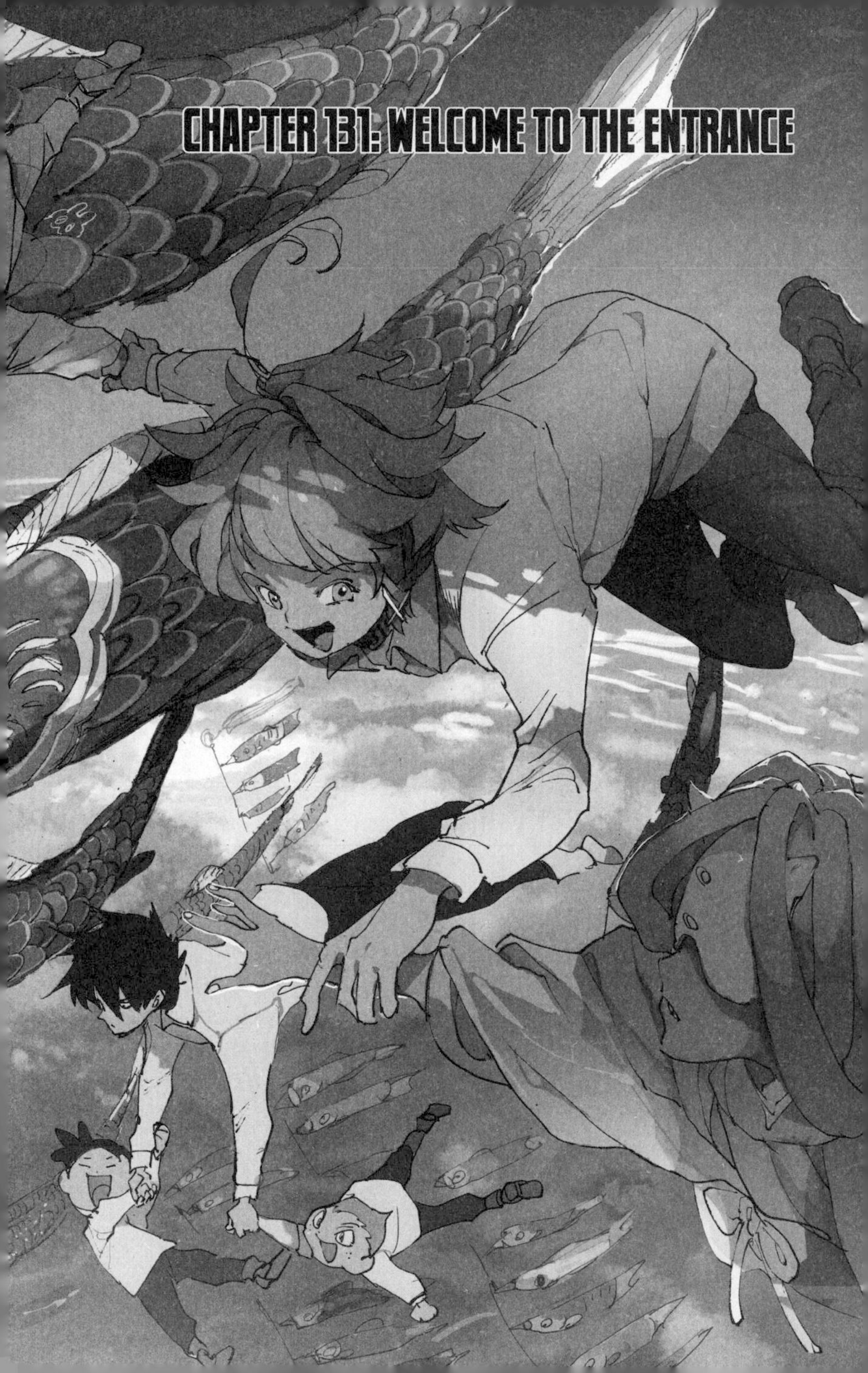
CHAPTER 131: WELCOME TO THE ENTRANCE

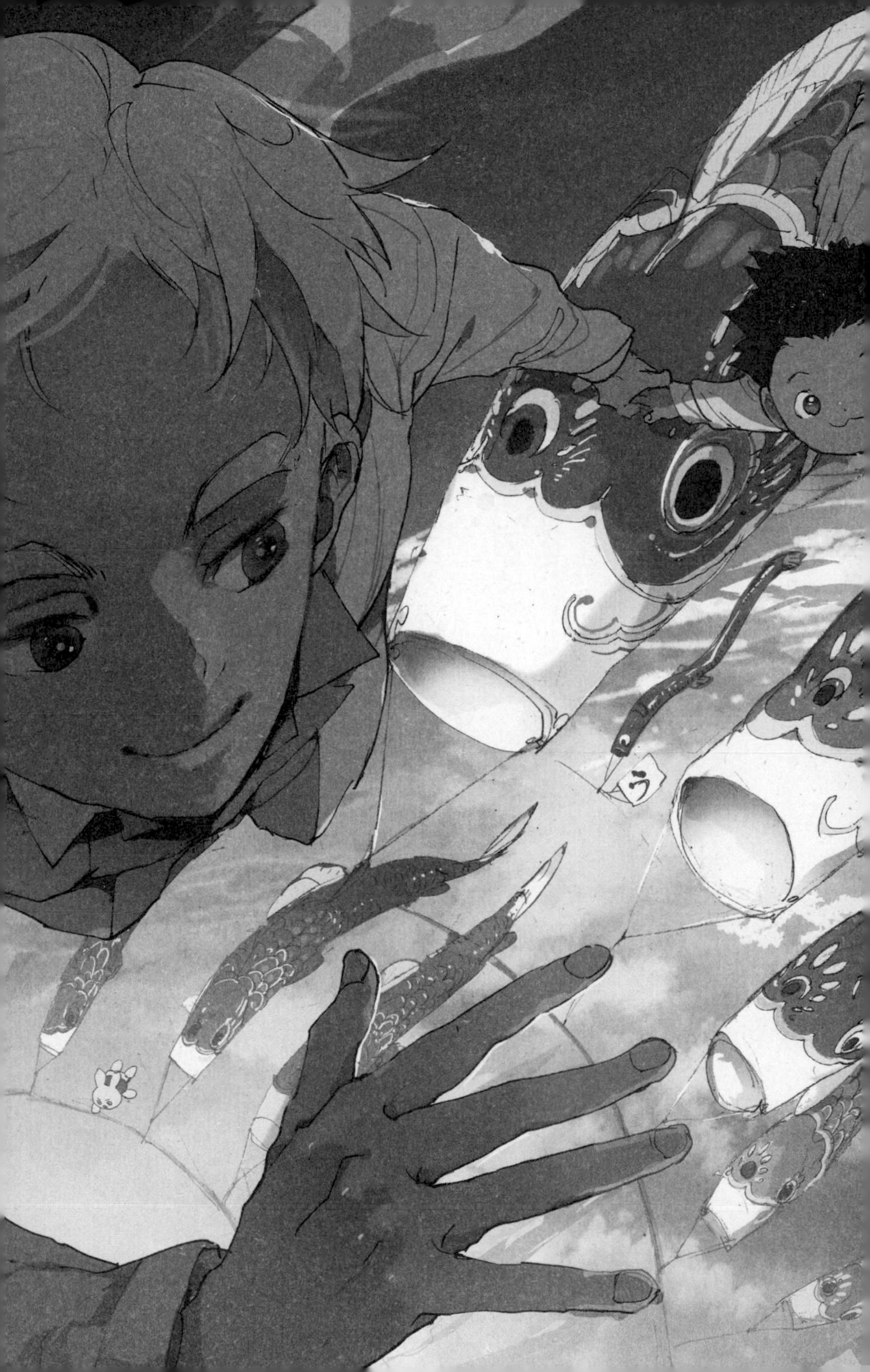
う

How to Draw NORMAN

HOW TO DRAW NORMAN

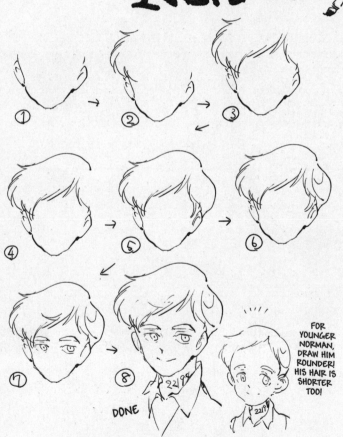

① ② ③

④ ⑤ ⑥

⑦ ⑧

DONE

22/19

FOR YOUNGER NORMAN, DRAW HIM ROUNDER! HIS HAIR IS SHORTER TOO!

22/19

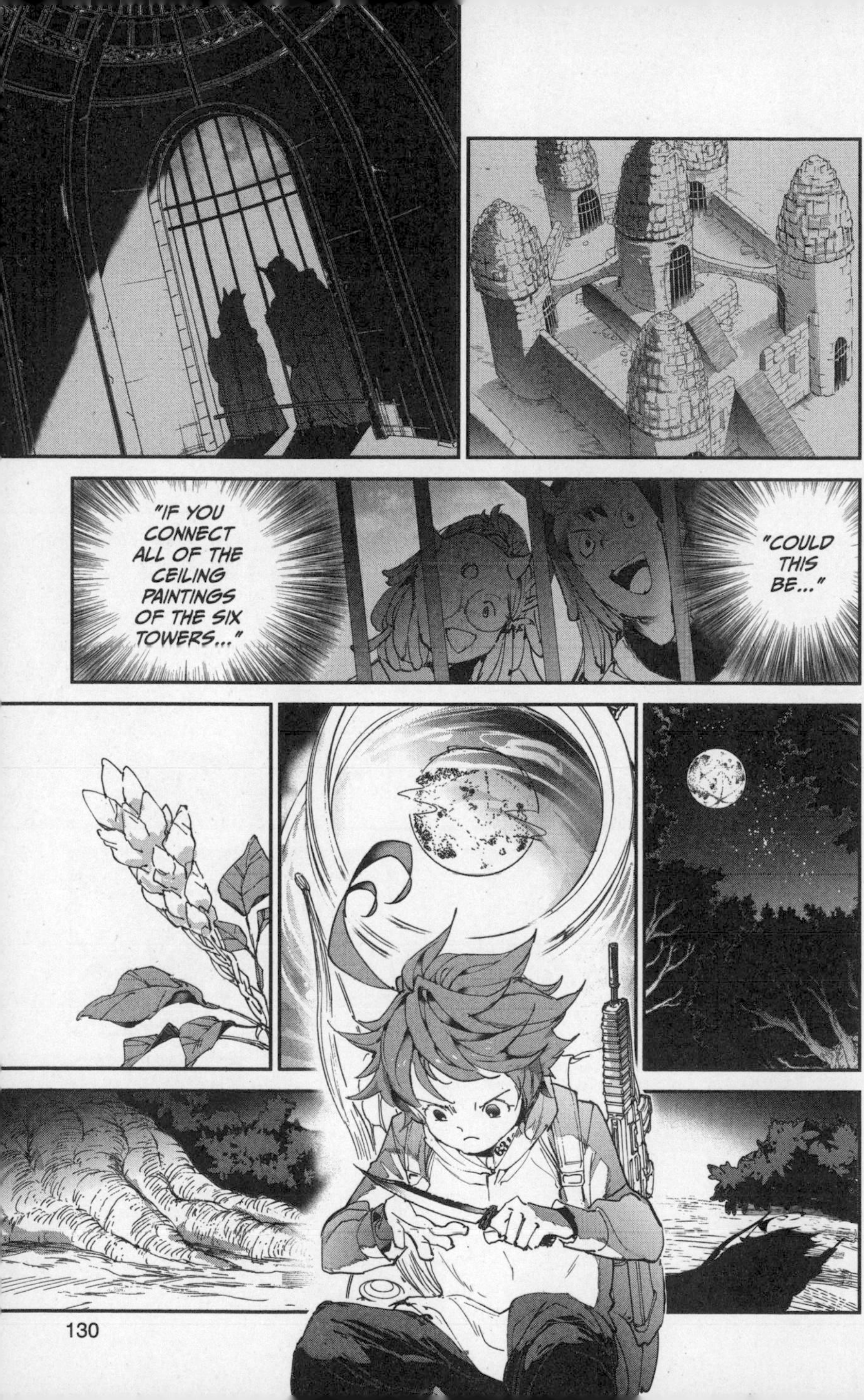
"COULD THIS BE..."
"IF YOU CONNECT ALL OF THE CEILING PAINTINGS OF THE SIX TOWERS..."

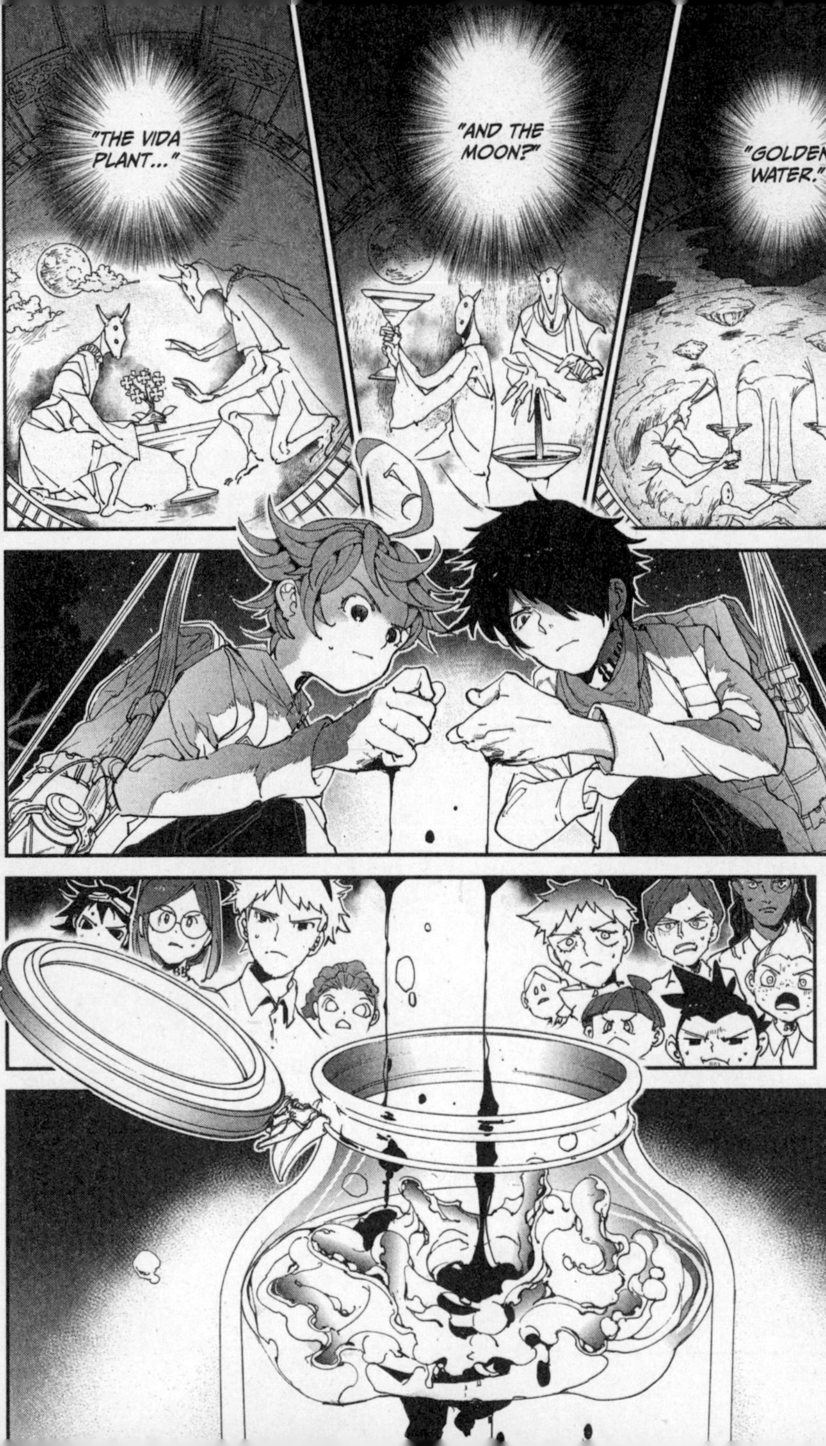
"GOLDEN WATER."
"AND THE MOON?"
"THE VIDA PLANT..."

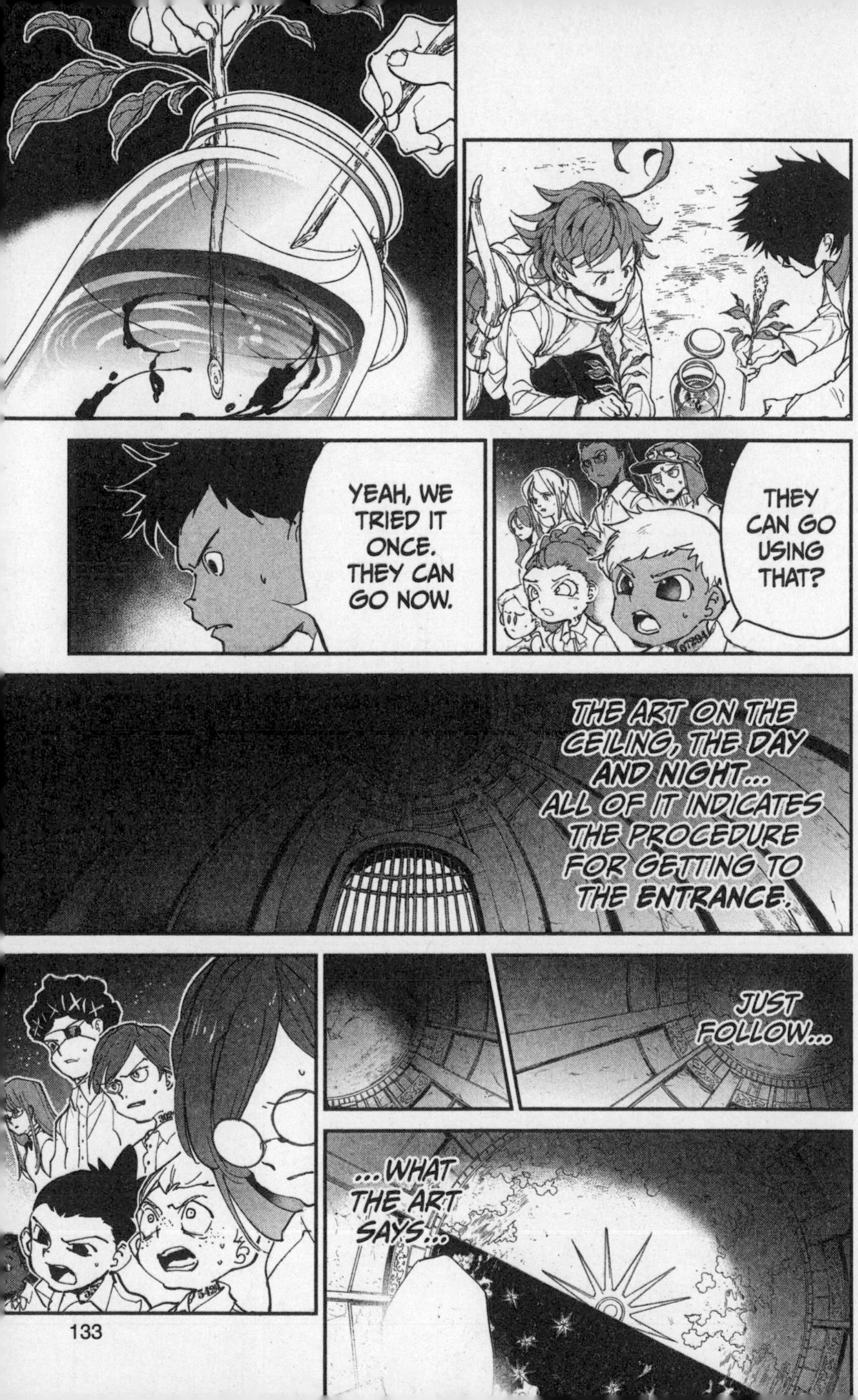
THEY CAN GO USING THAT?
YEAH, WE TRIED IT ONCE. THEY CAN GO NOW.
THE ART ON THE CEILING, THE DAY AND NIGHT... ALL OF IT INDICATES THE PROCEDURE FOR GETTING TO THE ENTRANCE.
JUST FOLLOW...
...WHAT THE ART SAYS...

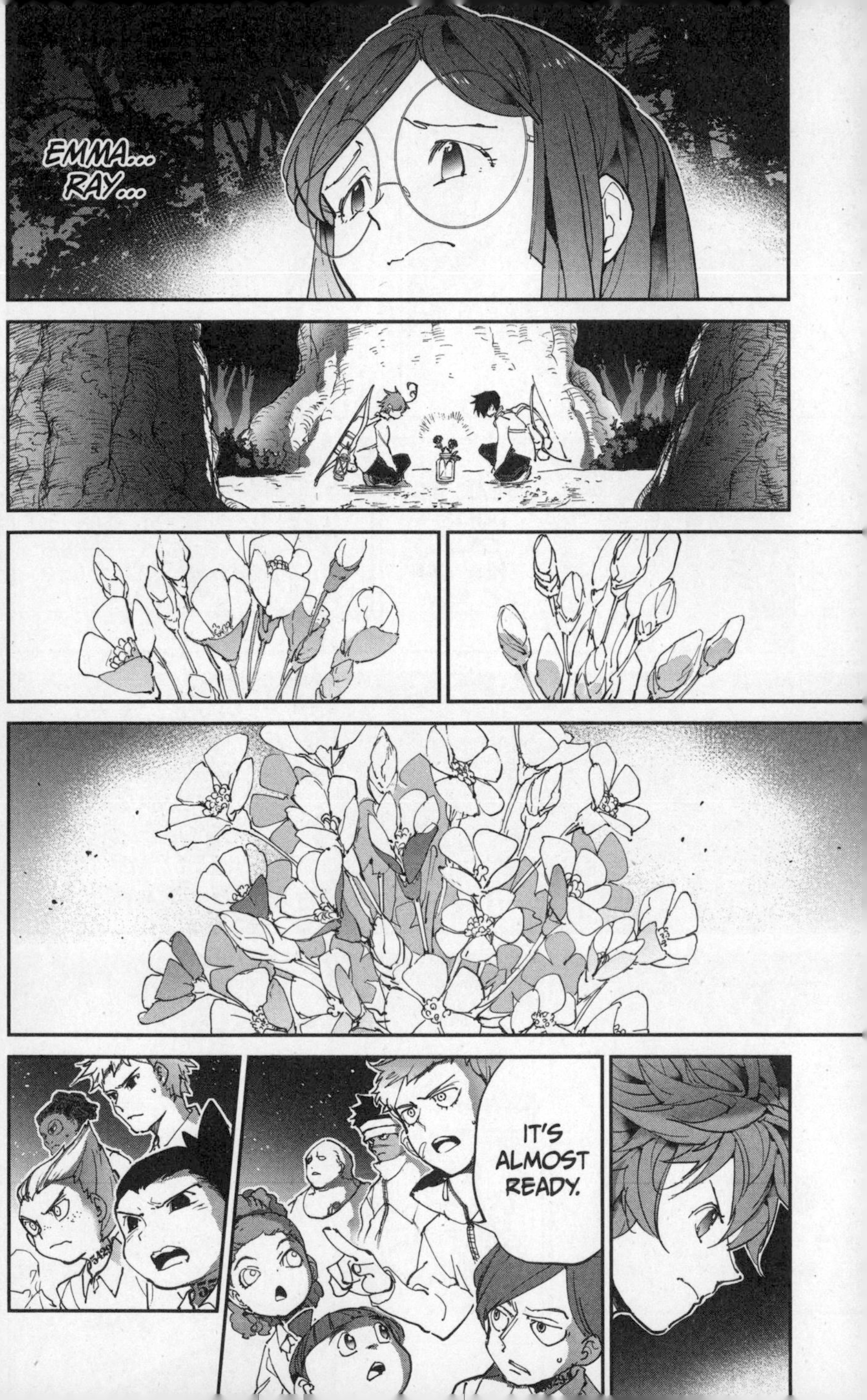
EMMA...
RAY...
IT'S ALMOST READY.

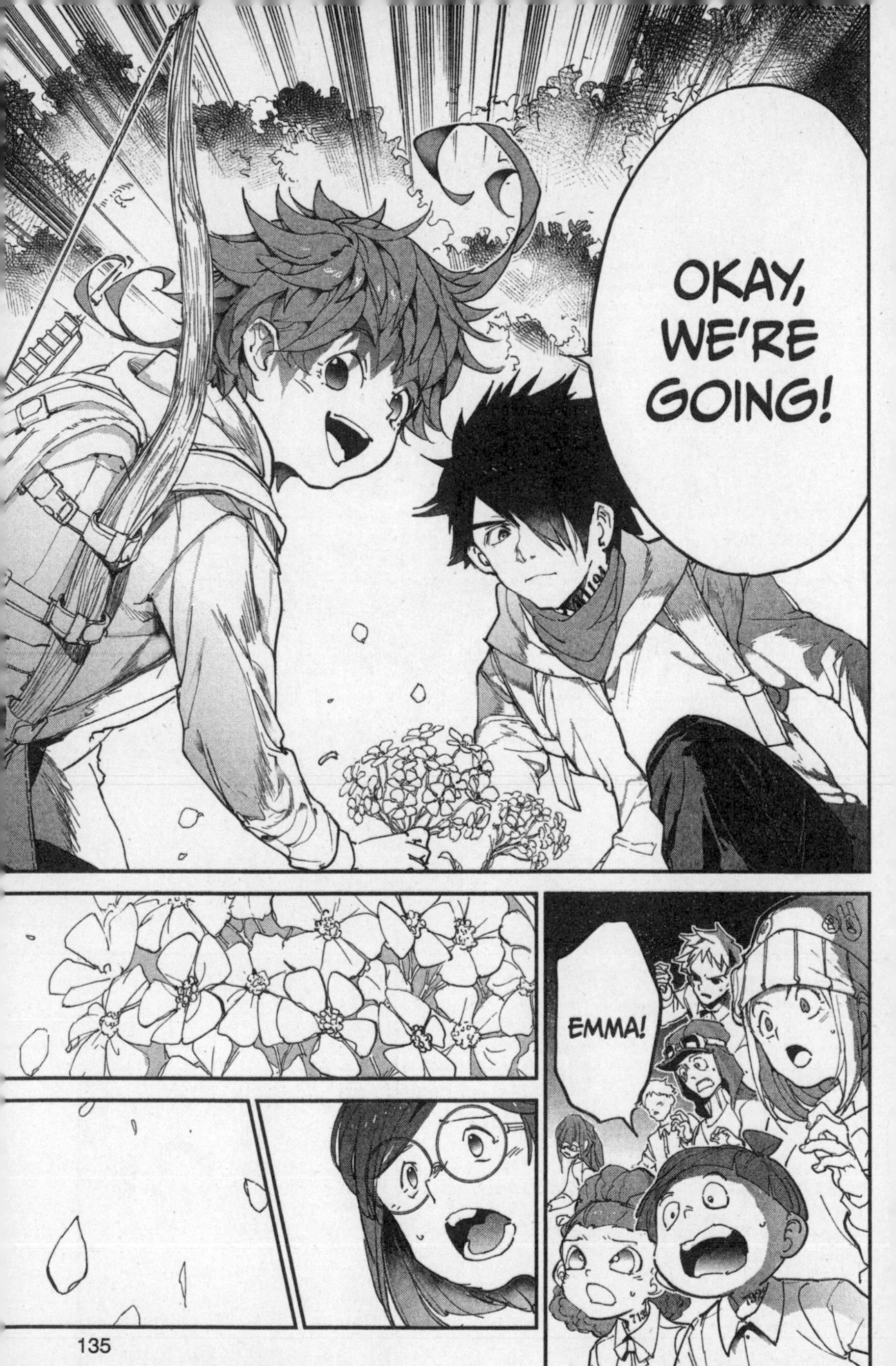
OKAY, WE'RE GOING!
EMMA!

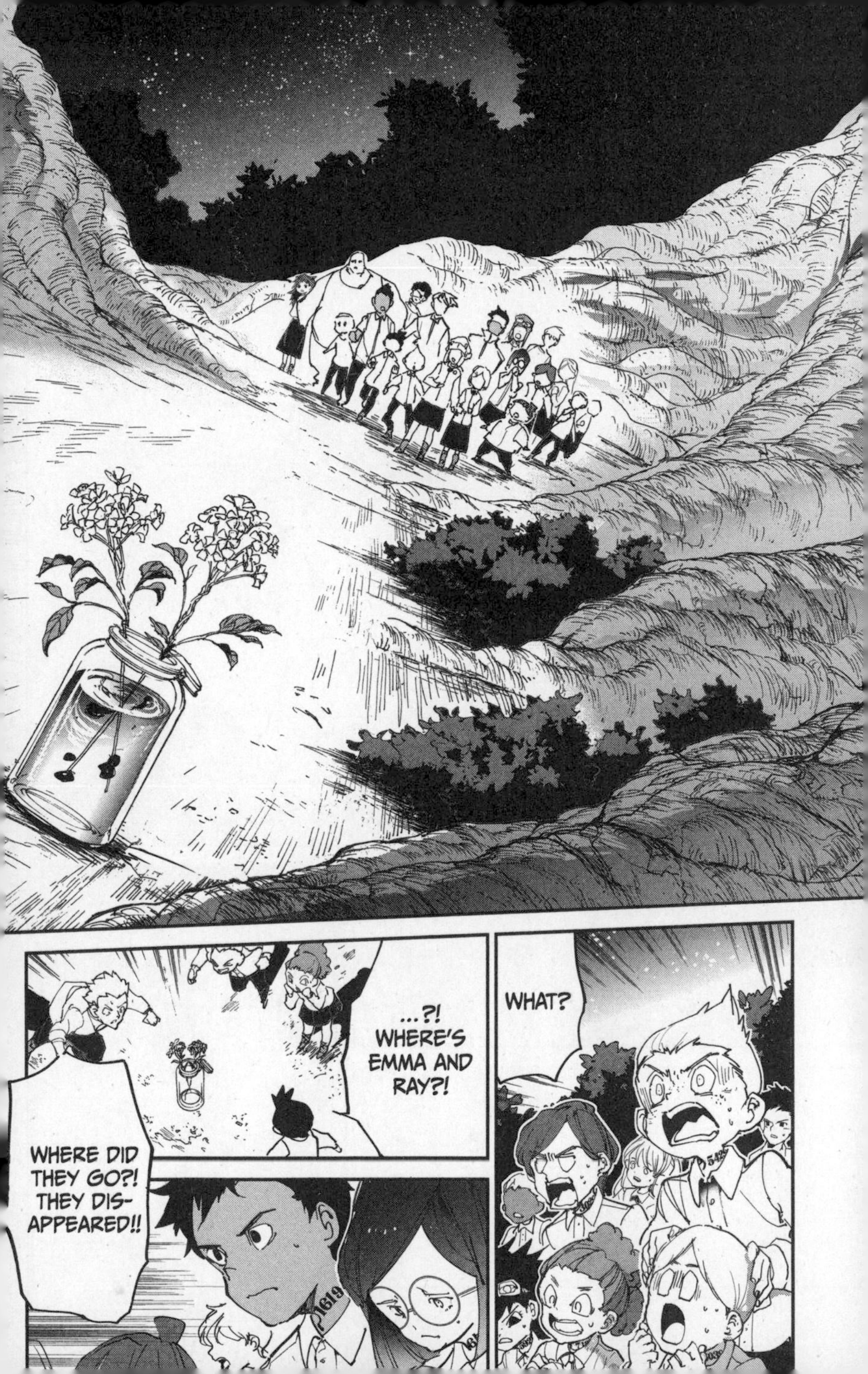
WHAT?
...?! WHERE'S EMMA AND RAY?!
WHERE DID THEY GO?! THEY DIS-APPEARED!!

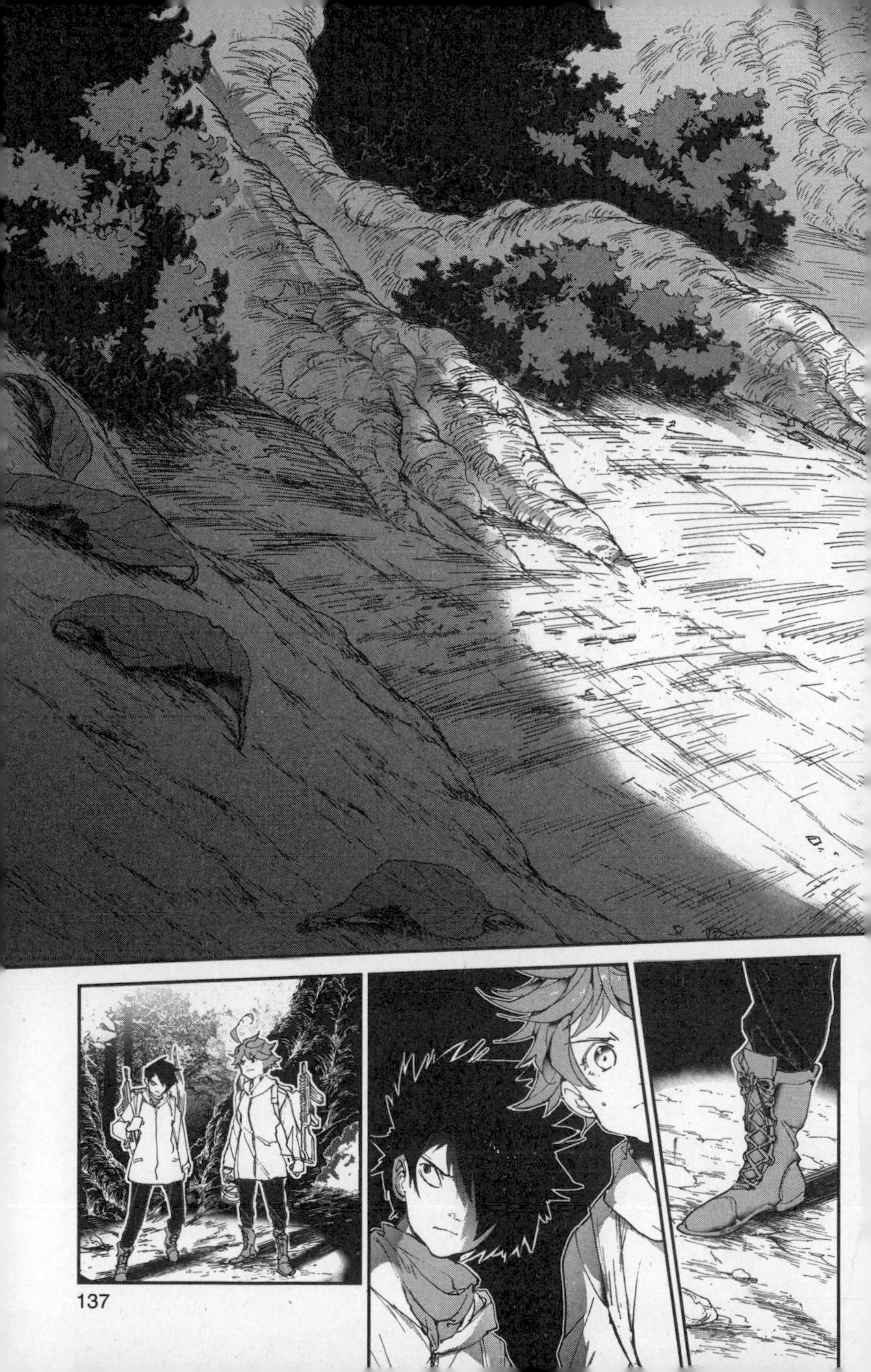

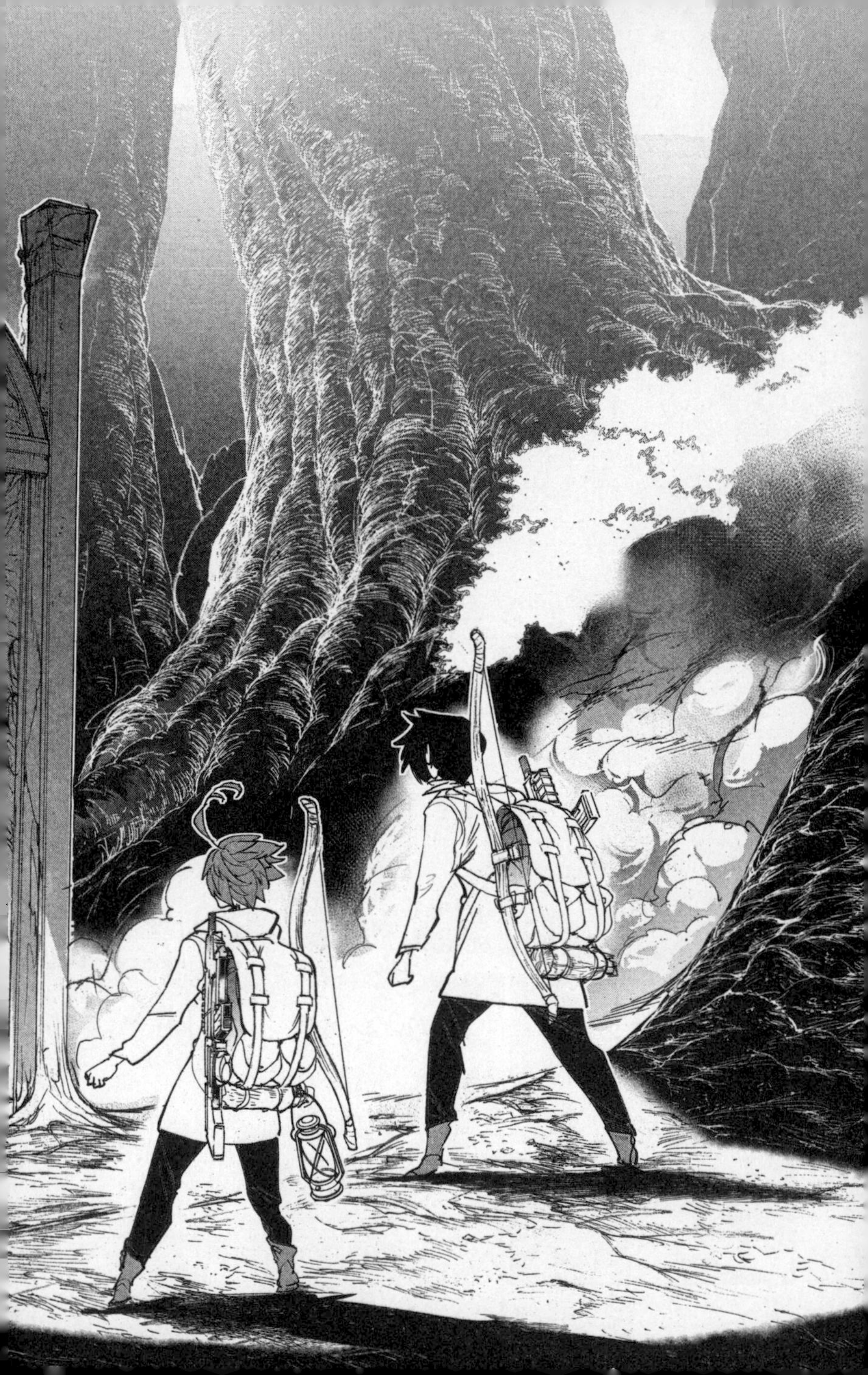

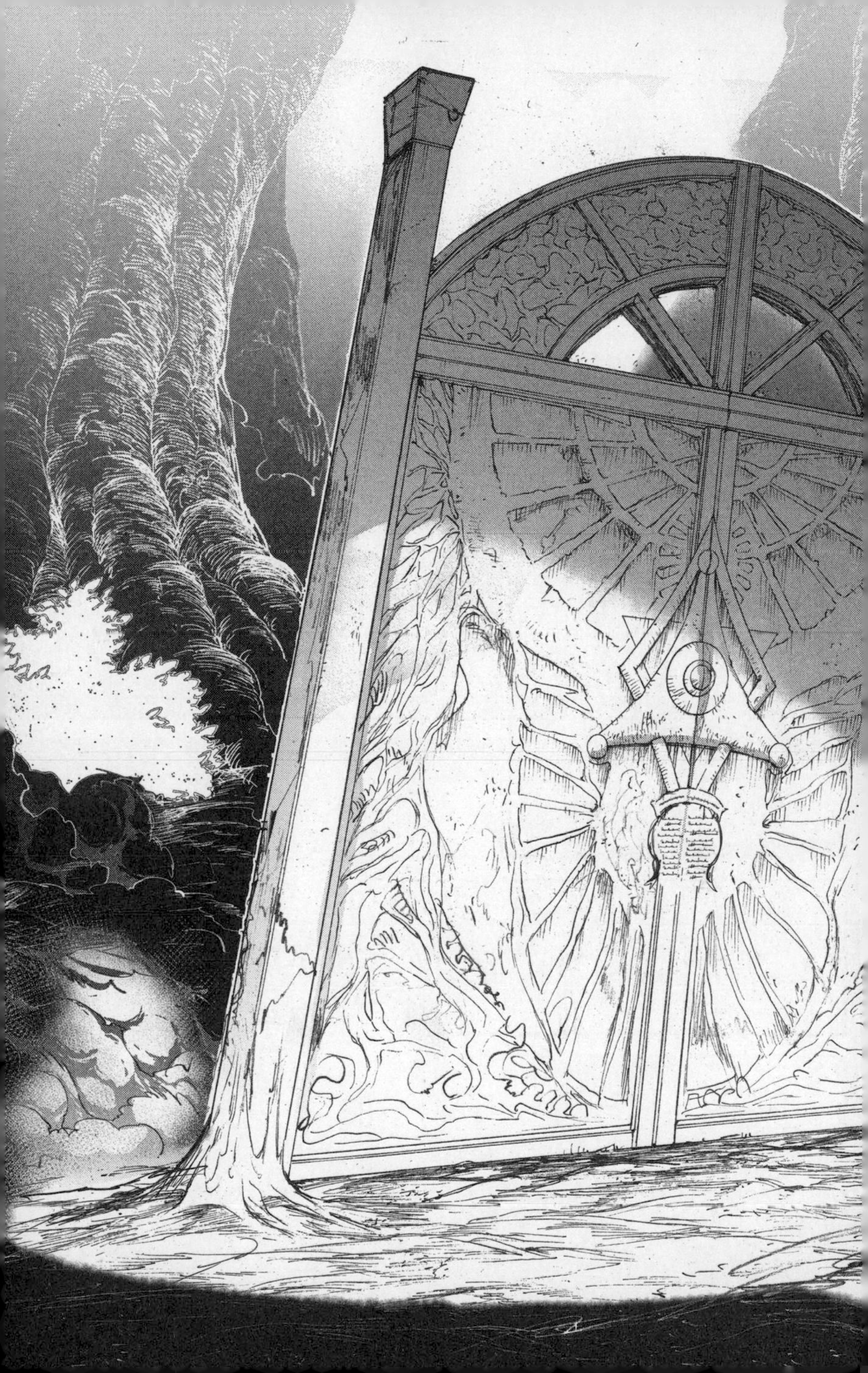

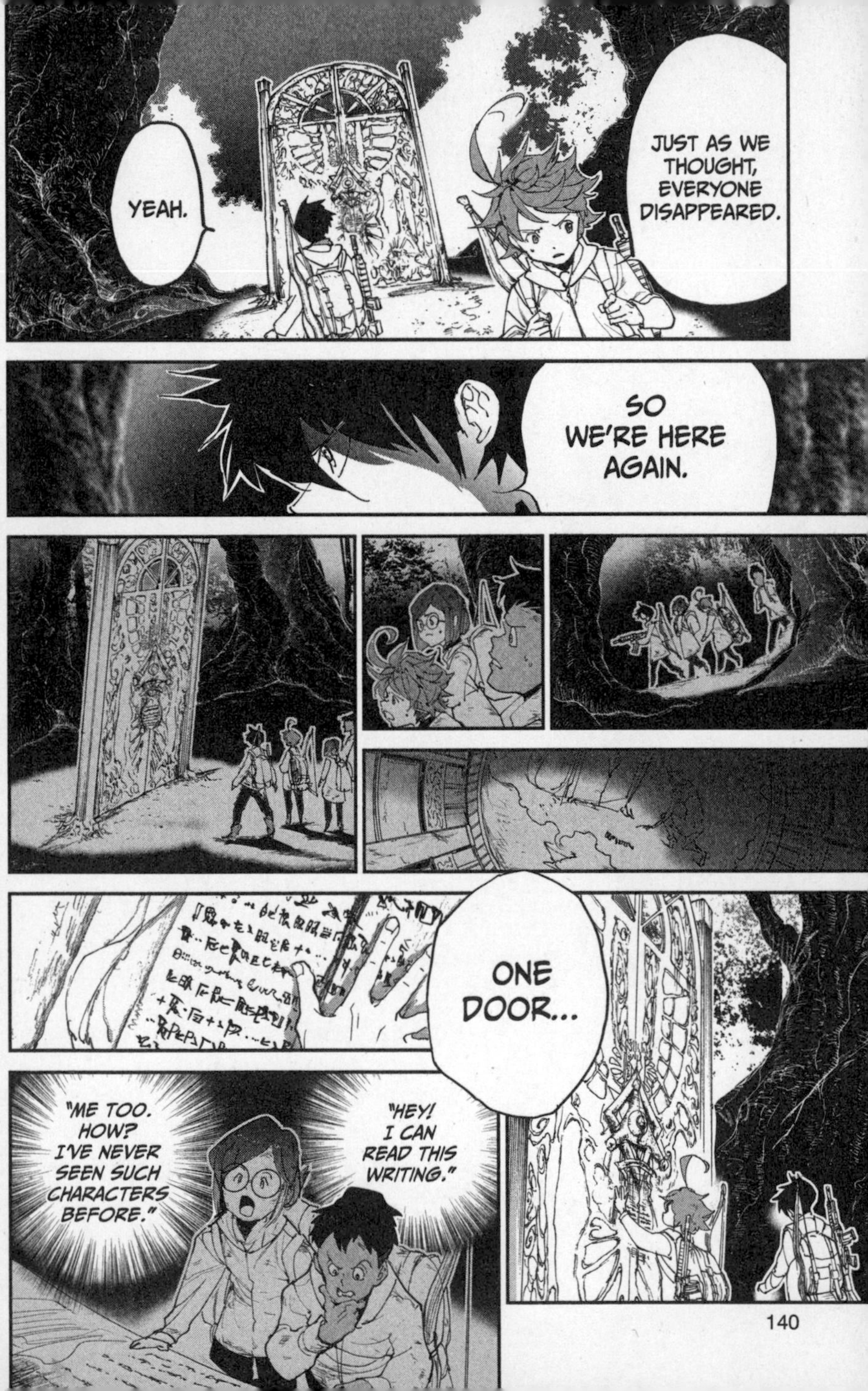
JUST AS WE THOUGHT, EVERYONE DISAPPEARED.
YEAH.
SO WE'RE HERE AGAIN.
ONE DOOR...
"HEY! I CAN READ THIS WRITING."
"ME TOO. HOW? I'VE NEVER SEEN SUCH CHARACTERS BEFORE."

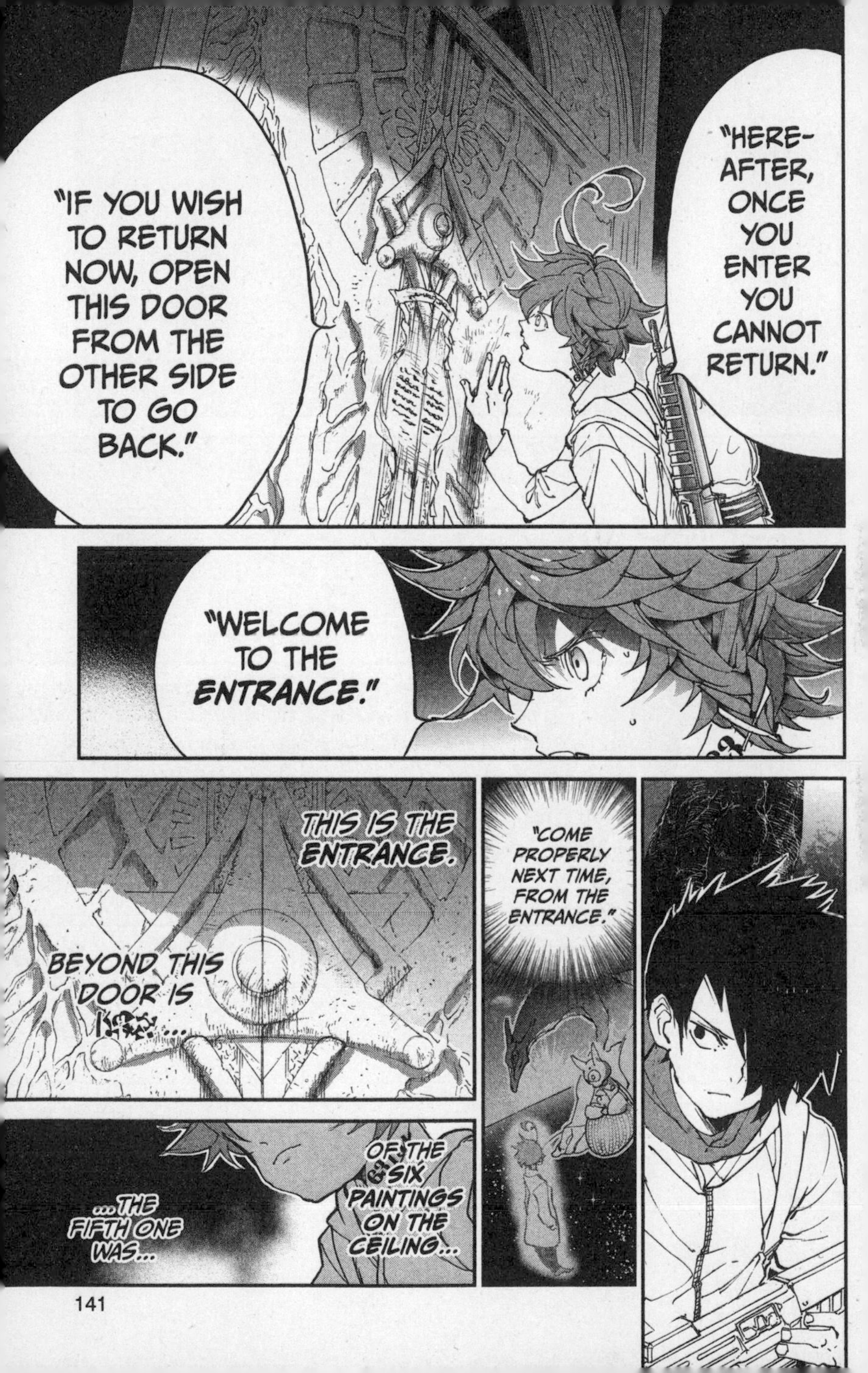
"HERE-AFTER, ONCE YOU ENTER YOU CANNOT RETURN."
"IF YOU WISH TO RETURN NOW, OPEN THIS DOOR FROM THE OTHER SIDE TO GO BACK."
"WELCOME TO THE ENTRANCE."
"COME PROPERLY NEXT TIME, FROM THE ENTRANCE."
THIS IS THE ENTRANCE.
BEYOND THIS DOOR IS ...
OF THE SIX PAINTINGS ON THE CEILING...
...THE FIFTH ONE WAS...

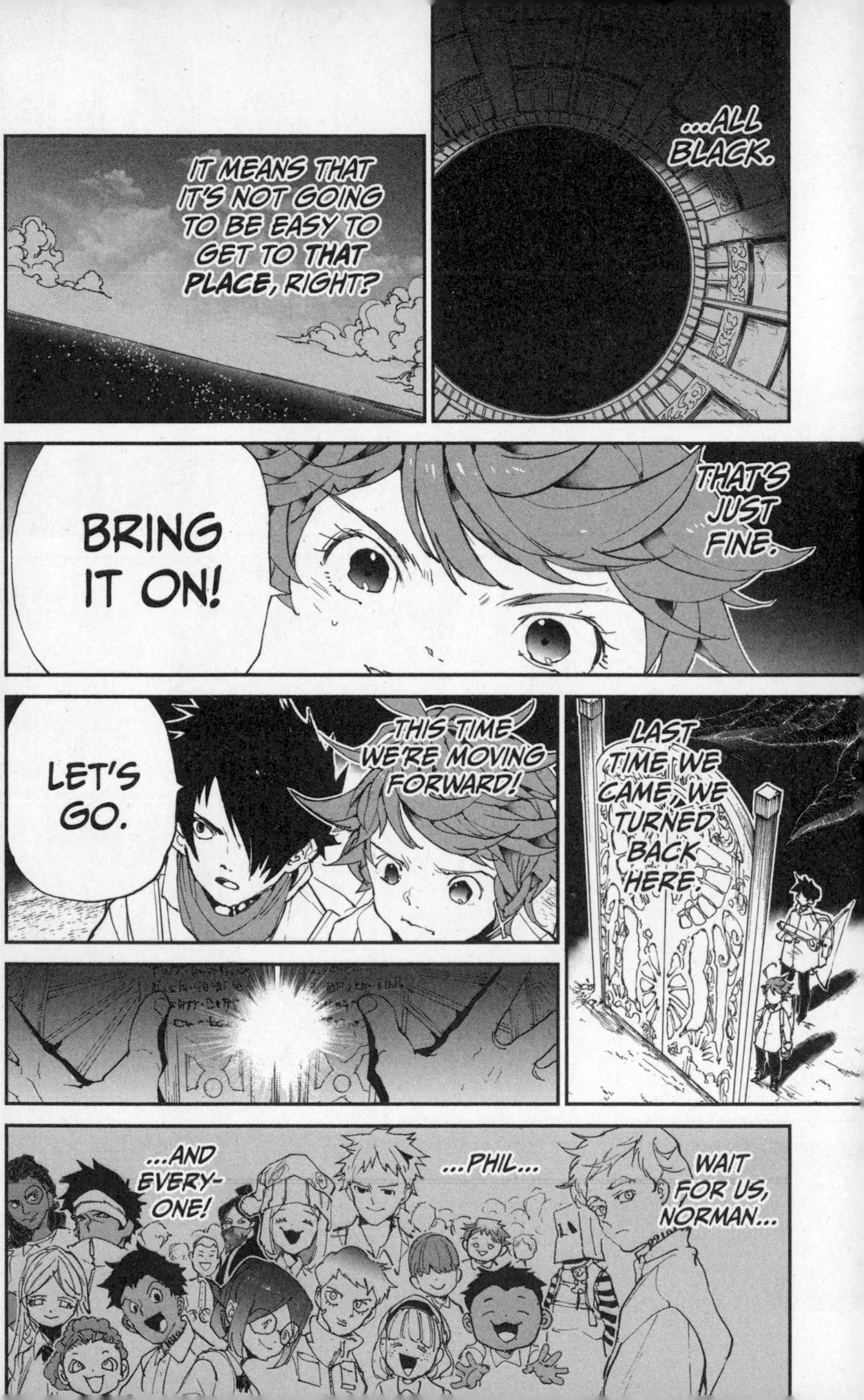
...ALL BLACK.
IT MEANS THAT IT'S NOT GOING TO BE EASY TO GET TO THAT PLACE, RIGHT?
THAT'S JUST FINE.
BRING IT ON!
LAST TIME WE CAME, WE TURNED BACK HERE.
THIS TIME WE'RE MOVING FORWARD!
LET'S GO.
WAIT FOR US, NORMAN...
...PHIL...
...AND EVERY-ONE!

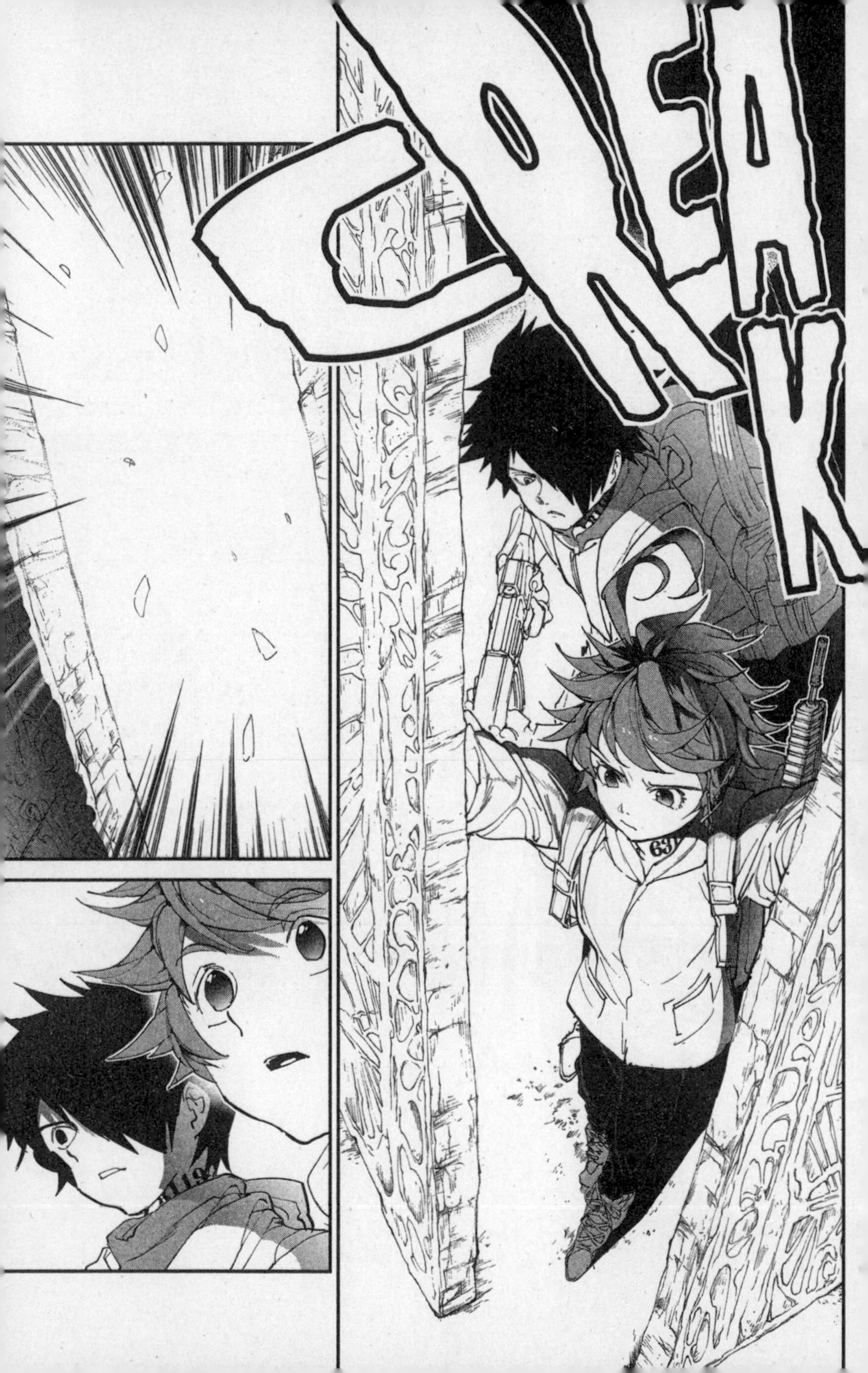
CREAK

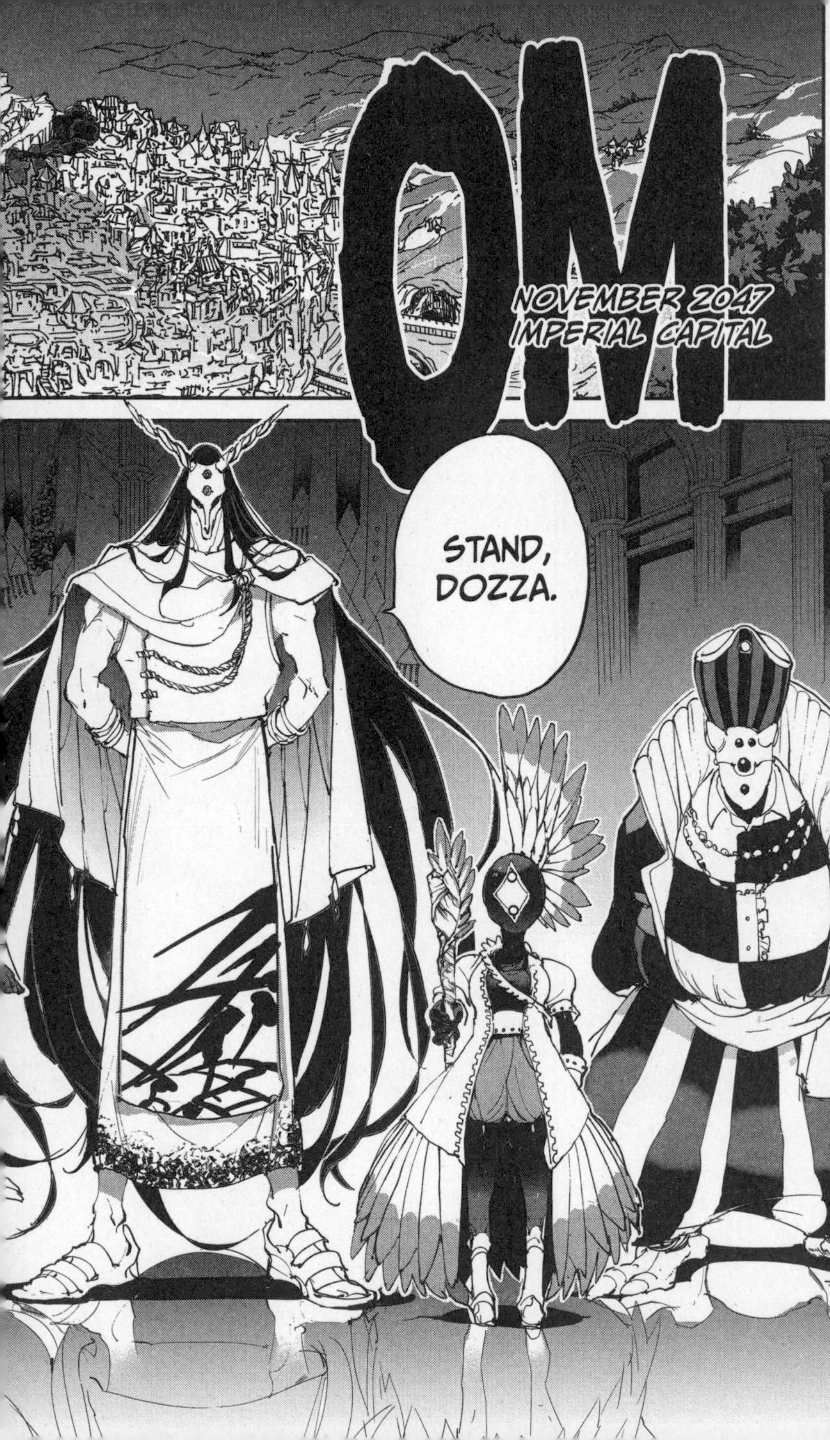
OM
NOVEMBER 2047
IMPERIAL CAPITAL
STAND, DOZZA.

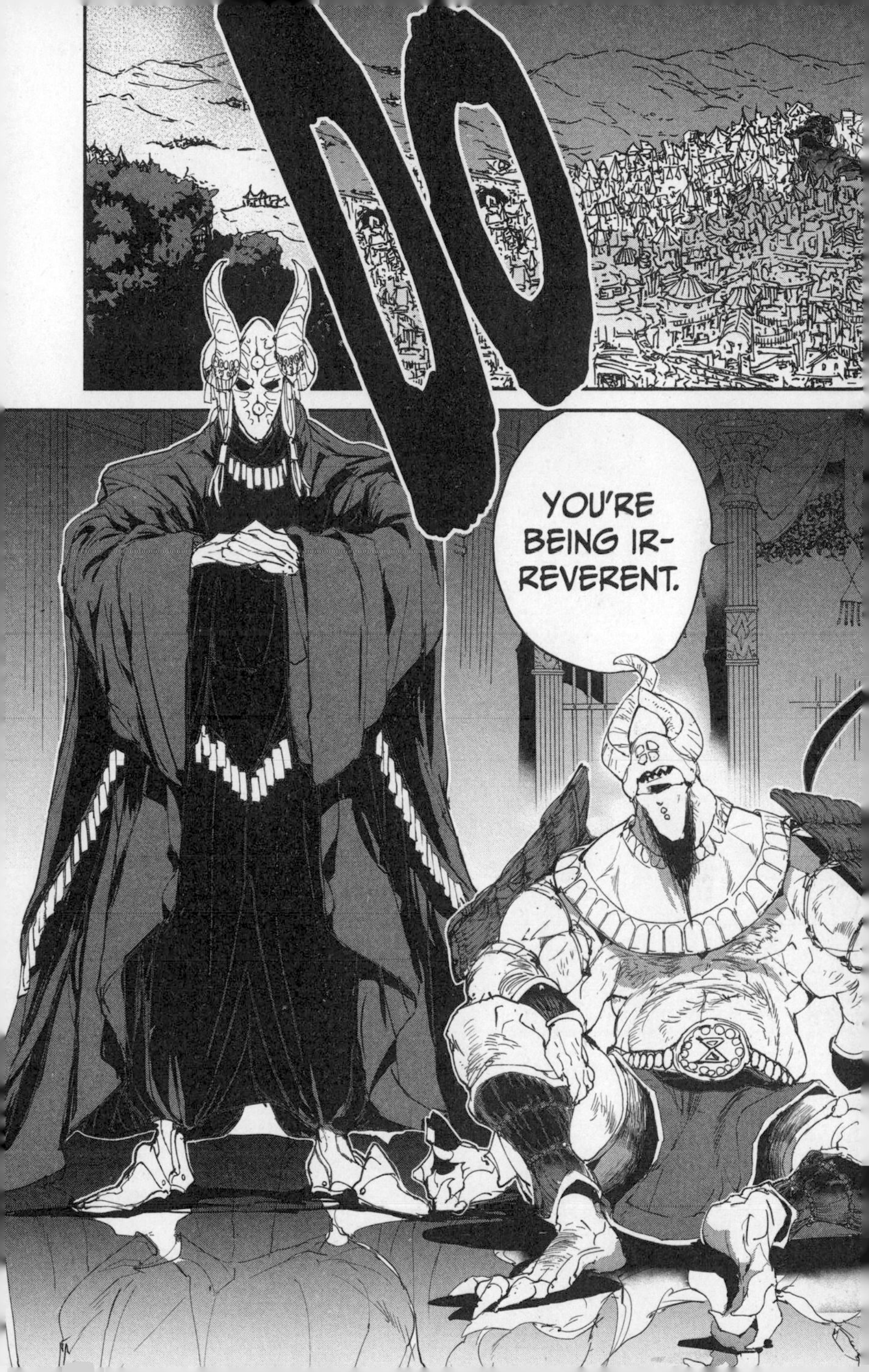
YOU'RE BEING IR-REVERENT.

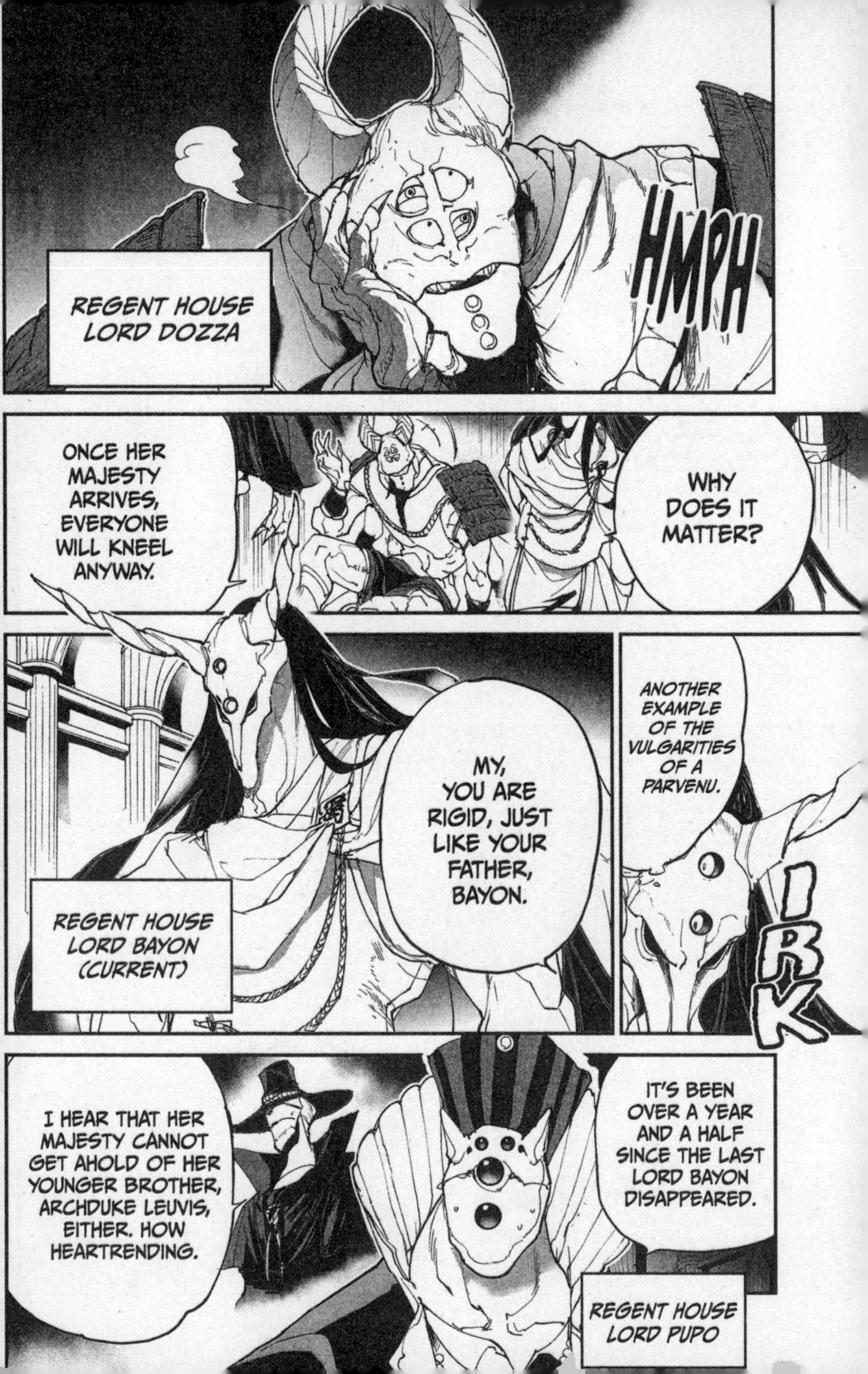
HMPH
REGENT HOUSE LORD DOZZA
WHY DOES IT MATTER?
ONCE HER MAJESTY ARRIVES, EVERYONE WILL KNEEL ANYWAY.
ANOTHER EXAMPLE OF THE VULGARITIES OF A PARVENU.
IRK
MY, YOU ARE RIGID, JUST LIKE YOUR FATHER, BAYON.
REGENT HOUSE LORD BAYON (CURRENT)
IT'S BEEN OVER A YEAR AND A HALF SINCE THE LAST LORD BAYON DISAPPEARED.
I HEAR THAT HER MAJESTY CANNOT GET AHOLD OF HER YOUNGER BROTHER, ARCHDUKE LEUVIS, EITHER. HOW HEARTRENDING.
REGENT HOUSE LORD PUPO

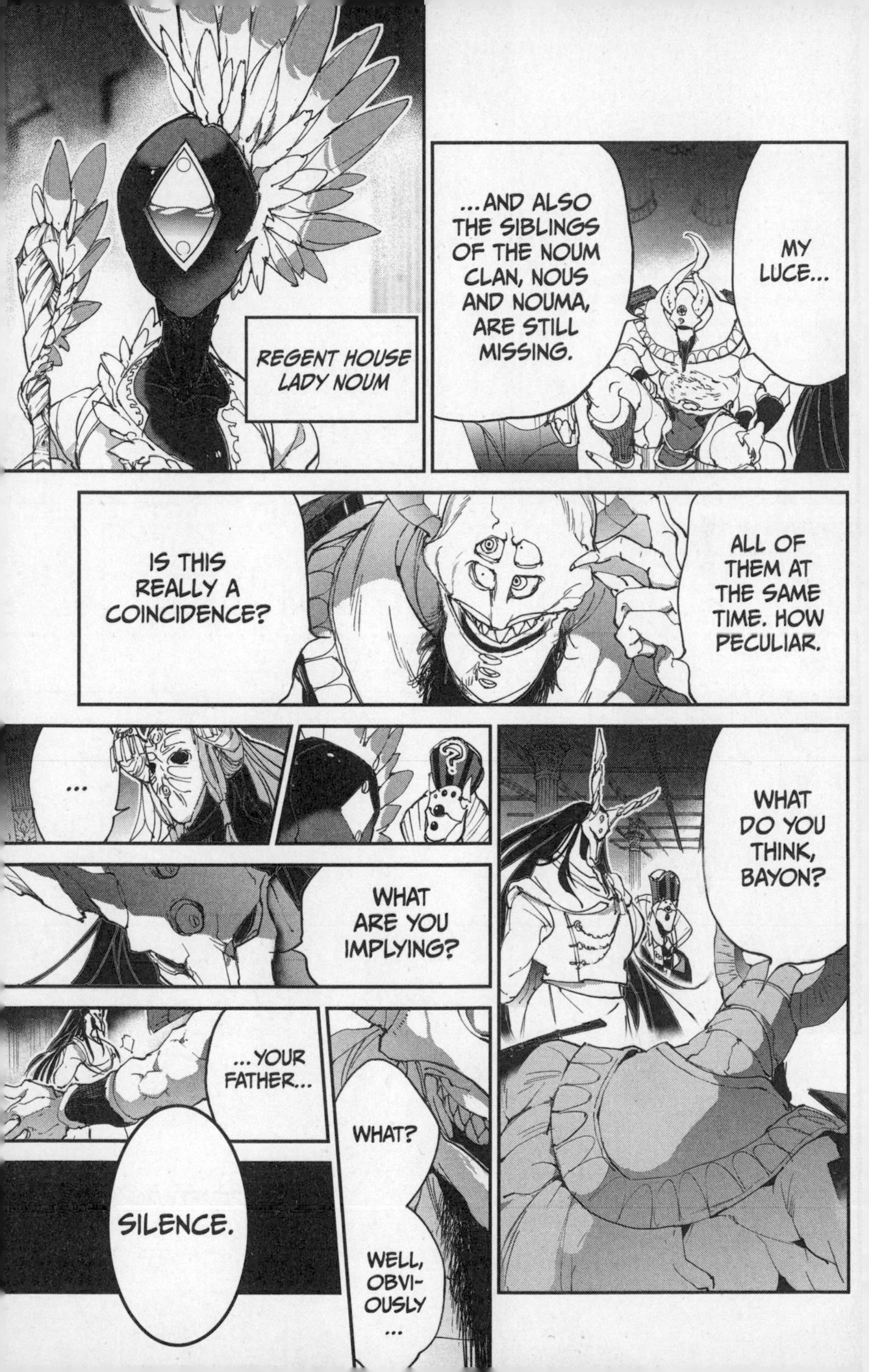
MY LUCE...
...AND ALSO THE SIBLINGS OF THE NOUM CLAN, NOUS AND NOUMA, ARE STILL MISSING.
REGENT HOUSE LADY NOUM
ALL OF THEM AT THE SAME TIME. HOW PECULIAR.
IS THIS REALLY A COINCIDENCE?
WHAT DO YOU THINK, BAYON?
...
WHAT ARE YOU IMPLYING?
WHAT?
WELL, OBVI-OUSLY ...
...YOUR FATHER...
SILENCE.

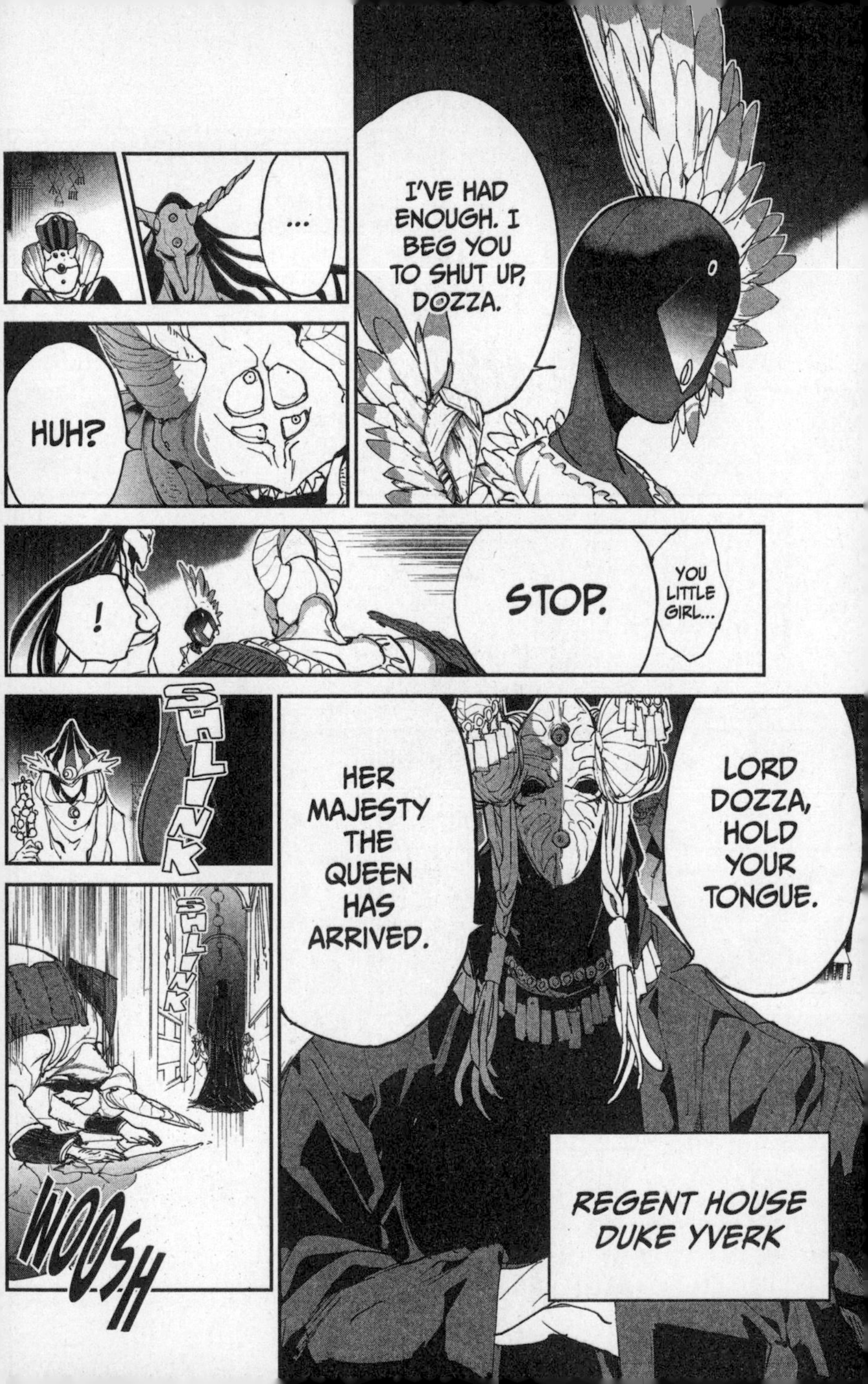
I'VE HAD ENOUGH. I BEG YOU TO SHUT UP, DOZZA.
...
HUH?
YOU LITTLE GIRL...
STOP.
!
LORD DOZZA, HOLD YOUR TONGUE.
HER MAJESTY THE QUEEN HAS ARRIVED.
REGENT HOUSE DUKE YVERK
SHLINK
SHLINK
WOOSH

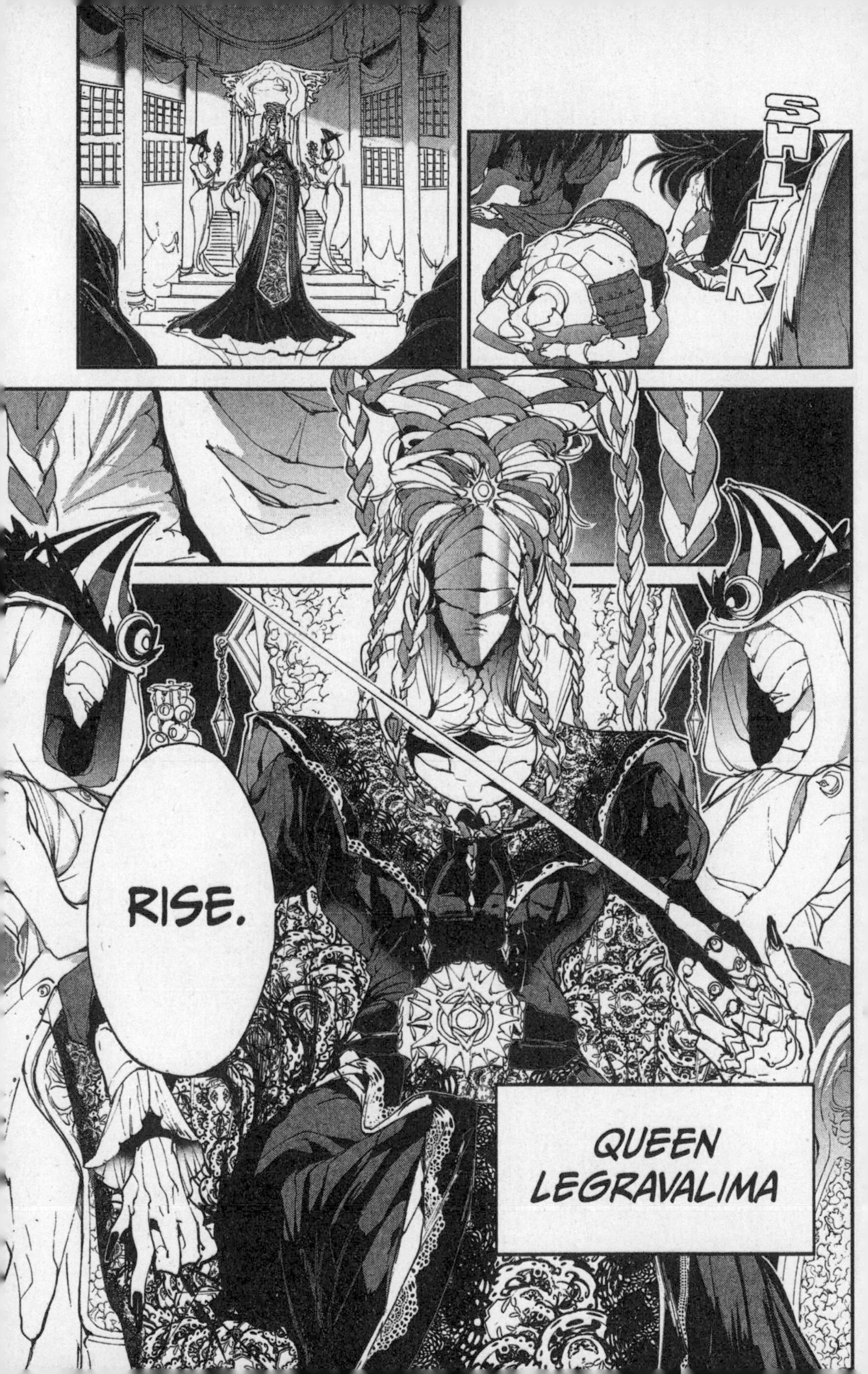
SHLINK
RISE.
QUEEN LEGRAVALIMA

THE PROMISED NEVERLAND SIDE SCENE 021

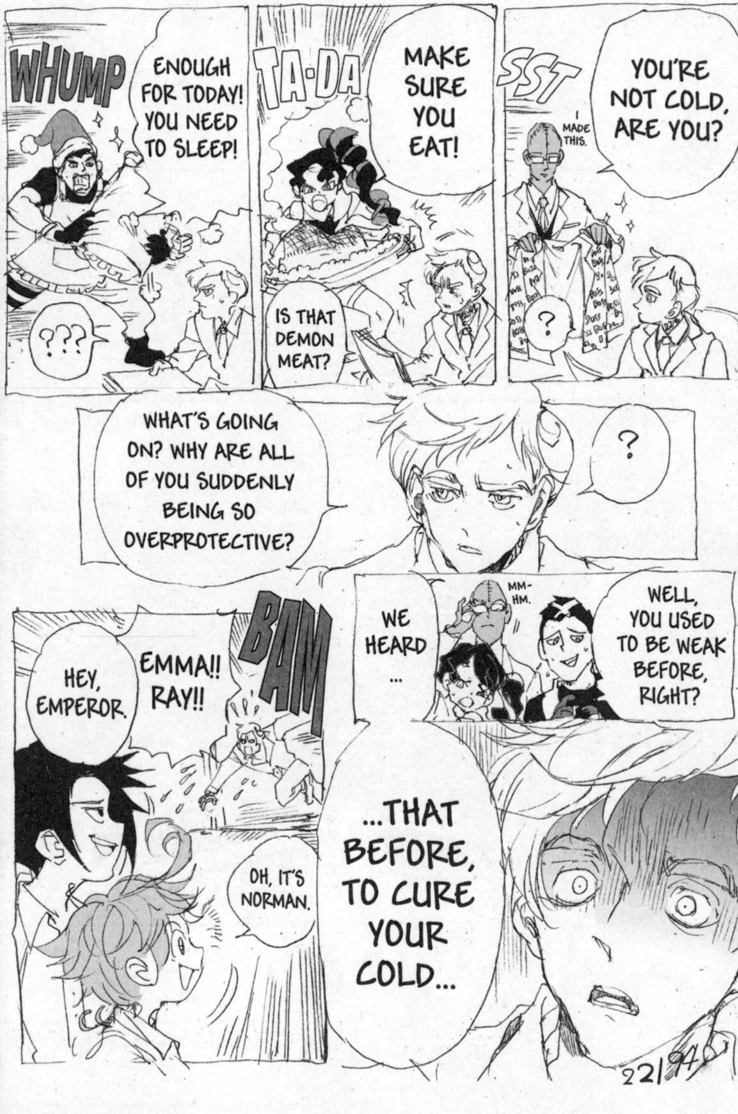
SST
I MADE THIS.
YOU'RE NOT COLD, ARE YOU?
?
TA-DA
MAKE SURE YOU EAT!
IS THAT DEMON MEAT?
WHUMP
ENOUGH FOR TODAY! YOU NEED TO SLEEP!
???
?
WHAT'S GOING ON? WHY ARE ALL OF YOU SUDDENLY BEING SO OVERPROTECTIVE?
WELL, YOU USED TO BE WEAK BEFORE, RIGHT?
MM-HM.
WE HEARD ...
...THAT BEFORE, TO CURE YOUR COLD...
BAM
EMMA!! RAY!!
HEY, EMPEROR.
OH, IT'S NORMAN.

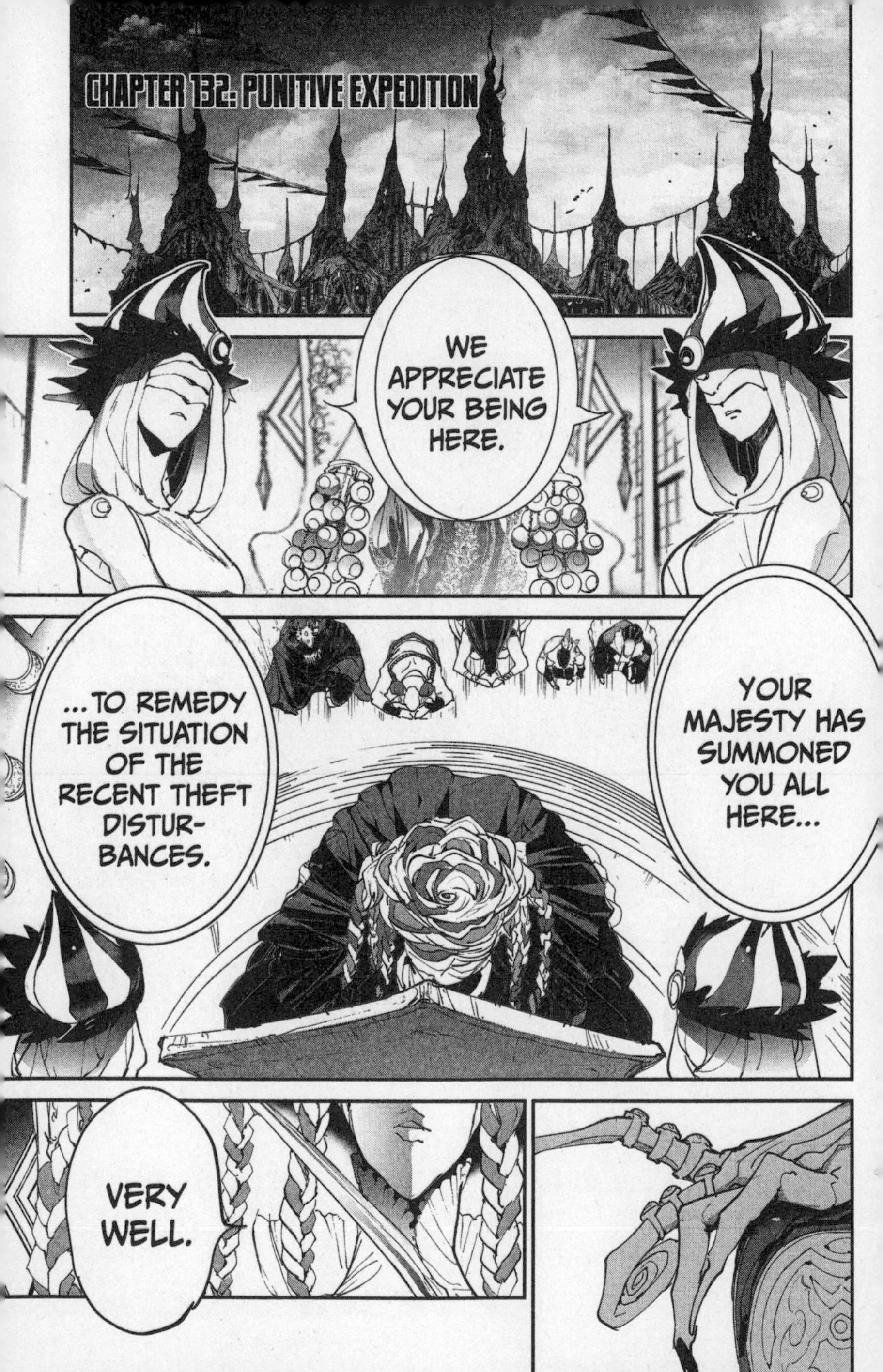
CHAPTER 132: PUNITIVE EXPEDITION
WE APPRECIATE YOUR BEING HERE.
YOUR MAJESTY HAS SUMMONED YOU ALL HERE...
...TO REMEDY THE SITUATION OF THE RECENT THEFT DISTUR- BANCES.
VERY WELL.

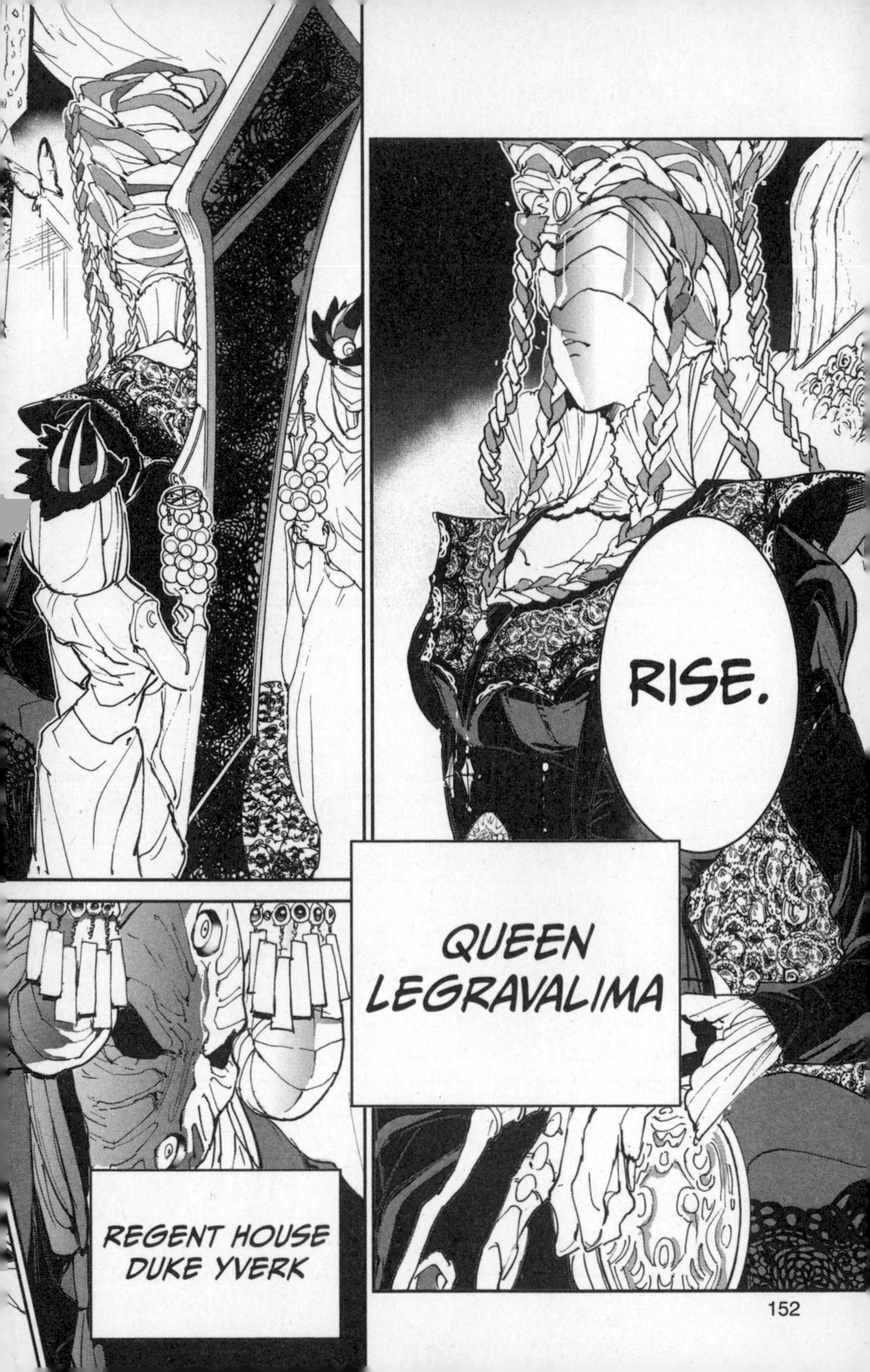
RISE.
QUEEN LEGRAVALIMA
REGENT HOUSE DUKE YVERK

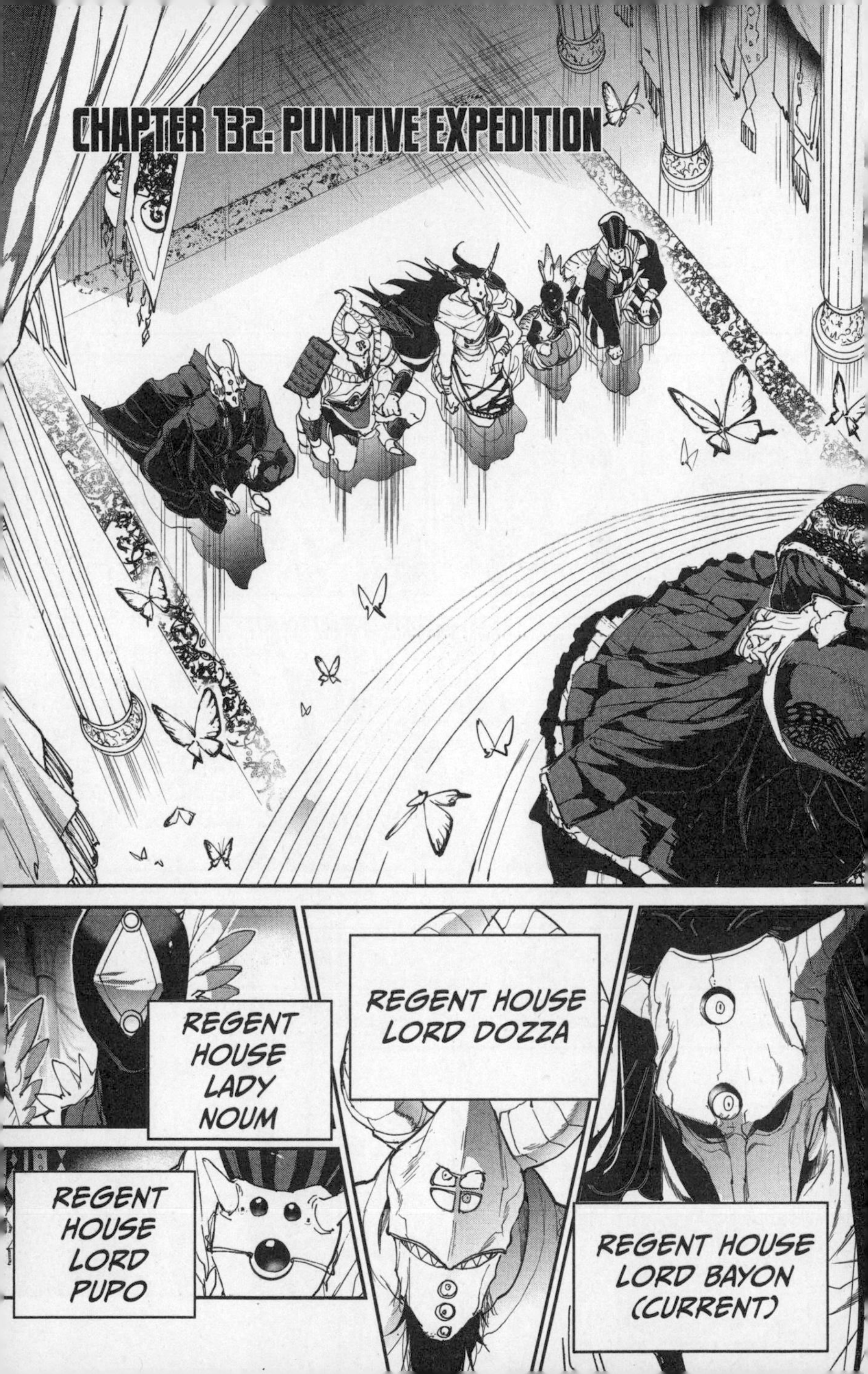
CHAPTER 132: PUNITIVE EXPEDITION
REGENT HOUSE LORD BAYON (CURRENT)
REGENT HOUSE LORD DOZZA
REGENT HOUSE LADY NOUM
REGENT HOUSE LORD PUPO

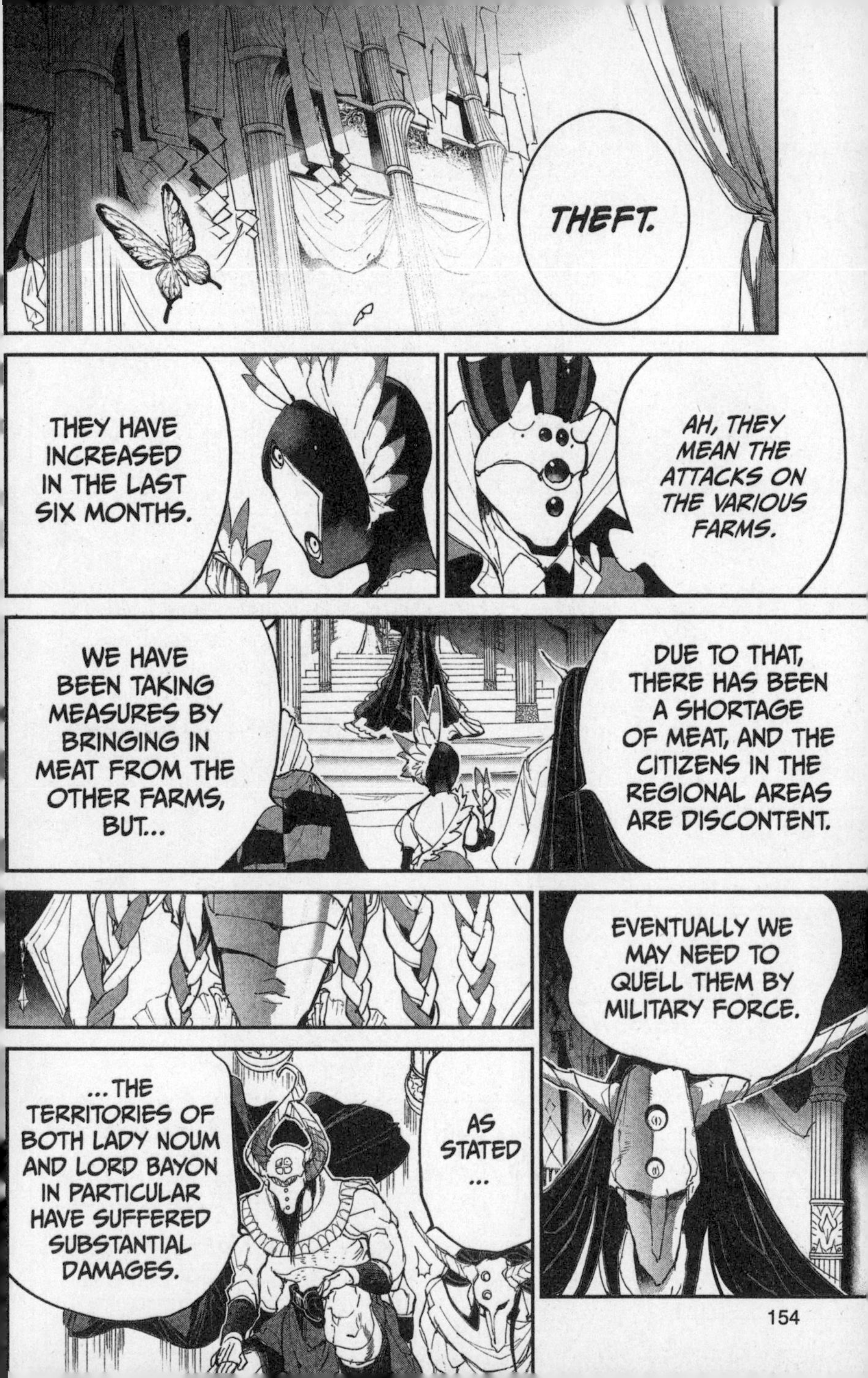
THEFT.
AH, THEY MEAN THE ATTACKS ON THE VARIOUS FARMS.
THEY HAVE INCREASED IN THE LAST SIX MONTHS.
DUE TO THAT, THERE HAS BEEN A SHORTAGE OF MEAT, AND THE CITIZENS IN THE REGIONAL AREAS ARE DISCONTENT.
WE HAVE BEEN TAKING MEASURES BY BRINGING IN MEAT FROM THE OTHER FARMS, BUT...
EVENTUALLY WE MAY NEED TO QUELL THEM BY MILITARY FORCE.
AS STATED ...
...THE TERRITORIES OF BOTH LADY NOUM AND LORD BAYON IN PARTICULAR HAVE SUFFERED SUBSTANTIAL DAMAGES.

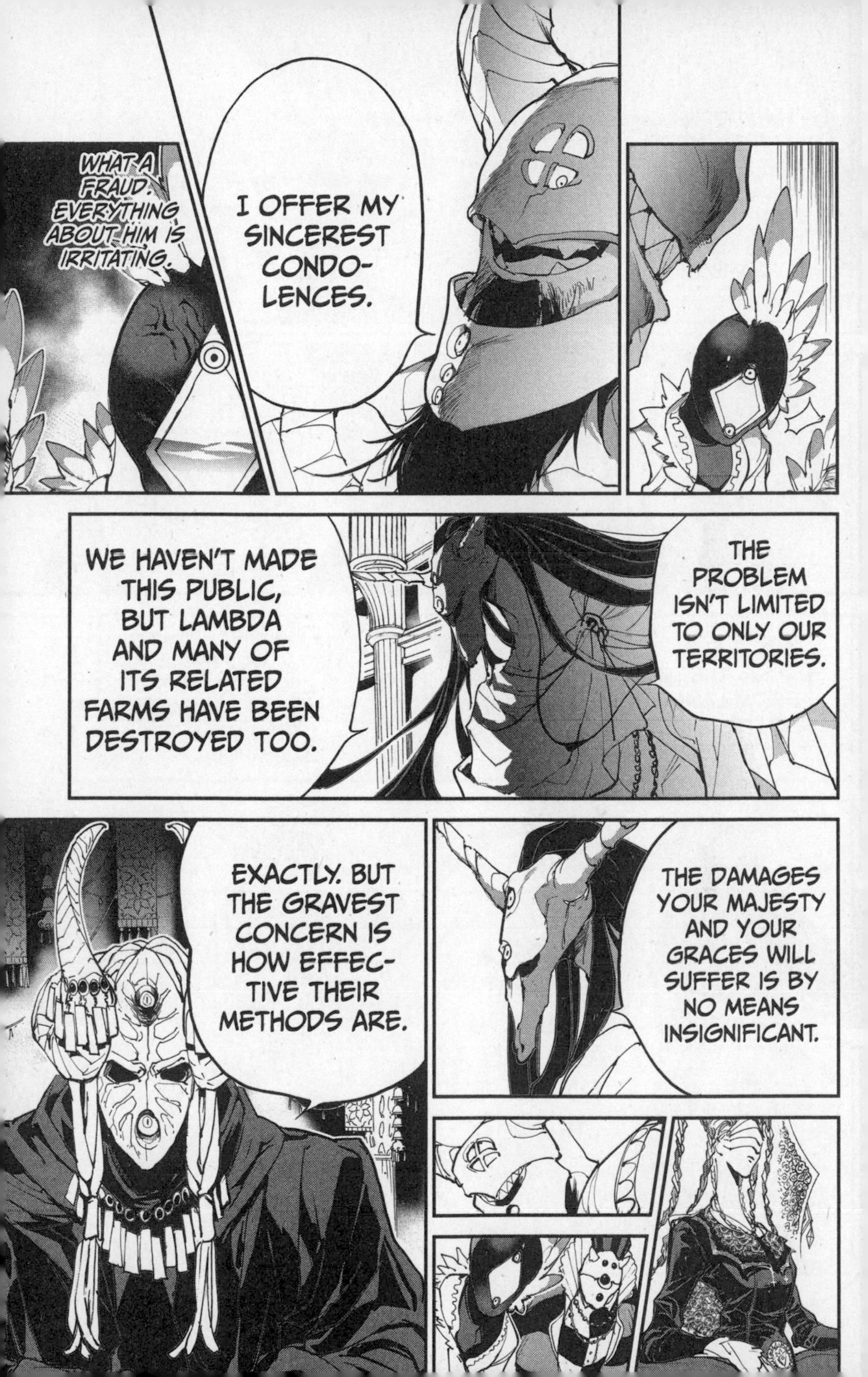
I OFFER MY SINCEREST CONDOLENCES.
WHAT A FRAUD. EVERYTHING ABOUT HIM IS IRRITATING.
THE PROBLEM ISN'T LIMITED TO ONLY OUR TERRITORIES.
WE HAVEN'T MADE THIS PUBLIC, BUT LAMBDA AND MANY OF ITS RELATED FARMS HAVE BEEN DESTROYED TOO.
THE DAMAGES YOUR MAJESTY AND YOUR GRACES WILL SUFFER IS BY NO MEANS INSIGNIFICANT.
EXACTLY. BUT THE GRAVEST CONCERN IS HOW EFFECTIVE THEIR METHODS ARE.

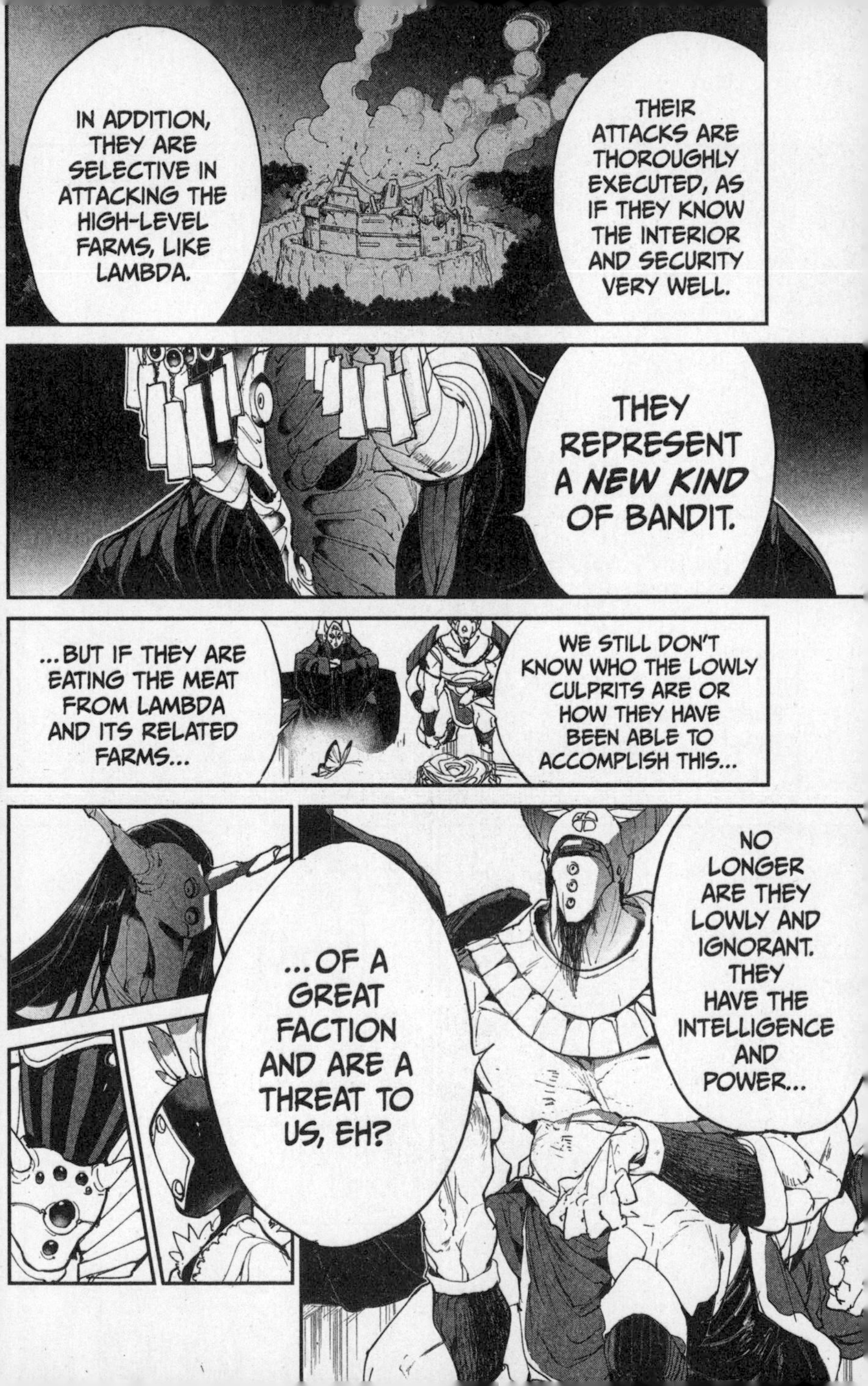
THEIR ATTACKS ARE THOROUGHLY EXECUTED, AS IF THEY KNOW THE INTERIOR AND SECURITY VERY WELL.
IN ADDITION, THEY ARE SELECTIVE IN ATTACKING THE HIGH-LEVEL FARMS, LIKE LAMBDA.
THEY REPRESENT A *NEW KIND* OF BANDIT.
WE STILL DON'T KNOW WHO THE LOWLY CULPRITS ARE OR HOW THEY HAVE BEEN ABLE TO ACCOMPLISH THIS...
...BUT IF THEY ARE EATING THE MEAT FROM LAMBDA AND ITS RELATED FARMS...
NO LONGER ARE THEY LOWLY AND IGNORANT. THEY HAVE THE INTELLIGENCE AND POWER...
...OF A GREAT FACTION AND ARE A THREAT TO US, EH?

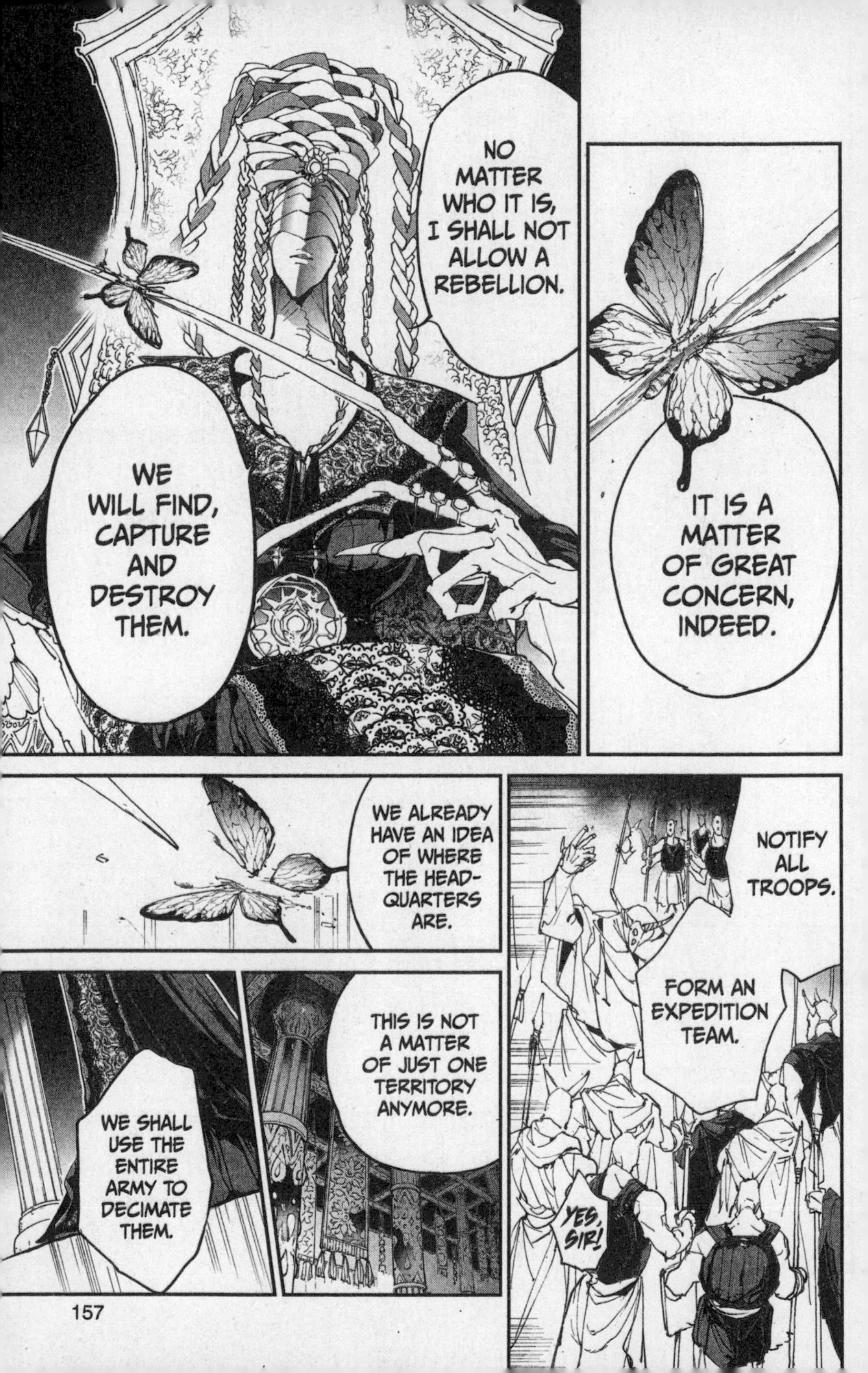
IT IS A MATTER OF GREAT CONCERN, INDEED.
NO MATTER WHO IT IS, I SHALL NOT ALLOW A REBELLION.
WE WILL FIND, CAPTURE AND DESTROY THEM.
NOTIFY ALL TROOPS.
FORM AN EXPEDITION TEAM.
YES, SIR!
WE ALREADY HAVE AN IDEA OF WHERE THE HEAD-QUARTERS ARE.
THIS IS NOT A MATTER OF JUST ONE TERRITORY ANYMORE.
WE SHALL USE THE ENTIRE ARMY TO DECIMATE THEM.

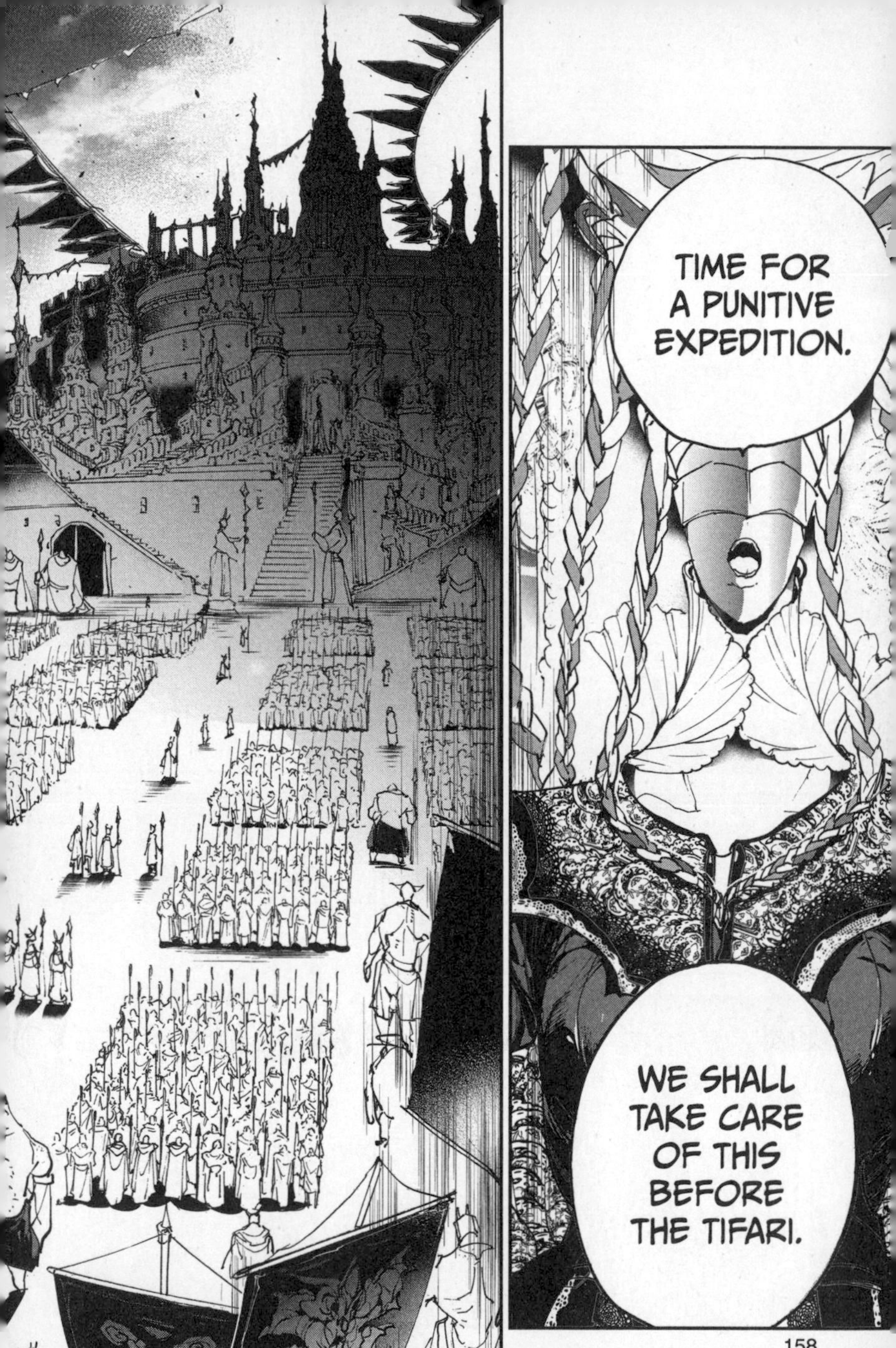
TIME FOR A PUNITIVE EXPEDITION.
WE SHALL TAKE CARE OF THIS BEFORE THE TIFARI.

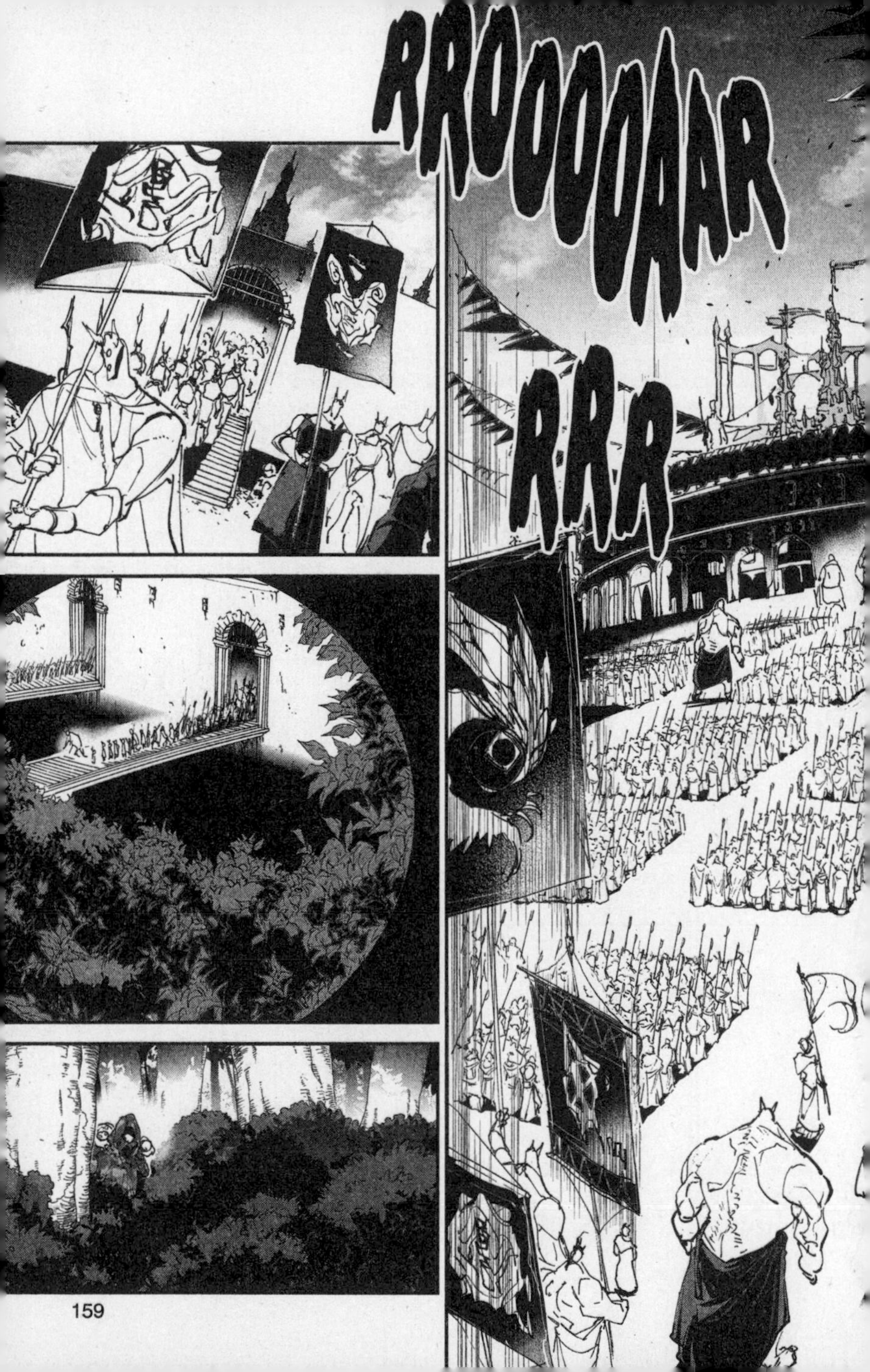
RROOOOAAR
RRR

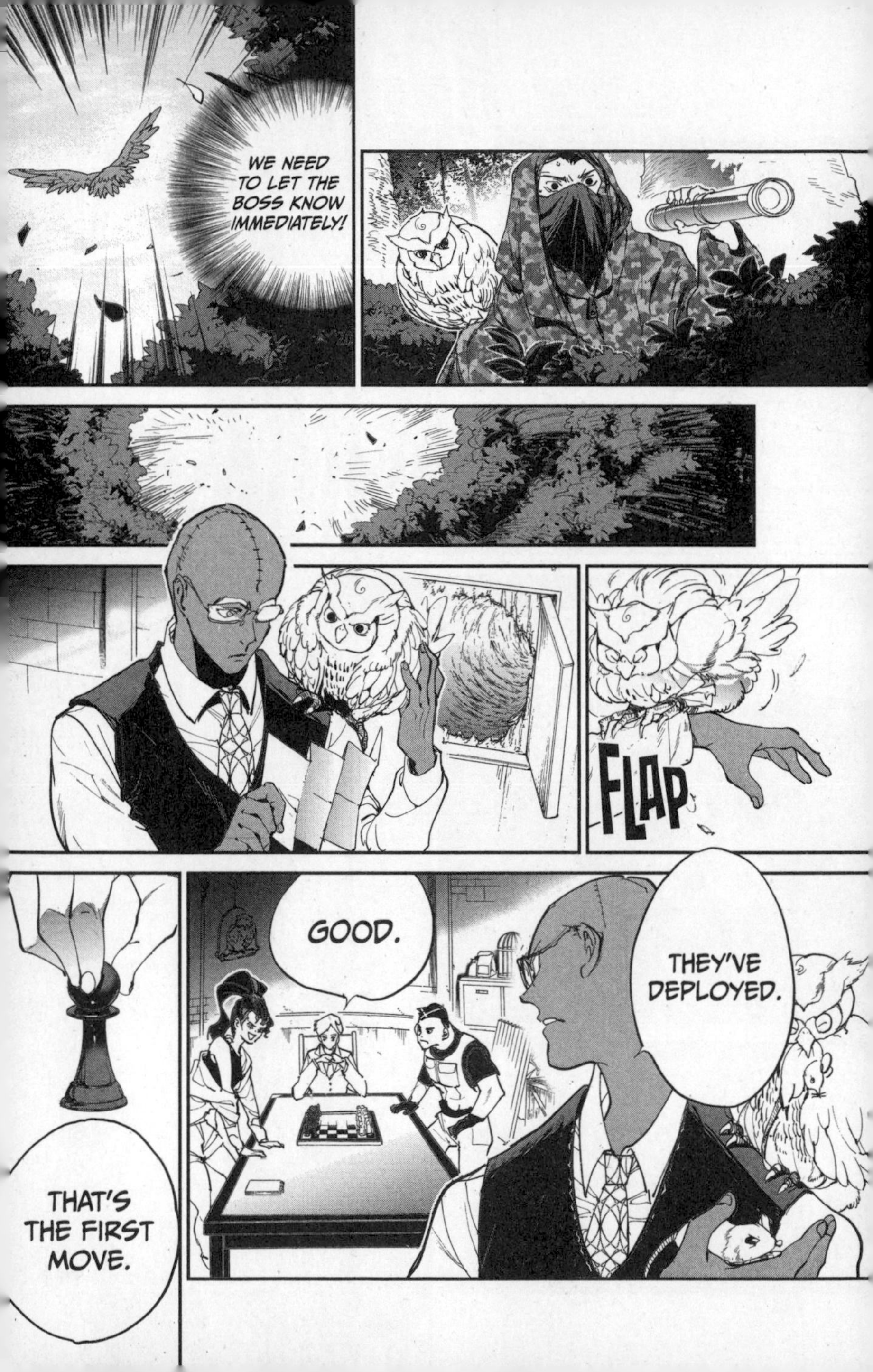
WE NEED TO LET THE BOSS KNOW IMMEDIATELY!
FLAP
THEY'VE DEPLOYED.
GOOD.
THAT'S THE FIRST MOVE.

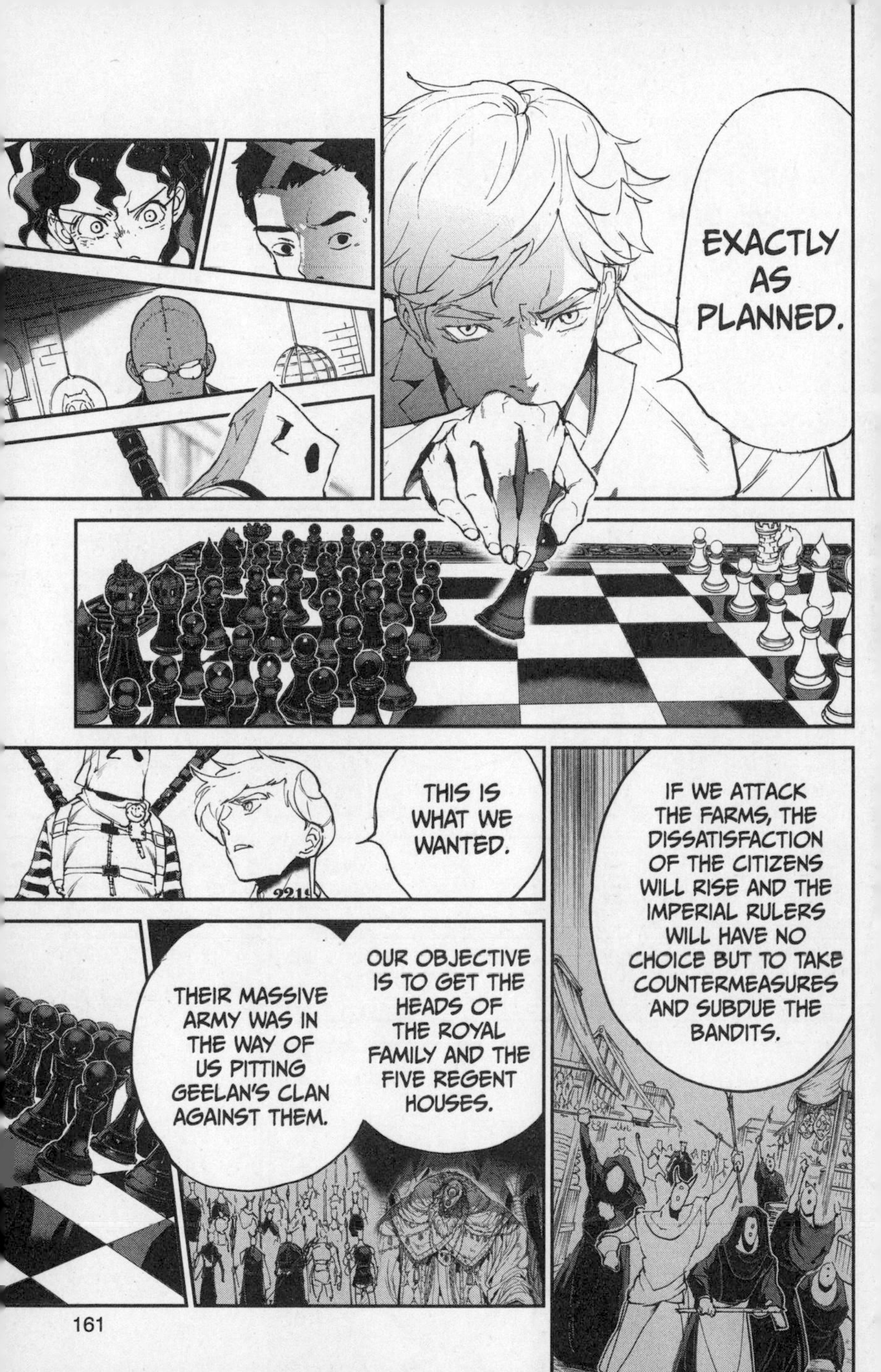
EXACTLY AS PLANNED.
IF WE ATTACK THE FARMS, THE DISSATISFACTION OF THE CITIZENS WILL RISE AND THE IMPERIAL RULERS WILL HAVE NO CHOICE BUT TO TAKE COUNTERMEASURES AND SUBDUE THE BANDITS.
THIS IS WHAT WE WANTED.
OUR OBJECTIVE IS TO GET THE HEADS OF THE ROYAL FAMILY AND THE FIVE REGENT HOUSES.
THEIR MASSIVE ARMY WAS IN THE WAY OF US PITTING GEELAN'S CLAN AGAINST THEM.

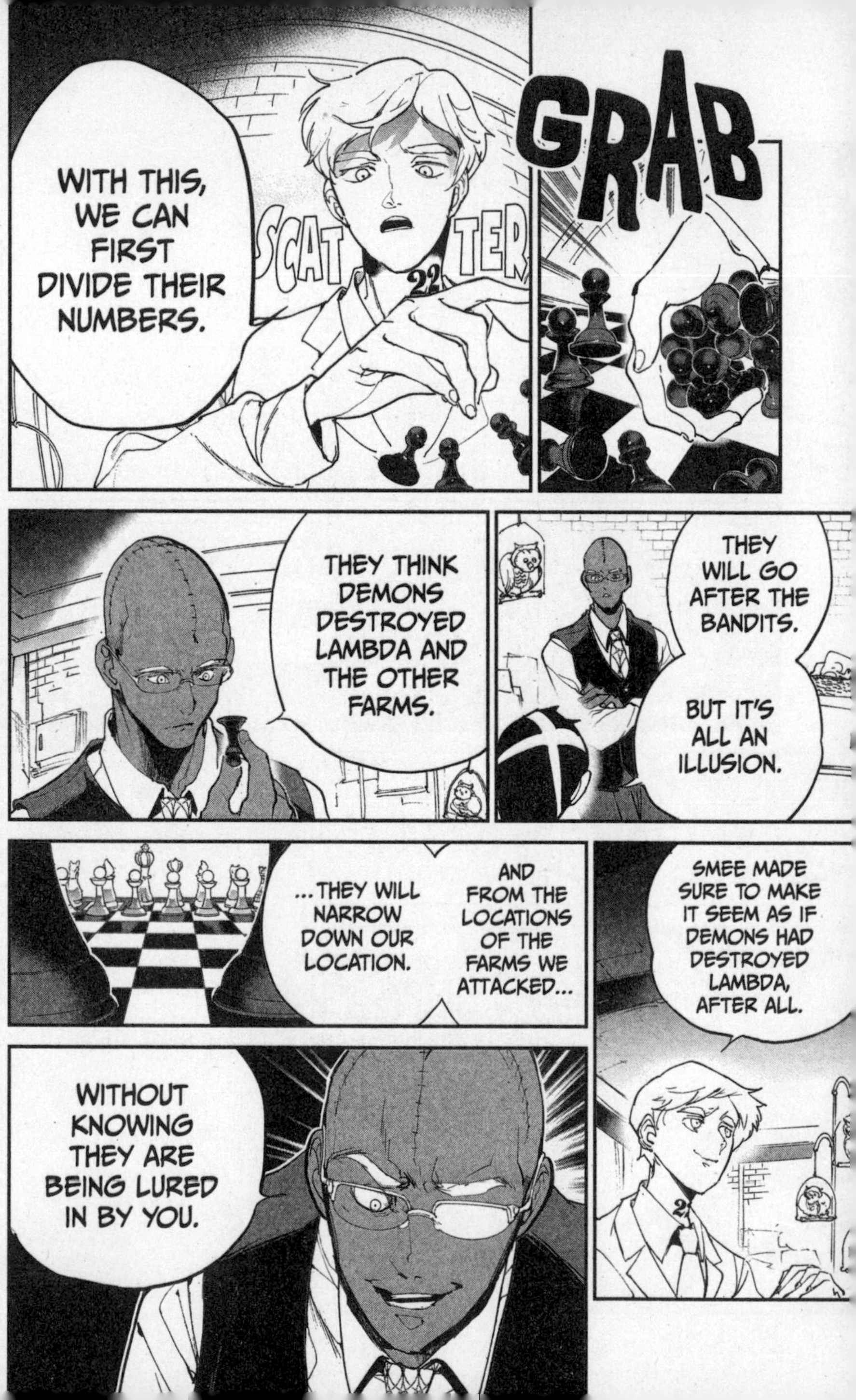
GRAB
WITH THIS, WE CAN FIRST DIVIDE THEIR NUMBERS.
SCAT TER
THEY WILL GO AFTER THE BANDITS.
BUT IT'S ALL AN ILLUSION.
THEY THINK DEMONS DESTROYED LAMBDA AND THE OTHER FARMS.
SMEE MADE SURE TO MAKE IT SEEM AS IF DEMONS HAD DESTROYED LAMBDA, AFTER ALL.
AND FROM THE LOCATIONS OF THE FARMS WE ATTACKED...
...THEY WILL NARROW DOWN OUR LOCATION.
WITHOUT KNOWING THEY ARE BEING LURED IN BY YOU.

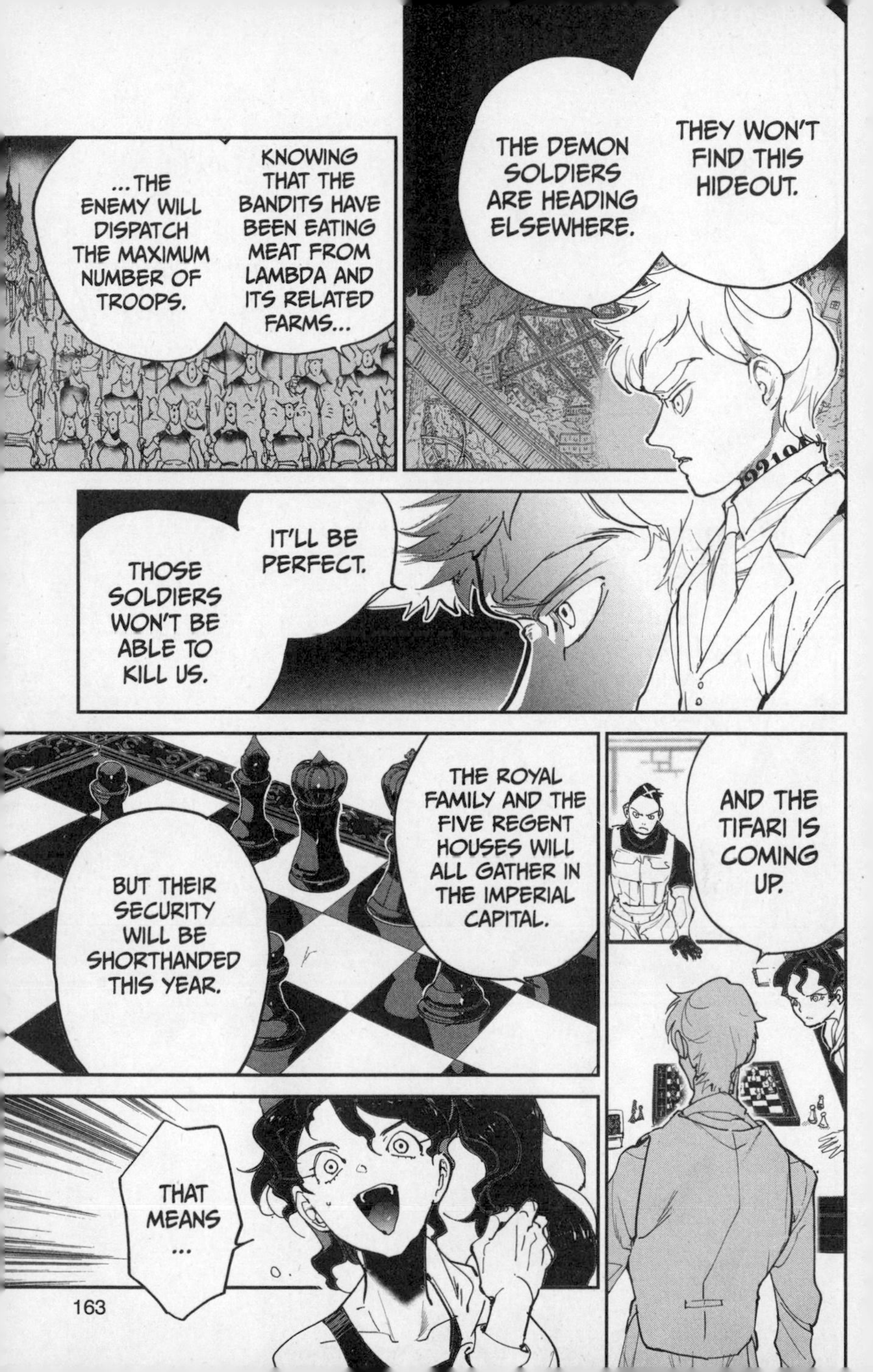
THEY WON'T FIND THIS HIDEOUT.
THE DEMON SOLDIERS ARE HEADING ELSEWHERE.
KNOWING THAT THE BANDITS HAVE BEEN EATING MEAT FROM LAMBDA AND ITS RELATED FARMS...
...THE ENEMY WILL DISPATCH THE MAXIMUM NUMBER OF TROOPS.
IT'LL BE PERFECT.
THOSE SOLDIERS WON'T BE ABLE TO KILL US.
AND THE TIFARI IS COMING UP.
THE ROYAL FAMILY AND THE FIVE REGENT HOUSES WILL ALL GATHER IN THE IMPERIAL CAPITAL.
BUT THEIR SECURITY WILL BE SHORTHANDED THIS YEAR.
THAT MEANS ...

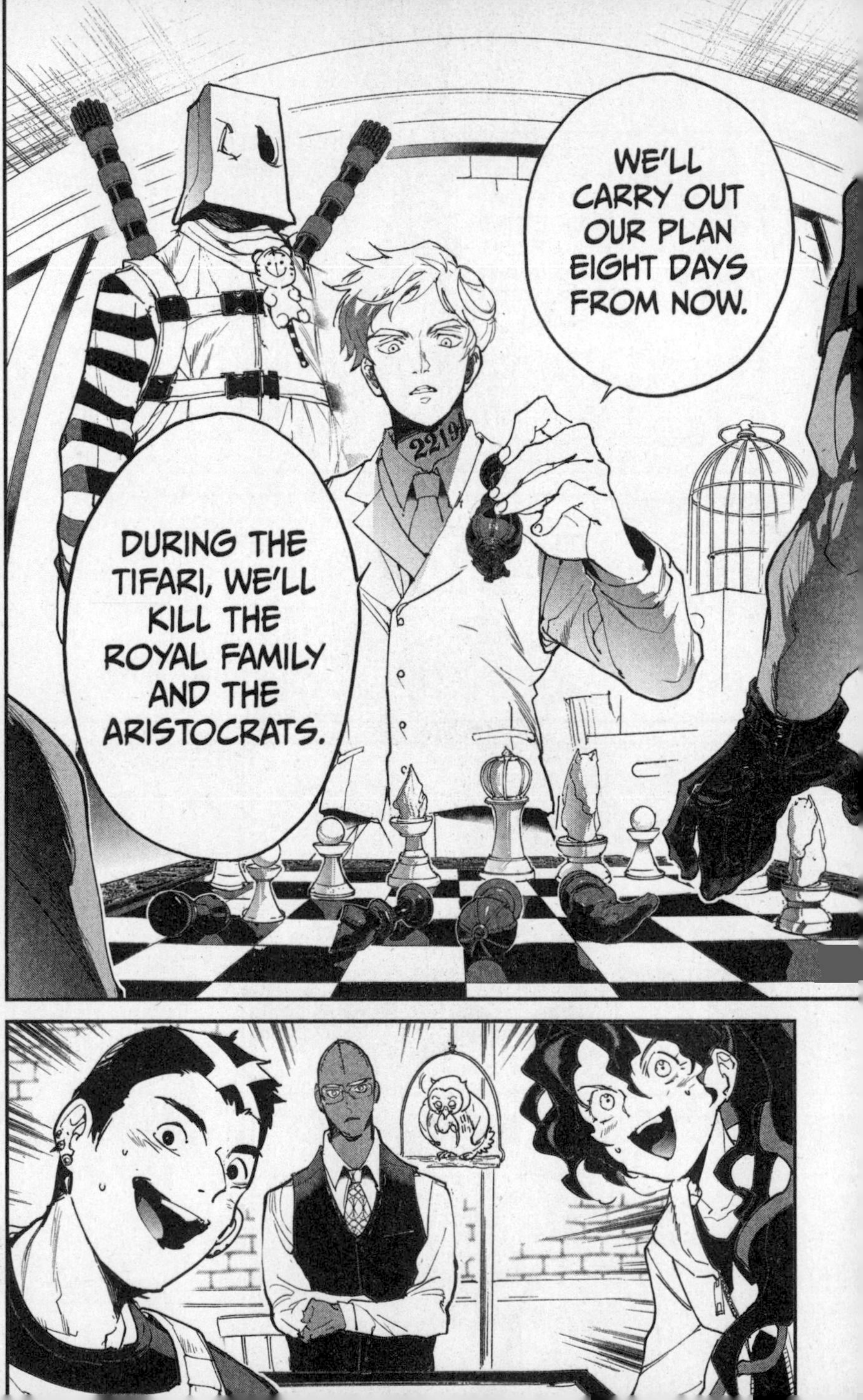
WE'LL CARRY OUT OUR PLAN EIGHT DAYS FROM NOW.
DURING THE TIFARI, WE'LL KILL THE ROYAL FAMILY AND THE ARISTOCRATS.

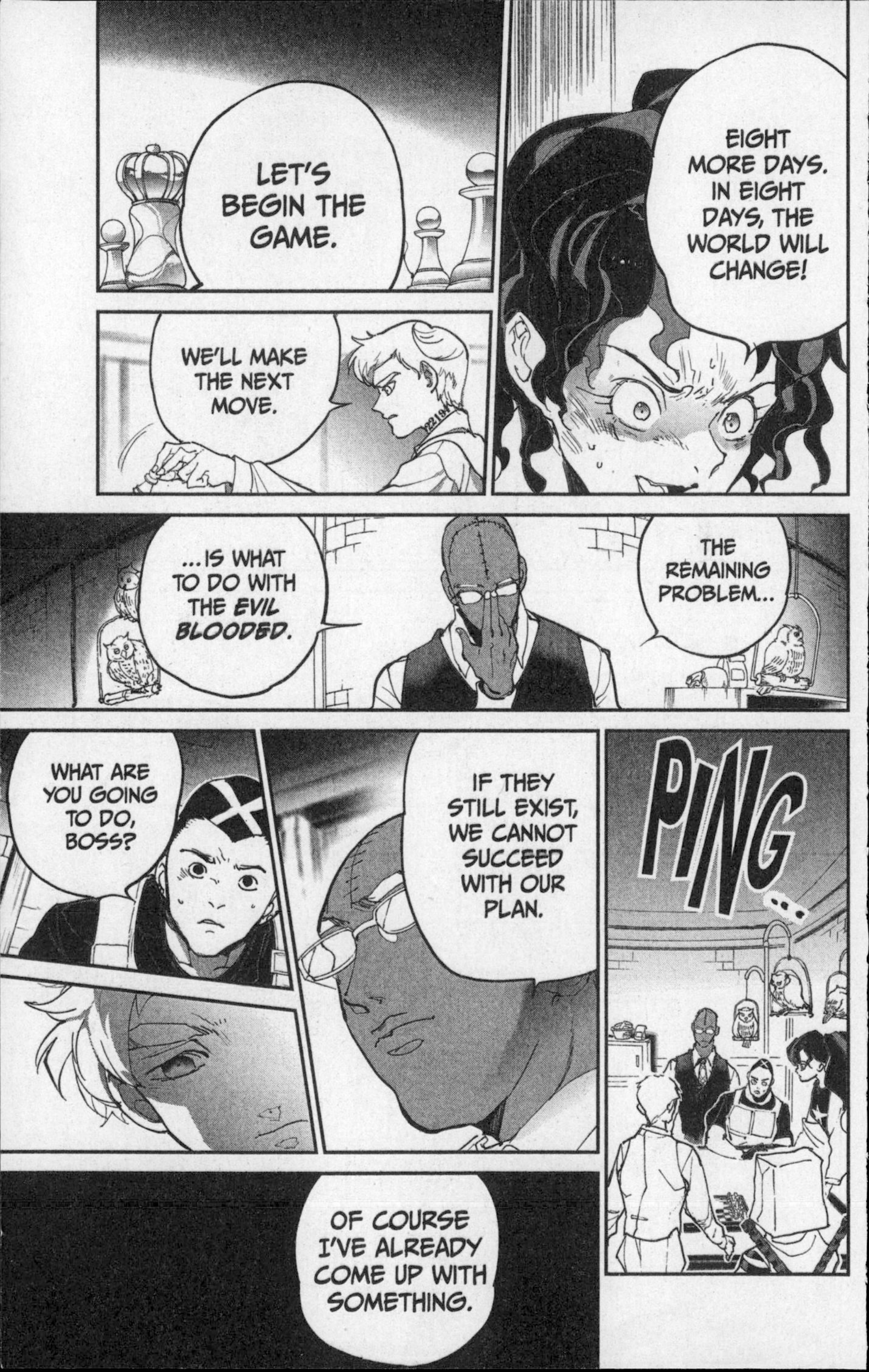
EIGHT MORE DAYS. IN EIGHT DAYS, THE WORLD WILL CHANGE!
LET'S BEGIN THE GAME.
WE'LL MAKE THE NEXT MOVE.
THE REMAINING PROBLEM...
...IS WHAT TO DO WITH THE *EVIL BLOODED*.
PING...
IF THEY STILL EXIST, WE CANNOT SUCCEED WITH OUR PLAN.
WHAT ARE YOU GOING TO DO, BOSS?
OF COURSE I'VE ALREADY COME UP WITH SOMETHING.

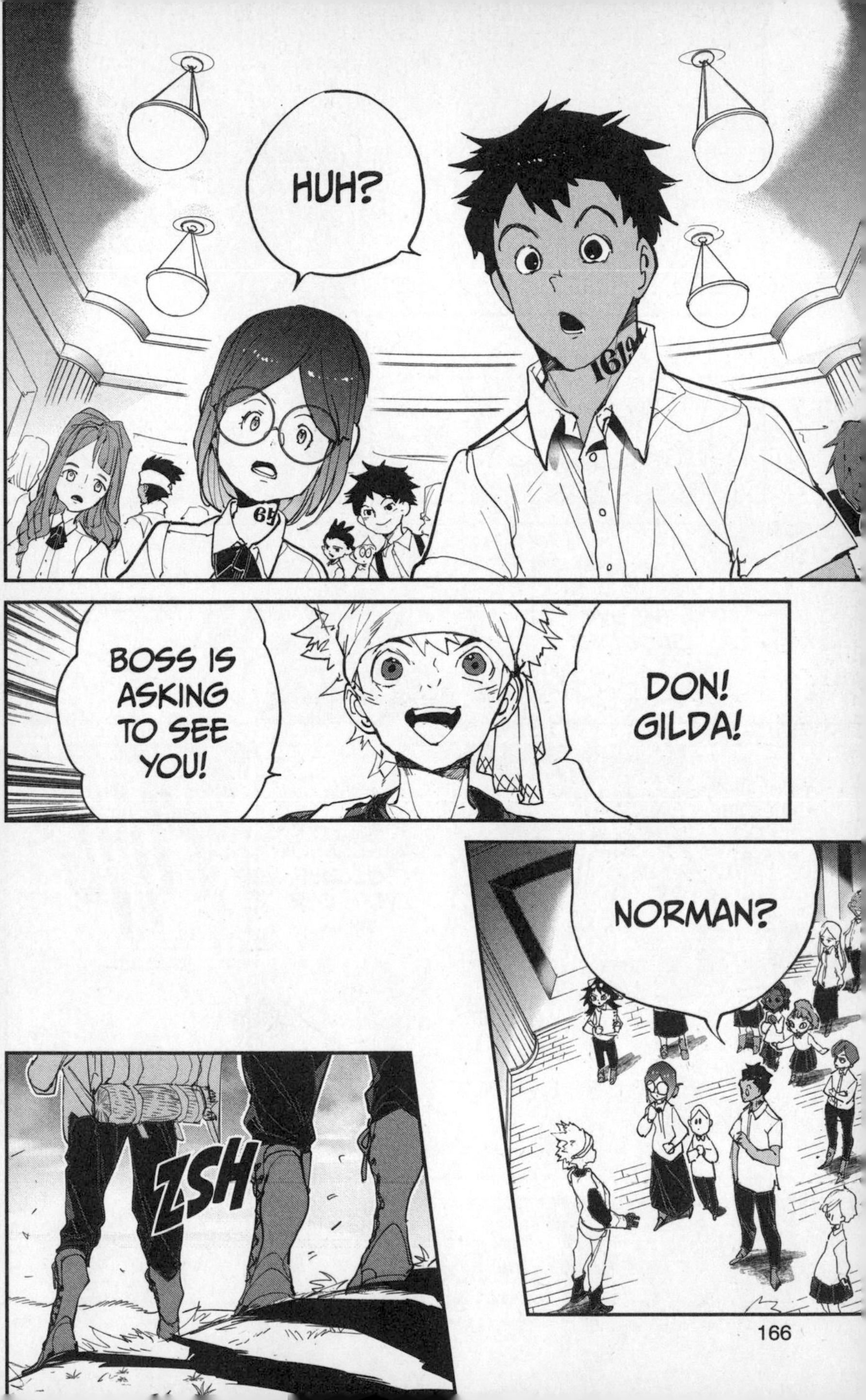
HUH?
DON! GILDA!
BOSS IS ASKING TO SEE YOU!
NORMAN?
ZSH

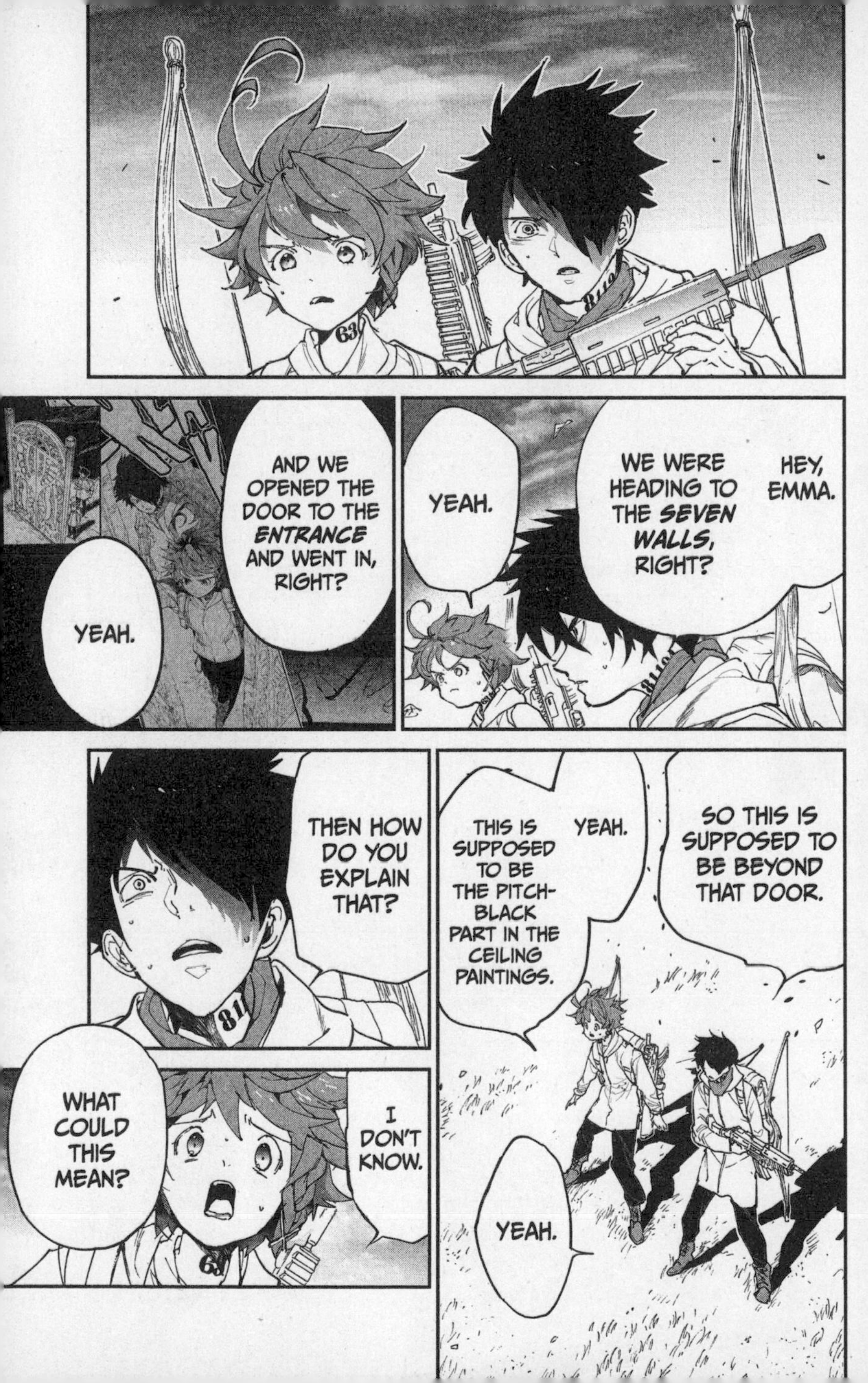
HEY, EMMA.
WE WERE HEADING TO THE *SEVEN WALLS,* RIGHT?
YEAH.
AND WE OPENED THE DOOR TO THE *ENTRANCE* AND WENT IN, RIGHT?
YEAH.
SO THIS IS SUPPOSED TO BE BEYOND THAT DOOR.
YEAH.
THIS IS SUPPOSED TO BE THE PITCH-BLACK PART IN THE CEILING PAINTINGS.
YEAH.
THEN HOW DO YOU EXPLAIN THAT?
I DON'T KNOW.
WHAT COULD THIS MEAN?

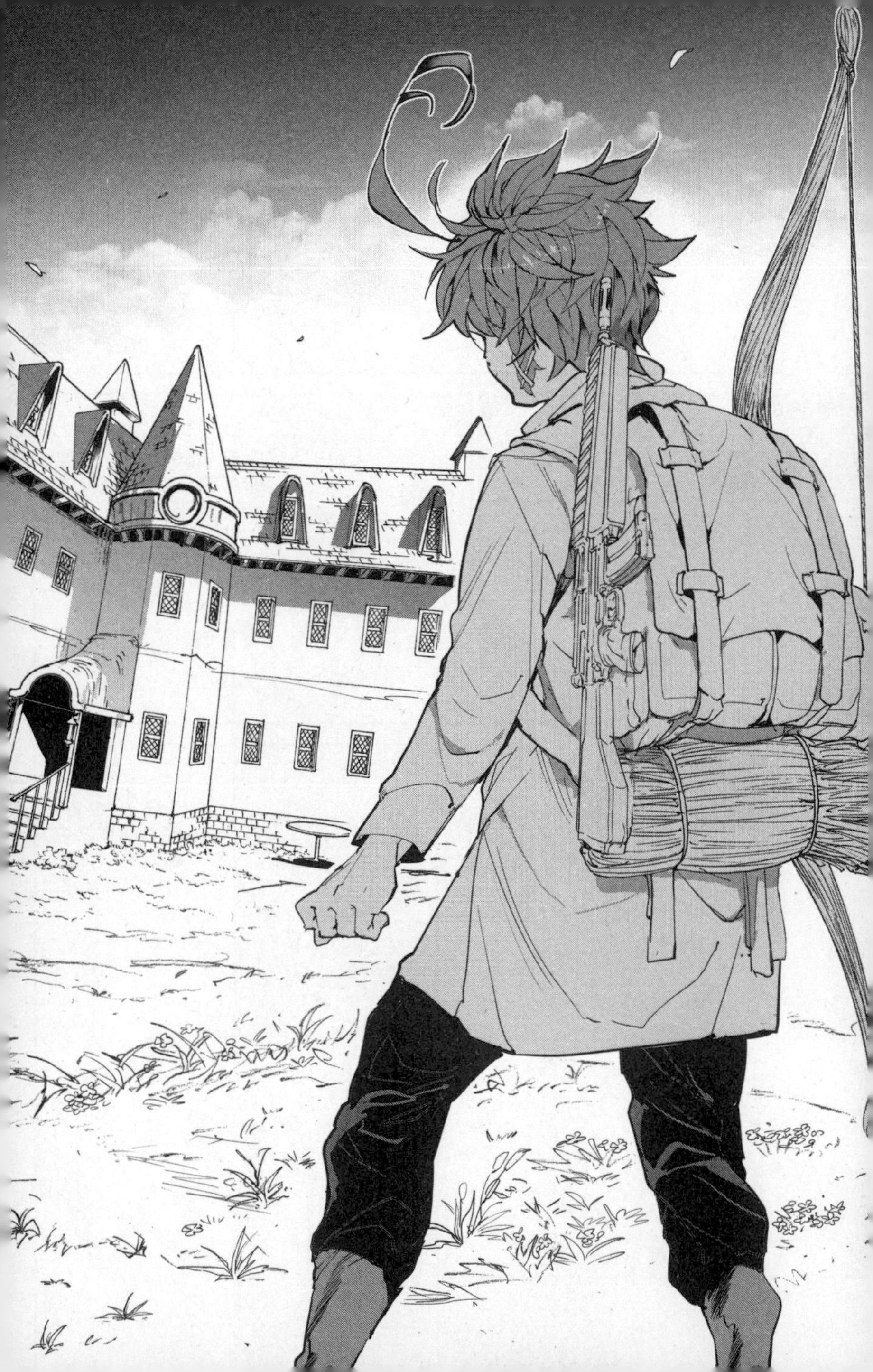

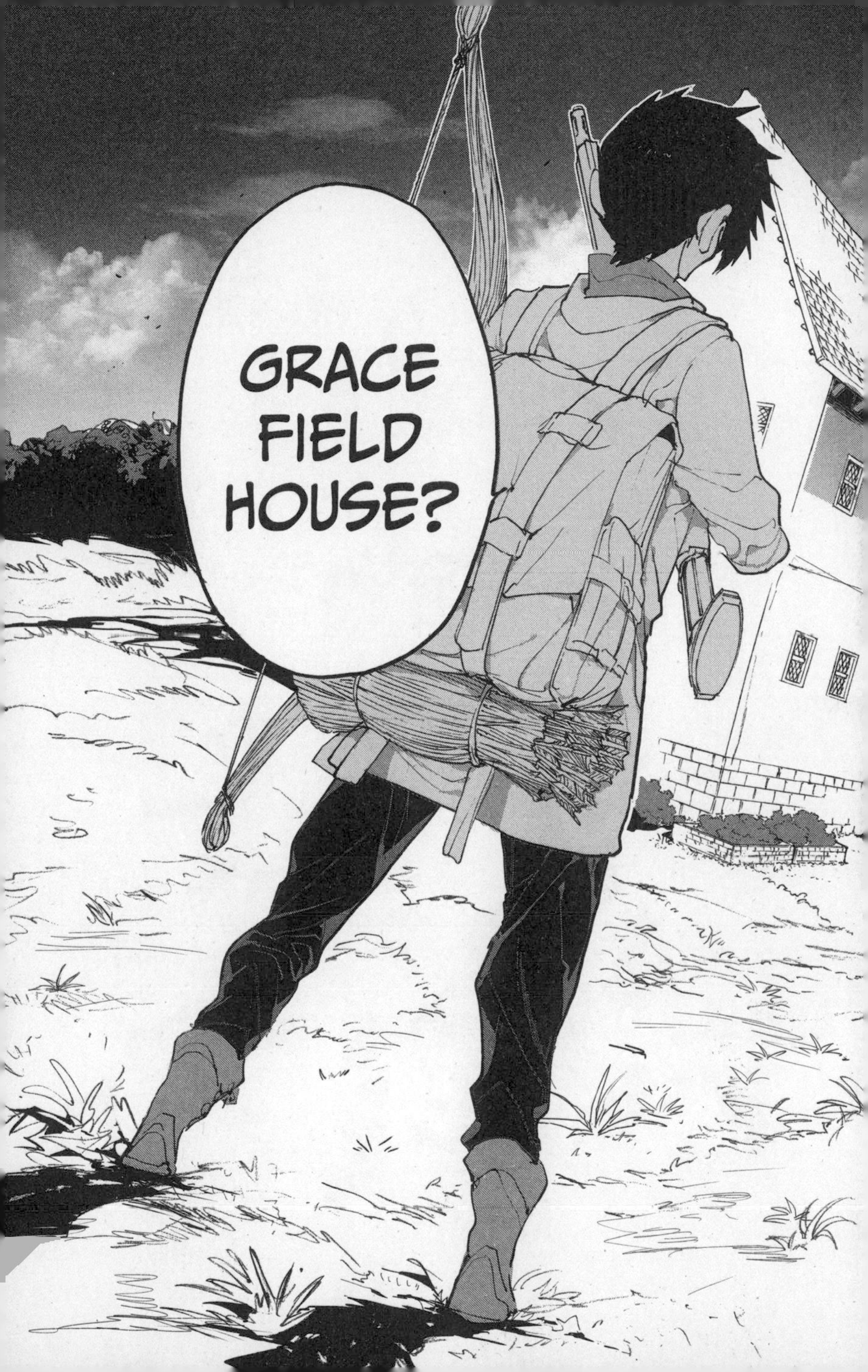
GRACE FIELD HOUSE?

THE PROMISED NEVERLAND SIDE SCENE 022

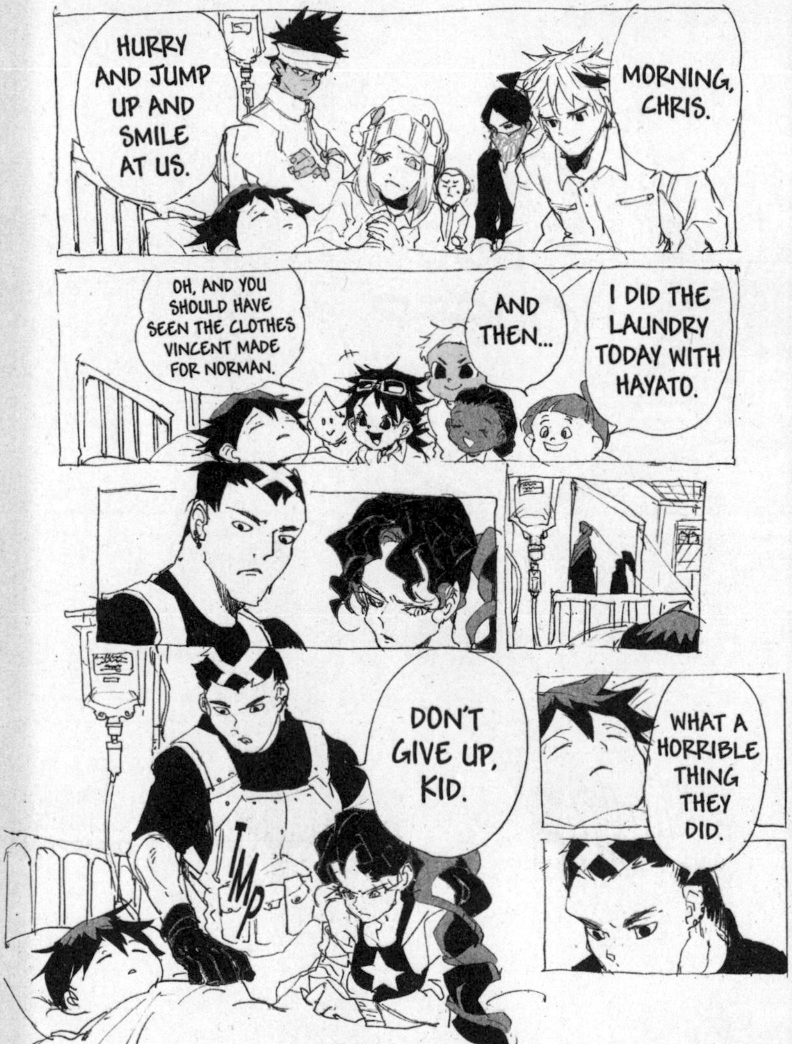
MORNING, CHRIS.
HURRY AND JUMP UP AND SMILE AT US.
I DID THE LAUNDRY TODAY WITH HAYATO.
AND THEN...
OH, AND YOU SHOULD HAVE SEEN THE CLOTHES VINCENT MADE FOR NORMAN.
WHAT A HORRIBLE THING THEY DID.
DON'T GIVE UP, KID.
TMP

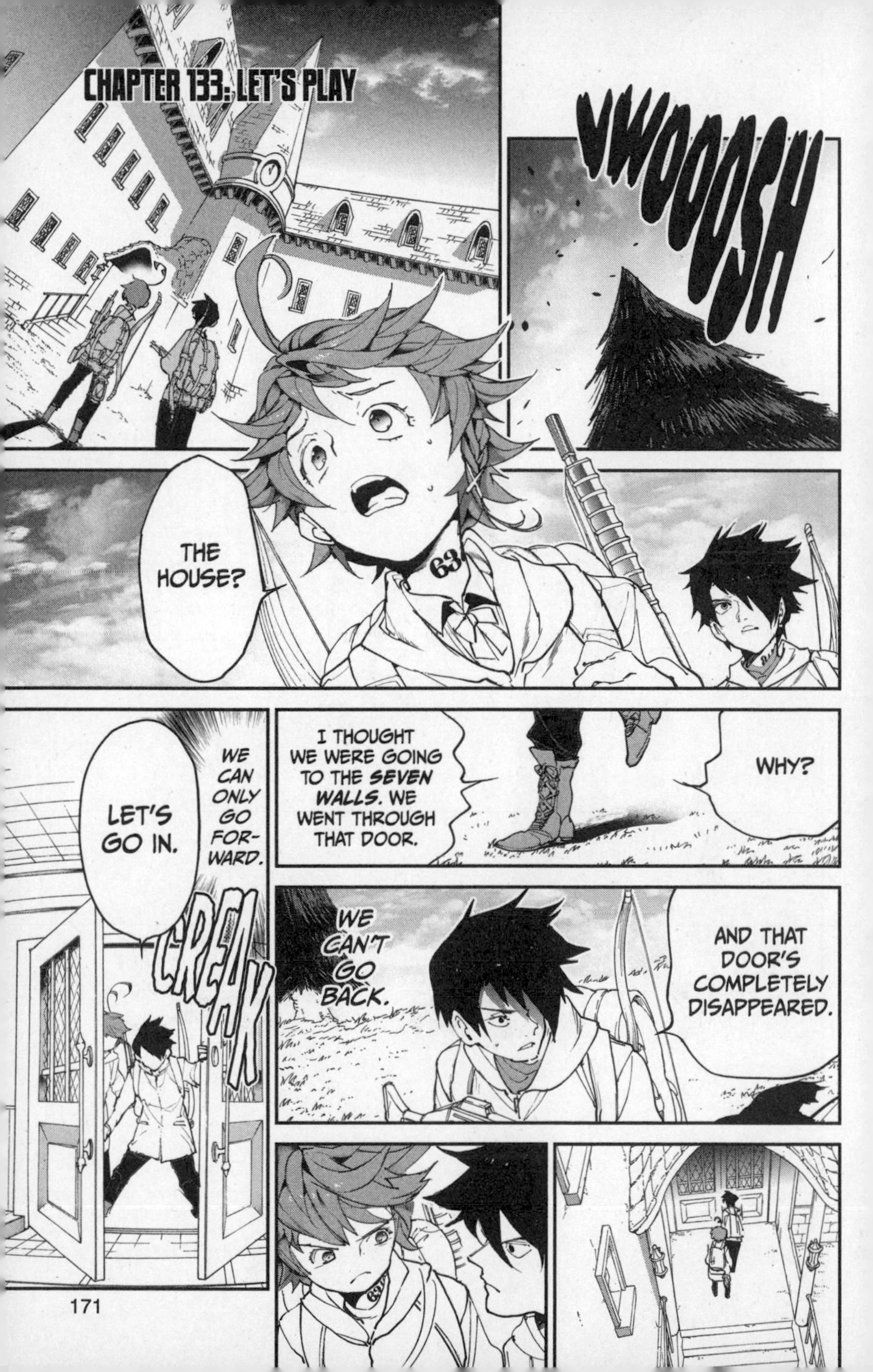
WOOOSH
CHAPTER 133: LET'S PLAY
THE HOUSE?
WHY?
I THOUGHT WE WERE GOING TO THE SEVEN WALLS. WE WENT THROUGH THAT DOOR.
AND THAT DOOR'S COMPLETELY DISAPPEARED.
WE CAN'T GO BACK.
WE CAN ONLY GO FOR-WARD.
LET'S GO IN.
CREAK

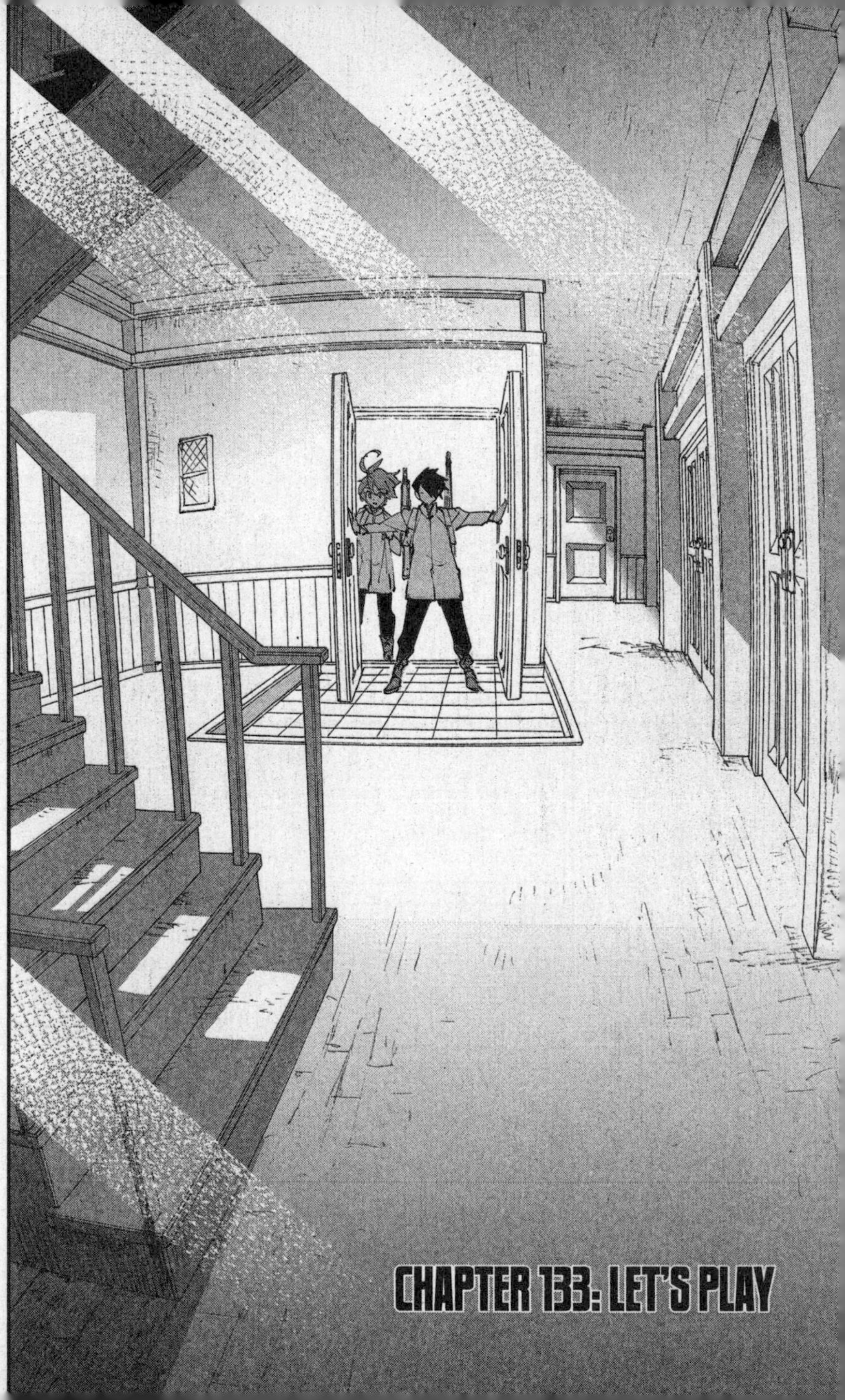
CHAPTER 133: LET'S PLAY

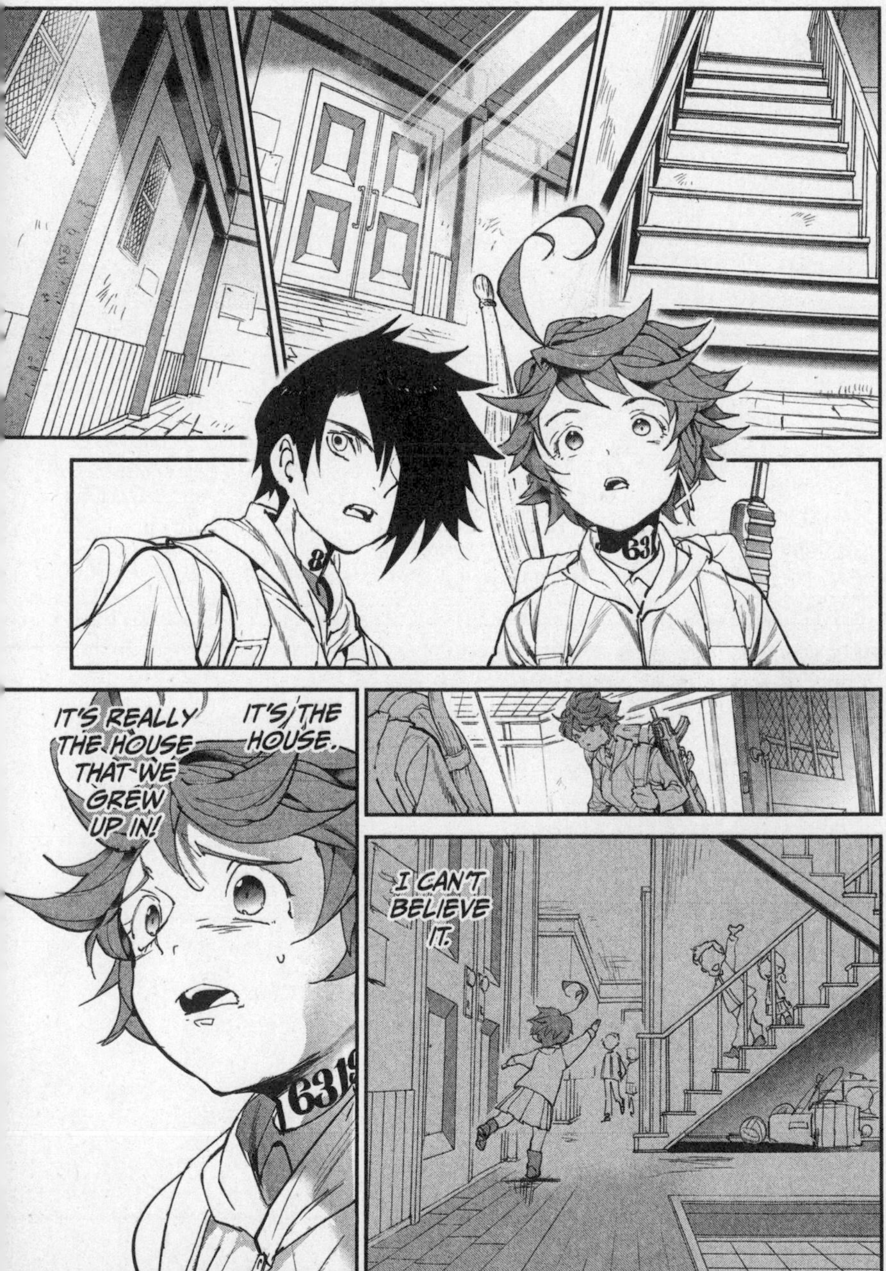
I CAN'T BELIEVE IT.
IT'S THE HOUSE.
IT'S REALLY THE HOUSE THAT WE GREW UP IN!

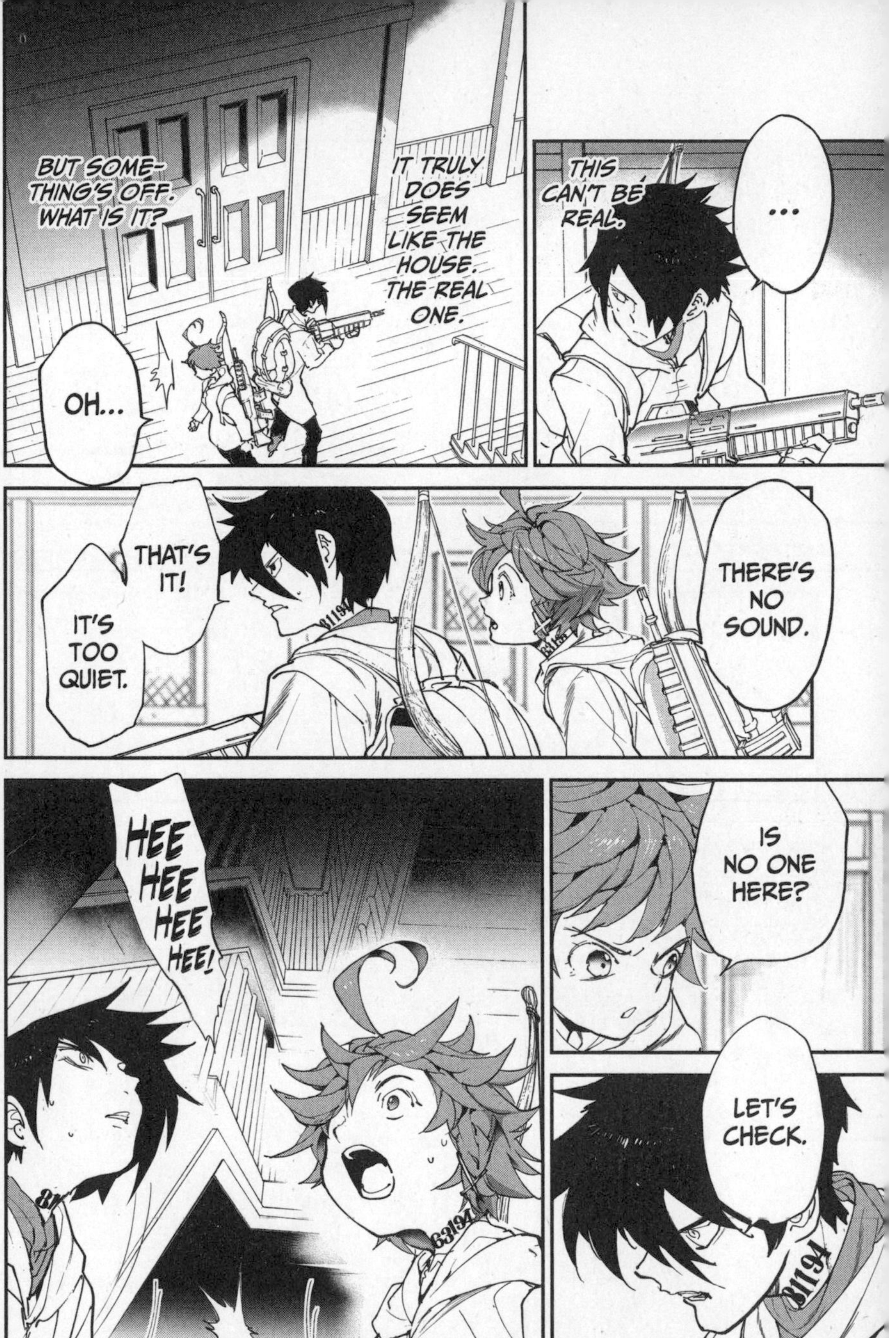
...
THIS CAN'T BE REAL.
IT TRULY DOES SEEM LIKE THE HOUSE. THE REAL ONE.
BUT SOMETHING'S OFF. WHAT IS IT?
OH...
THERE'S NO SOUND.
THAT'S IT!
IT'S TOO QUIET.
IS NO ONE HERE?
LET'S CHECK.
HEE HEE HEE HEE!

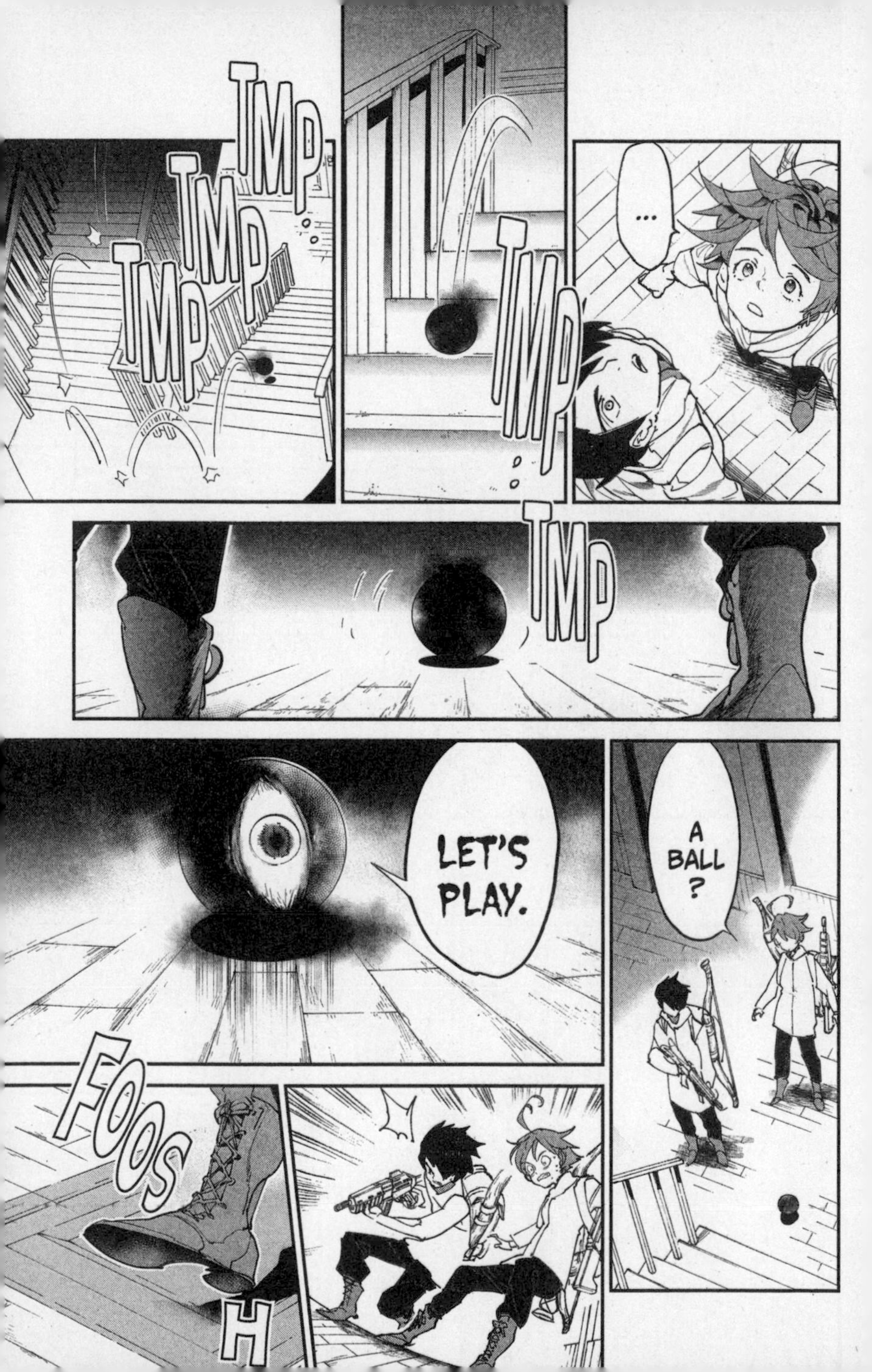
...
TMP
TMP
TMP
TMP
TMP
A BALL ?
LET'S PLAY.
FOOSH

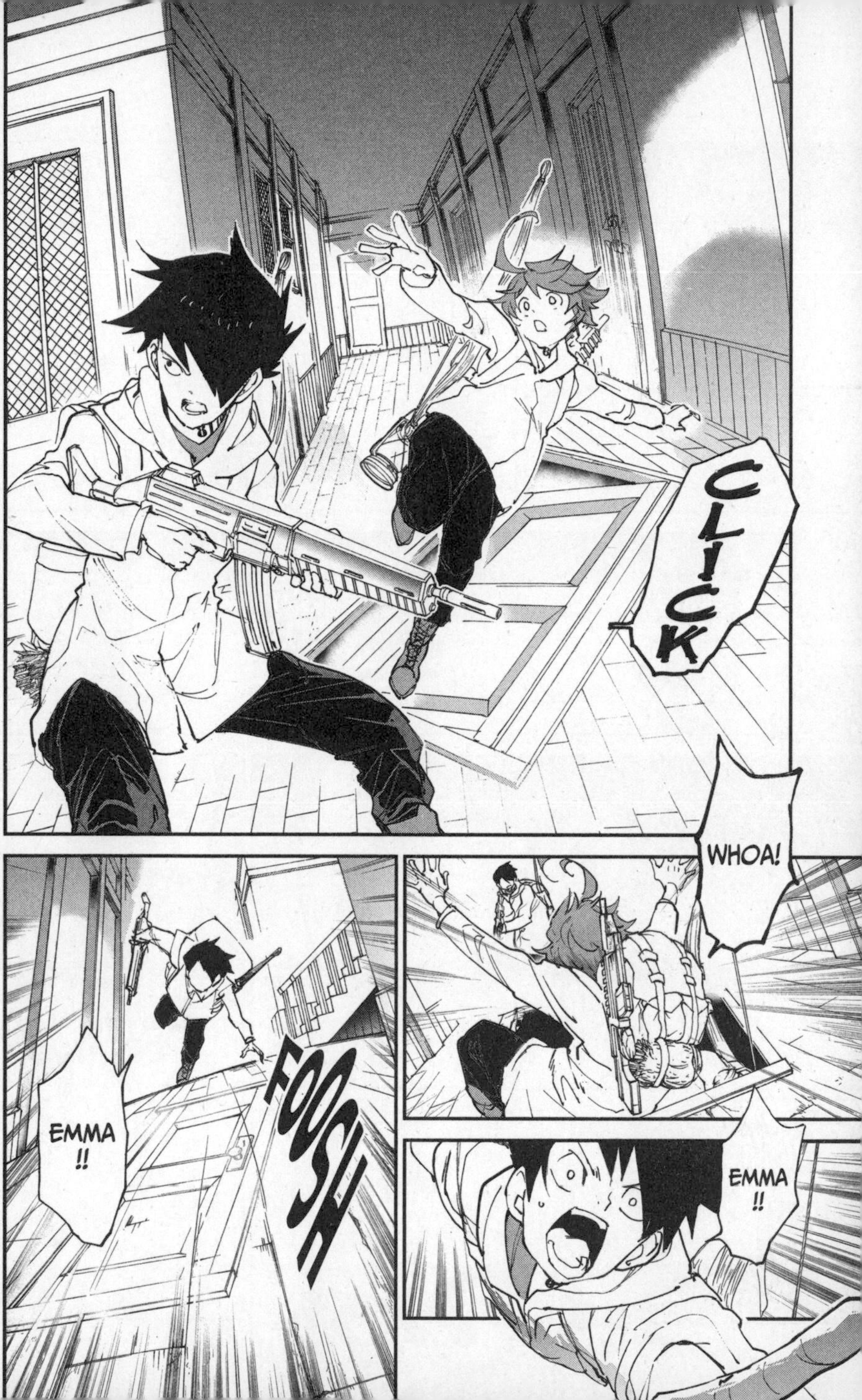
CLICK
WHOA!
EMMA!!
FOOSH
EMMA!!

HER VOICE IS COMING FROM THE SECOND FLOOR?!

RAY!

ANSWER IF YOU CAN HEAR ME!

WHERE ARE YOU?

EMMA!

WHAT'S GOING ON?

!!

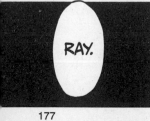

RAY.

177

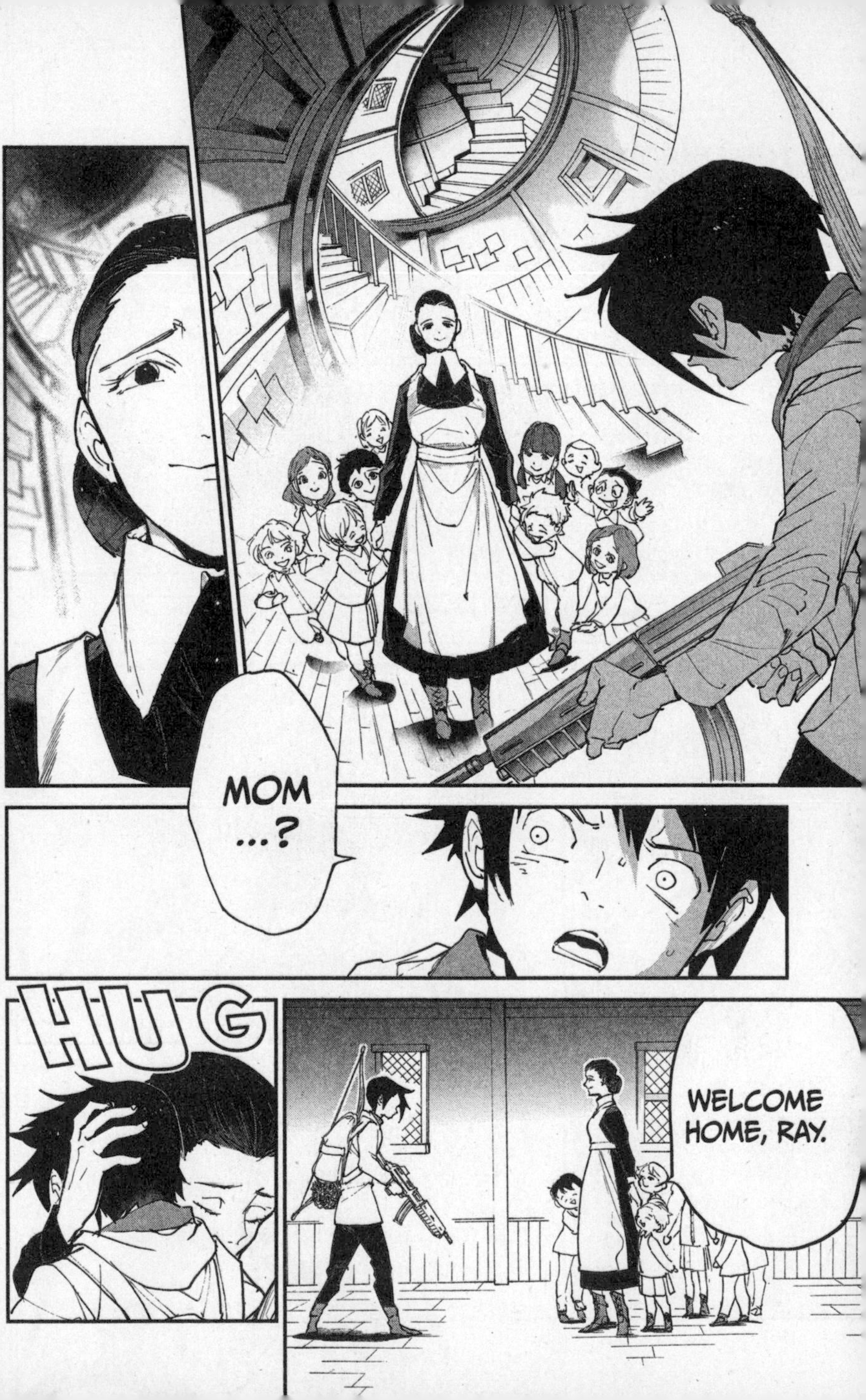
MOM ...?
WELCOME HOME, RAY.
HUG

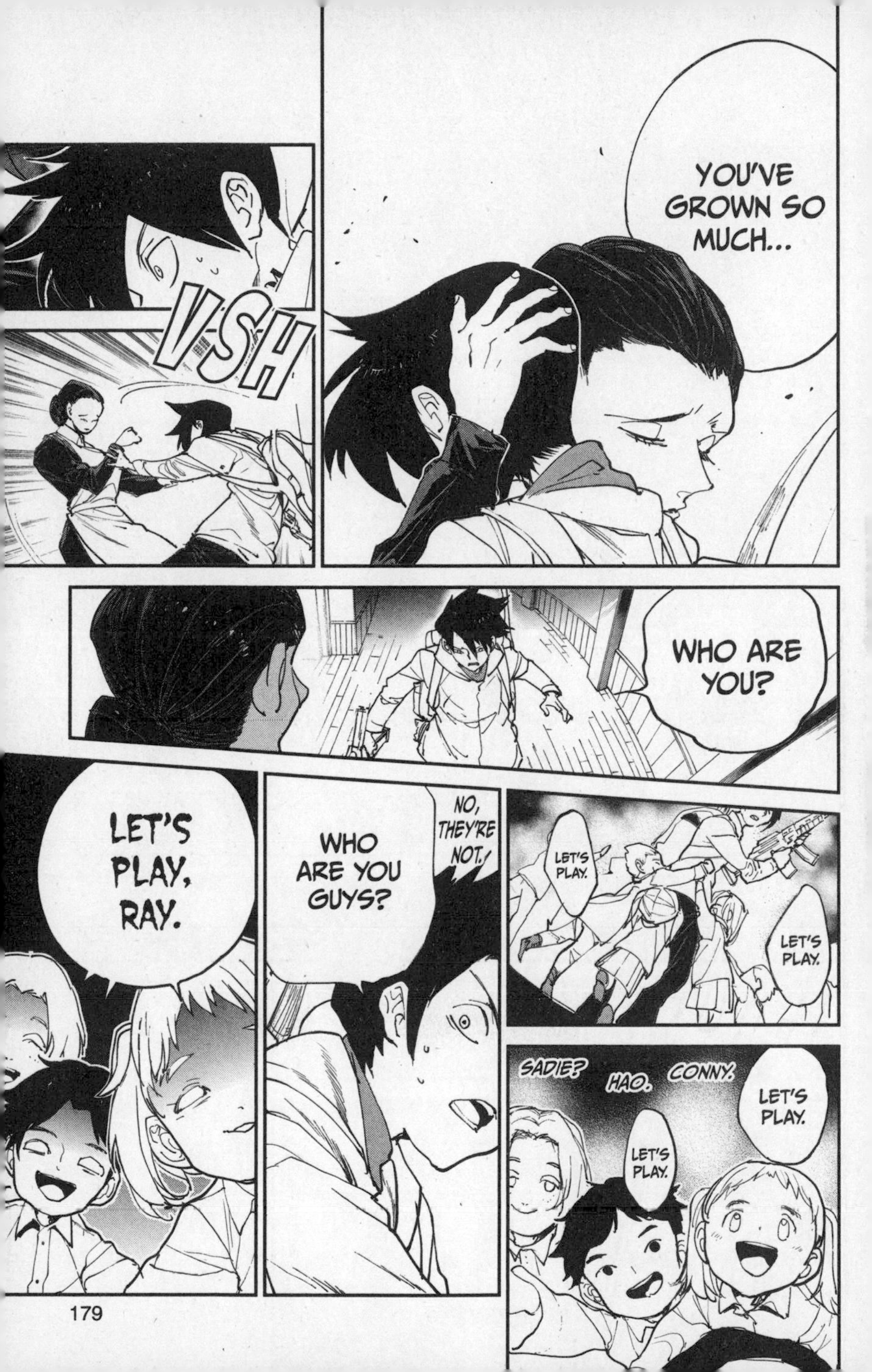
YOU'VE GROWN SO MUCH...
VSH
WHO ARE YOU?
LET'S PLAY.
LET'S PLAY.
SADIE?
HAO.
CONNY.
LET'S PLAY.
LET'S PLAY.
NO, THEY'RE NOT.
WHO ARE YOU GUYS?
LET'S PLAY, RAY.

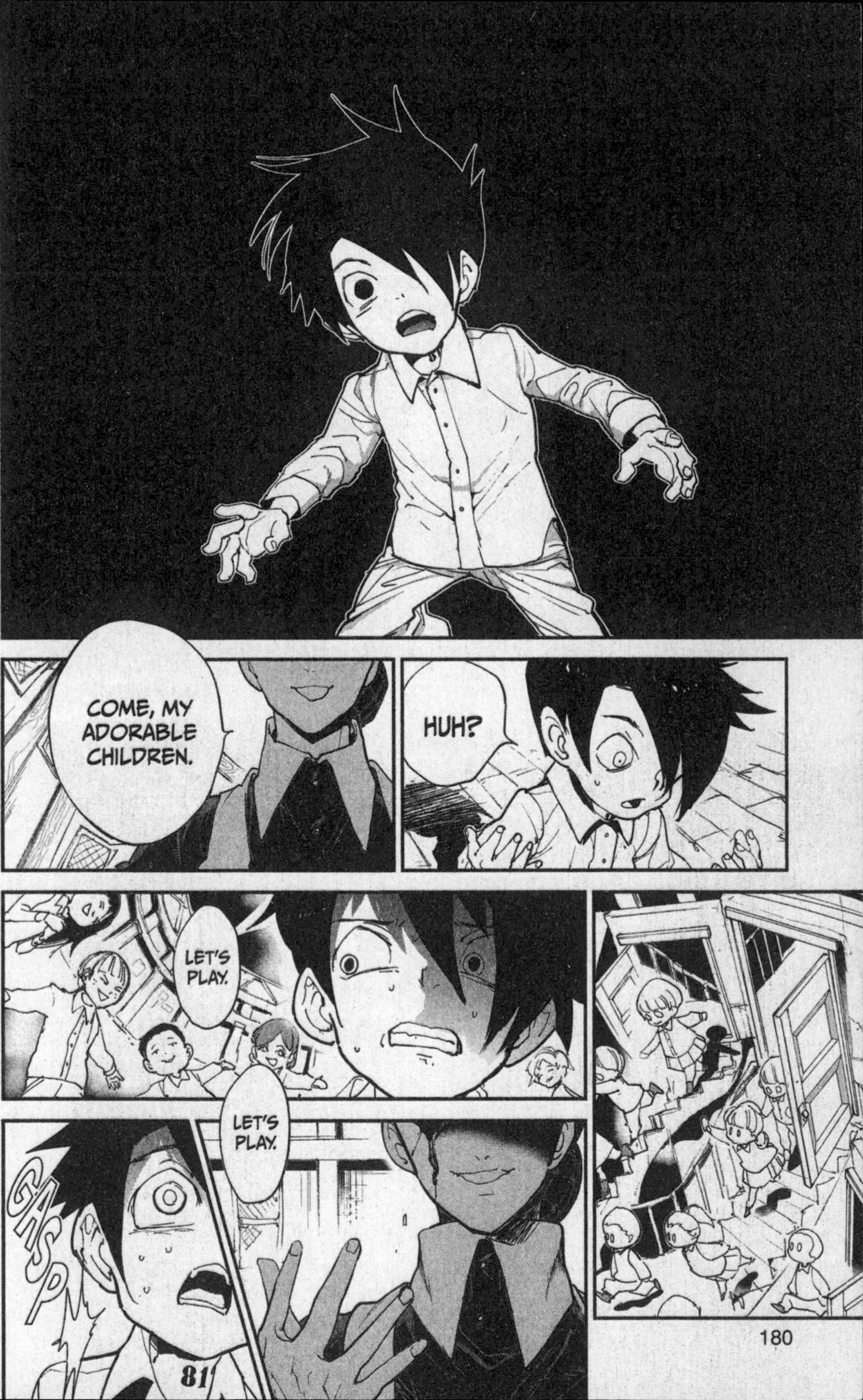
HUH?
COME, MY ADORABLE CHILDREN.
LET'S PLAY.
LET'S PLAY.
GASP

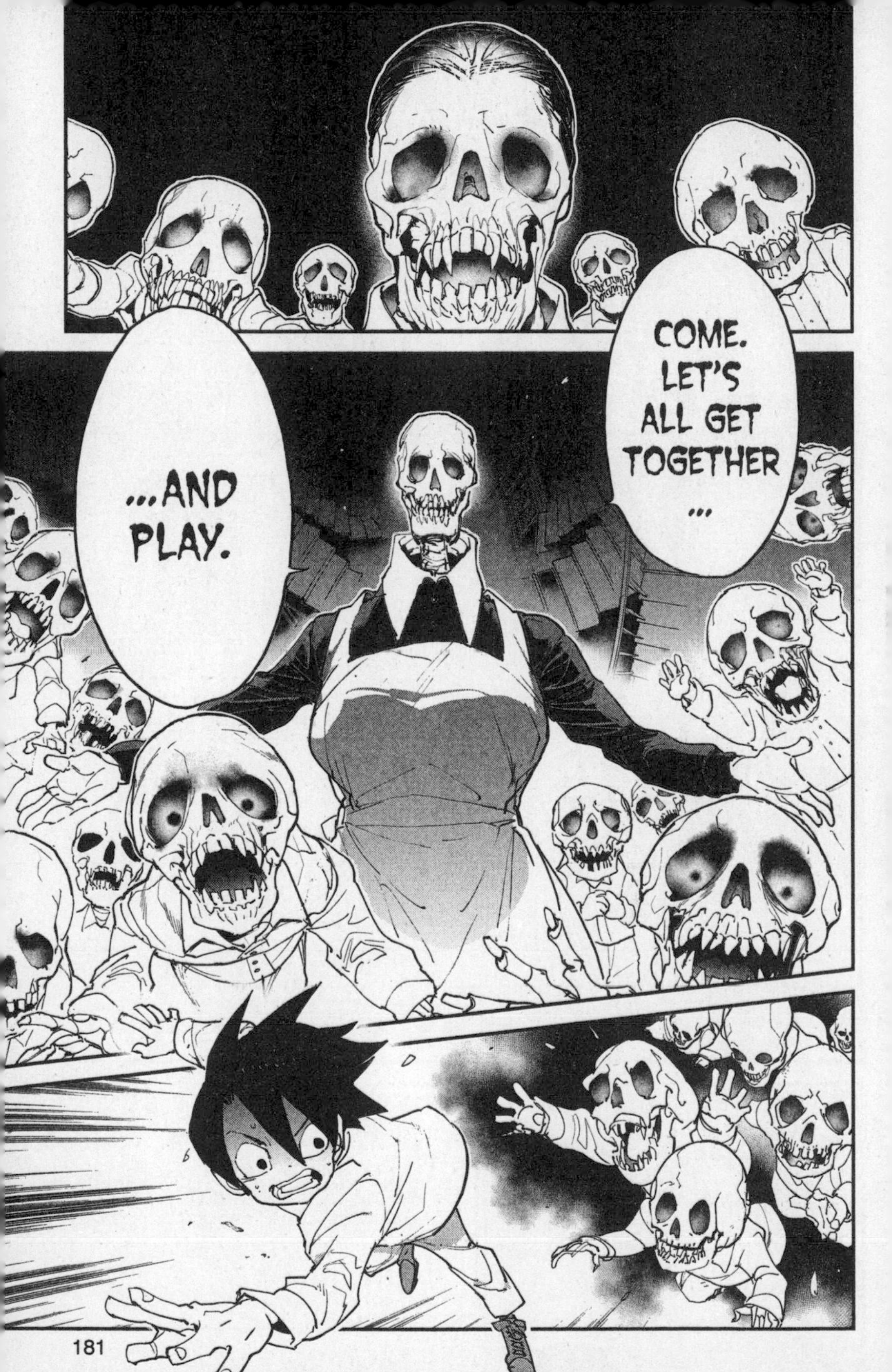
COME. LET'S ALL GET TOGETHER ...
...AND PLAY.

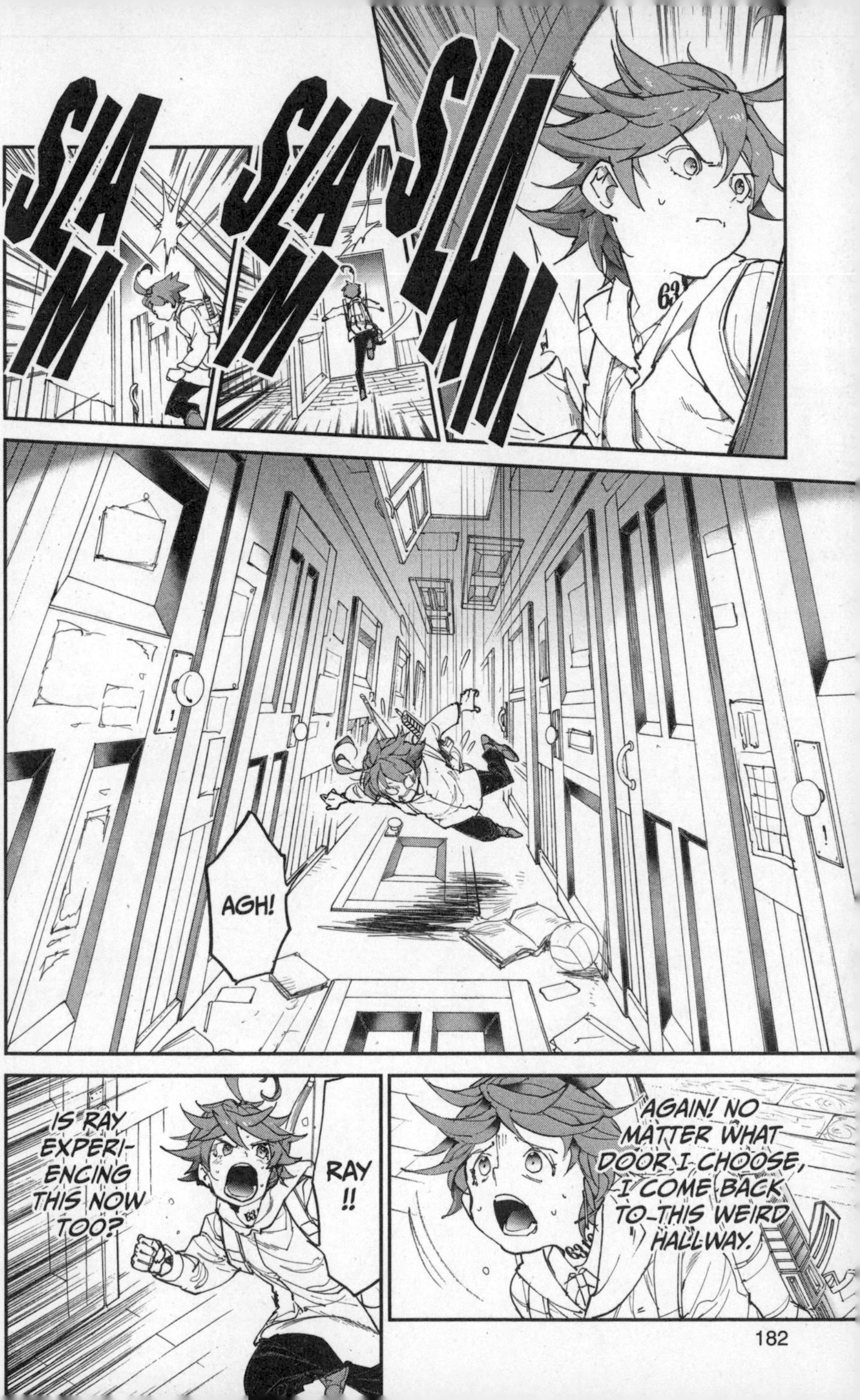
SLAM
SLAM
SLAM
AGH!
AGAIN! NO MATTER WHAT DOOR I CHOOSE, I COME BACK TO THIS WEIRD HALLWAY.
RAY!!
IS RAY EXPERI-ENCING THIS NOW TOO?

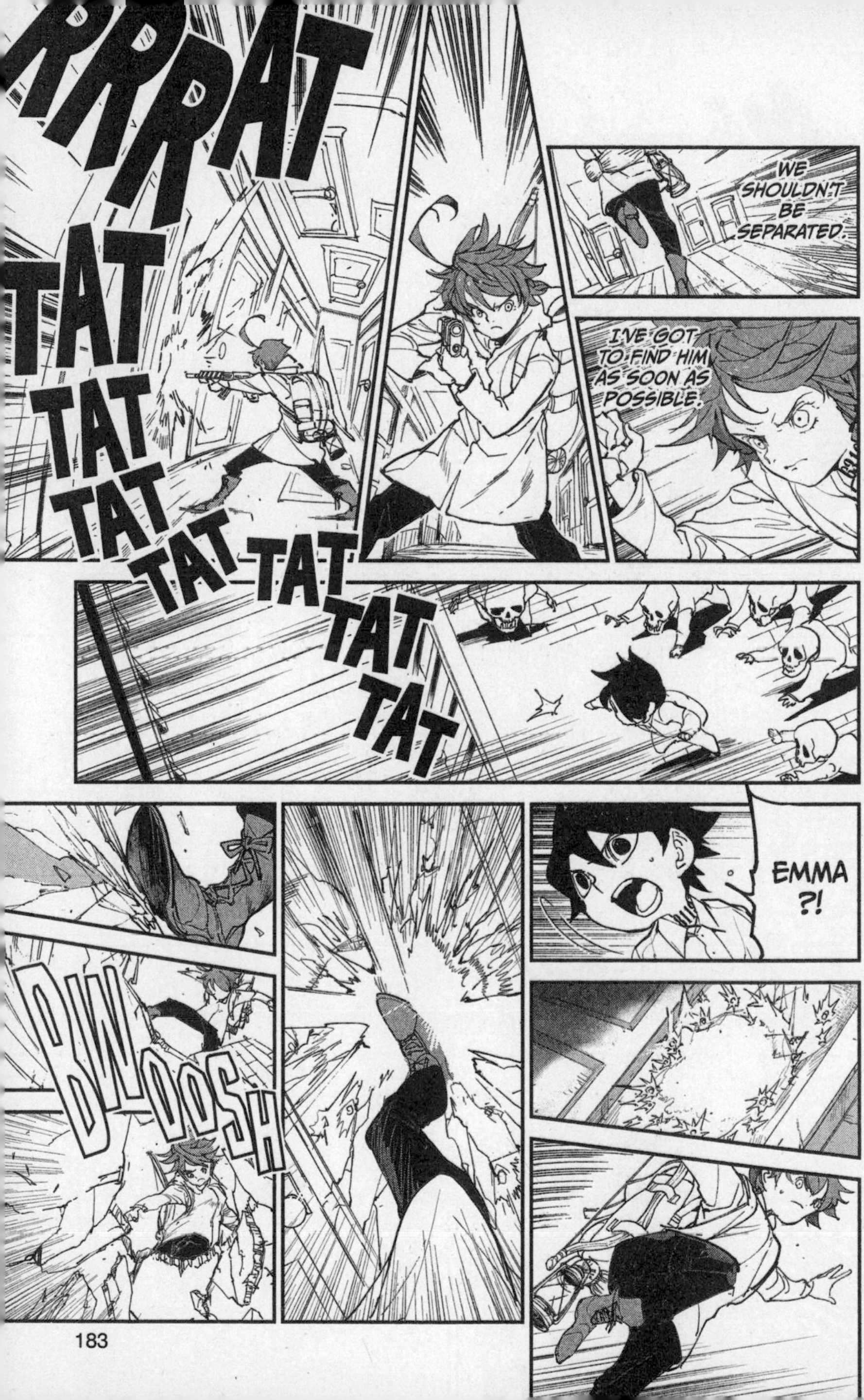
WE SHOULDN'T BE SEPARATED.
I'VE GOT TO FIND HIM AS SOON AS POSSIBLE.
RRRAT
TAT TAT TAT TAT TAT TAT TAT
EMMA?!
BWOOSH

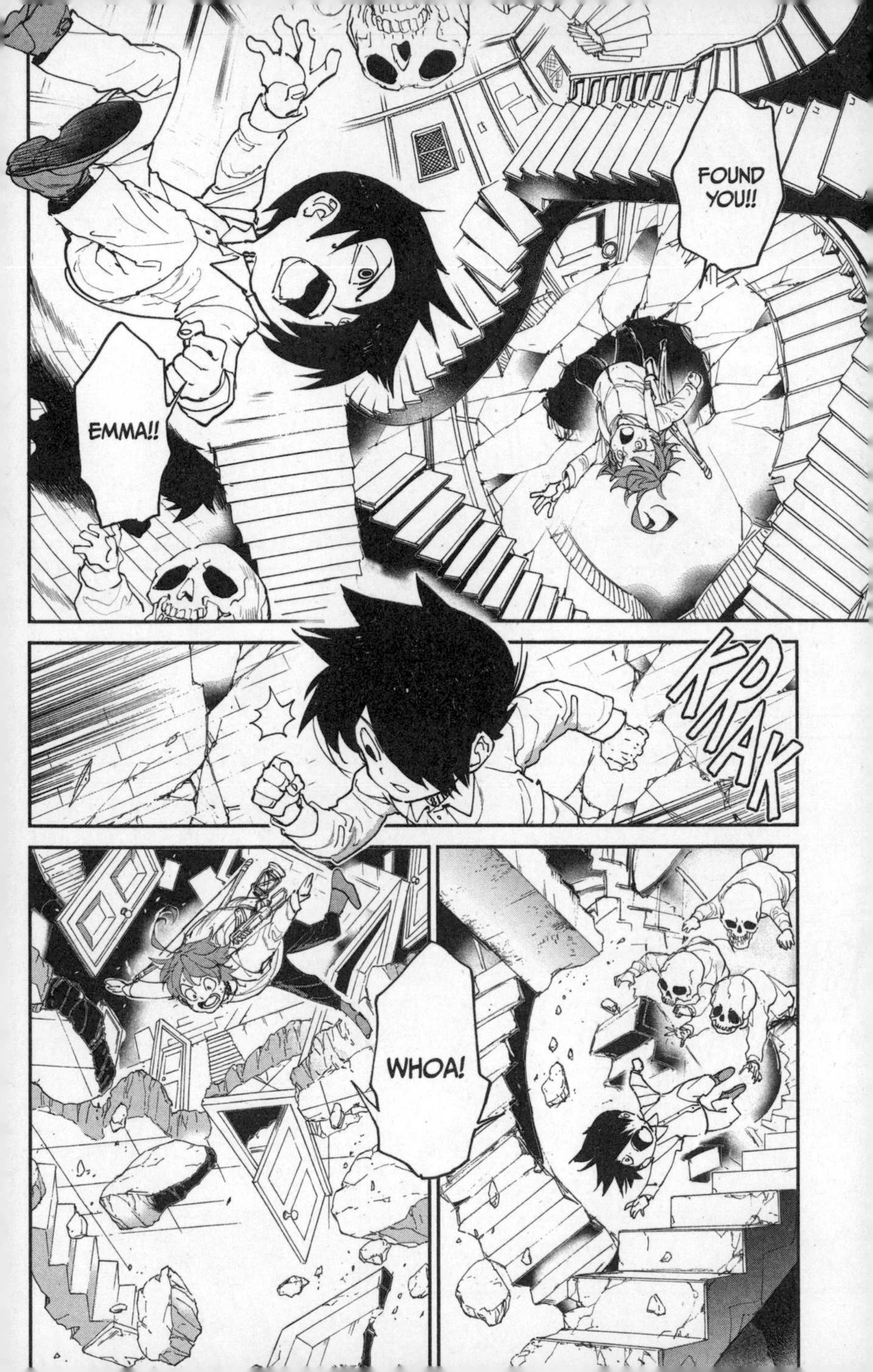
FOUND YOU!!
EMMA!!
KRAK
WHOA!

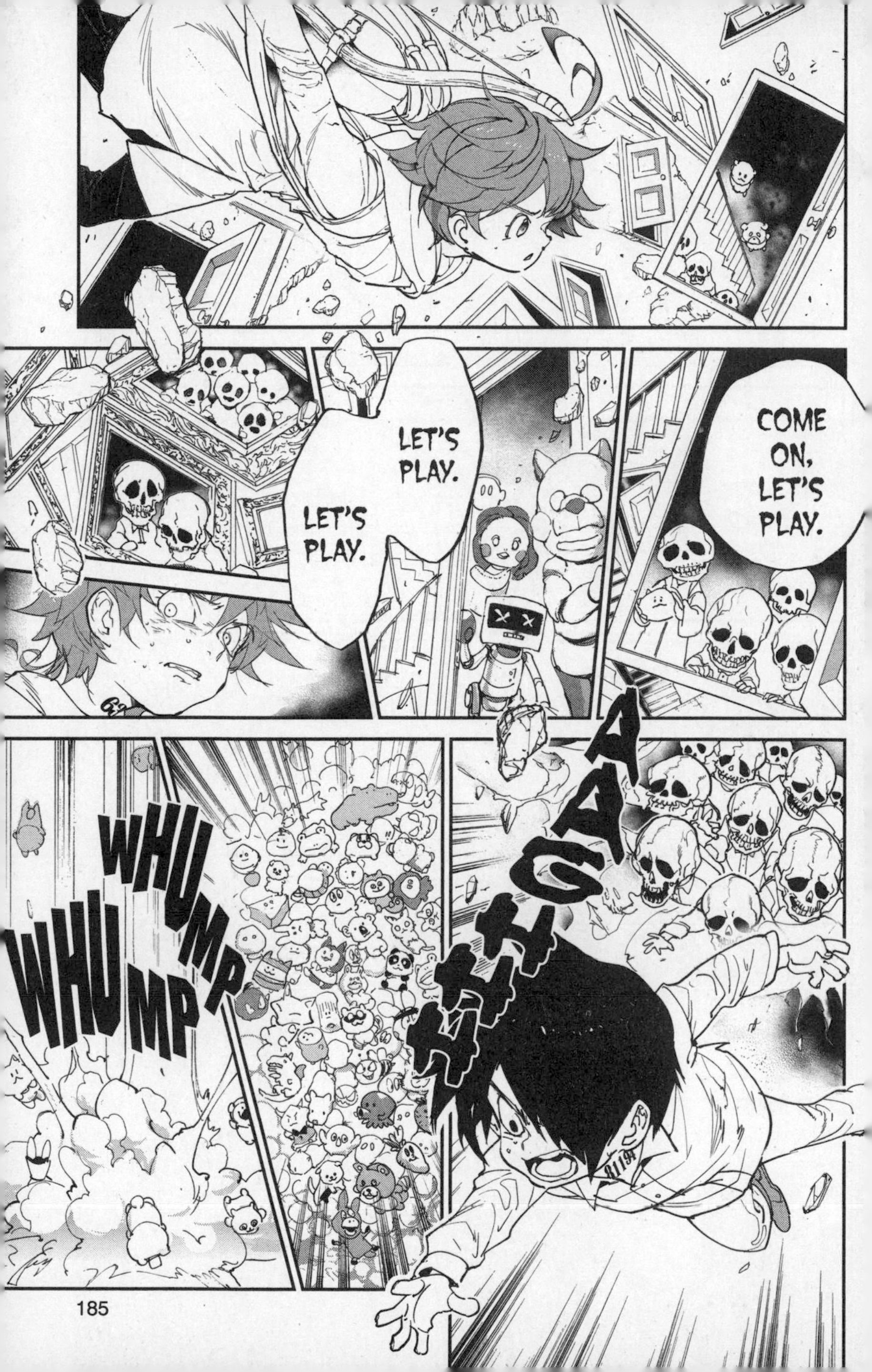
COME ON, LET'S PLAY.
LET'S PLAY.
LET'S PLAY.
WHUMP
WHUMP

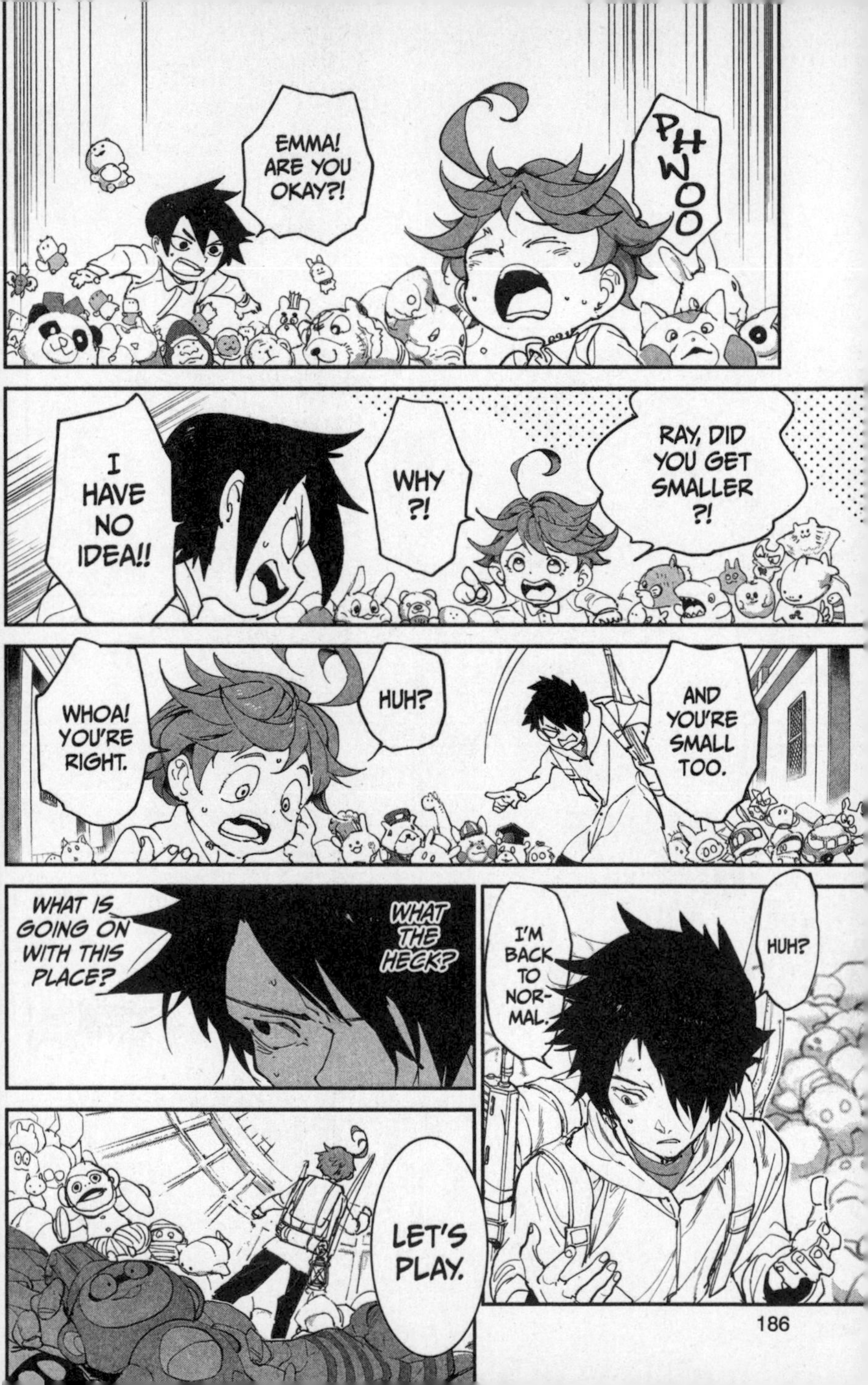
PHWOO
EMMA! ARE YOU OKAY?!
RAY, DID YOU GET SMALLER ?!
WHY ?!
I HAVE NO IDEA!!
AND YOU'RE SMALL TOO.
HUH?
WHOA! YOU'RE RIGHT.
HUH?
I'M BACK TO NOR-MAL.
WHAT THE HECK?
WHAT IS GOING ON WITH THIS PLACE?
LET'S PLAY.

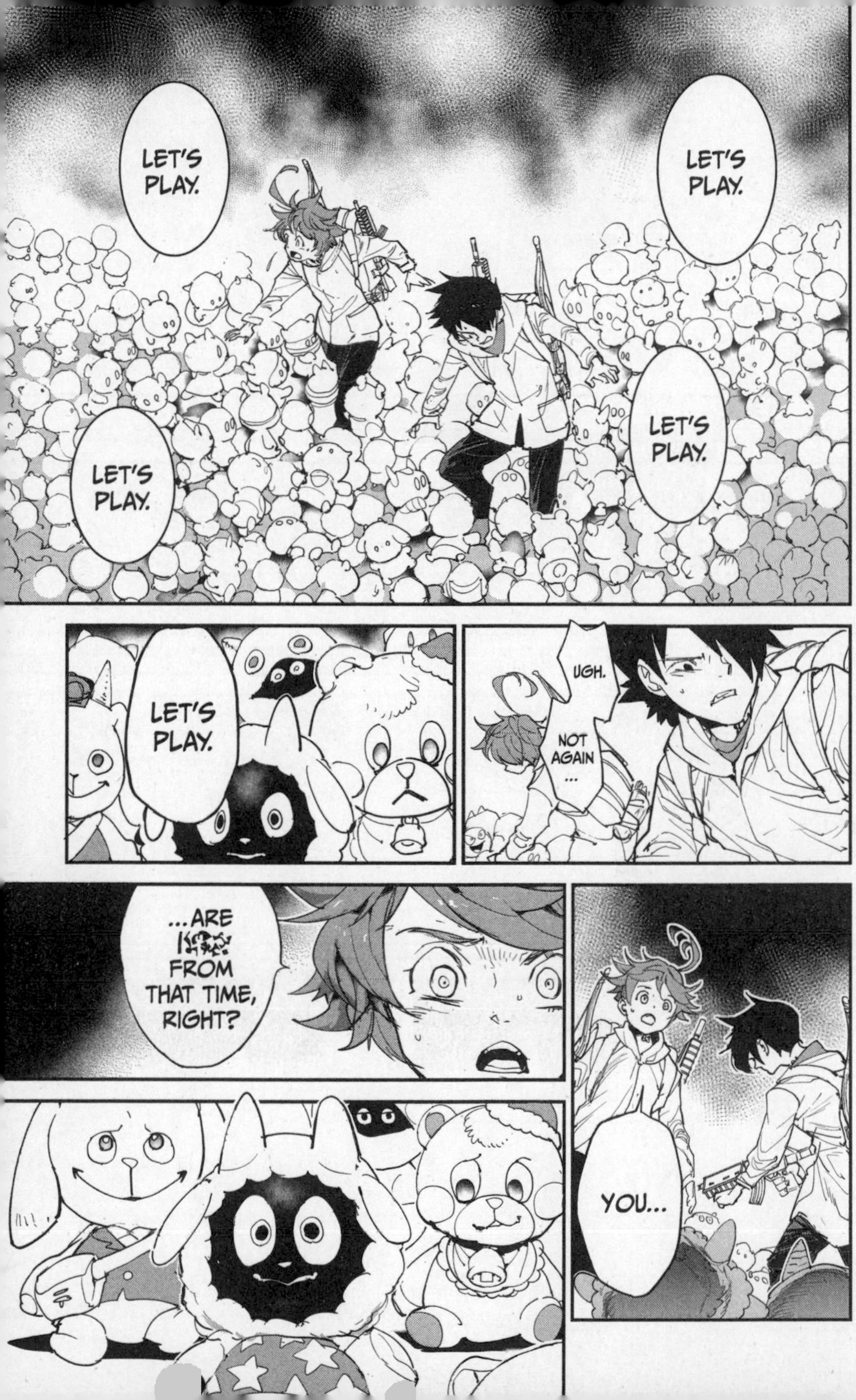
LET'S PLAY.
LET'S PLAY.
LET'S PLAY.
LET'S PLAY.
UGH.
NOT AGAIN ...
LET'S PLAY.
YOU...
...ARE FROM THAT TIME, RIGHT?

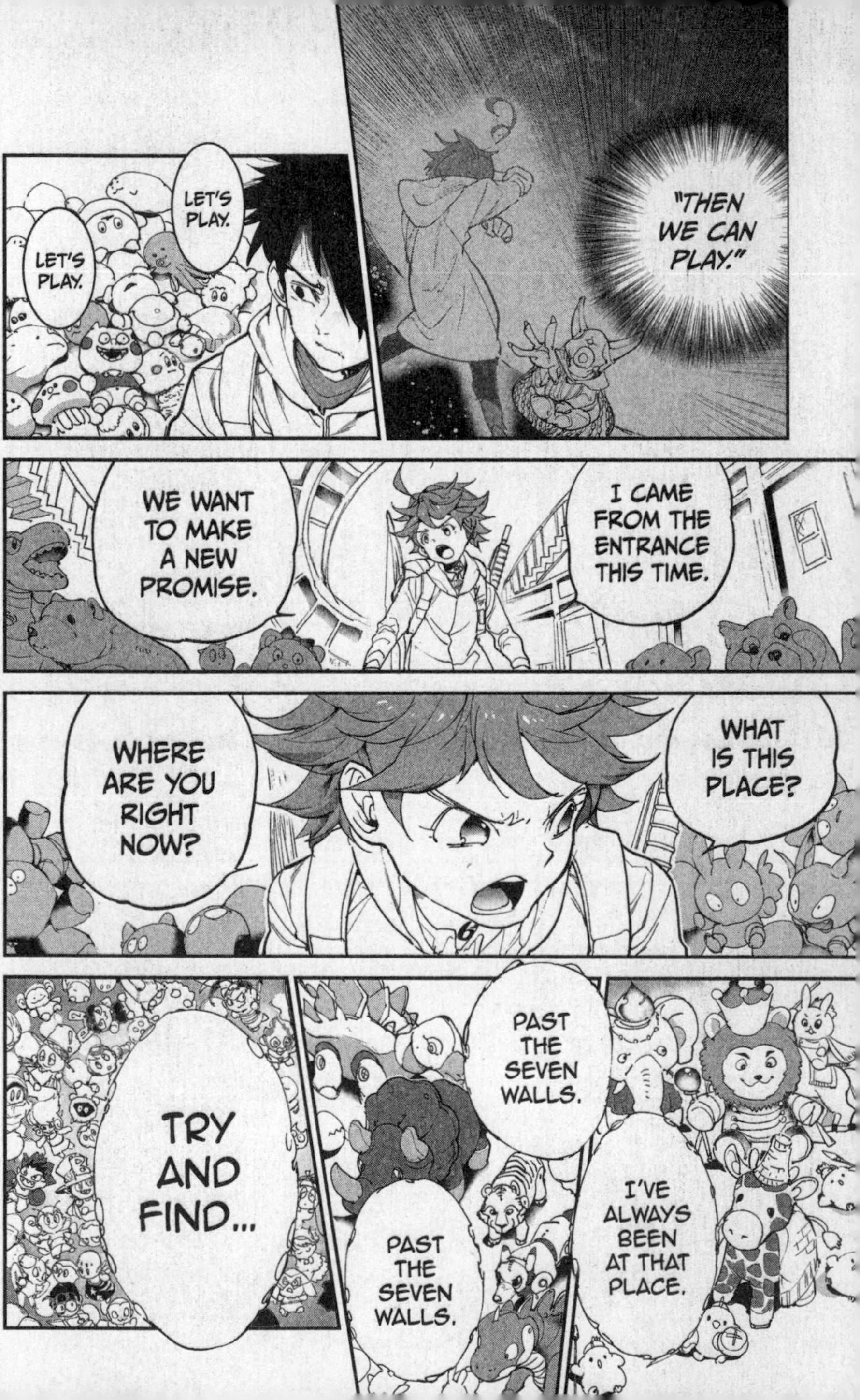
"THEN WE CAN PLAY."
LET'S PLAY.
LET'S PLAY.
I CAME FROM THE ENTRANCE THIS TIME.
WE WANT TO MAKE A NEW PROMISE.
WHAT IS THIS PLACE?
WHERE ARE YOU RIGHT NOW?
PAST THE SEVEN WALLS.
I'VE ALWAYS BEEN AT THAT PLACE.
PAST THE SEVEN WALLS.
TRY AND FIND...

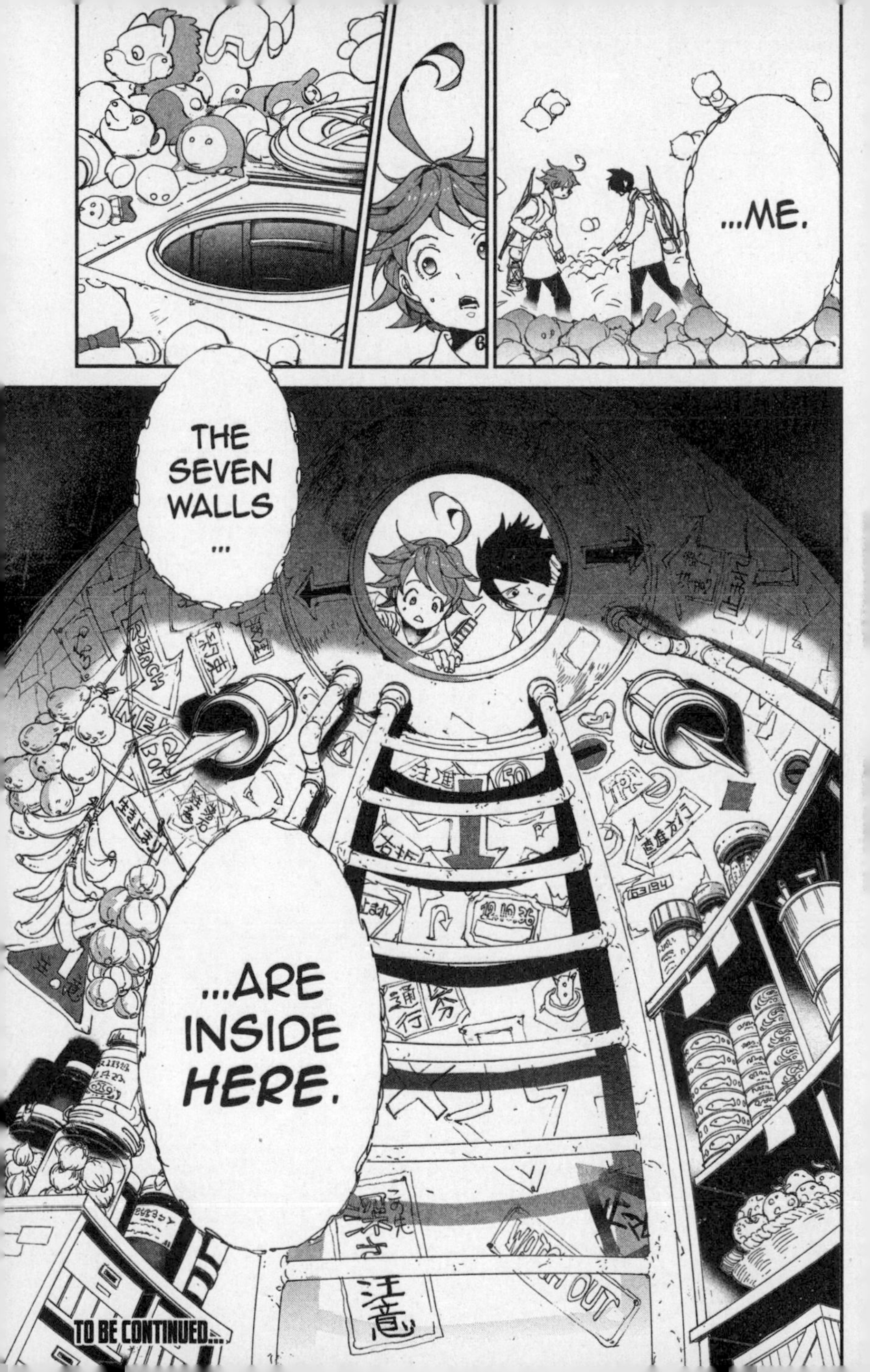
...ME.
THE SEVEN WALLS ...
...ARE INSIDE HERE.
TO BE CONTINUED...

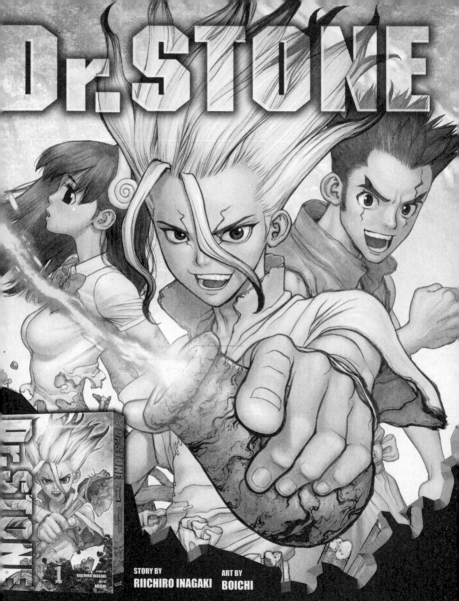

Dr. STONE

STORY BY
RIICHIRO INAGAKI

ART BY
BOICHI

One fateful day, all of humanity turned to stone. Many millennia later, Taiju frees himself from petrification and finds himself surrounded by statues. The situation looks grim—until he runs into his science-loving friend Senku! Together they plan to restart civilization with the power of science!

DEMON SLAYER

KIMETSU NO YAIBA

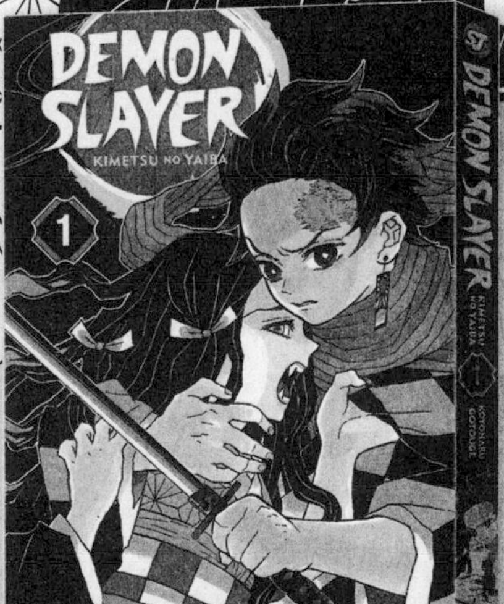

Story and Art by
KOYOHARU GOTOUGE

In Taisho-era Japan, kindhearted Tanjiro Kamado makes a living selling charcoal. But his peaceful life is shattered when a demon slaughters his entire family. His little sister Nezuko is the only survivor, but she has been transformed into a demon herself! Tanjiro sets out on a dangerous journey to find a way to return his sister to normal and destroy the demon who ruined his life.

YOU'RE READING THE **WRONG WAY!**

The Promised Neverland reads from right to left, starting in the upper-right corner. Japanese is read from right to left, meaning that action, sound effects and word-balloon order are completely reversed from English order.